D1252601

TO ÉRIC ROHMER

FRENCH
NEW WAVE

FRENCH NEW WAVE

BY **JEAN DOUCHET**

IN COLLABORATION WITH **CÉDRIC ANGER**

TRANSLATED BY **ROBERT BONNONO**

D.A.P./DISTRIBUTED ART PUBLISHERS, INC.
IN ASSOCIATION WITH **ÉDITIONS HAZAN/CINÉMATHÈQUE FRANÇAISE**

PREFACE: THE NEW WAVE, OR A CERTAIN QUESTION OF STYLE *8*

1. GROWING PAINS *10*

1955 *24*

2. REVIEWS AND AUTHORS *30*

3. FILM CLUBS AND THE CINÉMATHÈQUE *44*

4. FAVORITE DIRECTORS *56*
   THE SILENT FILM *58*
   FROM THE SILENT TO THE TALKIE *61*
   THE DIRECTORS OF THE TALKING PERIOD, 1945–1960 *66*

1956 *70*

5. THE FILM INDUSTRY *76*

1957 *82*

6. *CAHIERS DU CINÉMA* *88*

7. THE CONCEPT OF THE AUTEUR *98*

1958 *106*

8. THE STUDIO *112*

9. THE STREET *120*

1959 *128*

10. THE BODY *136*
   THE BODY WITHOUT TRUTH *137*
   BRIGITTE BARDOT *143*
   GESTURE, SPACE, MOVEMENT *149*

1960 *156*

11. HISTORY OF THE NEW WAVE *164*

1961 *174*

12. NARRATIVE *180*

13. DIALOGUE: TRUTH AND LIES *188*

14. LIGHT AND CAMERA *202*

THE CAMERA *204*
OPTICS *206*
FILM *209*
LIGHTING *213*

1962 *216*

15. SOUND *222*

16. BIOGRAPHICAL DICTIONARY OF THE NEW WAVE *232*

DIRECTORS *234*
SCREENWRITERS AND CINEMATOGRAPHERS *253*
SOUND TECHNICIANS AND EDITORS *255*
COMPOSERS *256*
ACTORS *257*
PRODUCERS *264*

1963 *266*

17. THE NEW WAVE AROUND THE WORLD *272*

USA *273*
QUÉBEC *279*
BRAZIL *280*
JAPAN *283*
EUROPE *284*
THE THIRD WORLD *290*
1968 *291*
CZECHOSLOVAKIA AND HUNGARY *291*
FEDERAL REPUBLIC OF GERMANY *297*
SWITZERLAND *300*
BELGIUM *301*
FRANCE *301*
THE UNITED STATES (REVISITED) *303*

1964 *310*

18. INFLUENCE AND DECLINE *314*

CHRONOLOGY *326*

INDEX *330*

ACKNOWLEDGMENTS *358*

THE NEW WAVE, OR A CERTAIN QUESTION OF STYLE

DOMINIQUE PAÏNI

In his latest book, philosopher Jacques Rancière presents a long but stimulating argument summarizing the two classic methods of linking cinema and history by making either one of the terms the object of the other. "The most interesting problems arise when we discard the subject/object relationship and attempt to grasp both terms simultaneously. Such a move reveals how the concept of cinema and the concept of history are intertwined and compose a history together."[1]

Rancière's statement is a fitting description of Jean Douchet's work. Douchet has managed to combine a chronicle of the sixties with the development of cinema, producing a history that is far more interesting than the sum of its parts, here current events and aesthetics. Although the book doesn't claim to offer a detailed historical analysis of the New Wave, it provides a superb overview of a period during which many of cinema's formal structures were reinvented. Douchet confronts the question of cinema's close relationship to history, which—to quote Rancière again—attempts to incorporate three separate stories: "the film's plot type, the memorial function it fulfills, and the way a film confirms its participation in a shared destiny [in this case, that of an entire generation]."

This represents a considerable gamble for the author given the scope of the book and the mythic overtones the New Wave has assumed in the history of art, where its impact is felt well beyond that of cinema. *French New Wave* is at once a chronological overview, an attempt to contextualize cinema in relation to the other arts and the evolution of society, a convenient tool for approaching key films, and an iconography. But aside from whatever reference value the book may have, it also supplies readers with a critical and theoretical analysis of film. It is unusual to combine both an inventory of events and their interpretation for there's always the risk of an author getting bogged down in anecdote and subjectivity. The Cinémathèque française knew this when it asked Douchet to write a historical and critical overview of the New Wave. It was a risk worth taking, however; Douchet produced a lively and entertaining book that successfully combines history and criticism.

The intelligence of Douchet's analysis is obvious throughout the book. Rather than trying to force theoretical assertions into capsule summaries, he allows his intelligence to range across the entire spectrum of film and social history, derailing conventional assumptions about the New Wave while providing insights into the movement.

For example, it's striking how obvious it is in retrospect that the New Wave was, fundamentally, a product of its time: impertinent, playful, inventive; emphasizing chance, rupture, improvisation, and brilliant intuition;

creating sequences that loop back on themselves like gags or that metonymically demonstrate the entire film. This is one of the reasons for the impression of speed in these films (one that is still strong forty years later), their dynamic brutality, and insolence—all reflections of a young generation in a hurry. At the same time it is to Douchet's credit that he reminds us of the importance of an earlier generation of filmmakers. The rediscovery of the silent film, for example, had considerable influence on the New Wave. Rohmer's love of Murnau, the use of quotation in Godard and Varda, and various other borrowings from silent film, were considered highly innovative in contemporary film. This cinema, which took its cues on the use of voice-over from Guitry, also looked to the silent film for a form of mise-en-scène in which the physical presence of the actor and the styles of editing could return to their origins. The silent and the talkie reunited at last! Henri Langlois launched a generation of filmmakers who discovered the cinema of the past at the Cinémathèque française, just as Matisse and Picasso reinvented twentieth century painting by imitating Ingres, Delacroix, and Manet in the Louvre. The New Wave was creative because it imitated Rossellini, Dreyer, Bresson, Lang, Hitchcock, and Renoir. All served as examples for filmmakers who were accused of destroying cinema through their indifference to its past. Douchet implicitly argues that the rebellion of the New Wave's "young Turks" was paradoxically fed by a very traditional notion of artistic heritage and a willingness—far wiser than it may have appeared at the time—to imitate cinema's masters.

A "collaborationist" mentality was still very much alive at the beginning of the sixties. Corporatist academicism and a leftist criticism, pervaded by a watered-down sense of surrealism, accused the New Wave (primarily the directors associated with *Cahiers du cinéma*) of destructiveness and an attitude of "anything goes." But such criticisms were nothing more than tired platitudes. It is the same anti-intellectual and resentful mentality that currently rejects contemporary followers of Duchamp and American conceptual art. That is why the intellectual, ideological, and artistic picture sketched by Douchet in this book remains remarkably current at the end of the nineties.

In spite of the range of personalities that helped make the New Wave what it was, there is little question that it represents a distinct approach to filmmaking. It was characterized both by its passion for the art of film and by a militancy embodied in a form of critical engagement— which predated the films themselves—distinguished by determination and anger (for example, Truffaut's articles in the magazine *Arts*). The title of the 1956 film by Jacques Rivette that Douchet presents as having launched the New Wave, *Le Coup du Berger*, is indicative of the movement as a whole.

Along with the victory of pictorial abstraction and the simultaneous return of the object in art (the New Realism exemplified by César, Raysse, Arman, and Tinguely), narrative deconstruction (the nouveau roman of Robbe-Grillet, Claude Simon, and Nathalie Sarraute), happenings (Allan Kaprow and Jean-Jacques Lebel), and the theater of the absurd (Ionesco, Beckett), the New Wave reflects an era of conquest, change, and growth. The word "new" is itself indicative of the optimism that preceded the general crisis after May 1968. But the conflagration resulting from the New Wave—"cinema doesn't make life, life makes cinema and gives the present its sense of immediacy"[2]—although of short duration (barely three or four years), decisively transformed the art of film and made it the century's quintessential *modern* art. No doubt it took the aesthetic excesses of the New Wave to also enshrine the cinema that preceded it. And this same excess provided us with criteria that enabled us to rank the history of cinema as a whole, based on a sense of artistic judgment. Such judgment was infused with morality and a sense of aesthetic discrimination that rejected any form of ugliness masquerading as nonconformity (in other words, obscenity). It promoted lucidity, truth, and beauty. The cinema experienced its own Renaissance. The Cinémathèque française was its Florence and Langlois its Vassari.

1   Jacques Rancière, *De l'Histoire au cinéma*, Series edited by Antoine de Baecque and Christian Delage. Paris: Éditions Complexe, 1998.

2   Jean Douchet.

Growing a
Graphi

What does it mean to be a fan? To be thirteen? To spend the afternoon in a darkened movie theater trying to escape the realities of a world at war? Although it may not be the obvious place to start, pushing the dawn of the New Wave back to the time of the Occupation can help explain both its development and its later success, for in large part, the New Wave resulted from the growing cultural aura of enthusiasm and excitement that emerged after the war ended, and it paralleled many of the social changes then occurring in post-war France.

The disturbances of 1940 resulted in a division, no less real for being invisible, within the film industry. At the same time, there was, of course, a significant generation gap among the members of what would become the New Wave cinema. There is a first, older group of filmmakers, those born between 1918 and 1925, that is represented by André Bazin, Jacques Doniol-Valcroze, Pierre Kast, Alexandre Astruc, Maurice Schérer (the future Éric Rohmer), Alain Resnais, Chris Marker, and Maurice Pialat (although not a New Wave director). A second, younger group, born between 1928 and 1932, is represented primarily by Jacques Rivette, Jean-Luc Godard, Claude Chabrol, François Truffaut, Jacques Rozier, and Jacques Demy.

Henri Langlois and Georges Franju, founders of the Cinémathèque française, in 1936
The 400 Blows (François Truffaut, 1959): Jean-Pierre Léaud and Patrick Auffray steal Monika's photograph

The first group was deeply caught up in the various artistic, social, and political currents that agitated French society between 1935 and 1939. Directly affected by historical events, the filmmakers of this generation were committed to voicing their political position—during the Occupation as well as the Liberation—both in life and art. In general, they came to film relatively late, and it was not cinema but rather literature, whether French or American, that was the dominant force in their intellectual lives. An indispensable medium in the world of ideas, polemics, and political commitment at the time, literature was an obsession for these young directors. This interest in writing would prove to be enormously productive for them and in time lead to the development of many new forms of cinematic expression, but it delayed their entry into film, an art they secretly felt to be essentially inferior. It was only later, after the war had ended, that they embraced film openly, and even having done so, they found they needed to justify cinema's uniqueness and status as a medium, if only to convince themselves of its worth. Their nostalgia for a failed life in literature clearly manifests itself throughout their later filmic work.

Their's was a generation that had little opportunity to learn the history of the craft. After *La Revue du cinéma,* the cinephile's bible, ceased publication in 1931, critical studies and articles on film appeared only sporadically, often written by Roger Leenhardt, Léon Moussinac, Georges Sadoul, or Jean Mitry. They thus lacked an active engagement with theory. And the practical situation wasn't much better. The Cinémathèque française—an archive and haven for cinephiles—had been created in 1936 by two young men, slightly older than this first generation of directors: Henri Langlois (b. 1914) and Georges Franju (b.1912), whose development paralleled that of the first generation of directors. Langlois was more directly involved in film than Franju, but they both became active participants in the creation of the New Wave. In 1936, however, they were unable to publicly screen the film treasures they had jealously gathered over the years. Because screening rights lasted only seven years, once this period was over, the young cinephiles of the time had to resort to a handful of prestigious repertory houses to see films: Studio 28, the Ursulines studio, the *Agriculteurs* theater, etc. Repertory houses generally showed films from the dawn of the talkies, which were then barely ten years old and, less frequently, the classics of silent film. These young directors, however, knew almost nothing about the silent film, except what they may have picked up as children. They had laughed at "Charlot" in 1925,[1] and in 1939 they found themselves face to face with Chaplin.

This first generation showed a fondness for American film, for their adolescence had been populated by Westerns and adventure films, cops and robbers, comedies by Ernst Lubitsch, Howard Hawks, Frank Capra, and Leo McCarey. They had also known love stories, the first Technicolor films, dance routines by Fred Astaire and Ginger Rogers, and musicals by Busby Berkeley. (They had to wait until the end of the war, however, before the mythic but overrated *Gone With the Wind* was shown in France.) During the Occupation, the nostalgia of this group for American films increased with their scarcity. Meanwhile, the numerous French and German productions of the time were no more than pale imitations, *ersatz* films. (The word has the ring of a brazen lie and belies its origin in the German chemical industry.) These imitations, did, however, serve to revive interest in the originals and at the same time underscored their absence. This sense of loss, added to the consequences of the war, led this generation of directors to yearn for freedom, which in turn was reflected in a growing awareness of the importance of political consciousness, a characteristic of directors such as Doniol-Valcroze, Kast, Resnais, Marker, and others.

This first group of directors was also characterized by a certain indulgence, mixed with admiration, for what seemed to them the best of French cinema during these dark years. Thus it is easy to understand why, during the fifties, they did not share the virulent antipathies to established cinema of their younger colleagues and why they decided to pursue their own interests. Although they discovered American film before the war, they were no less informed by a French cinema, which they considered, not without a certain sense of chauvinism, to be the best and most intelligent in the world. They were of course familiar with the most important filmmakers of the period—Julien Duvivier, Jacques Feyder, René Clair, Jean Grémillon, Marcel Pagnol, Sacha Guitry—but their final assessment of them remains unclear. The director

Jean-Pierre Léaud, *Le Pére Noël a les yeux bleus* (Jean Eustache, 1967)

who had the greatest influence on this first generation, however, was Marcel Carné, with his theory of "poetic realism," perhaps because Carné incorporated the best of German expressionism into his work. Éric Rohmer claimed that in 1938 *Quai des brumes* had determined his career as a filmmaker. He was eighteen at the time. And André Bazin, during his incessant travels in France and abroad between 1945 and 1950, always brought a copy of *Le Jour se lève* with him to explain cinema to audiences of students, workers, and peasants.

The second group of directors followed a radically different path. In 1940 they were between eight and twelve years old. They knew little about film, but during the four years of the Occupation, it became the center of their universe. For these children then entering adolescence, film provided both refuge and a source of enthusiasm, replacing the role that literature had played for their elders. It is true that during this period, literature generally had lost a great deal of its luster, as it no longer offered romantic or exalting hopes of shaking up the world. Literature—and its writers—had resigned itself, at best, to passive defense, at worst to sinister collaboration with the status quo.

The power to incite that had once belonged to literature now passed on to film. Cinema connected to the life around it, embraced it, blended with it. Truffaut's comment "I still ask myself the question that has tormented me since I was thirty years old: Is cinema more important than life?" could have been spoken by Godard, Rivette, and the others of his generation. Truffaut's question neatly summarized the concerns of the New Wave as a whole. This generation would transform the cinema, giving primacy to its sense of direction and possibilities.

It would be a serious error, however, to assume that this younger group wasn't interested in literature. They were passionate readers, just as the pre-1940 generation had been, and never abandoned a pronounced and enduring taste for books. It was fiction especially that stimulated their imaginations. But the sense of realism that characterized film was, in their eyes, more directly involved with life. This taste for realism can in turn be seen in their literary

Maurice Ronet, *Le Feu follet* (Louis Malle, 1963)
Jean-Paul Belmondo, *Pierrot le fou* (Jean-Luc Godard, 1965)

Barbet Schroeder, *The Baker of Monceau* (Éric Rohmer, 1963)

preferences: at the time of the *Cahiers du cinéma* of the 1950s, the group's favorite writer was Honoré de Balzac. And in *The 400 Blows*, the young Antoine Doinel gets so worked up over the creator of the *Comédie humaine* that he sets his bedroom on fire.

But film was in no way a substitute for literature. On the contrary, literature helped them appreciate film. To a much greater extent than the previous generation, they had lost their sense of direction during the war. The reviews and criticism of the time (with the exception of those by François Vineuil—aka Lucien Rebatet in *Je suis partout* or Jacques Audiberti in his *Comoedia*) were nonexistent, and repertory films, often the best ones, were banned. Without a living memory of film, they had to develop their own tastes and judgments. This was done as an entirely individual effort, driven by each person's sense of enthusiasm and sense of curiosity; and these young men, many of whom were from the provinces, did what they could under the circumstances, which was simply to watch as many films as possible. But the choices were limited. Aside from German productions, such as the imitations of Hollywood musical comedies starring Marika Rökk or Zarah Leander, a few melodramatic propaganda films, the two Agfacolor hits *Die goldene Stadt* and *The Fantastic Adventures of Baron Munchhausen*, and the rare Italian film, such as Alessandro Blasetti's *The Iron Crown*, they only had access to the 220 French films produced during this four-year period.

There was a ritual aspect to the young cinephile's behavior that consisted mainly of wandering around movie theaters, closely examining the stills of current or forthcoming films, fantasizing over the posters, imaginatively creating a climate of fear and danger around themselves, a sense of the forbidden, a sentiment of guilt that aroused desire. Sharing the projector's nocturnal secrets, they abandoned themselves to the solitary pleasures that their intense complicity with film engendered. Did it satisfy their needs? This was their first criterion, and their judgment was based primarily on a film's ability to provide pleasure or disappointment. They compared films, categorized them. Gradually a list of favorites took shape: *Goupi mains rouges* by Jacques Becker, *Lumières d'été* and *Le Ciel est à vous* by Jean Grémillon, *Douce* by

Jean-Paul Belmondo, *Pierrot le fou*
My Life to Live (Jean-Luc Godard, 1962)

Le Petit Soldat (Jean-Luc Godard, 1960–1963)
Anna Karina and Jean-Paul Belmondo, *Pierrot le fou*

Claude Autant-Lara, *Les Visiteurs du soir* by Carné and Prévert, *Le Destin fabuleux de Désirée Clary* and *La Malibran* by Sacha Guitry, *Les Anges du Péché* by Robert Bresson, and a few others. These were the films they saw over and over again. But the film that received the most attention was *Le Corbeau* by Henri-Georges Clouzot: the film had a profound effect on these adolescents and to them represented the summit of cinematic art.

During the forties, film and culture were poles apart, and intellectually speaking, cinema was considered off limits. Formal education, based on the study of literature, did, however, provide an intellectual structure for these budding truants, and combined with their own primitive apprenticeship—studying films on their own—resulted in two important things. First, far from rejecting the critical activity that the conjunction of circumstances and their passion for film imposed on them, these adolescents felt the need to nourish and develop it. Critical thought enabled them not only to approach film but to conquer it, and it became such an essential element of their intellectual growth that it came to symbolize the entire creative process for them. The films of Godard, Truffaut, or Rohmer, for example, at once engage and chart the trajectories of critical thought. Second, their own love for literature led them to the notion of the *auteur*, or author. This occurred quite naturally, since this was what they had been taught in school. At the same time the concept of the auteur in film was made that much easier by the fact that the 220 French films of the Occupation were made by only 83 directors, which amounts to roughly 3 films per director. Further, the fact that they could compare and, especially, categorize films reaffirmed, almost unconsciously, this idea. A decade later, after a period of productive gestation, the concept of the auteur would grow to full fruition. Reformulated, it became one of the key concepts of the New Wave.

1 Charlot was the name given to Charlie Chaplin's screen persona in France.

Pierre Fresnay, *Le Courbeau* (Henri-Georges Clouzot, 1943)

1955

JOHNNY GUITAR

LES DIABOLIQUES

LA STRADA

VIAGGIO IN ITALIA

FRENCH CANCAN

LES GRANDES MANOEUVRES

THE BAREFOOT CONTESSA

KISS ME DEADLY

LES MAUVAISES RENCONTRES

All reviews are excerpts from their respective publications.

JOHNNY GUITAR

Nicholas Ray

DREAMLIKE WESTERN

A young American director, a contemporary of Wise, Dassin, and Losey, by the name of Nicholas Raymond Kienzle, has become the hot new discovery of the "young critics." Nick Ray is an *auteur* in the best sense of the word. Ray's films all tell a similar story, the story of a violent man who wants to change his life and his relationship to a woman who is morally stronger than he is. Ray's hero is always weak, infantile, childish. His films are filled with moral solitude, vigilantes, and lynch mobs.

Johnny Guitar is a faux western, but not an "intellectual western." It's a dream western, a fairyland—unreal and manic. It's only a small step from dreams to Freud, a step our Anglo-Saxon colleagues have taken by introducing the "psychoanalytic western." But the qualities of this film, Ray's qualities, are different, and strictly invisible to someone who has never risked looking into the eyepiece of a camera. We film critics flatter ourselves—and in this we want to distinguish ourselves from other critics—in consciously returning to the sources of cinematic creation. Unlike

André Bazin, I believe we should be able to recognize the director in his films. Otherwise we have failed. The mark of Ray's imposing talent resides in his absolute sincerity, his heightened sensitivity. He's not a great technician. All his films are filled with unexpected continuity jumps, but it's obvious that Ray is less concerned with the traditional, overall impression of a film than with giving each scene a certain emotional quality. *Johnny Guitar* was "made" rather hastily from very long shots broken up into four sections. The editing is deplorable. But what makes this film interesting is, for example, the very beautiful way the actors are arranged within the frame.

The difference between Hawks and Ray is similar to that between Castellani and Rossellini. In Hawks we witness the triumph of the mind, in Nick Ray the triumph of the heart. We can prefer Hawks to Ray, *Big Sky* to *Johnny Guitar*, or accept them both, but to anyone who rejects them both, I would offer the following advice: Stop going to the movies. Stop looking at films. You'll never understand what inspiration means, or a viewfinder, or poetic intuition, or a frame, a shot, an idea, a good film—in short, cinema. Unbearably pretentious? Hardly. Just an unshakable conviction. ■

Robert Lachenay, *Cahiers du Cinéma*, April 1955

LES DIABOLIQUES

Henri-Georges Clouzot

DISCONCERTING VIRTUOSITY

Scathing dialogue, rapid-fire images, expressiveness, and an intelligent dynamism are the elements of what could be referred to as Clouzot's cinematographic style, an approach comprised of both literary fiction and visual invention. Clouzot applies his method with disconcerting virtuosity, enabling him to maintain dramatic tension within practically every scene, while modifying the sources of this tension throughout the film. Until the finale, until that startling scene the director has asked us not to reveal, the audience is kept breathless. ■

Louis Chauvet, *Le Figaro,* March 2, 1955

FLAWLESS WORK

No matter how skillfully crafted a film's screenplay, it obviously demands an even greater directorial skill to bring it successfully to the screen. That's certainly the case here. Clouzot's film serves as a model of a faultless production. With his straightforward style, Clouzot is careful not to push the psychology of his characters too far and sticks to fairly linear caracterizations. The film's subtlety and ambiguity, its rigor, lies in Clouzot's development of the action.

Has there ever been a directorial approach that was less gratuitous within the genre? There isn't a single scene, the slightest gesture or noise that doesn't serve a purpose and which doesn't have a clearly defined dramatic function. It would be pointless to speak of romanticism, poetry, the bizarre, cruelty, sadism, or black humor, for the film's style is perfectly apposite: although far from neutral, it is simply—and diabolically—exactly necessary, perfectly adequate. ■

Jacques Doniol-Valcroze, *France-Observateur,* February 3, 1955

LA STRADA

Federico Fellini

GENTLE, PROFOUND, PASSIONATE

There are "admirable" films, "quality" films, such as *On the Waterfront, Le Rouge et le Noir,* and *Romeo and Juliet,* to name only the most recent. And then there are those sublime films, films with a soul, like *La Strada.* Do such a film's "shortcomings" really matter? Does it matter that the story drags a little near the end, when each scene is of such astounding beauty?

Fellini dislikes the picturesque, and his taste for pathos is similar to Chaplin's. Giulietta Massina's performance, however, appears to be directly inspired by the best in Chaplin, but with a freshness and sense of timing that seem to have been invented for this film alone. *La Strada* is unlike any other film, and this is not the least of this gentle, profound, and passionate film's many qualities. Bitter, yet full of hope. A lot like life. ■

Jean Aurel, *Arts,* March 16, 1955

CRUEL AND TENDER OBSERVATION

Are there any legitimate criticisms of this film? There's the precarious mental condition of the three protagonists: an innocent, a bully who is sometimes struck with a touch of humanity, and an acrobat referred to as a "fool," whose bizarre, yet seductive, attitude is not always clearly explained. The film contains a number of "falsely Chaplinesque" aspects, but there's considerable disagreement over this point. Is Chaplin's influence clearly visible in *La Strada*?

The qualities of this film are many and they are quite extraordinary. The atmosphere of the drama is described with a visual strength that has rarely been equaled. The three-wheeled motorcycle, a kind of broken-down trailer that Zampano drives, is a device of epic proportion. The show put on by the strong man and the clown, the conditions in which they travel, all the small details that mark each moment of the film, Zampano's sentimentality when he

attempts to run away, his fights, his anger—there is a sense of poetry in all this, a sense of cruel and tender observation. And what a miracle for Fellini to have been able to translate with such depth the true nature of these difficult characters, who themselves defy analysis. (Sidestepping any psychological objections to this film by means of metaphysical affirmation, the director posits that every object is good for something in this world.) ■

Louis Chauvet, *Le Figaro,* March 14, 1955

VIAGGIO IN ITALIA

Roberto Rossellini

ADMIRABLE DRAMATIC PRECISION

Due to the film's novelty, what happens on screen in *Viaggio in Italia* will undoubtedly surprise a number of viewers. But most will see nothing out of the ordinary: a man and woman traveling by car, walking, going into houses, opening doors, climbing stairs, stretching out on a terrace in the sun, exchanging no more than a few brief words. Yet if this is all they see, they will miss the interior journey that sustains the

film with admirable dramatic precision. The things that the careful viewer will see are the Matisse-like universe (as Matisse himself noted), the world of failed actions, the unkept promises, and crowning it all, at the height of the film's dramatic arc, the sudden explosions, the sense of deliverance, those few brief but pathetic seconds during which Destiny suddenly turns inside out like a glove, when the mirror breaks and hearts collide, naked once more, pushed toward one another in a fury of passion.

In my opinion this is what the audience needs to see, not the film's technical imperfections. It belongs to a type of cinema (Bresson's, for example) in which the representation of a profoundly realist form of behavior is more significant than problems of continuity or the camera's shadow on the procession. Style is essential, not the mechanical perfection of style. A certain "roughness" is inherent in certain kinds of prose, just as in painting, when the meaning of a drawing or a sketch is not a function of inability but of necessity. Everything in Rossellini, stylization or negligence, works toward a final sense of perfection, which is not the perfection of a clock spring but the natural upsurge of his talent and message. ■

Jacques Doniol-Valcroze, *France-Observateur*

TOO LONG AND BADLY SHOT

Although *Viaggio in Italia* is a romantic documentary, this banal romance leaves a lot to be desired. As a documentary it is much too long and badly photographed. The exteriors resemble those washed out images that we attribute, with some generosity, to the poor quality of Italian film stock during the era of *Quatro Passi fra le Nuvole*. And since Rossellini is ambitious and Naples is large, its beauties are revealed in a series of traveling shots and panoramas that cause viewers to wonder if the director's vision isn't failing. The changes of perspective are linked to one another by interminable shots of Ingrid Bergman at the wheel of what she can see of her car. The film achieves a kind of paroxysm of giddiness; Bergman visits museums, parks, a catacomb, Vesuvius and Pompeii. Her husband goes to Capri. If this film were a documentary, we might be willing to extend our patience. Here practically any pretext is used to provide an opportunity for yet another visit. Ingrid Bergman trots around and generally behaves like a child. It's the first mistake acting students are taught to avoid. ■

Claude Martine, *Arts*, April 27, 1955

THE OLD RELATION BETWEEN SIGN AND IDEA IS SHATTERED

The public generally has a standard reaction to novelty. Reread the accounts of the first exhibitions by the Impressionists or Fauves, the first performance of Sacre du Printemps and you'll encounter comments like: "He doesn't know what he's doing." "I could do the same thing." "That's not painting." "That's not music." "That's not cinema." A convention of what is *natural* has been created in darkened theaters across the country, just as the dabblers of the last century constructed one about *modeling*. As Manet deliberately rejected the safety net of chiaroscuro, so too has the author of *Viaggio in Italia* discarded a facile cinematic language worn thin by fifty years of use. Before Rossellini, even the most brilliant, the most original director thought it his duty to try to learn from his predecessors. He knew that the way an actor blinked or held his head, the way he moved his body, awakened a conditioned reflex, a given emotional reaction in the viewer. The director played with those reflexes, he didn't try to subvert them. He made art, and by this I mean he created a personal body of work out of cinema's raw material. For Rossellini, this material doesn't exist. His actors behave like actors in other films only to the extent that they use the gestures and attitudes common to us all. But they evoke in us a desire to seek out something else behind their behavior, which our natural inclination as spectators is inclined to discover. The old relationship between sign and idea has been shattered and a new one has taken shape, and it is disturbing. ■

Maurice Schérer, *Cahiers du cinéma*, May 1955

FRENCH CANCAN

Jean Renoir

BRILLANT, SPIRITED

French Cancan represents a milestone in the history of color in cinema. Not wanting to make a picturesque film, Jean Renoir presents *French Cancan* as a kind of "anti-*Moulin Rouge*." Unlike Huston's film no gel filters are used to create blends of color; only pure colors appear. Every scene is a cartoon in movement. The blacks,

browns, and beiges are beautiful, and Madame Guibole's dance class reminds us of a Degas sketch. The final French cancan is an astonishing tour de force, an extended bravura performance that carries the entire audience along with it. While *French Cancan* may not be as important as *The Rules of the Game* or *The Golden Coach*, it is a brilliant and spirited film nevertheless. It is Renoir at the height of his power, as vigorous and youthful as ever. ∎

François Truffaut, *Arts*, May 4, 1955

AN ELABORATE CLICHÉ

The colors are beautiful, unreal and heavily applied in the style of an American musical. If only the prince (that ineffable prince) knew how to dance instead of talk! Maria Félix is unquestionably beautiful. The music by Van Parys falls, predictably, somewhere between a pastiche and a copy. But the interludes by that other grotesque, a hybrid between Zappy Max and Fernandel, are absolutely ridiculous. And the lyrics! The appearances of Edith Piaf and André Claveau are painful. Neither the embarrassment of nor the falsity of the oversize letters on the signboards are in any way redeemed by humor. The evening in Montmartre is an elaborate cliché far removed from the "shirtsleeve cinema" that Renoir is capable of. Everything in this film is clean and new, down to the buttons on the actors' spats, but something important is missing, which the costume designer can't provide. (It's worth mentioning in passing that the costumes by Rosine Delamare are more successful than Douy's sets. The designer vacillates, following the director.) The phoniness of the rue Lepic, with its vegetable carts and piles of artificial stones is painful to look at. The actors act. The audience gets bored. The dance rehearsals are all PG. They're Degas all right, but the kind that appears on Post Office calendars.

I'll admit that I still haven't seen *Moulin Rouge*, fearing it would be well done. I'll get over it. I venture there is more cinema (atmosphere, technique, color, excitement, brio) in the first two reels of *Moulin Rouge* than in ten *French Cancans*. This is a third-

rate film. And let's not get too worked up over the final cancan scene, which any American director could portray equally well. ∎

Bernard Chardère, *Positif*, November 1955

LES GRANDES MANOEUVRES

René Clair

NERVOUS ENERGY AND SPIRIT

When I mention René Clair I think of cinema. Those three crystalline syllables bring to mind a lengthy sequence of glorious images filled with grace and intelligence. Of course, many would find it unreasonable to claim that it was with René Clair that intellectualism entered French cinema. Nevertheless, there's an element of truth to the statement, and the refined and elegant silhouette of the director of *Le Million* will be a fitting symbol of an important aspect of French intellect in film's future Pantheon. Although somewhat cold, *Les Grandes Manoeuvres* is full of nervous energy and spirit.

A friend, who is rather critical of film, said to me "Look for the equivalent of *Les Grandes Manoeuvres* in literature and you'll find a second-rate love story." I disagree.

The development of intellect and creation takes place over time as a history of "relations" rather than of juxtapositions. Part of film's magic attraction is that the inspiration that leads to the creation of a character like Dolly or Bouguereau materializes on screen in masterful films, like *Les Grandes Manoeuvres*.

Everything about this film reminds me of an operetta—the set, the uniforms, the music kiosk, the marionettes and old maids from the province. Still the music that reverberates in our ear is substantial. A pleasant, precise mechanism, wound by a delicate hand, is set in motion and advances without interruption. We smile, laugh, are astonished, smile again, and feel our hearts ache. For these reasons alone it would be a mistake to underestimate *Les Grandes Manoeuvres*, as I understand some people have. ∎

Jacques Doniol-Valcroze, *France-Observateur*, November 3, 1955

THE BAREFOOT CONTESSA

Joseph L. Mankiewicz

A FILM, FULL OF ANGER AND HATE

Does *The Barefoot Contessa* signify the disorder of the Cartesian mind? The French public is a victim of literary allusions. It is also a victim of its own stupidity, demanding adult films and guffawing like a hackney driver when it finds one.

The biggest mistake one can make in viewing this film is to take it at face value. The on-screen spectacle is only a means to show us the film's true meaning, which can be found in the viewing audience itself. Obviously, the characters have an off-screen existence: they look different, have different names, perhaps several. To attach a name to the face of a mystical and sexually obsessed billionaire producer is hardly difficult. It's even easier when you can associate two or three. Without looking too hard it would

also be easy to find four or five tipsy heads of state "between Nice and Monte-Carlo," and just as many rich South American playboys and yacht owners. Who would dare list the number of impotent Italian counts? This film's allusions are wonderful in their plentitude and they are all appropriate. Mankiewicz's objective is not an intimate dinner, but a massacre, full of anger and hatred.

When the count admits his infirmity to his wife, the audience's laughter soon turns to embarrassment. I'll wager that they would never have made the connection on their own. When Ava Gardner enters the Mediterranean in a white bathing suit and leaves in a green one, the audience assumes Mankiewicz is an idiot. But when she turns around and reveals she is wearing a two-color suit, green on one side and white on the other, it's Mankiewicz who shows the audience that they're the idiots.

This helps explain the film's principal character, perfectly embodied by the beautiful Ava. Frigid with the libertines, a nymphomaniac with the puritans, she is everything the audience isn't. She is, most importantly, the woman they'll never possess themselves, since they identify too closely with the male characters in the film, who could just as well have appeared as chauffeurs, guitar players, or bohemians. I'll wager that their dignity

would have been offended by this, however. What's more, these same men would never be able to mislead their Cinderella for long, for there's a sleeping Italian count in all of them. They get drunk on champagne, roulette, and fast cars, and their wives are stupid, alcohol soaked, and ugly. The only time they sleep with their mistress is when she's "tired or frightened." This Beauty, turned into a barefoot statue, will evade them. In the end, she belongs to no one, except perhaps the man who is willing to protect her without wanting to possess her: Mankiewicz, in the guise of Bogart's chiseled features. ∎

Claude Chabrol, *Cahiers du cinéma*, July 1955

KISS ME DEADLY
Robert Aldrich

A FRENZY OF LYRICISM

Aldrich obviously tries to salvage a banal subject: a second-rate Mickey Spillane detective novel—a kind of super-Cheney, with an excess of violence, dead bodies, bad taste, and vulgarity. To do this he plunges the viewer into a frenzy of lyricism, a kind of deliriously unhinged world that ultimately results in a form of cruel poetry, with images redolent of Cocteau's *Blood of a Poet*.

We're a long way from the standard detective novel here. In challenging the rules of the genre, Aldrich throws everything he can into this film: lyricism, pathos, extremes of emotion, the way he cuts short his best screen effects, his preference for detailed, pitiless faces, his profound sense of sound balance, and his success with basic filmic procedures (such as shooting a character's feet whenever they're on screen for any length of time). Aldrich possesses the kind of talent that can't be acquired: a style characterized by surprising energy and density. Some things in the film don't work; the direction is often poor ... but this was most likely the result of Aldrich's limited budget. ∎

Jacques Doniol-Valcroze, *France-Observateur*, November 22, 1955

OFTEN SURREAL, DELIBERATELY BIZARRE

Spillane's world is always more or less the same. It's one in which the bad guys always seem to fall for "exciting" women, bombshells who prefer to display their legs rather than their intelligence. In Spillane we also find the detective as superman. He feels contempt for women, rejects their lustful advances, sacrifices a night of romance for adventure, and isn't afraid of danger. The resulting mixture is more amusing than pernicious. Still, it's hard to deny that director Robert Aldrich (recent winner at the Venice festival) has considerable and wide-ranging talent. The film contains some examples of this talent; they are served with intelligence and accordingly seasoned for the genre.

The style in this film is often surreal, intentionally bizarre. And although there are times when Aldrich's way of telling a story gets in the way of the film, and even threatens to destroy it, his style also helps advance the plot. This is especially true when the film's more unlikely fantastic aspects involve serious trompe-l'oeil and other stratagems that threaten to sidetrack the story for good. But Aldrich handles this confusion easily and efficiently. In the end his style is what makes the film interesting. The hero is part of a barely credible story, and the circumstances are too obviously fictitious. A kind of nuclear device is left in a coat room by some devious characters whose intelligence leaves plenty of room for improvement. The plot could easily have become ridiculous. Carefully edited, with a forward-moving rhythm, however Aldrich's technique gives the film a kind of inflexible logic that could almost be called Cartesian. What better way to sidetrack the viewer?

The film's atmosphere, the characters' faces, even the extras, who add an element of irony, all make this an interesting film. The meal is only as good as the recipe. Let's not belittle the recipe. ∎

Louis Chauvet, *Le Figaro*, September 18, 1955

THE FIRST FILMMAKER OF THE ATOMIC AGE

Aldrich, a phenomenon whose visual imagination is without equal, continues to

astonish and confuse audiences. For Aldrich, there are no laws, no taboos: his scenes are dizzying and diametrically opposed. "Impossible" is not in the American vocabulary. He makes us witness the implacable struggle between black and white: masses of shadow intersect one another, are riddled with flashes of white. The laws of editing appear to have disintegrated: the image explodes. Aldrich is the first filmmaker of the atomic age. ∎

Charles Bitsch, *Cahiers du cinéma,*
October 1955

LES MAUVAISES RENCONTRES

Alexandre Astruc

BEAUTY LIES IN ACCURACY

A portrait of Alexandre Astruc would naturally begin "Frivolity is not Astruc's strong point." And such a comment wouldn't be out of place. What is most characteristic of youth—and I don't believe this is true only of our generation—is not, as our aging roués seem to think, vitality, nonchalence, or frivolity, but, on the contrary, seriousness, a penchant for

morality, and a constant questioning of everything, especially oneself. This would be a fine subject for film and here's a director who appears perfect for the job, "a young film by a young director, for the young." That's the slogan I would proudly display if I were in charge of advertising for *Les Mauvaises Rencontres*. It is precisely this gravity, this seriousness that some people find unpleasant. A comparison with *The Rules of the Game* and *Les Dames du bois de Boulogne* is inevitable, given the condescending reception they were given in Paris. In both cases the films were treated with the same ironic hostility on the part of a public that felt uncomfortable, realizing it had been surreptitiously caught in a trap. For once the bad guys aren't on screen but among the judges. The elite has a hard time admitting such a reversal of roles.... How does Astruc go about this? His critics claim he's a formalist. I would, on the contrary, say that Astruc's approach is that of someone who has something important to say, someone who wants to be heard, and who has made sure that all the elements of his work advance his beliefs. His efforts converge toward a single direction: clarity, precision, directness. It is most likely this absence of ambiguity that most bothers the "impressionist" critic, who is always more comfortable with the absence of avowed ambition. Anyone who speaks like Astruc generally wants to be heard, and rightly so. Beauty, he suggests, is found in accuracy, and Astruc's ambition was to make an accurate film. Anyone wanting to criticize the film will have to address this issue. However, our journalists are unable to discuss the truthfulness of something they are ignorant of: the accuracy of the description of a world not their own. What is important is that today's younger generation recognizes itself in this film, not only through the action, characters, and dialogue, but by its tone, its point of view, and the director's profound preoccupation with the story.

We speak of the use of *technique* in this film, but technique is simply a name, film jargon for the will of the sublime. Think of Hitchcock, Welles, or Lang. The effective

use of technique signals a soul naturally inclined to greatness and deserves reproach only when it fails. Shakespeare used it to present an image in verse. In this light every movement of the camera is subject to the movement of the soul, the film's direction is entirely based on the belief in correspondence, in the secret effluvia that emanate from human beings, and on the effect of their intellect, whose waves attract or repel the camera, on the structure of the film. I assume this mysticism of the dolly shot will appear ridiculous to many, but Astruc's film will certainly be incomprehensible to anyone who doesn't believe in the quasi-physical reality of ideas, of their struggles and mysterious affinities, their perpetual movement, which ultimately constitutes their lyricism. Such precision, such accuracy are the products of an impassioned individual, someone who can't be identified by the trembling of his hand but by a certain nervous tension, an edgy control over the reflexes of the flesh, which is so obvious here as to be disturbing. ∎

Jacques Rivette, *Cahiers du cinéma,*
November 1955

REVIEWS & AUTHORS

It has often been asked why young cinephiles, during the fifties, rejected official French film with such vehemence. And worse still, why were they so quick to defend American cinema? The political explanation is obvious.

The Liberation introduced a period (1945–1950) that proved to be fertile for film as a whole but not very favorable to French film. Even so, 1945 turned out to be a blockbuster year in France, with the release of Marcel Carné's *Children of Paradise*, Robert Bresson's *Les Dames du bois de Boulogne*, and Jacques Becker's *Falbalas*. Begun in 1944, these films were the crowning glory of French cinema during the Occupation. Each was, in it its own way, a film *of* resistance, but it wasn't until 1946 and René Clément's *La Bataille du rail* (Clément was also working as Jean Cocteau's technical advisor on *Beauty and the Beast*) that films *about* the Resistance began to appear. Adhering to the national policy of reconciliation advanced by the dominant political parties of the time, these films were designed to absolve French society of its Pétainist tendencies during the war. *Le Père tranquille* remains the model for this form of kindhearted apathy and programmed forgiveness. Directed in 1946 by René Clément, the author–actor Noël-Noël played the role of a kindly grandfather who, in spite of his worn slippers and middle-class demeanor, possessed the burning

courage of an energetic and effective Resistance leader. This collective fantasy, this desire to forget the sense of hidden and burning shame, ensured the film tremendous commercial success.

Inevitably, this process of turning away from, of rejecting, reality turned out to be a serious disappointment to the two generations that would become the future New Wave. At a time when Italian neorealism turned to the street for inspiration, French film confined itself to the studio and wallowed in a pessimistic and morose vision of daily life. The failure of Marcel Carné's *Portes de la nuit* (1946) should have served as a warning, but instead it signaled an even deeper escape into pessimism. Henri-Georges Clouzot, Claude Autant-Lara, Julien Duvivier (with *Panique* in 1947, after his return from Hollywood), Henri Decoin, and many others, simply built on the theme, which a caricature of Sartrian existentialism had made popular, of an ontologically defiled universe populated with reprobates. The summit was reached by Yves Allégret and his screenwriter Jacques Sigurd in their trilogy *Dédée d'Anvers* (1948), *Une si jolie petite plage* (1949), and *Manèges* (1950).

This had nothing to do with the cinema that the young film fanatics had dreamed about during the Occupation, and it outraged them. They felt as if they had been betrayed by the filmmakers that they had so deeply admired. The violence displayed by Truffaut, Rivette, Godard, Chabrol, and

Maria Casarès, *Les Dames du bois de Boulogne* (Robert Bresson, 1945)

N° 132 - 6 Janvier 1948

L'ECRAN français

Paris-Cinéma

L'HEBDOMADAIRE INDÉPENDANT DU CINÉMA ★ L'HEBDOMADAIRE INDÉPENDANT DU CINÉMA

HENRY FONDA a fait une création impressionnante du personnage de Tom Joad, le héros des RAISINS DE LA COLERE que John Ford a réalisé d'après le roman de John STEINBECK (Voir p. 4 et 5)

Les Films de la Semaine

AMIRAL NAKHIMOV : Peinture de bataille (Sovietique v. o.)

L'AMIRAL NAKHIMOV
Scén. : I. Loukovsky. Réal. : Vsevolod Poudovkine. Interp. : Alexis Diky, Rouben Simonov, Vsevolod Poudovkine, E. Samoïlov, V. Vladislavsky. Images : A. Golovnia et T. Lobova. Décors : V. Egarov, A. Vaisfeld. 1945.

Ce n'est certainement pas pour nous un événement comparable à *Ivan le Terrible*. Si contestable que soit l'esthétique du dernier film d'Eisenstein, elle était, du moins, une révélation sensationnelle sur l'évolution d'un des plus grands metteurs en scène du monde. Ceux qui en espéraient autant de Poudovkine seront déçus. Cela dit, relativement au metteur en scène de *La Mer* et de *Tempête sur l'Asie*, *Amiral Nakhimov* est pourtant une œuvre importante, la meilleure à bien des titres du cinéma soviétique depuis sept ou huit ans (*Ivan le Terrible* mis à part). Elle souffrira, malheureusement, en France, de l'indifférence inévitable du public pour des événements et un héros historique à peine connus chez nous. Il est vrai que le nom de Tchapaiev n'était pas plus populaire que celui du vainqueur de la bataille de Sinope, mais il incarnait un aspect de la révolution russe. Poudovkine, à l'inverse d'Eisenstein, s'est systématiquement refusé à la transposition épique ou esthétique. Son film frappe tout au long par une impression d'honnêteté scrupuleuse tant dans la psychologie des personnages que dans la mise en scène. L'ampleur exceptionnelle de celle-ci n'est tout simplement qu'à la mesure des événements. C'est d'ailleurs par là qu'au delà de notre relative indifférence à l'intrigue, *Amiral Nakhimov* devient rapidement attachant. Il est inhabituel que le cinéma dépense de si grands moyens sans spéculer malhonnêtement sur leurs effets. La mise en scène d'*Amiral Nakhimov* ne serait pas, quant au nombre des figurants et des vaisseaux coulés, indigne de Cecil B. de Mille, mais la bataille navale ou l'attaque de Malakoff sont traitées sur le même ton que la conversation de Nakhimov et du prince Menchikoff. Tout au plus, les cadrages, le décor, les costumes évoquent-ils parfois, dans les dimensions du cinéma, les tableaux d'Horace Vernet ou de Detaille. Mais cette référence picturale n'est pas déplaisante, on dirait d'une sorte d'honnêteté esthétique supplémentaire.

André BAZIN.

LE FORT DE LA SOLITUDE : Un peu de fort, beaucoup de faible (Fr.)

Scén. et dial. : Bernard Zimmer, d'ap. René Guillot. Réal. : Robert Vernay. Interp. : Paul Bernard, Alexandre Rignault, Lucien Nat, Michel Marsay, Claudine Dupuis, Georges Hubert, Henri Coutet. Images : Maurice Barry. Son : C. Evangelou. Décors : Renoux et Gabutti. Musique : Habib Iguerbouchem. Prod. : U.G.C. et Temara-Film. 1947.

Il paraît que, ne trouvant pas dans tout le Maroc de « bordj » à sa convenance, Robert Vernay, le réalisateur du Fort de la Solitude, *en fit construire un tout exprès pour lui. Mais, bien entendu, il ne pouvait être question de dépenser les six cents millions de* César et Cléopâtre... *Si bien qu'on ne nous montre, en définitive, qu'un bordj miniature, des murs derrière lesquels nous sentons qu'il n'y a rien, un « quartier réservé » de mirliton et, malgré le sable, un bled de pacotille.*

S'efforce-t-on, pourtant, à grand renfort de cris, de convulsions et de sueur, de nous la suggérer, cette couleur locale qui constitue la raison d'être du film ! Ce précieux trésor, cette photo de femme, de « sa » femme, que garde jalousement la brute primitive qu'est Alexandre Rignault et que convoitent tous ses compagnons d'infortune dans ce coin de désert maudit, il n'a été mis là que pour corser encore l'atmosphère irrespirable de ce lieu de fin du monde. Mais il ne nous émeut jamais. Parce que nous n'avons pas chaud avec les héros du drame, nous ne souffrons pas avec eux, nous ne les « connaissons » pas. Et qu'ils s'agitent en vain devant nous.

Et quand survient, comme une cassure, la seconde partie — métropolitaine et policière — de l'histoire, nous l'admettons comme un tout, plus varié, plus humain et plus proche, et nous nous hâtons d'oublier le préambule un peu long qui devait être cependant — sinon dans le livre de Guillot que je n'ai pas lu, du moins dans l'intention de son adaptateur Bernard Zimmer — pesant comme chape de plomb, lancinant comme une rage de dent. Mais, c'est là qu'il manque cette conviction, cette pénétration, cette poésie (noire ou rose) qui font les grandes œuvres. Et que l'on sent poindre, de temps à autre, dans La Septième Porte, *par exemple.*

Le personnage inquiétant de Paul Bernard, marlou faussement repenti ; celui, sommaire et assez répugnant, de Rignault ; la figure falote et imprécise du capitaine Lucien Nat, nous laissent, hélas ! le contrôle de tout notre esprit critique, parce qu'ils n'ont qu'un cadre, physique et moral, mal défini, inachevé et maladroit. Quant à Claudine Dupuis, l'émotion qu'elle provoque (chez le public mâle tout au moins) est d'une tout autre espèce. J.-J. Delbo, dans un rôle ingrat, montre son habituelle habileté.

Jean NERY.

TOUJOURS DANS MON CŒUR : A l'eau de rose (Am. v. .o)

ALWAYS IN MY HEART
Scén. : A. Comondini, d'ap. D. Bennett et I. White. Réal. : Jo Graham. Interp. : Kay Francis, Walter Huston, Gloria Warren, Patty Hale, Frankie Thomas, Una O'Connor, Borrah Minevitch et ses vagabonds. Images : Sid Hickox. Musique : H. Roemheld. Prod. : Warner Bros. 1942.

Le titre peut sembler ironique, si l'on pense qu'il s'agit là d'une tentative sans lendemain pour lancer la jeune Gloria Warren, qui devait, en principe, concurrencer Deanna Durbin et Judy Garland. Gloria Warren est une de ces mille petites actrices sans grand talent qui chantent agréablement, jouent passablement et dansent à l'occasion. *Toujours dans mon cœur*, taillé à sa mesure, nous introduit dans cet univers périmé où les directeurs de prison sont de bons bougres, et où les détenus jouent au base-ball et sont relâchés quand ils sont mélomanes. Car tel est le sujet : Walter Huston a été condamné par erreur; sa femme (Kay Francis) et sa fille (Gloria Warren) croient à son innocence et lui vouent un impérissable amour. Il compose une mélodie intitulée *Toujours dans mon cœur*. L'air est repris par Borah Minevitch et ses boys, par Gloria Warren qui le chante en swing et en berceuse, et par tous les crooners américains. Walter Huston devient célèbre et on le libère illico. Elle est d'ailleurs assez nostalgique et fort potable, cette mélodie.

Un film à l'eau de rose, à l'usage des midinettes sentimentales. Les autres verseront une larme apitoyée en retrouvant une Kay Francis vieillie, avachie, médiocre et insupportable. Walter Huston est sobre. Rien à dire sur la réalisation terne et médiocre. Les boys de Borah Minevitch sont bons, particulièrement le petit nain bossu au nez crochu.

G. DABAT.

LA DAME EN BLEU : Opéra-comique en technicolor (Anglais v. o.)

THE LAUGHING LADY
Scén. : S.-J. Wittingham, d'ap. Ingram d'Abbes. Réal. : Paul L. Stein. Interp. : Anne Ziegler, Webster Booth, Félix Aylmer, Francis L. Sullivan, Peter Graves. Images : Edward Scaife. Musique : Hans May. Prod. : British National Films.

Il y a des chœurs. Des bateliers, par exemple, qui s'interrompent de bateler pour pousser la romance. On reconnaît qu'on est au cinéma au fait que le bateau ondule. Les bateliers, nonobstant le mal de mer, ténorisent comme devant. Il y a la profondeur du champ, dans un décor unique et voué aux vertus du grand spectacle : la couleur de fond dans des demi-teintes indiscernables et les visages des figurants s'uniformisent dans une pâte figée. Il y a de la soldatesque, des chansons à boire, du folklore d'époque et des haillons révolutionnaires. Il y a des épisodes multiples, et des bons sentiments à la pelle, à défaut de tout découpage. Il y a des tableaux de bravoure. Il y a des sans-culottes et des chaises à porteurs, et la guillotine, et des personnages qui s'appellent M. Pitt et M. Robspear, également connu sous le nom de Robespierre. Bref, un mélange d'Opéra-Comique, de Châtelet et de Paul Reboux.

Là-dessus, le public emboîte le film. Il a tort et il a raison. Il a tort parce qu'il semble incapable de dépayser ses catégories, d'accepter ce spectacle pour ce qu'il est : un opéra-comique filmé, et de juger les œuvres selon leurs intentions. Il a raison en ceci que le film n'ajoute rien à l'opéra-comique et s'éloigne du cinéma sans rien apporter de valable à cet art synthétique qu'il deviendra sans doute un jour (et qu'annonce un film de grande classe comme Henry V). *Je ne m'avance pas plus avant dans ces vues, car ce serait ridicule, à partir d'un prétexte aussi dépourvu d'ambition.*

Comme le moraliste peut trouver à discourir sur la confusion des langues, le technicien peut commenter la couleur indéfiniment. Il aime que le technicolor rappelle parfois l'agfacolor, il regrette toutes les facilités accordées au bariolage par le scénario, il salue la réussite de tel ou tel flash et il déplore l'effroyable échec de la profondeur du champ.

Jean QUEVAL.

LE MINOTAURE vous conseille...

Ne manquez pas...

La Bataille de l'eau lourde (Un fait d'armes authentique. Fr. Nor.). — **Les plus belles années de notre vie** (Le drame des démobilisés américains. Am.). — **Les Raisins de la colère** (Une grande fresque sociale. Am.).

Allez voir...

L'Amiral Nakhimov (La bataille navale de Synope. Sov.). — **Brève Rencontre** (L'aventure d'une femme honnête. Ang.). — **Café du Cadran** (Un bistrot de Paris. Fr.). — **Crossfire** (Un assassin antisémite. Am.). — **Dame de Shanghaï** (Orson Welles. Am.). — **Danger de mort** (Le drame d'un pharmacien. Fr.). — **Dumbo** (Walt Disney. Am.). — **Grandes Espérances** (Dickens vu par David Lean. Ang.). — **Heureux Mortels** (Une famille anglaise. Ang.). — **L'Idole** (La boxe. Fr.). — **Maria Candelaria** (Dolorès del Rio. Mex.). — **Les Maudits** (Dans un sous-marin nazi. Fr.). — **Monsieur Vincent** (Pierre Fresnay. Fr.). — **The Overlanders** (A travers l'Australie. Ang.). — **Quai des Orfèvres** (Policier. Fr.). — **Le Tournant décisif** (Stalingrad. Sov.). — **Le Père Tranquille** (Un Français moyen résistant. Fr.).

Pour passer le temps...

L'Affaire Macomber (Un drame dans la jungle. Am.). — **L'Arche de Noé** (Burlesque intellectuel. Fr.). — **Le Bandit** (L'après-guerre. It.). — **Pavillon noir** (Corsaires, en technicolor. Am.). — **Rio, rythme d'amour** (Sambas. Am.).

Et si vous ne les avez pas vus...

Les Bas-Fonds (D'après Gorki. Fr.). — **La Bête humaine** (Zola vu par Renoir. Fr.). — **Pépé le Moko** (La Casbah d'Alger. Fr.). — **Pontcarral** (Les bonapartistes sous Louis-Philippe. Fr.).

Pour Paris et la banlieue parisienne, consulter les programmes dans notre supplément gratuit.

MICHIGAN KID : Un western, c'est tout (Am. v. o.)

MICHIGAN KID
Scén. : Roy Chanslor, d'ap. Rex Beach. Réal. : Ray Taylor. Interp. : Jon Hall, Victor McLaglen, Andy Devine, Rita Johnson, Griff Barret. Images : Virgil Miller. Décors : Russell Gausmann. Prod. : Universal. 1947.

Connaissez-vous le cinecolor ? Non ? Vous avez de la chance. Ce mystérieux ersatz du technicolor prête aux images les apparences des fruits et légumes de mauvaise qualité où dominent les teintes du jaune passé-décomposé. *Michigan Kid* est un film bas en couleurs. Sa couleur n'est pas l'unique défaut de ce western qui n'est pas tout à fait un de ces produits de série pour paysans attardés de l'Ouest américain et pas davantage un de ces films dont un des mérites essentiels de John Ford est d'avoir montré qu'ils ne ressortissent pas d'un genre mineur.

Pourtant le metteur en scène de *Michigan Kid*, Ray Taylor, a fait ses premières armes comme assistant de John Ford. Rien ne le confirme. Sa technique reste clouée au traditionnel découpage du film d'aventures et son seul mérite est de ne pas prendre très au sérieux les péripéties de son film dont le début ressemble à une parodie du western avec les quatre copains bagarreurs, la belle fille du saloon, le troupeau de bandits, les bouteilles cassées derrière le comptoir et le sheriff qui ne comprend rien à rien. Il faut dire que ce sheriff est excusable car, si le casse-tête chinois n'existait pas, on pourrait dire que les scénaristes de *Michigan Kid* l'ont inventé. Il se passe beaucoup de choses dans ce film et la plupart du temps les héros sont à cheval, ce qui donne au film l'aspect d'une course hippique où les jockeys manieraient le revolver en guise de cravaches et porteraient des chemises à carreaux au lieu de maillots de soie.

Je ne sais pas si vous l'avez déjà remarqué mais il y a toujours dans les westerns un héros qui s'appelle Curly et ce Curly est, en général, le bandit. Pour ne pas faillir à cette singulière tradition, Victor Mac Laglen joue le rôle de Curly mais avec une mollesse qui étonne chez cet acteur dont la carrière se trouve définitivement derrière lui. Jon Hall est un Kid de 1 m. 90 (et autant de tour de poitrine). Andy Devine a une trop bonne tête pour qu'on ne le prenne pas pour un bandit. Rita Johnson, la jeune première, est fort maigre et on regrette tout au long du film les charmes anonymes d'une danseuse de saloon dont l'exhibition onduleuse rachète l'ennui d'une soirée.

Roger-Marc THEROND.

ais" n'accepte aucune publicité cinématographique

Page from *L'Écran français*

other associates of the future *Cahiers du cinéma* in response to this so-called "tradition of French quality" results from this deep sense of disillusionment. The decline manifested in Carné's transition from *Children of Paradise* to *La Marie du port* (1950) or Clouzot's from *Le Corbeau* to *Wages of Fear* (1953), explains the young directors' feelings of anger, injustice, and even bad faith, of which Truffaut, the youngest of the group, was the uncontested master.

Becker was one of the first (*Antoine et Antoinette,* 1947, *Rendez-vous de juillet,* 1949, *Édouard et Caroline,* 1951) to break with French film's two-bit pessimism and to attempt to represent a younger generation that was enterprising and contemporary, that did not feel it had been tainted by some form of congenital despair. Cocteau showed it was possible to create individual works of art outside the general malaise (*Orpheus,* 1950). Guitry returned with the splendid

Diable boiteux (1948), a triumph of elegant intellect (its young characters are not only refined but somewhat precious). René Clair returned from Hollywood to release the academic *Le silence est d'or* (1947), a film full of old-fashioned charm (that was ultimately disappointing). Then came the meteoric arrival of a relative unknown, Jean-Pierre Melville, whose faithful adaptations of *Silence de la mer* and *Enfants terribles* returned to the idea of resistance. But Bresson would have to wait

until 1950 to film his interpretation of a rebellious and disobedient soul (the young girl in *Journal d'un curé de campagne*), and Grémillon saw three of his projects, films about combat and hope, shelved: *La Commune de Paris* (1945), *Le Massacre des innocents* (1947), and *Le Printemps de la liberté* (1948). During this time he filmed a single documentary, *Le Six Juin à l'aube* (1946), and *Pattes blanches* (1949), a film in keeping with the sordid mentality of the time, from which, in spite of his scriptwriter Jean Anouilh, he managed to extract a fine film.

In hindsight it appears that the future New Wave made, although intuitively and unconsciously, an essentially moral choice that would serve as the basis for its aesthetic opinions, unaware of the extent to which it acted from political conviction. This young generation felt that beauty was refracted through goodness and truth, lucidity and struggle, in short, by a spirit of resistance, and that ugliness often prolonged a collaborationist mentality, frequently disguised as the "advanced" opinions maintained by former members of the Resistance. While the script, the setting, or one or two virtuous characters propagated ideas that were superficially politically correct, these ideas had no substance. The content took precedence over the form, but the form was so murky that the content remained nearly invisible. A certain part of French

Nicole Stéphane and Howard Vernon, *Silence de la mer* (Jean-Pierre Melville, 1949)

cinema of the period was clearly out of phase with the reality of a society that, in practice, refused what that kind of film offered: a spurious discourse of struggle, a feeling of abandonment and abdication.

One wonders if this conflict between young and old, between two different points of view, still exists in the nineties. Based on recent attacks by official French cinema against the decline of the New Wave, with their only criterion of judgment being commercial success, it appears doubtful. After nearly fifty years only a single element has changed—American film. During the years 1945–1950, American film liberated the tastes, the vision, and the imagination of the young rebels. The vitality of American film pointed to the sclerosis of French quality cinema as a source of evil. Today, it is American film that is diseased, and filmmakers from all countries, Americans included, must struggle against it. "From the

crowd to resistance," as Jean-Marie Straub and Danièle Huillet, his wife, would say. To claim, in the name of competition, that one must submit to the rules established by an enormous machine designed to pulverize—commercially, artistically, and ideologically—all genuine creation, all difference and originality, implicates one in a hypocritical illusion. The "collaborators"—whether decision-makers, producers, or directors—will always be prepared to comply in the name of supposedly general interests and profit from their own slice of the pie, no matter how small. It is the same today as it was for the directors of the New Wave.

Arriving with explosive force, the Liberation was aptly named, sweeping the country clean not only of the occupying force and its collaborators, but also, and especially, of a reprehensible ideology. It was a form of redemption, which awakened an immense need for communication, expression, reflection, and understanding. In film, as in many other fields, speaking out became a necessity. The Liberation also reinstituted two phenomena that were born at the end of the First World War, were close to extinction during the thirties, and were invisible during the Occupation: film reviews and magazines, and film clubs. All blossomed again in 1945.

At the time film was immensely popular. The only distraction available to the public, it represented a living force and thus something of significance. Its aura generated a strong need for information. A number of new film journals appeared immediately following the war, which were restricted in length only because paper was in short supply. But three years later many of them had disappeared or merged with the others. This was true of both *L'Écran français* and *La Revue du cinéma*. These journals, however, served as vehicles for the first generation of the New Wave—from Bazin to Astruc, from Doniol-Valcroze

Henri Langlois and Jean-Pierre Melville sometime during the 1950s

André Bazin in the offices of Travail et Culture

Festival de Tours 1957. In the first row, François Truffaut; in the second row, Janine et André Bazin; third row, second from the right, Jacques Doniol-Valcroze

to Rohmer—to theorize and analyze their love of film. They helped the second generation affirm its tastes and structure its thought. After the Liberation film was no longer considered a product but a plant that had to be propagated.

L'Écran français was initially introduced in 1943 within the Resistance. It was a clandestine newsletter that gathered together writers with a range of backgrounds (both moderates and members of the Communist party) along with filmmakers such as Jacques Becker, Jean Grémillon, René Clément, and Louis Daquin. At the time of the Liberation, it became a weekly and split off from *Lettres françaises* (the cultural journal of the French Communist party) as an independent publication. Bringing together the best critics of the period (Georges Sadoul, Roger Leenhardt, Georges Altman, Nino Frank), it was as involved with the life of the French cinematographic industry as it was with the art of film. The format, graphics, variety of information and articles, the minotaur logo (designed by Maurice Henry) whose expression, ranging from joy to sadness, expressed the critic's opinion of a film, turned the review into the essential accessory of the authentic cinephile. It stimulated the mind, provoked disagreement, anger, enthusiasm—especially with the release of *Citizen Kane*; in short, it perfectly fulfilled its role as educator, initiator, and provocateur.

The individual whose influence was most clearly felt on the review was, of course, André Bazin. In August 1945 he brought several articles to Jean-Charles Tacchella, the review's nineteen-year-old editorial secretary who had been a young cinephile stranded in the countryside and who had later come to Paris, as so many others had done—just as Bazin himself had done. Struck by the fevered and impassioned atmosphere of the review, Bazin decided to actively participate in its production. For four years he wrote on a wide variety of subjects. Bazin's biographer Dudley Andrew[1] notes that film was, in Bazin's opinion, a way of involving the public not only in artistic questions but also in sociology, science, geography, and other matters. This educational mission, which Bazin associated with his function as a critic, was taken up by his protégés. Most significant to the New Wave, however, were Bazin's film criticism and essays. He grasped the importance of a two-sided phenomenon that included the film and the critic. First, recent events and, in a larger sense, historical evolution had radically modified his contemporaries' relationship to, and apprehension of, the world. Second, if those involved in cinema were to account for this change, they would need a new approach, a different, modern, style. The artist had to seek out contemporary forms, and critics had to analyze them to facilitate under-

Georges Sadoul and Paul Éluard in 1929

standing (see, for example, Bazin's work on Orson Welles, William Wyler, Roberto Rossellini, Vittorio de Sica, or on Chaplin and *Monsieur Verdoux*). The question of form thus became preeminent. The battle was joined by members of the review's editorial team, in particular Alexandre Astruc and Roger Leenhardt. In March 1948 *L'Écran français* published "Birth of a New Avant-Garde: The Camera as Pen," an article felt by both generations of the New Wave to be their manifesto. Astruc, whose elaborate and flamboyant style marked the article as his own, dared to claim that like literature and philosophy, film could tackle any subject, that the subject was part of the writing, and the camera the pen of modern times. Shortly after, Leenhardt, less abrupt but equally violent, uttered his battle cry on those same pages, "Down with Ford! Long live Wyler!" The idea of contrasting two filmmakers, at the time considered no more than mere craftsmen, on the basis of form, turned out to be scandalous. Moreover, the two directors were Americans.

With the Liberation, however, *L'Écran français* divided into two opposing camps. One, fundamentally political, promoted the idea of film's commitment in the ideological struggle between East and West. The other, basically aesthetic, led by Alexandre Astruc and André Bazin, continued the work of artistic criticism, which was simultaneously taking place in *La Revue du cinéma*. The latter camp didn't hesitate to praise American film, which the other camp fired on at will. The Byrnes-Blum agreement[2] of May 1946, at the onset of the cold war, turned their disagreement into a full schism, and the review became a weapon in the arsenal of the Communist press.

John Ford, a star of the many film clubs that were guided by the French Communist party, alone received favorable treatment, primarily because of *The Grapes of Wrath* (1940), which Stalin was fond of. Of course, Leenhardt's attack in his famous article, "Down with Ford! Long live Wyler!" which was theorized and developed by André Bazin, dealt with purely artistic matters. But the confiscation of this great director by the communist camp—*their* American filmmaker (even if, several years later, the communists rejected him as being too reactionary)—didn't prevent them from ostracizing him under the pretext of academicism and formalism. Such disputes over Ford lasted well into the sixties.

The schism turned out to be a serious error, but it is partly explainable by the polemic climate of the years 1945–1950. The generation of those who were twenty years old in 1950—a generation only moderately involved with the conflict—was less shocked by the partisan positions of the communist critics of *L'Écran français* or the

Naissance du cinéma (Roger Leenhardt, 1946)

NAISSANCE D'UNE NOUVELLE AVANT-GARDE

LA CAMERA STYLO

*Ce qui m'intéresse au cinéma,
c'est l'abstraction.*

(Orson WELLES.)

par ALEXANDRE ASTRUC

IL est impossible de ne pas voir qu'il est en train de se passer quelque chose dans le cinéma. Nous risquons de devenir aveugle devant cette production courante qui étire d'un bout de l'année à l'autre ce visage immobile où l'insolite n'a pas sa place.

Or le cinéma aujourd'hui se fait un nouveau visage. A quoi cela se voit-il ? Mais il suffit de regarder. Il faut être critique pour ne pas voir cette transformation étonnante du visage qui s'opère sous nos yeux. Quelles sont les œuvres par où passe cette beauté nouvelle ? Précisément celles que la critique a ignorées. Ce n'est pas un hasard si de *La Règle du jeu* de Renoir aux films d'Orson Welles en passant par *Les Dames du Bois de Boulogne*, tout ce qui dessine les lignes d'un avenir nouveau échappe à une critique à qui, de toute façon, elle ne pouvait pas ne pas échapper.

Mais il est significatif que les œuvres qui échappent aux bénissements de la critique sont celles sur lesquelles nous sommes quelques-uns à être d'accord. Nous leur accordons, quand on ne fait pas de ce petit domaine d'élection des photographes. Aucun domaine ne doit lui être interdit. La méditation la plus dépouillée, un point de vue sur la production humaine, la psychologie, la métaphysique, les idées, les passions sont très précisément de son ressort. Mieux, nous disons que ces idées et ces visions du monde sont telles qu'aujourd'hui le cinéma seul peut en rendre compte ; Maurice Nadeau disait dans un article de *Combat* : « Si Descartes vivait aujourd'hui il écrirait des romans. » J'en demande bien pardon à Nadeau, mais aujourd'hui déjà un Descartes s'enfermerait dans sa chambre avec une caméra de 16 mm. et écrirait le discours de la méthode en film, car son *Discours de la méthode* serait tel aujourd'hui que seul le cinéma pourrait convenablement l'exprimer.

Il faut bien comprendre que le cinéma jusqu'ici n'a été qu'un spectacle. Ce qui tient très exactement au fait que tous les films sont projetés dans les salles. Mais avec le développement du 16 mm. et de la télévision, le jour n'est pas loin où chacun aura chez lui des appareils de projection et ira louer chez le libraire du coin des films écrits sur n'importe quel sujet, de n'importe quelle forme, aussi bien critique littéraire, roman, qu'essai sur les mathématiques, histoire, vulgarisation, etc. Dès lors il n'est déjà plus permis de parler d'*un cinéma*. Il y aura *des* cinémas comme il y a aujourd'hui *des* littéra-

Suite page 40

caractère annonciateur. C'est pourquoi je parle d'avant-garde chaque fois qu'il arrive quelque chose de nouveau.

PRECISONS. Le cinéma est en train tout simplement de devenir un moyen d'expression, ce qu'ont été tous les autres arts avant lui, ce qu'ont été en particulier la peinture et le roman. Après avoir été successivement une attraction foraine, un divertissement analogue au théâtre de boulevard, ou un moyen de conserver les images de l'époque, il devient peu à peu un langage. Un langage, c'est-à-dire une forme dans laquelle et par laquelle un artiste peut exprimer sa pensée, aussi abstraite soit-elle, ou traduire ses obsessions exactement comme il en est, aujourd'hui de l'essai ou du roman. C'est pourquoi j'appelle ce nouvel âge du cinéma celui de la *Caméra stylo*. Cette image a un sens bien précis. Elle veut dire que le cinéma s'arrachera peu à peu à cette tyrannie du visuel, de l'image pour l'image, de l'anecdote immédiate, du concret, pour devenir un moyen d'écriture aussi souple et aussi subtil que celui du langage écrit. Cet art doué de toutes les possibilités, mais prisonnier de tous les préjugés, ne restera pas à plocher éternellement ce petit domaine du réalisme et du fantastique social qu'on lui a accordé aux confins du roman populaire, il n'est pas de

tures, car le cinéma comme la littérature, avant d'être un art particulier, est un langage qui peut exprimer n'importe quel secteur de la pensée.

Cette idée de cinéma exprimant la pensée n'est peut-être pas nouvelle. Feyder disait déjà : « Je peux faire un film avec *L'Esprit des Lois*. » Mais Feyder songeait à une illustration de *L'Esprit des Lois* par l'image comme Eisenstein à une illustration du *Capital* (ou à une imagerie). Nous disons, nous, que le cinéma est en train de trouver une forme où il devient un langage si rigoureux que la pensée pourra s'écrire directement sur la pellicule sans même passer par ces lourdes associations d'images qui ont fait les délices du cinéma muet. En autres termes, pour dire que du temps s'est écoulé il n'est nul besoin de montrer la chute des feuilles suivie de pommiers en fleurs et pour indiquer qu'un héros a envie de faire l'amour il y a tout de même d'autres moyens de procéder que celui qui consiste à montrer une casserole de lait débordant sur le gaz comme le fait Clouzot dans *Quai des Orfèvres*.

L'expression de la pensée est le problème fondamental du cinéma. La création de ce langage a préoccupé tous les théoriciens et les auteurs de cinéma depuis Eisenstein jusqu'aux scénaristes et adaptateurs du cinéma parlant. Mais ni le cinéma muet, parce qu'il était prisonnier d'une conception statique de l'image ni le parlant classique, tel qu'il existe encore aujourd'hui, n'ont pu résoudre convenablement le problème. Le cinéma muet avait cru s'en tirer par le montage et l'association d'images. On connaît la déclaration célèbre d'Eisenstein : « *Le montage est pour moi le moyen de donner le mouvement (c'est-à-dire l'idée) à deux images statiques.* » Et quant au parlant, il s'est contenté d'adapter les procédés du théâtre.

L'EVENEMENT fondamental de ces dernières années, c'est la prise de conscience qui est en train de se faire du caractère dynamique, c'est-à-dire significatif de l'image cinématographique. Tout film, parce qu'il est d'abord un film en mouvement, c'est-à-dire se déroulant dans le temps, est un théorème. Il est le lieu de passage d'une logique implacable, qui va d'un bout à l'autre d'elle-même, ou mieux encore d'une dialectique. Cette idée, ces significations, que le cinéma muet essayait de faire naître par une association symbolique, nous avons compris qu'elles existent dans l'image elle-même, dans le déroulement du film, dans chaque geste des personnages, dans chacune de leurs paroles, dans ces mouvements d'appareils qui lient entre eux des objets et des personnages aux objets. Toute pensée, comme tout sentiment, est un rapport entre un être humain et un autre être humain ou certains objets qui font partie de son univers. C'est en explicitant ces rapports, en dessinant la trace tangible, que le cinéma peut se faire véritablement le lieu d'expression d'une pensée. Dès aujourd'hui il est possible de donner au cinéma des œuvres équivalentes par leur profondeur et leur signification aux romans de Faulkner, à ceux de Malraux, aux essais de Sartre ou de Camus. D'ailleurs, nous avons sous les yeux un exemple significatif : c'est celui de *Espoir* de Malraux où, pour la première fois peut-être, le langage cinématographique donne un équivalent exact du langage littéraire.

EXAMINONS maintenant les concessions aux fausses nécessités du cinéma.

Les scénaristes qui adaptent Balzac ou Dostoïevsky s'excusent du traitement insensé qu'ils font subir aux œuvres à partir desquelles ils construisent leurs scénarios en alléguant de certaines impossibilités du cinéma à rendre compte des arrière-fonds psychologiques ou métaphysiques. Sous leur main, Balzac devient une collection de gravures où la mode tient la plus grande place et Dostoïevsky tout d'un coup se met à ressembler aux romans de Joseph Kessel avec saoulerie à la russe dans les boîtes de nuit et

courses de troïka dans la neige. Or, ces interdictions ne sont que le fait de la paresse d'esprit et du manque d'imagination. Le cinéma d'aujourd'hui est capable de rendre compte de n'importe quel ordre de réalité. Ce qui nous intéresse au cinéma aujourd'hui, c'est la création de ce langage. Nous n'avons nullement envie de refaire des documentaires poétiques ou des films surréalistes chaque fois que nous pouvons échapper aux nécessités commerciales. Entre le cinéma pur des années 1920 et le théâtre filmé, il y a tout de même la place d'un cinéma qui dégage.

Ce qui implique, bien entendu, que le scénariste fasse lui-même ses films. Mieux, qu'il n'y ait plus de scénariste, car dans un tel cinéma cette distinction de l'auteur et du réalisateur n'a plus aucun sens. La mise en scène n'est plus un moyen d'illustrer ou de présenter une scène, mais une véritable écriture. L'auteur écrit avec sa caméra comme un écrivain écrit avec un stylo. Comment dans cet art où une bande visuelle et sonore se déroule développant à travers une certaine anecdote (ou sans anecdote, il importe peu) et dans une certaine forme, une conception du monde, pourrait-on faire une différence entre celui qui a pensé cette œuvre et celui qui l'a écrite ? Imagine-t-on un roman de Faulkner écrit par quelqu'un d'autre que Faulkner ? Et *Citizen Kane* serait-il convenable dans une autre forme que celle que lui a donnée Orson Welles?

Je sais bien encore une fois que ce terme d'avant-garde fera penser aux films surréalistes et aux films dits abstraits de l'autre après-guerre. Mais cette avant-garde est déjà une arrière-garde. Elle cherchait à créer un domaine propre du cinéma; nous cherchons au contraire à l'étendre et à en faire le langage le plus vaste et le plus transparent qui soit. Des problèmes comme la traduction des temps des verbes, comme les liaisons logiques, nous intéressent beaucoup plus que la création de cet art visuel et statique rêvé par le surréalisme qui d'ailleurs ne faisait qu'adapter au cinéma les recherches de la peinture ou de la poésie.

Voilà. Il ne s'agit pas d'une école, ni même d'un mouvement, peut-être simplement d'une tendance. D'une prise de conscience, d'une certaine transformation du cinéma, d'un certain avenir possible et du désir que nous avons de hâter cet avenir. Bien entendu, aucune tendance ne peut se manifester sans œuvres. Ces œuvres viendront, elles verront le jour. Les difficultés économiques et matérielles du cinéma créent ce paradoxe étonnant qu'il est possible de parler de ce qui n'est pas encore, car si nous savons ce que nous voulons, nous ne savons pas si, quand et comment nous pourrons le faire. Mais il est impossible que le cinéma ne se développe pas. Cet art ne peut pas vivre les yeux tournés vers le passé, remâchant les souvenirs, les nostalgies d'une époque révolue. Son visage est déjà tourné vers l'avenir et, au cinéma comme ailleurs, il n'y a d'autre souci possible que celui de l'avenir.

MAURICE SCHÉRER

Le cinéma, art de l'espace

L'emploi systématique que des réalisateurs comme Orson Welles, Wyler ou Hitchcock ont fait du plan fixe vient depuis peu nous rappeler que l'art du cinéma ne se réduit pas à la seule technique du changement de cadre et que, même aujourd'hui la valeur expressive des rapports de dimensions ou du déplacement des lignes à l'intérieur de la surface de l'écran peut faire l'objet d'un soin rigoureux.

On aurait pu, au contraire, caractériser l'évolution du cinéma jusqu'à ces dernières années par l'affaiblissement d'un certain SENS DE L'ESPACE qu'il ne faut pas confondre avec un sens de l'image ou une simple sensibilité visuelle. Il est remarquable que cette évolution n'ait commencé d'être vraiment sensible que dix ans environ après la découverte du montage. Si la naissance du cinéma en tant qu'art date de l'époque où « le découpeur imagina la division de son récit en plans », ce n'est pas, comme l'affirme André Malraux (1), parce que la photo mobile est un moyen de reproduction non d'expression, mais, bien plutôt parce que la technique de la succession des plans a contribué à renforcer le caractère expressif de chacun de ceux-ci : par exemple en rendant perceptibles des mouvements de très faible amplitude (battement des paupières, crispation des doigts) ou en permettant de suivre ceux dont la trajectoire dépasse de beaucoup l'étendue du champ visuel. L'espace cinématographique se définirait ainsi par rapport à celui de la scène à la fois par l'étroitesse de la surface de visibilité et l'étendue du lieu de l'action; ce n'est donc pas seulement l'intérieur de chacun des plans que le réalisateur doit déterminer en fonction d'une certaine conception de la spatialité, mais la totalité de l'espace filmé : dans *Le Mécano de la Générale* de Buster Keaton le mouvement d'aller et de retour du train correspond à une obsession spatiale très précise.

Ce souci d'expression spatiale est donc apparu de très bonne heure dans l'histoire du cinéma (et on peut se demander, en fin de compte, si l'*Hydrothérapie fantastique* de Méliès n'est pas aussi purement cinématographique que tel montage savant des années 1925-1930). Premier historiquement, il l'est aussi, si l'on peut dire, logiquement, dans la logique d'un art qui, étant par excellence l'art du mouvement, se doit d'organiser le code de significations qu'il utilise en fonction d'une conception générale soit du temps, soit de l'espace, sans qu'il y ait *a priori* aucune raison pour que le temps joue ici un rôle privilégié. L'espace, au contraire, semble bien être la forme générale de sensibilité qui lui est la plus essentielle, dans la mesure où le cinéma est un art de la vue. Aussi les œuvres auxquelles on décerne en général le nom de cinéma pur — les films dits d'avant-garde — se sont-elles attachées surtout à des problèmes d'expression plastique, à la constitution d'une « cinéplastique » du geste (2). Prenons garde, toutefois qu'un certain nombre d'entre elles, qu'il s'agisse du *Sang d'un poète* de Cocteau ou d'*Un Chien andalou* de Buñuel nous révèle un mode de significations qui se rattache à des conceptions plus littéraires ou picturales que vraiment cinématographiques : ce n'est pas par son degré d'abstraction qu'on pourra déterminer le degré de pureté d'un film, mais par la *spécificité* des moyens qu'il emploie.

Il ne s'agit donc pas ici de montrer une fois de plus comment certains réalisateurs

---

(1) Voir toutes les notes en fin d'article.

3

An article by Maurice Schérer (Éric Rohmer), which appeared in *La Revue du cinéma*, no. 14, 1948

conformity of a smug left than by the stupidity and vulgarity of the aesthetic judgment that followed. Typically, a European film—whether Russian (Stalinism was in full swing), Italian, English, or French, (to the extent that it showed a worker or a contemptible bourgeois)—received immediate praise, whereas a film by Walsh or Hawks was considered beneath contempt. The screening of early films (silent and talkies) at the Cinémathèque, along with new releases, required the more independent thinkers to reject this primitive duality. Film called for, demanded, open comparison among all its constituents. There could be no prejudice about a film's country of origin. Bazin, for example, wrote a number of serious and favorable essays about Stalinist works. Critical reflection followed comparison quite naturally and was primarily directed at professional skill and the quality of this skill. It quickly became evident, however, that the American cinema was better than the Russian, Scandinavian, English, or French. This served as an additional incentive for "discovering" Roberto Rossellini, Boris Barnet, Ingmar Bergman, Robert Bresson, etc., who were not only recognized but defended. Within this context the concept of the auteur was—had to be—born, for it was the only response aesthetics and ethics could make in the face of dogmatic, sectarian, and dead-end politics. For Bazin, as Dudley Andrew notes, "normal cinema" was American cinema. Some of these films displayed a new aesthetic or, as Bazin said,

represented "an evolution in the language of cinema." Many of his contributions to *L'Écran français* addressed this discovery, such as the one he wrote in the summer of 1946, entitled "The New American Style." This point of view was antithetical to the formalist, academic conception of the French cinematographic profession. The clash between the two camps occurred after an interview with Hitchcock in January 1949, conducted by Jean-Charles Tacchella and Roger Thérond, who admired *Rope*. The Stalinist old guard soon cut off debate by promulgating an article of dogma: "Content, yes. Form, no." And as an added precaution—more prosaically because of their financial difficulties—*L'Écran français* was absorbed by the communist press. In 1949 the Hollywood camp had lost their mouthpiece but won over France's future directors and young cinephiles.

La Revue du cinéma remained. Founded in 1928 by Jean-Georges Auriol and Denise Tual as an attempt at true critical reflection about the cinema, it had disappeared in 1931 after 29 issues had been published. The announcement by two of its founding members that it would reappear in 1946, with the help of Gallimard, was a major event. Directed by J.-G. Auriol, with the assistance of Jacques Doniol-Valcroze, it was little concerned with political orientation or social commitment: it was an "art" publication, open to the other arts (painting, theater, literature, music, decoration, and fashion) and involved with aesthetic refinement.

Alexandre Astruc and Lydie Doniol-Valcroze in the offices of *Cahiers du cinéma*

What it lacked in cinematic conviction was more than offset by its overall presentation. The idea of the auteur had now become fairly commonplace; there were studies on Griffith, Lang, Eisenstein, Ford, Dreyer, and Lubitsch. Welles, Rossellini, and Italian neorealism were defended in its pages. American film was very much discussed—even more so than French film—in its critical articles, although these lacked conviction and accuracy. The journal's judgments were often quite lucid, however. Writing of Roberto Rossellini's *Miracle* in issue 17 (September 1948), Jean-Georges Auriol implored the film-maker to "rediscover his style or any style for that matter . . . [for] his latest films are formless . . . [and] it would be painful to see a man of Rossellini's talent commit screen 'suicide.' Coasting on his 'genius,' he is satisfied with producing a product instead of creating a work of art." Hitchcock caused almost as many problems as he had for *L'Écran français.* In issue 15 five critics set their sights on him. Even Rohmer displayed some discomfort in defending *Notorious,* one of his favorite films by the master of suspense. At this point in time, however, they were still a considerable way from the Hitchcock–Hawkes debates of the future *Cahiers du cinéma.*

But *La Revue du cinéma,* quite independently of the many worthwhile articles in it, such as those by Doniol-Valcroze and Pierre Kast, had two points in its favor. First, a number of articles by Bazin appeared. Overwhelmed by his numerous contributions to other journals (he was a daily critic for *Le Parisien libéré,* produced weekly articles for *L'Écran français*, and essays for *Esprit,* a monthly for Christian intellectuals), his writings for *La Revue du cinéma* were infrequent but of high quality. They include a superb article, "The Myth of *Monsieur Verdoux*" (issue 9), and a two-part essay on depth of field, "William Wyler or the Jansenist Director" (issues 10 and 11). Second, there was Rohmer's article, "Cinema, the Art of Space" (issue 14, June 1948), which together with Astruc's essay on the camera-as-pen, was the article that had the greatest influence on the second generation of the French New Wave.

1   Dudley Andrew. *André Bazin.* Paris: Éditions de l'Étoile/Cinémathèque française, 1983.

2   The Byrnes–Blum agreement (Washington, May 28, 1946) between France and the United States dealt with monetary, economic, and social issues. In particular, France obtained from its powerful ally the concession that its war debt would not be reimbursed but used for national reconstruction. In exchange the French negotiators agreed to allow American products to enter the country. One provision of the agreement details a massive distribution of American films, a return to French screens after years of absence.

Jacques Doniol-Valcroze

Film Clubs, Ciné-mathèque

History, it is said, repeats itself. Fortunately, so do film clubs. The concept and the name originated with Louis Delluc and date back to 1920; it was his idea to launch a weekly newsletter entitled *Le Journal du ciné-club* or *Ciné-Club*. More importantly, he came up with the idea of a meeting place where filmmakers and film viewers could mingle. Delluc's idea was put into practice in November 1921. The club's purpose, as he saw it, was as follows:

- expand the "seventh art," as it was referred to by Italian film critic Riccioto Canudo; extend awareness of film's power of expression; build a bridge and open a dialogue between the public and filmmakers
- try to escape the influence of money on film
- subvert the destructive effects of an ever-present and impenetrable censorship

It is worth noting in passing that *Battleship Potemkin*, which had been banned in France for 20 years, was first shown at a film club in Paris in 1926.

Between 1920 and 1930, the final and most brilliant period of the silent film, film clubs developed, proliferated, and became politicized. They were part of the intellectual and artistic movements of the time and a natural component of a pervasive avant-garde mood. Their potential for education was immediately recognized. Jean Vigo created a film club in Nice. Before arriving in Paris Luis Buñuel ran the first Spanish film club at the University of Madrid. But with the arrival of sound, the film club's influence, like the influence of the first generation of New Wave directors, began to wane. Nonetheless, when Georges Franju and Henri Langlois formed the modest Cercle du cinéma in 1935, they laid the foundations for the future Cinémathèque française. After 1940 and the beginning of the Occupation, however, such associations were banned and the film clubs went into hibernation. André Bazin and Jean-Pierre Chartier, then a philosophy student at the Sorbonne and avid film fan, succeeded nonetheless in creating a film club sponsored by the Maison des Lettres, a local cultural organization, which had the approval of the Vichy government and the occupying forces. They screened 8 or 9.5 mm copies of old, worn films, obtained with difficulty from collectors for an audience of rarely more than 40 people.

The Liberation arrived like a string of exploding volcanoes. With the need for self-expression that shook up post-Pétainist France came an increased urgency in disseminating, understanding, and, most importantly, *recognizing,* the language of cinema. The environment was again favorable for the sudden growth of the film clubs, and the movement took off and began to consolidate. In 1946 the Fédération française des ciné-clubs (FFCC), a "non-sectarian" organization, came into being along with the Marxist Fédération loisir et culture (FLEC).

Although national education continued to ignore film's importance (it wasn't until the eighties that it was finally integrated into the curriculum), many teachers understood its relevance. Such teachers were often the founders or leaders of local film clubs. This was especially true in the countryside, where there was no vehicle for viewing recent or repertory films, whether French or foreign. (The industry considered recent films impossible to commercialize because they were "too difficult or artistic.") But film club leaders' own taste, based largely on their literary and university training, distanced them from any true understanding of film as a means of expression. There were some exceptions to this, of course, the best known being that of André Bazin.

Film clubs generally began their evening programs with a long and boring presentation based on a compilation of articles by well-known historians and critics, which had been laboriously prepared by the evening's host. This introduction was designed as an orientation for the public to the evening's film and encouraged a fundamentally orthodox interpretation. After the film was shown a discussion period began, consisting of a series of superficial statements that usually provoked arguments among the same four or five individuals, who would hurl their political, ethical, or philosophical opinions back and forth at one another. Hardly profound, their arguments were typically absolutist, a grab-bag of popular opinions that had little to do with the subject treated by the evening's film. Did anyone in the audience, anyone who had not fled by this time, remember the words of their host? "Now that we've discussed the film's content, does anyone have anything to say about the form?" A long silence would then precede an acknowledgment that "Well, the photography was beautiful and the director did a good job. That's all for tonight."

But it was just the beginning. And ideas swirled in the minds of a few enthusiastic adolescents who were infuriated by the mindless arguments exchanged during these discussions about the so-called subject of the film. It was a period of intellectual darkness, during which the enthusiasts feverishly tried to build a critical appeciation for cinema. They perceived, obscurely, that the value of the film lay outside the claims of the script, that it had nothing to do with the superficial aspect of the story. Slowly they discovered that the formal qualities of the film had to be addressed before all else, for these held the key to the true subject of the film. They learned that, strictly speaking, the film's form "contained" the content. By fostering reactions that were sometimes positive, sometimes negative, and often rebellious, the film club, the new element of provincial life, however, played a key role in the development of cinema and enabled a few young men of the second generation of the New Wave to graduate, cinematically speaking, from their stagnant classes.

In Paris, where people were more open-minded and better informed about film in general, film clubs were sprouting up all over. In the capital, a young film enthusiast like François Truffaut had the opportunity to watch films once or twice a day. By the time he was 12 (1944), film had become his passion and at 16 he founded his own film club so he would have access to the films he loved. The next step is familiar to anyone who has seen *The 400 Blows*: the theft of a typewriter to finance the project, reform school, etc. There was also the decisive, real-life meeting with André Bazin that radically changed his life. During the nineteen-eighties, shortly after his illness, the FFCC offered Truffaut the presidency of the organization. His response was immediate, and it would be the only presidency he would accept with joy, for it was to the film clubs that he owed his real aesthetic education and love of cinema.

Rohmer, who was born in 1920, was part of the first generation of the New Wave. Until 1945 he remained more closely attached to the traditional arts, primarily literature and music, than to film. And although he went to the movies, it was strictly as an amateur. Rohmer himself has stated that, at the time, he probably knew less about film than Truffaut, who was twelve years his junior. But he began attending the film clubs and his enthusiasm for cinema soon followed. Rohmer contends that, in spite of his close association with the aesthetics of that first generation of New Wave directors, which included Resnais, Doniol, Kast, etc., he was not a part of that generation. Rather, he belonged to the second generation of Truffaut, Godard, and Chabrol, with whom he remains closely associated. It is not so much that he wants to deny his ties to the first, but his initiation as a cinephile

1. François Truffaut and Jean-Marie Straub, two cinéphiles on the move

2. *The 400 Blows* (François Truffaut, 1959)

3. Antoine Doinel (played by Jean-Pierre Léaud)

4. The theft of the typewriter, one of Antoine Doinel's four hundred "blows"

1. Daniel Gélin, Christian Marquand and, on the right, Annie Girardot in *La Proie pour l'ombre* (Alexandre Astruc, 1961)

2. Maurice Ronet in *The Pit and the Pendulum* (Alexandre Astruc, 1963)

3. *Une vie* (Alexandre Astruc, 1958)

4. Christian Marquand and Maria Schell in *Une vie*

5. Christian Marquand in *Une vie* (Alexandre Astruc, 1958)

chronologically paralleled that of the second generation. Inevitably he shared their tastes, enthusiasms, dislikes, and opinions.

The proof, although indirect, can be found in examining the development of Alexandre Astruc, the other young theoretician, who in 1948, along with Rohmer, helped revolutionize thinking about film. Like Rohmer he had been a young cinephile and was an avid participant at the film clubs. But his tendency was to align himself with those ready to dictate matters of taste rather than to look and learn for himself. His literary background serving as a guide, his Malrauxian fascination with genius led him to attack Orson Welles's detractors and defend *Citizen Kane*, the focus of a new struggle between classicists and romantics. A landmark film considered emblematic of the new post-classical cinema that young cinephiles had placed their faith in, *Citizen Kane* exposed new fields of possibility to filmic language, made the camera as docile and easy to use as a pen in grasping the most subtle variations of thought.

Like the young American prodigy, the "wonder boy" he wanted to be compared to, Astruc, at 25, began his directing career with *Aller-Retour* (1948). In 1953 he produced *Le Rideau cramoisi*, a wildly successful short, followed by several features: *Mauvaises Rencontres* (1955), *Une vie* (1958), *La Proie pour l'ombre* (1961), *L'Éducation sentimentale* (1962). In the eyes of both New Wave generations, Astruc appeared to be the precursor of what each of them individually aspired to. In this sense he is rightly considered the first filmmaker of the New Wave. But his temperament as an essayist and novelist locked him into a formal system and a strongly controlled and encoded directorial style, at a time when the New Wave was about to break the rules of narrative and technical practice. The result was that Astruc was ignored by the very New Wave he had helped form. In 1968 he ended his career in film and took refuge in literature, journalism, and occasional projects for television.

Bazin felt that film clubs prolonged and enriched his activity as a critic and sharpened his theoretical approach. It was part and parcel of his work. In Dudley Andrew's book Jean-Charles Tacchella wrote that "In the aftermath of the war, Bazin concentrated his efforts on explaining films for and with the public. He saw himself primarily as a teacher. His activities for Travail et Culture, a government-supported cultural organization, were completely revolutionary (it was also the first time anyone had associated the word culture with the word film). Bazin showed films, in schools, factories, anywhere he could. He soon became the most sought after speaker in the film clubs."[1] Bazin's office was the busiest at Travail et Culture. Intellectuals of all stripes, who had never given a moment's thought to the cinema, now spent long hours analyzing and dissecting films. It was here that Alain Resnais, while preparing his film on Van Gogh, met Chris Marker. And Marker, who loved theater, was "so fascinated with Bazin's personality that he left the theater department to help him sort the mountains of paper that had accumulated in his office."[2] Bazin served as a magnet for intellectuals, Resnais and Marker became friends for life. The two young men eventually developed a more abstract and distanced approach to narrative, based on a documentary attention to concrete details. Together they directed *Les statues meurent aussi* (1953), a film about African art, the anticolonialist stance of which brought down the wrath of political censure.

The incessant back and forth that Bazin enacted between writing (anything from articles in *Esprit,* to simple, journalistic reports for *L'Écran français*) and speaking in the film clubs, which enabled him to sketch out new ideas, was disrupted in 1949 with the disappearance of *La Revue du cinéma* and his dismissal from the currently very communist *L'Écran français*. The film club was no longer an educational podium from which to disseminate fine phrases about the cinema; it became a weapon of the new criticism. This led to the creation of Objectif 49. Founded by Bazin, Astruc, Jacques Doniol-Valcroze, Pierre Kast, and Tacchella, and sponsored by Jean Cocteau, Jean Grémillon, Robert Bresson, Roger Leenhardt, Raymond Queneau, and René Clément, this film club presented unknown films from new directors such as Rossellini, Sturges, Welles, Wyler, Grémillon, Leenhardt, etc., who introduced and discussed their films for a hand-picked audience. To lend strength to its actions, Objectif 49 decided, not without some humor, to launch their own festival, which would be the antithesis of the commercial and artistic spirit found at Cannes. The Festival du Film Maudit took place in July 1949 in Biarritz. The young directors arrived in force, among them Truffaut, Chabrol, Godard, Rivette, and in spite of the age difference, Éric Rohmer. These young filmmakers, who had little inclination (especially since they were rarely invited) for social events, gorged themselves on film and talked through the night in the dormitory of the Biarritz lycée. For the first time both generations of the future New Wave were together. Together, but not united. For while there was obviously some common ground, there was a great deal more to disagree about.

It was the Cinémathèque française that was to form strong bonds among the different members and unite them into a team. The manner in which Henri Langlois had saved his

collection of films during the Occupation, the recognition of the need to preserve the cinematic heritage, the interest that politicians and intellectuals finally showed for film led to the opening of a new facility dedicated to the cinema in 1948. No longer the Cercle du cinéma, which had functioned as a kind of film club for 12 years, the Cinémathèque achieved the status of a museum. It opened on Avenue de Messine in Paris, and initially served as a meeting place. In 1945 an exhibition space was created and in 1948 it became a venue for screening films.

The screening room was miniscule and had no more than 50 seats. But they were always full. The importance of the Cinémathèque française naturally arose from its work in collecting, exhibiting, and conserving films, which were its principal functions. But its primary significance for cinema is based on Henri Langlois's notion of his curatorial mission. Unlike the other scattered film

Document 1:

```
MUSEE du CINEMA                    1954                    CARnet 10-58
7, avenue de Messine
PARIS ( 8ème )
              LE   MUSEE   DU   CINEMA
                dans son Cycle d'Eté présente :

           LES GRANDS CLASSIQUES DE L'ECRAN

    1er Septembre  : THE KID - Chaplin, 1921
     2     "        LA RUE SANS JOIE - Pabst, 1924
     3     "        L'OPERA DE QUAT' SOUS - Pabst, 1931
     4     "        LA LIGNE GENERALE,- Eisenstein, 1928
     5     "        M. LE MAUDIT - F. Lang, 1931
     6     "        NOSFERATU LE VAMPIRE - Murnau, 1921
     7     "        LE CABINET DU Dr CALIGARI - Wiene, 1919
     8     "        NANA - J. Renoir, 1926
     9     "        CHARLOT SOUS L'AVERSE - Chaplin, 1914
                    LE SOUS-MARIN PIRATE - M. Sennett, 1915
                    LES DEUX FONT LA PAIRE - M.Sennett, 1915
    10     "        L'AURORE - Murnau, 1927
    11     "        ALEXANDRE NEWSKY - Eisenstein, 1939
    12     "        LE CIRQUE - Chaplin, 1928
    13     "        BOUDU SAUVE DES EAUX - J. Renoir, 1932
    14     "        LOUISIANA STORY - Flaherty, 1948
    15     "        HOMMAGE à Germaine DULAC :
          18h30 ( LA CIGARETTE, 1919      GOSSETTE (ext.) 1923 ) 20h30
                ( FETE ESPAGNOLE, 1919    DIABLE DANS LA VILLE 1924(
                ( LA MORT DU SOLEIL (ext.) 1920 AME D'ARTISTE (ext.) 1925)
                ( LA SOURIANTE Mme BEUDET, 1922 ANTOINETTE SABRIER 1927 (
                  22h30  INVITATION AU VOYAGE (Ext.) 1927
                         LA COQUILLE ET LE CLERGYMAN, 1927
                         ARABESQUES - DISQUE 957, 1929
                         INEDITS - 1933-38
    16     "        LE MILLION - R. Clair, 1930
    17     "        L'AGE D'OR - Luis Bunuel, 1930
    19     "        L'ANGE BLEU - Sternberg, 1929
    20     "        HOMMAGE à DELLUC
          18h30 ( LE CHEMIN D'ERNOA 1920   LA FEMME DE NULLE PART, 1922) 20h30
                ( LE TONNERRE, 1921        LE PELOTE BASQUE )
                ( FIEVRES, 1923            L'INONDATION ....        22h30

    Projections à 18h30 - 20h30 - 22h30
    A l'attention des Etudiants de la Cité Universitaire: Moyens de correspondance de
    la Cité Universitaire au Musée du Cinéma : Métro MIROMESNIL - Autobus nº 21, Cité
    Universitaire - Gare St-Lazare et 84 : Luxembourg - Avenue de Messine .
```

Document 2:

```
             LA CINEMATHEQUE FRANCAISE
             -:-:-:-:-:-:-:-:-:-:-:-:-:-:-
                    MUSEE du CINEMA
       Présente à l'INSTITUT PEDAGOGIQUE NATIONAL - 29 rue d'Ulm  PARIS V°
                              -o-

Lundi 26 Octobre:
    18 h 30 - LES FILMS DE LA PLEIADE - BONJOUR Mr LA BRUYERE, Doniol-Valcroze 1957
              LE COUP DU BERGER, Rivette 1957 - O'SAISONS, O'CHATEAUX, A.Varda 1957
              LE CHANT DU STYRENE, A.Resnais 1958 - LE CARNAVAL A NEW ORLEANS, 1958
    20 h 30 - SUBIDA AL CIELO (La Montée vers le Ciel) de Luis Bunuel 1951 avec Lilia
              Prado, Carmelita-Gonzales, E.Marquez, L.Aceves Castaneda      (Mexique)
    22 h 30 - TIGRIS de Denizev 1911 (Italie) DONA NUDA de Carmine Gallone 1912
              ASSUNTA SPINA de Serena 1915 avec Francesca Bertine, G.Serena (Italie)

Mardi 27 Octobre:
    18 h 30 - THE RIVER de Lore Parentz 1938 (U.S.A.)
              THE LAND de Robert Flaherty 1942 (U.S.A.)
    20 h 30 - BOUDU SAUVE DES EAUX de Jean Renoir 1932 avec Michel Simon, Severine
              Leszozinska, Marcelle Haina, Charles Granval, Jacques Becker  (France)
    22 h 30 - TERRE D'ESPAGNE de Joris Ivens 1937  (Espagne)

Jeudi 29 Octobre:
    18 h 30 - LES NIEBELUNGEN I (La Mort de Siegfried) de Fritz Lang 1923/24 avec
              Paul Richter, Hans-Adalbert von Schlettow, Bernhart Goetzke, M.Schoen
    20 h 30 - LES VACANCES DE MONSIEUR HULOT de Jacques Tati 1951 avec J.Tati, Louis
              Perrault, André Dubois, L.Frégis, R.Lacourt, R.Carl, N.Pascaud  (France)
    22 h 30 - TARTUFFE de Murnau 1925 avec Emil Jannings, Lil Dagover (Allemagne)

Vendredi 30 Octobre:
    18 h 30 - LES NIEBELUNGEN II (La Vengeance de Kriemhild) de F.Lang(Allemagne)
    20 h 30 - PRIX DE BEAUTE (Miss Europe) de Genina 1929 avec Louise Brooks
                                                                         (France)
    22 h 30 - OCTOBRE de S.M.Eisenstein 1928 (U.R.S.S.)

Dimanche 1 Novembre:
    18 h 30 - METROPOLIS de Fritz Lang 1926 avec Brigitte Helm, Alfred Abel, Rudolf
              Klein-George, Heinrich George, Fritz Rasp, Gustav Fröhlich(Allemagne)
    20 h 30 - THINGS TO COME (La Vie Future) de William Cameron 1936 avec Raymond
              Massey, Ralph Richardson, Margaretta Scott, J.Clément  (Gde Bretagne)
    22 h 30 - LA BATAILLE DU RAIL de René Clément 1945 avec Clarieux, Durand,
              Desagneux, Laurent et les Cheminots de la S.N.C.F.       (France)
```

1. Program from the Cinémathèque Française, Avenue de Messine, summer 1954

2. Program from the Cinémathèque Française, Rue d'Ulm, 1959

3. The screening room on the Rue de Courcelles, showing a film by Jean Herman, 1962 (photograph from *La Cinémathèque Française*)

4. Festival du film maudit, Biarritz, August 3, 1949. Seated, from left to right: Alexandre Astruc, André Bazin, Claude Mauriac, Mitsou Dabat, and Lydie Doniol-Valcroze. Standing: Grisha Dabat, René Clément, Jean Grémillon, Raymond Queneau, Jacques Doniol-Valcroze, Éric Rohmer, Jean Cocteau, Léonide Keigel, Jean-Charles Tacchella, Jean Tronquet, Rogher Thérond, France Roche, Pierre Kast, Jean-Pierre Vivet, and Jacques Bourgeois

11 DECEMBRE **1929 - STERNBERG** . . .	L'Ange bleu (Allemagne). avec M. Dietrich, E. Jannings, H. Albers.	**21 NOVEMBRE** **1934 - RENOIR**
18 OCTOBRE **1929 - CLAIR**	Sous les toits de Paris (Fr.) avec P. Iléry, A. Préjean, G. Mo- dot.	**22 NOVEMBRE** **1934 - RAIZM**
12 DECEMBRE **1930 - GREMILLON** . .	La petite Lise (France). avec N. Sibirskaïa, Alcover, P. Bernard.	**19 OCTOBRE** **1935 - ROBISC**
13 DECEMBRE **1930 - BUNUEL**	L'Age d'Or (France). avec G. Modot.	**20 OCTOBRE** **1935 - RENOI**
11 NOVEMBRE **1930 - CLAIR**	Le million (France). avec Annabella, R. Lefebvre, R. Cordy.	**17 DECEMBRE** **1936 - LANG**
12 NOVEMBRE **1930 - PABST**	Die Dreigroschenoper (Al- lemagne). avec C. Neher, V. Gert, R. For- ter, F. Rasp.	**18 DECEMBRE** **1937 - WYLER**
13 NOVEMBRE **1930 - LANG**	Le maudit (Allemagne). avec P. Lorre.	**19 DECEMBRE** **1938 - EISENS**
14 NOVEMBRE **1931 - EKK**	Le chemin de la vie (U.R. S.S.). avec Batalov, Kyrla, Vesnovsky.	**20 DECEMBRE** **1938 - RENOI**
14 DECEMBRE **1931 - SAGAN-** **FROELICH.**	Jeunes filles en uniforme (Allemagne). avec H. Thiele, D. Vieck.	**24 NOVEMBRE** **1938 - DONS**
15 NOVEMBRE **1931 - FLEMING-** **FAIRBANKS.**	Around the world in 80 mi- nutes (U.S.A.). avec D. Fairbanks.	**21 OCTOBRE** **1939 - MALRA**
16 NOVEMBRE **1932 - RENOIR**	La chienne (France). avec J. Marèze, M. Simon.	**21 DECEMBRE** **1939 - DOVJE**
17 NOVEMBRE **1932 - CLAIR**	A nous la liberté (France). avec R. Cordy, H. Marchand.	**22 DECEMBRE** **1939 - CARNI**
18 NOVEMBRE **1932 - PABST**	Tragédie de la Mine (All.- France). avec Granach, Mendaille, Wendt, Manson.	**25 NOVEMBRE** **1939 - DONS**
19 NOVEMBRE **1932 - HAWKS**	Scarface (U.S.A.). avec A. Dvorak, P. Muni, G. Raft, B. Karloff.	**22 OCTOBRE** **1939 - RENO**
15 DECEMBRE **1932 - EISENSTEIN** . .	Que Viva Mexico (Mex.).	**23 OCTOBRE** **1939 - WITN**
16 DECEMBRE **1933 - LANG**	Le testament du Dʳ Mabuse (Allemagne). avec Klein-Rogge.	**26 NOVEMBRE** **1940 - DONS**
20 NOVEMBRE **1934 - VIGO**	L'Atalante (France). avec D. Parlo, Dasté, M. Simon, Margaritis.	**27 NOVEMBRE** **1940 - FORD**

libraries of the time, Langlois did not conceive of his role to be solely that of a curator who saves, accumulates, and jealously guards ancient treasures, but as a ferryman who brings treasures of the past to the people of the present. Langlois saw himself, in his tiny room, as an usher, who with his flashlight helps to define and to illuminate the future. Using the films of the past, he projected the cinema of tomorrow. In his eyes the function of the museum was to make use of consummate works of art by yesterday's artists to initiate, inspire, and train the potential but still immature filmmakers to come.

The Cinémathèque became, quite naturally, the country's true film school. The future filmmakers of the New Wave, then in their early twenties, refused without exception to enroll in IDHEC, the Institut des hautes études

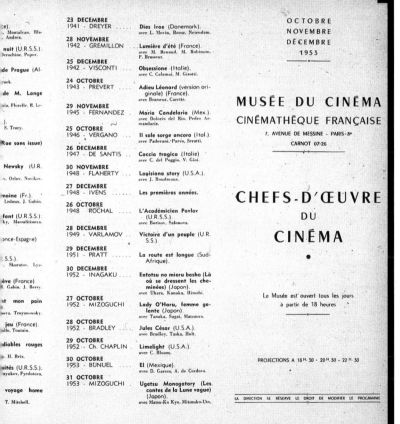

cinématographiques.[3] Alain Resnais and Louis Malle left the Institute before their first year of study was completed. At the time IDHEC had based its teaching methods on the national education system, and everything was drawn from books and oral presentations. Based on what were already

outdated theories, students learned and practiced by reading manuals that had long ceased to be relevant (it wasn't until 1968 that a more radical and welcome reform of such teaching methods took place at IDHEC). IDHEC did, however, supply the majority of the creative talent for television, as well as the first film technicians, who often ended their career as directors, some of them rather gifted. The latter came every evening to the Cinémathèque to nourish their immense but frustrated dreams of filmmaking.

What was Langlois's secret? He had complete confidence in the sensitivity and judgment of the individual spectator. His programming was extremely subtle, and he gambled on the "fan" who refused to give up his seat for the entire evening. It became his practice to screen films that were very different from one another in tone (drama and comedy), genre (western and melodrama), period (silent and sound), origin (Russian and American), etc. He chose them because he had himself established secret links between the films, which he left up to the public to discover. Because he wanted the viewer to actively participate in understanding film he screened silent films without any musical accompaniment, and often without insert titles. He showed films in Czech, Azerbaijan, or Javanese, without an accompanying translation. He believed that the public should make the effort to grasp what took place on the screen. Occasionally this gave rise to hilarious errors of interpretation, but more than anything it drew the viewer's attention to what was taking place on screen. Langlois forced the viewer to abandon whatever literary understanding he or she associated with a film story and to penetrate a magical universe based on a new form of dramaturgy that was brought into existence by the visual treatment of and plastic interpretation of space. The viewer was forced to examine the film's form, what was later to be known as *mise-en-scène*, which contained, delivered, and explained the work's true meaning.

Langlois loved to say that if film hadn't been born silent, cinematic art would never have been born at all, or only belatedly and incompletely. It would have been nothing more than canned speech, without any genuine visual or auditory innovation. After a childhood spent wearing out the seat of his pants in the darkened halls of the popular cinema, in the "school of silent film," he retained a handful of important truths. Langlois understood that the language of cinema, week after week, month after month, year after year, had been forged between a cinematically illiterate public and novice filmmakers, equally ignorant, but bold and intuitive. This dialogue evolved throughout the silent period. As soon as one cinematic effect had been understood and assimilated, directors tried out new ones, risked unknown expressions, combined increasingly bold grammatical forms. Beginning in 1920, the most audacious techniques of the various avant-gardes were immediately integrated, absorbed, and exploited by commercial cinema.

Langlois was convinced that the silent film provided the best way to learn the art of cinema. This was the reason for his 1948 decision to program primarily films from this period. The young intransigents who stretched out on the floor in front of the first row of seats, their heads just above the bottom of the screen (the only way to get into the film for free) were barely twenty years old. They had been born the same year as the talkies and, with the exception of the films of Chaplin, knew nothing about silent film. This group included Godard, Truffaut, Rivette, and others of their generation. Yet within two years they possessed an extensive vision of the history of cinema and an increasingly accurate idea of the art and its language. At the same time Langlois presented a number of audacious, lesser-known films that had been banned (Jean Genet's *Chant d'amour*, Kenneth Anger's *Fireworks*) but whose modernity was without question. Every young filmmaker who showed up with a can of film under his arm was welcome, and his work was screened by the master of the house, shown that evening after the program, without warning. Langlois's Cinémathèque was his home, always open to cinema's past, present, and future.

The educational role that Langlois sought had been achieved. The proof of this came in 1968, when the French bureaucracy tried to remove him from his position as head of the Cinémathèque française. The revolt was spontaneous, and included the filmmakers of the New Wave and their fans, frequently resulting in violent demonstrations with the police. Removing Langlois led to a general mobilization within cinema and brought together some of the greatest filmmakers in the world—Chaplin, Kurosawa, Welles, Bergman, Satyajit Ray, Nicholas Ray, Renoir, Rossellini, Lang, Hitchcock—as well as the intervention of the major Hollywood studios, who threatened to withdraw all the films they had lent to Langlois (which made up nearly the entirety of the holdings of the Cinémathèque française). The government was forced to back off. For the first time, in ten years in power, De Gaulle yielded. Historians consider the "Langlois affair" to be the precursor to May '68. Whether or not that is true, in 1968 people of all ages, from every walk of life, recognized the global importance of Henri Langlois to the life of the cinema.

The question naturally arises, without Langlois's (and Mary Meerson's, Lotte Eisner's, Marie Epstein's, Musidora's, etc.) Cinémathèque française, would there have been a New Wave? Certainly. But it wouldn't have had the same force, the same brilliance, or the same effect. It would simply have been French.

1 Dudley Andrew. *André Bazin*. Paris: Éditions de l'Étoile/Cinémathèque française, 1983.

2 Andrew. *André Bazin*.

3 Institute for Advanced Film Studies.

1. Éric Rohmer

2. The Committee for the Defense of Henri Langlois, April 18, 1968: Robert Bresson, François Truffaut, Pierre Kast, Marcel Carné, Maître Kiejmann, Henri-Georges Clouzot, Alain Resnais (photograph by Raymond Depardon)

Auteurism favored reflection and implied selectivity. As in all the arts, such a process operated by means of selections that evolved slowly over the years. Films and filmmakers were compared with one another: some were kept, others rejected. Even though such a system was known to be unfair, it was absolutely necessary, and the new criticism embodied in *Cahiers du cinéma* was deliberately partisan. Thus while auteurism was developing as an approach to cinema, it was also rewriting cinema's history, and

Favorite

it did so in such a way that its choices and values are still current. Auteurism has been criticized, particularly by those who want to attack the spirit and work of the New Wave, slightly refined, and updated for modern tastes, but overall, the great figures that emerged from this reevaluation of the history of cinema are still widely recognized today.

Reexamination was necessary. First, because during the years 1945–1950, the cinema was only around fifty years old, and cinema's past was still manageable enough that students could familiarize themselves with its entire history. Yet there was enough of it to enable students to distance themselves from the past and form new judgments. Second, because auteurism was associated with a combative strategy that was more internal than external, and revolved around the only question that mattered to filmmakers during this period of initial assessment (What is cinema?), the Hitchcock–Hawks approach—or auteurism—naturally served as a line of attack. This did not imply that the young writers at *Cahiers*

audacious enough to serve as a guide. It could be used to evaluate new directors and determine who was and who was not an auteur (or a member of the inner circle) on the basis of only one or two films. It helped "create" the contemporary directors who appeared after 1945. The pertinence of the choices made at the time, today obvious to all but a few hysterical renegades, was generally sufficient enough to justify the validity of the auteur concept itself. The concept of the auteur has often been attacked, never replaced, and appears now to be more necessary than ever.

Londres, entrée du cinématographe (Lumière, 1896)

La Sortie des usines Lumière (Lumière, 1895)

du cinéma, unlike their elders Bazin, Doniol, Kast, etc., believed that Hitchcock or Hawks were the greatest filmmakers, but simply that they were the most exemplary. By accepting the film industry's technical and professional rules, and by integrating them into their work, these two directors illustrated in ideal fashion the concept of the director-as-auteur. They served to define and focus auteurism.

And because film history was revised, the concept of the auteur was able to function on two levels. It verified past accomplishments, drew attention to forgotten directors, and altered their rankings, raising some directors (Murnau, for example) and pushing others from the Olympus they had occupied up until 1950 (Pudovkin and René Clair). But more importantly, the idea was

Although not exhaustive, the following is a list of those filmmakers who have had the greatest influence on the New Wave since 1895.

The silent film

David W. Griffith. Discovered at the Cinémathèque française, he dazzled, fascinated, and excited audiences. His approach to film combined all the possible forms of cinema: from the familial intimacy of the amateur film to the sweeping mise-en-scène of the spectacle. He had a stupefying ability to create a canvas out of everything he filmed, to make the frame dynamically responsible for all the movements in the film (in particular, human emotions), to cut up spatial unity through editing into multiple fragments and then reunite them again. Without exception the entire New Wave admired Griffith, remembered him, and used him as a source

The Outlaw and the Wife (Victor Sjöström, 1917)

Enfants pêchant des crevettes (Lumière, 1896)   *Intolerance* (D. W. Griffith, 1916)

The Lumière brothers were preferred to Méliès for theoretical, moral, and artistic reasons. They approached cinema as a mechanical and scientific instrument. It was the device itself—the film camera and projector—that recorded life and was able to restore and observe it. The device was able to cut through space to expose things to *view*, able to frame and tease out a sense of immediate plastic drama, provoked by the eruption of an event that was captured as "news" or "reportage." It was the triumph of machinery and all its marvels. Méliès represented a return to theatricality and the stage, its fantasy and "imagined" reality. These two approaches to film have remained the guiding forces in the history of cinema.

of inspiration. One of the best loved of Griffith's films: *True Heart Susie* (1919).

Victor Sjöström and Mauritz Stiller.

The New Wave admired these Swedish directors and their dramatic use of natural elements, which emphasized the immensity of space in Scandinavia. But it never updated their approach. Sjöström's *The Outlaw and His Wife* and especially *The Wind* (1928, filmed in the United States) were preferred to *The Phantom Chariot*. Among Stiller's films, the New Wave favored *The Treasure of Arne*, *Erotikon*, *The Legend of Gösta Berling*.

Buster Keaton. While Keaton was still remembered as a great burlesque comedian in 1945, he had been completely forgotten as an auteur. The New Wave, Rohmer in particular, rediscovered him. In "Le cinema, art de l'espace" (*La Revue du cinéma*, no. 14, 1948), Rohmer makes Keaton the focal point of his argument, claiming that his greatest strength is as a creator of form. Keaton systematically constructs the shot, fixing it to the flat surface of the screen. He uses this horizontality as a way to superimpose and reveal parallel universes, piercing them with a perpendicular axis that dynamically opens and wears away the depth of field. Keaton's methods made sense to the New Wave and served as a lesson in cinema and mise-en-scène. Through gales of laughter, the New Wave revitalized itself with Keaton's purity, abstraction, and

screen as a blank canvas, a unique object upon which he could work the cinema's magic. It served as a frame to delimit the field of existence. A character *exists* only if he is visible within the frame (thus the importance of appearances and disappearances, veils, and hiding places) but *no longer exists* once he crosses that limit (this explains the strong sense of dramatization that results from entrances and exits on screen). Murnau's plastic composition contrasted a succession of spaces, each of which was designed on the basis of preceding and succeeding spaces. The rhythm of his films speeds up and slows down, reflects and justifies movement, including that of the camera, which attempts to overcome stasis. The editing is worked around the idea of the insert, etc. Such techniques became "seminal figures" of cinematic expression, to

Buster Keaton in *The Navigator*, 1924

George O'Brien in *Sunrise* (F. W. Murnau, 1927)

intelligence. The films that never failed to find an enthusiastic audience: *The Navigator* and *The General*.

Friedrich W. Murnau. The New Wave freed him from purgatory. He was considered the greatest director in the world during the twenties, but had been forgotten by the critics and historians of the fifties, who attributed *Tabu* entirely to Flaherty. For *Cahiers du cinéma* Murnau's defense became more than a necessity, it was the crux of their aesthetic stance. Here was a director who had used every expressive means available to film and had explored each of its constituent elements (using daylight and night light, soft light or brilliant light). He used the

use Rohmer's expression, and left an indelible mark on future filmmakers.

In addition, Murnau had an enormous influence on many of the directors favored by the *Cahiers*, including Hawks, Hitchcock, Ford, Mizoguchi, Minnelli, and others. Earlier critics, who worked on a film by film basis rather than focusing on the auteur, had been forced to ignore one of the most inventive, if not the greatest, of all directors. After the dazzling, stupefying discovery of *Nosferatu*, *The Last Laugh*, *Faust*, and especially *Sunrise*, a film the entire future New Wave chose as the most beautiful film in the history of cinema, the similarity with *Tabu* became obvious from the opening shot. The story bore Murnau's indelible mark. This was something that historical research could easily have shown, since Flaherty had left Tahiti before shooting for the film had begun. This having been said, the attribution of *Tabu* to Murnau alone in no way harmed the New Wave's admiration for Robert Flaherty, another great director of space. *Nanook of the North*, *The Man of Aran*, and the later *Louisiana Story* (1948) were, for the writers of *Cahiers du cinéma*, cinematic jewels that served, and continue to serve, as a way of approaching the distinction between documentary and fiction.

other director. This was what Rivette thought most remarkable about von Stroheim. His sense of realism led to a baroque and flamboyant delirium. Stroheim invented a form of cinema that his contemporary Antonin Artaud (with reference to the stage) called the "theater of cruelty." Von Stroheim also had been Renoir's teacher, and influenced Welles, along with many other directors. This absolute auteur and outcast was central to the directors and critics of the New Wave, for whom he was an enduring

Queen Kelly (Erich von Stroheim, 1928)

Erich von Stroheim. In 1950 Erich von Stroheim's films were as bold and sensational as they had been in the twenties. Moral censorship also had an effect on social mores. But what was even more astonishing was a naturalist realism so exacerbated that it drew out and dissected each situation slowly and minutely, down to the smallest (and often most intimate) detail. A scene in von Stroheim lasts two or three times longer than the same scene shot by any

source of inspiration. Their favorite film? All of them, without exception.

From the Silent to the Talkie

special issue of *La Revue du cinéma* to him, he is said to have been forgotten after his death in 1947 by the second generation. This was far from the truth. Lubitsch remained as deeply admired as ever, but because his films weren't shown, there was little opportunity for this admiration to express itself. In reality, there was little to criticize in the work of the man with the cigar between his teeth. The scriptwriter (*To Be or Not to Be* was felt to be the greatest script ever written in the history of cinema), the brilliant writer of dialogue, the elliptical director who created the famous "Lubitsch touch," continued to fascinate. The directors of the New Wave all learned from Lubitsch (screenplay in Truffaut, for example, tone in Chabrol, light in Godard, etc.). Lubitsch's rise resulted in the downfall of the very Parisian René Clair, whose French "delicacy" suddenly appeared heavy-handed compared to the racy but

To Be or Not to Be (Ernst Lubitsch, 1942)

Beyond a Reasonable Doubt (Fritz Lang, 1956)

Charlie Chaplin. Chaplin remained in favor with both the first and second generation of the New Wave, from issue 1 to issue 159 of the *Cahiers du cinéma*. It is unfortunate that no study of Chaplin (except for Bazin's essay on *Verdoux* or that of Jean Mitry, neither of which were published in the *Cahiers*) ever introduced a new point of view about a body of work as fundamental as this. It is especially unfortunate that a critical examination of his style has never been attempted. Cinematic language has never achieved such pure and limpid classicism as that found in *The Circus*. Too pure perhaps for the young directors who hoped to break with such perfection.

Ernst Lubitsch. Although much admired by the first generation of the New Wave, which devoted a

artificial futility and true Germanic gravity of the genial director from Berlin.

Fritz Lang. A fall from grace—such was the general opinion of the conservative critics in 1950, and a single thread ran through their discussions of Lang: What had become of the great director of the German period (1920 to 1932)? The New Wave responded: He went to Hollywood and has never been better. The visible apparatus of the mise-en-scène in the *Nibelungen*, *Metropolis*, and even *M* become interiorized. The stasis of plastic composition has been abandoned for a dynamic of inexorable movement: a scene is the cause of the following scene, which, in its movement, becomes the cause of the third scene, and so on until the final credits. The scene no longer serves as a support for a formalist intention. Rather, it is a neutral yet inevitable place of transition (see, for example, *The Big Heat*, *The Blue Gardenia*, *While the City Sleeps*, *Beyond a Reasonable Doubt*, all of which the *Cahiers* championed). Although it is still a "scene," it serves to trace the projection of an intention that hides behind anonymity and indifference. There is no finer manifestation of the essence of mise-en-scène than that found in Lang. Like so many other directors, those of the New Wave without exception, from Franju to Straub, willingly submitted to the rigors of Langian necessity.

Alexander Dovzhenko, Dziga Vertov, Sergei Eisenstein.
Often shown at the Cinémathèque française, Soviet films of the end of the silent

Godard, Dovzhenko for Rohmer, Eustache, etc. The cinematographic design of *Battleship Potemkin*, however, was rejected as being too psychological.

Boris Barnet.
Considered a sympathetic but second-rate Russian director until he produced three important films, Barnet turned out to be something of a revelation in the eyes of the young directors of the fifties. Based entirely on the principle of association—idea, emotion, sensibility—his style broke with narrative tradition for the sake of the freedom and creativity of poetic language. Recourse to the art of the circus clown favored the constant rupture of linearity. Discontinuity had the force of dramatic law. Godard, more than any other director, was influenced by Barnet, and it is

Renée Falconeti, *The Passion of Joan of Arc* (C. T. Dreyer, 1928)

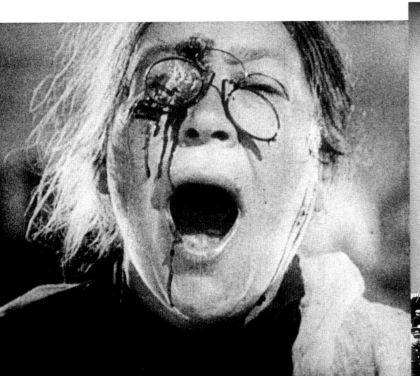

The Battleship Potemkin (S. M. Eisenstein, 1926)

La mort !

The Man with the Movie Camera (Dziga Vertov, 1929)

The Girl with the Hatbox (Boris Barnet, 1

period and beginning of the talkies, left a strong and favorable impression on future directors. The stylistic audacity of the young Bolshevik revolutionaries awakened a desire for disruption in the French cinema. Eisenstein's towering genius (from *Strike* to *Ivan the Terrible*, especially part II), Dovzhenko's telluric lyricism (from *Earth* to *Poem of the Sea*), and the conceptual poetry of Dziga Vertov's *Kino-Pravda* and *Man with a Movie Camera* magnified the individual theoretical approaches to editing these directors established. The New Wave had its own favorites: Eisenstein for Resnais and Marker, Vertov for

impossible to understand his work without referring to Barnet. *Charlotte et son jules*, which was indebted to *The Young Girl with the Hatbox*, was an obvious homage to Barnet's work. And every New Wave director without exception regarded *By the Bluest of Seas* as one of their favorite films. Gradually, even in the USSR, Boris Barnet came to be considered one of the greatest, most exciting, and most original of Soviet directors.

Carl Theodore Dreyer.
A summit in film history. Dreyer reduced everything to a sign, essentialized

form, achieved an almost physical concretization of the most important of all emotions, love—as force, as form, as a truth of nature, and especially human nature. Asceticism, the magical power of a felt abstraction, makes Dreyer's films supremely unique. Image, light, sound, and the interaction of the actors hypnotize the spectator, key his breathing to the rhythm of the film. Dreyer was not just a model filmmaker, he was a model for filmmakers. And it is in this way that Rohmer, Rivette, and the others regarded him.

Jean Renoir.

First there was the shock of *Rules of the Game*. In 1947–1948 the film was still in poor condition, and François Truffaut ran from film club to film club to locate scenes that had been cut from the various versions. From the very beginning, his work stood out. The immense admiration for his later

was, and remains, the essential reference for any director, or any true cinephile.

Abel Gance.

His capacity for clairvoyance and delirium, which skirted the boundaries of genius and ridicule, demand our respect and admiration.

Jean Vigo.

Truffaut's imaginary older brother (his Rusty James). He was the comrade-in-arms of Demy, Rozier, Eustache, and Godard. Vigo's poetic vision of reality, the cruel tenderness that emanates from his work and his characters, their euphoria, the anarchic force that liberates them, their freedom, the misfortune that his only two feature films (*Zero for Conduct* and *L'Atalante*) were the victims of censorship and Gaumont Studios, and especially his premature death at 32 (he was along with Renoir, destined to

Sacha Guitry in *Quadrille*, 1937.

Sylvia Bataille, *Une partie de campagne* (Jean Renoir, 1936)

Jean Vigo at the camera during the early nineteen thirties

films (*The River*, *The Golden Coach*, *French Cancan*, etc.) was reinforced by the simultaneous discovery of his pre-war films, which slowly began to appear. The majority of these were unknown to the young filmmakers of the nineteen fifties. *Boudu Saved from Drowning* had been considered a flop, and the negative almost destroyed. *A Day in the Country* and *Grand Illusion* overwhelmed audiences. *La Chienne* fascinated them. *Toni* shocked them. Renoir was called a genius so often that the adjective seemed prosaic. Very quickly, Renoir became the focus of the struggle to establish auteurism in French film. A special issue of *Cahiers du cinéma* (no. 78) was entitled "Renoir le patron." Renoir was held up as the master of French cinema and one of the pivotal figures in the history and formation of cinematic art. Renoir

become the greatest of French directors), have left a lasting impression on us all. Truffaut called him Saint Vigo. Equally striking are Vigo's use of dissociation and association, which were influenced by the work of Dziga Vertov through the intermediary of his brother, Boris Kaufman, Vigo's head cameraman and friend.

Sacha Guitry.

Guitry was an unabashed proponent of theatricality, which he filmed straight on, without hesitation. He was able to shrug off the grammatical rules of a cinematic language that was still new but already academic. Because fantasy was the guiding spirit of his work, the New Wave defended Guitry throughout the course of his career (from Resnais to Doniol, from Demy to Eustache—they all claimed to draw inspiration from him). They conferred upon him the title—so strongly coveted by numbers of conscientious and serious directors—of *cinéaste*. Guitry's *Le Roman d'un tricheur* became a worldwide success and his use of narration to lighten the story and magnify its dynamics became a significant force of change in the cinema.

Josef von Sternberg.
Like Lubitsch, von Sternberg was one of the favorite directors of *La Revue du cinéma*. The succeeding generation did not renounce him, however. They were enthusiastic in their admiration for *Shanghai Gesture*. *I, Claudius* was a

to rebellion so characteristic of Vidor's films that had the greatest effect on his audiences (*The Fountainhead*, *The Man Without a Star*, etc.). The sense of Hollywood action carried away by an epic lyricism that exhausts itself in excess made Vidor, along with Dovzhenko and Gance, one of the three great visionaries of the period.

Leo McCarey.
Laughter and tears. Joy and pain. The director of the Laurel and Hardy of the silent period, Leo McCarey's nervous, clear, and efficient comedies lean toward sadness over time and give way to the tears of melodrama. McCarey's ability to reverse course and suddenly change register continues to astonish. But it's possible that he, like Frank Capra, was too American in his ideological discourse and formal methods—too correct, too direct, too much of a realist,

Marlene Dietrich, *Morocco* (Josef von Sternberg, 1930)

She Wore a Yellow Ribbon (John Ford, 1946)

favorite of Chabrol; *Jet Pilot* was admired by Truffaut, Godard, and Rivette; and the entire staff of the *Cahiers du cinéma* defended his last film, *The Saga of Anatahan*, tooth and nail. Although Bresson drew inspiration from his extremely sophisticated style, it had a lasting influence only on Chabrol and Demy. Bresson's stylistic experiments, based on the work of von Sternberg, infiltrated the work of the entire New Wave.

King Vidor.
Although the Vidor of the silent film and the beginning of the talkie is almost unanimously admired, it is his later work that excited the young critics of the New Wave. More than intellect was involved. While the torrid sensuality, both biblical and puritanical, of *Duel in the Sun* and *Ruby Gentry* were rousing, it was the call

and demagogically too close to the people—to really inspire French directors. Admired, acknowledged, and celebrated, yes, but he was not really New Wave.

Other American filmmakers of the period, although equally admired, had only an indirect influence on the French New Wave. This is true of George Cukor, Raoul Walsh, and others. But the New Wave had a fondness for several of the so-called "Z series" directors, like Edgar G. Ulmer or those who had been marginalized because of their independence, like Tay Garnett. William Wyler, however, who was extolled by Bazin in 1950, was practically laughed at in 1960. During this same period, George Stevens was highly regarded by many of Hollywood's best directors because he was able to adapt a distinct personality to the demands of the producers and the studios. None of this redeemed him in the eyes of the *Cahiers* and Stevens was metaphorically executed.

Three filmmakers, however, were the victims of obvious New Wave injustice during the fifties: John Ford, Louis Buñuel, and Jean Grémillon.

John Ford.
Though his trial was couched in the guise of an aesthetic debate, Ford fell victim to the uncertainties of the Cold War. His rejection took the form of a New Wave indifference to masterpieces like *The Sun Shines Bright* and *The Prisoner of Shark Island*. It was strange that the future New Wave could

Lya Lys, *L'Âge d'or* (Luis Buñuel, 1930)

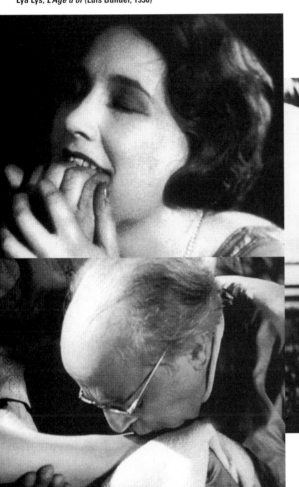

El (Luis Buñuel, 1952)

not or would not see the obvious connection between Ford and Murnau. Not until the sixties was Ford recognized as one of the leading directors of his time, something his peers had known for years. He is, with Griffith, not only the quintessential American director but one of the greatest in the world.

Luis Buñuel.
Buñuel experienced a fate similar to Ford's. Because he was a "surrealist" and monopolized by the *Cahiers'* adversaries at *Positif*, his star waned with the rise of the review's second generation (Bazin, Kast, and Doniol maintained their friend-

ship and admiration for him). There was a certain element of bad faith involved in this, however. During the early fifties, the future New Wave universally admired *Un chien andalou*, *L'Âge d'or*, *Land Without Bread*, and *Los olvidados*. *El* and *The Criminal Life of Archibaldo de la Cruz* continued to win praise. But Buñuel disturbed and intrigued viewers. It was impossible to remain indifferent to his work. This was not only because of his discourse, however; it was the formal qualities of his work that caused difficulties. The audience's reticence first had to be overcome before he could be appreciated. It was important to acknowledge the absolute freedom of the story (which advanced in zigzag fashion), recognize the audacity of a directorial style that involved a flattening out of the elements of representation and accept the absolute primacy given to the force of an image that is always explosive, blinding, and shocking, as if it rose

Mireille Balin and Jean Gabin, *Gueule d'amour* (Jean Grémillon, 1937)

intact from the depths of the unconscious. Once the principle of Buñuellian construction was accepted, and this occurred only at the start of the sixties, his entire body of work was able to be recognized.

Jean Grémillon.
Grémillon never had a chance. Perhaps because he was supported by Doniol, Bazin, and especially Pierre Kast (who was his assistant and co-screenwriter), Grémillon earned no more than the polite attention of the *Cahiers*. In fact, its writers classified him among the directors of the French quality tradition. It's unfortunate that they failed to see what is so obvious today: the strong influence in his films, starting with those of the late thirties (*Gueule d'amour*, *Remorques*), of Howard Hawks, Grémillon was the only typically French director to film in the American style.

The Directors of the Talking Period, 1945–1960

film world was divided in two: pre- and post-Rossellini. And by 1950 the future New Wave had made its decision in favor of a post-Rossellinian cinema. Rossellini's modernity harmonized with the needs of the young generation who wanted to take part in the evolution of cinematic art. Rossellini radically changed the nature of representation, starting with the position of the spectator. In his work the filmmaker (and the spectator) no longer guide the action; the event forces its own time frame upon the film and directs the flow of the story. The spectator-as-witness, like a person in an accident, becomes a helpless victim.

Ingmar Bergman. In 1953 *Monika* simultaneously deepened the audience's love of film and aroused their sexual fantasies, and in *The 400 Blows*

Roberto Rossellini, Henri Langlois, and Jean Renoir during the nineteen sixties (photograph by Man Ray)

Harriet Anderson, *Monika* (Ingmar Bergman, 1953)

Roberto Rossellini. The New Wave's big brother and the director who had the greatest influence on it, he completely revolutionized the concept of cinema and its history. Rossellini's genius stems from the fact that he was able to adjust the cinematic clock back to zero. He threw out fifty years of theater dramaturgy and romanticism. In Rossellini, we return to film's origins, to the first pictures by the Lumière brothers, to news and current events. He was able to acknowledge the dramatic force found in any event important enough to be observed. With *Paisan*, *The Flowers of St. Francis*, and *Germany Year Zero*, the

Truffaut projected this adolescent excitement onto Antoine Doinel, who unveils a photograph of Monika in a movie theater in Pigalle. *Monika* was immediately perceived to be the work of a true *cinéaste*. The scene in which some see the beginnings of the New Wave is one in which for several moments Monika stares at the camera and, without blinking, sustains the disapproving, accusatory gaze of the audience. In *Monika* the position of the viewer (already shifted by Rossellini) is, suddenly, literally reversed. The viewer has been flushed out of the comfort of his armchair, attacked as a hedonistic voyeur, driven into the open. Swept up in the agony of guilt that circulates throughout Bergman's films, his role in the film is now different. Previously, the viewer judged; now, he is judged, held responsible. The New Wave remembered Bergman's lesson, and echoes can be found in the many close-ups in early films of the New Wave, the most celebrated being that of Antoine Doinel at the end of *The 400 Blows*. After 1953–1954 *Cahiers du cinéma* helped establish Bergman's reputation in France and worldwide. Every contributor to the magazine wanted to write about his films. In 1958, after *The Seventh Seal* and *Wild Strawberries* were released, Bergman was globally recognized as one of the pivotal directors of the post-War period.

Nicholas Ray. From his very first film, *They*

Scott Brady, Joan Crawford, and Sterling Hayden in *Johnny Guitar* (Nicholas Ray, 1954)

Ava Gardner and Humphrey Bogart, *The Barefoot Contessa* (Joseph L. Mankiewicz, 1954)

sidered the quintessential poet–director, as Vigo and Barnet were before him, Nicholas Ray was the subject of the most unconditional and enthusiastic articles published in *Cahiers du cinéma* (they mounted an aggressive defense of both *Bigger Than Life* and *Johnny Guitar*). It was as if the essential characteristics of the concept of the auteur were concentrated in him and his work. Ray didn't write his own screenplays and didn't always choose his subjects or his cast, but the choices he made were those of a man who thought for himself. His rebellious lyricism, especially when it appeared arbitrarily, his belief in strong values, such as self-esteem, make Ray a modernist director. As the years pass, his position as one of the key sources of inspiration for the New Wave—for all contemporary cinema in fact—seems more assured.

Jean-Paul Belmondo and Samuel Fuller in *Pierrot le fou* (Jean-Luc Godard, 1965)

Live by Night, which was shown at the Festival du Film Maudit in Biarritz, Nicholas Ray was adopted by the future New Wave as a kind of American older brother. In their eyes he embodied the American filmmaker of the fifties, whose films captured America's emotional malaise by means of a poetics of space. In Ray's hands the new CinemaScope technology became the ideal format for a style that oscillated dramatically between an almost fetal need to vanish within a maternal and protective environment, and the virile desire to confront the exaltation and solitude of an immense, cosmic space. Con-

Joseph L. Mankiewicz. He produced a cinema of the intellect. He turned speech into the instrument of intelligence and the weapon of its action. For Mankiewicz sound structured the story, produced the image; it became the subject of the film. This was the reason for Mankiewicz's repeated use of flashback. By showing that sound *creates* the image, has primacy over it (Godard later named his studio Sonimage), and that theatricality dissolves into pure cinematography, he had a profound influence on the New Wave (from Rohmer to Eustache). Two of Mankiewicz's films became New Wave favorites: *The Barefoot Contessa* and *The Quiet American*.

Other young filmmakers were also championed by the New Wave: Otto Preminger (Hollywood directorial style carried to perfection), Samuel Fuller (action is emotion, emotion is action), Anthony Mann (the mental

space that reflects its neurosis in and through the healthy immensity of physical space), Robert Aldrich (Big Bob), Douglas Sirk (American melodrama intentionally exacerbated by an expressionist realism that later inspired Fassbinder), Vincent Minnelli (admired as much for his melodramas as for his success at musical comedy).

Yet, until 1960, John Huston, Stanley Kubrick, and Elia Kazan were all rejected as being too demonstrative. Houston for his subject matter, Kubrick for his form, and Kazan for his renegade behavior as a witness during the McCarthy trials.

Orson Welles.
He was a genius, a prodigy— and the absolute model for each and every New Wave director. As a filmmaker he demonstrated a passion for craftsmanship. As a writer he displayed Shakespearean

Chaplinesque sentimentalism, which Bazin revered. *Cronaca di un amore*, by Michelangelo Antonioni, who was discovered in 1950 along with Nicholas Ray, at the Festival du Film Maudit, earned the director a reputation for a "modernity" that would shock many.

Kenji Mizoguchi.
Mizoguchi won the Lion d'Argent twice in Venice, in 1953 and 1954, but was discovered only in 1956, in Paris. He was immediately acknowledged (by Rivette, Godard, Demonsablon, Rohmer) as a great director and eventually as one of the

Les Anges du péché (Robert Bresson, 1943)

Francisco Reiguera, *Don Quixote* (an unfinished film by Orson Welles, 1955–1972)

Le Plaisir (Max Ophuls, 1951).

dimension in his themes. He provided an expressively dramatic vision of a world seen in close up. And as a director he was dedicated solely to his art.

Luchino Visconti.
The New Wave still has questions. They accept his theatricality, admire the lyrical, operatic realism of *Senso*, but are troubled by the aesthetic vision of *The Earth Trembles*. Doniol and Bazin were enthusiasts; the others somewhat more circumspect. Nearly the entire New Wave, however, admired Visconti's sketch for Rossellini's *Amore*, "The Miracle," in which he plays the role of Saint Joseph. They were more circumspect toward the Fellini of *La Strada* and *Il Bidone*, which Bazin praised effusively. And they were equally unanimous in their condemnation of De Sica's feigned

cinema's greatest artists. Because of the time it took to assimilate his work, he had no direct influence on the New Wave. But the New Wave absorbed his moral attitude, his aesthetic in its approach to filmmaking: that of a portraitist. Like Velasquez, Mizoguchi was content to paint all of reality and nothing but reality, without prejudice. Godard's *My Life to Live* would have been impossible without *Street of Shame* (1956), Mizoguchi's last and most sublime film.

In some respects Mizoguchi's glory eclipsed that of Akira Kurosawa, who was subsequently ignored. Ozu wasn't discovered until 1960. Naruse not until 1970. At the start of the New Wave, Japanese cinema in general was practically unknown in France. So little was known, in fact, that it was naively assumed that Resnais's *Hiroshima mon amour*, released in 1958, was influenced by the Japanese cinema.

Robert Bresson.
Along with Renoir, Bresson served as a model for the New Wave. After two films, one of which was *Les Dames du bois de Boulogne*, he became indispensable. More than any other filmmaker, Bresson raised the question of style, and the need to find a new style that would eliminate the theatricality of cinematic representation. His was a style reluctant to show too much, preferring instead to suggest what should be seen and hostile to any intentionality that would interfere with

based on a careful attention to everyday life. Becker's realism, however, was free of any trace of the contemptuous familiarity that characterized the films of his more conventional colleagues, who were steeped in the tradition of French quality cinema. Truffaut's esteem for Becker's work is thus easily understandable.

Max Ophuls.
It was the Ophuls who returned from Hollywood that the New Wave admired, the Ophuls of the last four films. His dancing camera, the precious brilliance of the sentiments that words, attitudes, lights, costumes, and sets evoke as they conceal, conceal as they reveal, had a profound effect on many directors, Demy most of all. *Lola Montès* was one of the proud symbols around which the New Wave rallied.

The New Wave was also influenced by Jean

Mon oncle (Jacques Tati, 1958)

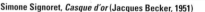

Simone Signoret, *Casque d'or* (Jacques Becker, 1951)

auditory comprehension. A maniacally attentive style that accented the artificiality of its means to grasp the truth of relationships. Bresson's work with framing, light, sound, and his clipped use of dialogue and narration, editing, and rhythm, fascinated and influenced Godard, Demy, and Rivette. Bresson managed to make only three films between 1944 and 1959, but he shot *Pickpocket* in 1960 at the moment of the New Wave's triumph. The film was quite naturally associated with the movement, and from then on Bresson's career was assured.

Jacques Becker.
While Renoir's assistant, Becker was generally well received. With good reason. The New Wave appreciated his sharp, concise, aristocratic style, which promoted a precise realism

Cocteau, in particular for *Les Parents terribles* and the two Orpheus films. They admired his refusal to accept a poetics that fled reality and his willingness to affirm that such a poetics is intrinsically associated with the physics and mechanics of the world. Roger Leenhardt, a writer and art enthusiast who loved and defended film, directed *Les Dernières Vacances* in 1948. The film's post-Impressionist tones, redolent of Louis Delluc, also impressed young filmmakers, who because of this film understood that it was possible to make a distinctly personal film independently. This was Jacques Tati's approach, as well, when he shot *Jour de fête* in 1947, but it was with *Les Vacances de M. Hulot* and *Mon oncle*, that the great comic director finally entered the ranks of the New Wave's "favorite directors."

1956

LOLA MONTÈS

REBEL WITHOUT A CAUSE

NIGHT AND FOG

NIGHT OF THE HUNTER

ASÍ ES LA AURORA

LE MYSTÈRE PICASSO

THE MAN WITH THE GOLDEN ARM

SMILES OF A SUMMER NIGHT

LOLA MONTÈS

Max Ophuls

THE BAROQUESCREEN

It's one of the few and most astonishing examples of baroque art to make its way to the screen. Whether or not we care for the baroque is a matter of personal preference, but the baroque as a tendency should be discussed with respect and not with the same contempt we heap upon childish tantrums and involuntary physical disorders. The prodigious skill of Ophuls's technique interests me only to the extent that it results in a style. The beauty, scope, and self-confidence of this style should overcome any reticence about this film. The result is unusual and may disturb a public that has grown accustomed to technical skill, bad taste, simplification, and a kind of narrow "dogmatism" that adversely affects the appreciation of the beautiful and natural aspiration toward the qualitative perfection of art. But Ophuls has attempted to reverse the popular trend. He decided to trust the public, and *Lola Montès* signals his respect. For this, as well as the overall value of his work, Ophuls deserves our admiration and recognition. ■
Jacques Doniol-Valcroze, *Les Lettres Françaises*, January 18, 1956

AN ENORMOUS CONFECTION

Someone who knows and loves the cinema recently explained to me, in discussing this film, that bad taste has become a sign of genius for someone with the courage to take it to extremes. It's probably a worthwhile theory, but it doesn't really apply to Max Ophuls because, in spite of his excess, he hasn't gone as far as he could have, hasn't reached that point of extreme outrage that would have broken through the wall of monstrosity to reach the divine. He has succeeded, however, in providing us with an incomplete and complex body of work from which anyone can pick and choose as they please, assigning motives to Ophuls nearly at random, including philosophical ones. Of course, it would be impossible to easily divide this enormous confection into conveniently anthologized pieces. A skillful editor could use these same elements to create an astonishing symbolic documentary on the circus and its splendors and miseries.

Others, more modest in their aspirations, would find nothing more than the exhausted efforts of an author who wallows in his subject, gets mired in it, and tries to redo *La Ronde*, employing the same gimmicks, the same cheap symbolism, and a big budget—a big budget and a wide screen that gives poor Ophuls nothing but headaches.

Ophuls apparently spent a large part of his time wondering how to shorten his diabolical fresco, which he buries in shadow on either side when he can't find the right drapery with which to wrap— courtyard and garden included—the principal scene. Once in a while, tired of such tricks, he makes do with a matte and denies CinemaScope the breadth that makes it unsuitable for so many things.

Lost in this vast field, Martine Carol is like a target getting hit with potshots. Bang! (The makeup man.) Bang! (The hairdresser.) Bang! (The gaffer.) Bang! (The color specialist.) Bang! (The cameraman.) Bang! (The makeup man again, who plasters her with greasepaint to simulate anguish.) For Ophuls actors are merely objects, like lamps or plaster statues, and he treats them accordingly, loading them down with the German rococo trappings he's so fond of. Only Peter Ustinov is impervious, protected by his personality—carefree, impertinent, equivocal. He's a worthy successor to Charles Laughton, including both his talents and shortcomings.

Lola Montès is a gigantic parade, a wedding cake in the window of a pastry shop, which the whole town turns out to gawk at: we may admire it, but if we go inside, it's only for a slice of pie. ∎

R.-M. Arlaud, *Combat,* January 2, 1956

A CATHEDRAL BETWEEN HEAVEN AND EARTH

Great artists are careful never to "make art." One way or another they try to make us believe in the practical necessity of their work, of their lack of responsibility for its creation. Aware of the immorality associated with trying to "fabricate life," the true artist resorts to subterfuge. Ophuls masks what he presents on screen to the point of completely removing it from view. This is the reason for the lace and veils, the gates and fences, even those stovepipes and ropes that are placed between the action and the lens, between the recreated life and the viewer, who can only look on lazily. The extreme of this sense of dissimulation in Ophuls's work can be found in the silence that followed *Madame de.* The same sense of reserve determines the speed with which his camera moves, the overly quick takes. It is what causes Ophuls to remove from his final cut both Lola's leap and her striptease, which would have been misinterpreted in a film by a moralist. Imagine a painter, who, ashamed of the miniature he wants to exhibit, hides it from his visitors by surrounding it with a three-hundred pound frame.

Martine Carol, like Marilyn Monroe, is simply a courageous and flirtatious young woman who, through the mysterious laws of the box office and the demands of producers, finds herself playing roles that would be perfect for Ingrid Bergman, Greta Garbo, or Joan Crawford. Max Ophuls, who quickly realized that Martine Carol had as much in common with Lola Montès as he himself had with the Pope, decided to turn Lola into a plaster statue endowed

with the capacity for suffering. Lola Montès doesn't exist? What difference does it make! By piling stones on this ethereal construction, Ophuls has managed to build a cathedral between heaven and earth, an Oratorio. It's no coincidence that *Lola Montès* reminded me of Joan at the stake, which is another film about which quite a lot of nonsense has been written. ∎

François Truffaut, *Cahiers du cinéma,* January 1956

REBEL WITHOUT A CAUSE

Nicholas Ray

HARDENED VITELLONI

Nicholas Ray, together with Robert Aldrich, is the standard bearer for the young critics who admire American cinema and see these two directors as proof of its vitality, in spite of everything, and in spite of Hollywood. I don't agree with my young colleagues in many instances, even taking into account a polemic margin of safety, but in the case of Nicholas Ray, I have to admit that they're right.

Like the heroes of *The Wild One,* those in *Rebel without a Cause* suffer from their spiritual emptiness. Between childhood

and manhood they have to cross a no-man's land of morality where play soon turns to tragedy. They are in some respects like the hardened characters in *I Vitelloni,* reflecting an American society that is brutal and efficient, where the proof of existence counts for more than a peaceful life. These young men don't hang around the beach, they play at mimicking murder, as in that extraordinary scene in which the gang leader challenges the newcomer to a knife fight or the absurd game of chicken that combines stock-car racing and Russian roulette, and which ends in death for one of the participants. The scene, in retrospect, takes on a tragically premonitory coloration after James Dean's death in an automobile accident. ∎

André Bazin, *France-Observateur,* April 6, 1956

A BITTER AND PESSIMISTIC POET

The subject of *Rebel without a Cause* can't be described because the screenplay isn't structured from the point of view of a screenwriter but from that of a director, something far more valuable. This isn't an "illustrated novel" or a literary source "brought to the screen," but a series of abstract ideas that take shape through their formulation on screen as pure mise-en-scène.

If *Rebel without a Cause* is head and shoulders above other films about American adolescence, it's because the poet Nicholas Ray has done a better job than Benedeck the sociologist or Brooks the reformer. Yes, Nicholas Ray is a poet, bitter and pessimistic. His films bear witness to a sensibility and sincerity that are rarely seen in Hollywood.

And who would reproach Ray for his pessimism? *Rebel without a Cause* isn't a reformer's film. It's obvious that the problems of adolescence, when they are honestly expressed, have no solution. The adolescent must cross the "great divide" to adulthood alone. Cocteau and *Les Enfants Terribles* often comes to mind in this context. Like Cocteau, there is a sense of realism in Ray's work, which violently bursts to the surface, and ricochets back and forth in a flurry of words, a theatrical realism that possesses the sudden energy of a musical beat.

It's not necessary to go into the details: the cinematography, color, acting, directing—all are very good. Along with *The Big Knife* and other films, *Rebel Without a Cause* inaugurates a new era in Hollywood, a period when filmmakers have won back their freedom. ∎

François Truffaut, *Arts*, April 4, 1956

NIGHT AND FOG

Alain Resnais

AN OVERWHELMING FILM

Night and Fog is the most overwhelming film I've seen in a long time. It is the most penetrating as well. Raw, lucid, directed with an obvious concern for objectivity, the film moves forward like a well-oiled machine, implacably unfolding its string of horrors as it attempts to stir the viewer's dormant conscience, a goal not without merit.

No courtroom has ever heard a more damning indictment. I have never seen anything more moving than this slow 1955 procession through the abandoned remains of the death camps, overrun by verdant foliage, nearly forgotten beneath the growth of successive springs. The pastel tints of the photography contrast with the brutal reminders of Nazi atrocities, and the authentic documents in black and white, which produce a strangely balanced symphony of effects. ∎

Jean Dréville, *Les Lettres Françaises*,
April 12, 1956

PORTRAIT OF A MONSTER

Alain Resnais' *Night and Fog* is a film that, in principle, has little need of film criticism. The subject matter of this requiem commands our respect, and creates a silence that can be broken only at the risk of sacrilege. Let's assume for a moment that, cinematically speaking, *Night and Fog* were a bad film. It's not too far fetched to imagine that, even using the same documents and having access to the

same physical conditions, another director would have ended up with something other than this simple accumulation of horrors or, worse, a hate-filled indictment, narrow-minded and demagogic. Even if such were the case, it would be pointless to criticize the film; the mere presence of these images arouses feelings that are beyond the reach of criticism.

We could avoid this dilemma by saying that Resnais has displayed tremendous seriousness, discretion, and conscientiousness in making this film. That would be a sign of false modesty, however, and this film, in which everything we see is true, demands our honesty above all. To me it is important to know that *Night and Fog* is a masterpiece of editing and that Resnais has managed to blend documentary scenes, color footage shot in Poland, Jean Cayrol's commentary, and Hans Eisler's music, into an extraordinary film that resonates with a unified voice. That's the incredible paradox of this film, which after several viewings, continues to appear both perfect and harmonious in its ineluctable progression. In this sense it resembles the sufferings depicted by Goya or the cruelest moments in Kafka. *Night and Fog* wouldn't have such power if it weren't first and foremost a great work of art, the most terrifying of all documentaries, if its gestation hadn't required the detached abstraction of composition necessary to achieve its realization. In this film nothing counts beyond an impenetrable phenomenon, the unforgettable portrait of a monster. ∎

Jacques Doniol-Valcroze, *Cahiers du cinéma*,
May 1956

NIGHT OF THE HUNTER

Charles Laughton

BLOOD-SOAKED HUMOR

The directing, although full of novel touches, staggers between the Nordic and German sides of the street, even grasps an expressionist lamp-pole, but fails to

navigate Griffith's minefield. More stop lights and splayed policemen! There are some problems in the way Laughton directs his actors, a few facile scenes, and a final moment of odious sentimentality.

But thanks to its blood-soaked humor, its poetry (both good and bad), and especially its contempt of commercial and aesthetic convention, *Night of the Hunter* is a pretty good minor film. It's an unusual film too, and one you should see if you like films that push boundaries and allow viewers to make their own discoveries, for this film pushes and discovers. ∎

François Truffaut, *Arts*, May 23, 1956

SULFUR AND INCENSE

Is there any relationship between Charles Laughton the director (of the present film) and Charles Laughton the actor? We've grown accustomed to referring to the actor as being colorful and larger-than-life, to the point where it's become a cliché. If "being colorful" is a way of expressing one's enjoyment in life, then we can see both director and actor in the same Laughton. In *Night of the Hunter* he combines a range of extremes: a puritanism that finds an outlet in collective religious hysteria, madness, a child's heroism, and an old woman's devotion.

Yet, the film's conception of good and evil remains inflexible. One of the strangest things in this odd story, which is laced with sulfur as much as with incense, is that throughout the film we don't find the same character repeated in various forms. For here, it's only a matter of degree, in spite of appearances and what we're supposed to believe, between the mad preacher and the old woman. Both of these people move in opposite directions, but they start at the same point and are triggered by the same mechanism, the safe harbor of puritan morality. Yet they are linked together. The widow, who is herself seized with a mystical passion, represents one of these links. Although it is no more than the pale reflection of her new husband's passion, it is a reflection nonetheless.

In this sense the film is certainly interesting. The story is told in a hybrid style, where everything is jumbled together: excess and restraint, a poetic sentiment that is often quite touching, the use of a compelling counterpoint thats adds a sense of lyricism to the film when it suddenly bursts through the surrounding silence. ■

José Zendel, *Les Lettres Françaises*,
May 17, 1956

ASÍ ES LA AURORA

Luis Buñuel

OPEN SEASON ON COUNTRY, FAMILY AND RELIGION

Buñuel has incorporated the techniques formerly used by surrealism to attack Country, Family, and Religion. The director is careful not to hit below the belt, however, and throughout this film of misfortune, Buñuel doesn't arouse our pity so much as our sense of injustice. Jean Ferry's dialogue, direct and as sharp as if it were struck from a medal, leaves no room for doubt. Both pity and sentimentality are constantly under siege, the former through the cruelty of the depiction, the latter through a typically sadistic need to destroy the lyricism of a love scene by introducing unusual elements to it, whether they be

commonplace (a comb), humorous (a tortoise), or poetic. In this way Buñuel rediscovers the time-tested recipe of surrealist metaphor. ■

André-S. Labarthe, *Cahiers du cinéma*,
June 1956

SURREALIST CLICHÉS

Buñuel is a joker. But that's his concern. I assume this outdated surrealist has little need for bourgeois seriousness. His sophomoric tricks, heavy with intention, are nuanced with insights that are themselves not without grace. He is comfortable with "mistakes," with the liberty he takes with the story. It's an inventiveness that is redolent of literature, but it's inventiveness just the same. For example, the comb and tortoise that manage to slip beneath the lovers during their embrace doesn't add to the film, but neither does it "destroy" anything; it's not a sign of great, or even good, directing, but frankly, I hold nothing against it. A policeman reads Claudel and hangs Dali's Christ on a wall. Since Buñuel insists, why not laugh it off?

The story itself is compelling, but does Buñuel take himself seriously? The question doesn't interest me. Instead let's look at his basic philosophical approach (his and that of his collaborators on the film, Roblès and Ferry), and compare it to his previous work. It's clear that the rich are bastards and the poor are good, that the law is always wrong and love excuses everything. It's not simply the naiveté of this attitude that annoys me but the narrowmindedness it implies.

Very little remains of Breton's myth of *amour fou*, except for what you'd find in a pulp novel; the *aggressiveness* of the twenties has become the complacency of a college student with time on his hands. It's enough to turn you into a bigot, a cop, or a fascist—nothing but clichés, another way of knocking down a straw horse. The "key" to the film may be the father-in-law who lays down the law to his son-in-law and young wife, who has returned home "to be with mother." Did the screenwriter come up with this idea? Buñuel has an excuse for this as well: in Spain, or Mexico, such

customs are still alive. How long will the dueña be around? Oh, France! Oh, twentieth century!

The film's direction is both good and bad. The *good* part is the fantasy element (since there is no real humor in the film): A feeling for beautiful landscapes, careful and natural framing, a taste for bric-a-brac, the picturesque, a "miniaturist" feeling. What's *bad* about this film, however, is the actors, whose performances are unbelievably stilted. Our entomologist is interested in cats, and they act very well. ■

Eric Rohmer, *Arts*, May 16, 1956

A CRAZY AFFECTION FOR REVOLT

Even though the name "Luis Buñuel" doesn't appear on screen, before the first images of the rock-strewn island, violent and secret, where the action is ready to explode, there are a hundred telling signs of the artist's signature. Those cats devouring a dead cat, the children who play at capital punishment and throw stones at one another, the terrified white chickens that announce death's approach, the love scene in front of the bed of the little girl who has been raped, the obsession with gates, which criss-cross so many scenes, the contempt for the powerful and the crazy affection for revolt, that same cruel light that washes across the faces of the unjust and caresses, through the shadows, the eyes and lips of desire, the dryness of the air and the lightning bolts of friendship that streak across the night sky—who else but Buñuel could present them with such energy and loyalty? ■

Claude Brule, *Paris-Presse*, May 12, 1956

AN IMPASSIONED, DESPERATE CALL TO MURDER

Neither pessimistic nor cruel, Buñuel is a moralist, and a real one. If he uses violence to denounce oppression, if he lets loose his cocks so you cage your chickens, if he sharpens his razor to cut the throat of a nun, it's because he wants to prevent you from calmly sipping your morning coffee in bed, satisfied with yourself and your world. "If I could illuminate love and its reasons, its straw tragedy, its comedy of lead, would I have words enough to destroy hatred and show the victim crushing the hangmen? Would I be able to color the word revolution?" These lines from Paul Éluard belong to Buñuel as well. A surrealist in the best sense of the word, he lives freely in a state of purity and revolt, protesting an intolerable reality, shouting an "impassioned, desperate call to murder," but all the while hoping for imminent human salvation, and nonstop departure for the marvelous world of love's images. ■

J. Trébouta, *Cinéma 56*, December 1956

LE MYSTÈRE PICASSO

Henri-Georges Clouzot

THE COLOR AND VIOLENCE OF A STORM

"You have to stick around a while to become young." The words aren't from Socrates but a fearful adolescent of 75, who could pass for his brother, with his boxer's nose and fiery eyes, his insolent hunger and spirited outbursts. Pablo Picasso is like an old tree made of young shoots. The first thing we notice about *Le Mystère Picasso*, the

new masterpiece from Clouzot, who has just returned from a wildly successful trip to Cannes, is that it offers us a simultaneously hot and cool glimpse of the painter's secret youthfulness: the old Andalusian lion has kept his cub's heart.

The ambitious Clouzot captures a hundred minutes of inspiration and the painter's struggle with his own demons. Through the use of ink that magically appears through paper, he was able to film the complete genesis of a painting, the author's hesitations and regrets, his failures and victories. Mounted behind the blank canvas, the camera records the birth of those lines . . . without ever revealing the hand that drew them, the hand of this extravagant, irrepressible, joyful, and always surprising, genius. Picasso the sorcerer.

The meeting of these two men—Picasso and Clouzot—has the color and violence of a storm. The resulting film is a document, not a documentary. Like a good detective novel or thriller, the murderer and victim are hard to tell apart. Faced with a dumbstruck Picasso, Clouzot introduces Picasso, man of a thousand stratagems, pursuing Picasso the pitiless. There is a bit of *Le Corbeau* and *Quai des orfèvres* in this silent race, overflowing with impatience and anger, It adds an extraordinary emotional unity to the film's technical innovations.

This is a unique film, an admirable film, a film that, thank God, violently forces us to take sides. To say that I am strongly "in favor" of it doesn't amount to much, though. Anyone for whom painting is more than a Post Office calendar will be deeply affected by *Le Mystère Picasso*. As for those who smirk when they see *Les Demoiselles d'Avignon*, the way people laughed at Manet and Van Gogh or yelled with anger in Cannes when they saw Clouzot's film, they may make so much noise that it's hard to ignore their presence. But it's even more difficult to attach any importance to it. ■

Claude Brule, *Paris-Presse*, May 20, 1956

CONCESSIONS

Le Mystère Picasso is both better than what we expect and more disappointing. The

subject matter of the film is admirable, but it's pulled in several different directions at once, and the production obviously suffers from having been produced under conditions typical of a commercial film with a budget of only 460,000 francs. To appeal to the public, Clouzot made concessions, some of which may prove fatal for the film. For example, the most imperceptible and unacknowledged acceleration during the execution of several drawings will shock painters—and with good reason. But it's mostly due to Georges Auric's score that the public isn't as excited by this film as it should be. More can be said about *Le Mystère Picasso* (which will be even more controversial when it is released in Paris than here), but the rudeness shown by certain viewers who left the theater during the screening required a more direct response. ■

François Truffaut, *Arts*, May 9, 1956

THE MAN WITH THE GOLDEN ARM

Otto Preminger

VOYAGE TO THE END OF THE NIGHT

Frank Sinatra's hero is one of the most complete, most appealing, and most amazing characters to have appeared in American cinema during the last ten years. This man with the golden arm (the arm he uses to shoot up, the arm that deals at poker, the arm that plays in the orchestra) is, quite seriously, a "good hearted" character. We are constantly aware of his internal struggles and it's our ability to feel him move into action that makes the film unusual, involving us personally in this otherwordly adventure, this voyage to the end of the night, which leaves us exhausted and moved. Of course, none of this would have been possible without Preminger's remarkable direction. ■

Jacques Doniol-Valcroze, *France-Observateur*, May 23, 1956

AN HOMAGE TO LOVE AND COURAGE

It's not easy to get over Otto Preminger's film. It sticks with you, awakens images, and, without ever appearing to be a film about "ideas," manages to evoke them anyway. This drama, which concerns a heroin addict who manages to go straight, get hooked again, and finally kick the habit once and for all, could have been a rather ordinary film. It isn't. An homage to love and courage, this is one film that manages to avoid being pedantic.

Preminger's heroes evolve within a narrowly circumscribed universe—a bar, a clandestine nightclub, a flop house, a street with newspapers swirling in the wind. After detoxing, it's here that Frankie (Frank Sinatra), the "man with the golden arm," returns to practice dealing cards. A professional gambler and ex-junkie, Frankie wants to change jobs, change his life, start out all over again, but everything works against him and, little by little, caught inside some type of infernal machine, he gives up. ■

Martine Monod, *Les Lettres Françaises*, May 23, 1956

SMILES OF A SUMMER NIGHT

Ingmar Bergman

NORDIC FARCE

Ingmar Bergman is unable to create characters with firm and clearly defined feelings. He constantly hesitates between two different genres and four or five different styles. He casually drags us from slapstick to intellectual theater, from vaudeville (one character is in pajamas, and a bed decorated with a trumpeting cupid is dragged from one room to another) to advanced philosophy (an old woman, vaguely resembling a witch, presides over a strange banquet, muttering incantations after her guests drink a potion). He throws together Courteline, Feydeau, Jean Anouilh, and Shakespeare, but without the least subtlety.

The vaudeville is unquestionably the best part of the film. There's quite a bit to laugh at, especially if you like farce, blurry images, misunderstandings, off-color stories, bawdy remarks, and stock characters, like his monocled officer. He's aggressively virile, insanely jealous, vulnerable, cynical, insolent, and fond of duels. We do have to credit the director with a certain understanding of cinematic poetry, however. If he were better able to control his gifts, Bergman's humor could be put to better use. ■

Louis Chauvet, *Le Figaro*, June 22, 1956

AN IRRESISTIBLE FASCINATION

With its sense of "court and kitchen," its balletic approach to frivolous love affairs bordering on drama, its literary resonances resembling Musset and Beaumarchais, you would swear *Smiles of a Summer Night* was adapted from a play. Yet judging by the screenplay and dialogue, it's clearly Bergman's work. It immediately brings to mind Jean Renoir's *The Rules of the Game*, but during the festival at Cannes, Bergman kindly acknowledged that, in spite of his admiration for Renoir, several of whose films he was familiar with, he had never seen *The Rules of the Game*. And this seems quite plausible, once you've seen Bergman's other films.

Bergman's recent themes find their logical culmination in *Smiles of a Summer Night*. Handled in a style that is clear and precise and softly illuminated by a kind of lunar light, it's both one of the most enjoyable films to look at and one of the most intellectually suggestive to appear within the last fifteen years. The direction isn't always in keeping with Bergman's intentions or the literary and psychological value of the text, but the way he directs his actors carries the film along with irresistible fascination, imparts to it a delightful sense of movement. The actors themselves are remarkable. ■

Jacques-Doniol Valcroze, *France-Observateur*, June 1956

BETWEEN REALITY AND DREAM

Everything, or nearly everything, about *Smiles of a Summer Night* is done well—the luminous clarity of the shimmering, almost milky photography (the film looks as if it were shot during a full moon), the delicate interweaving of the scenes, the tone of the dialogues, with their continuous sing-song of tenderness and humor, the sense of abandon and leisure, reality and dream, common sense and madness. If we had to compartmentalize Bergman and separate his inspiration from his directorial ability, it would be the latter that sometimes falters for lack of rigor, suffering from a slight clumsiness and needless repetition. Bergman the director isn't always the equal of Bergman the author. He manages to betray himself on the screen and diminish some aspects of his intellect, weaken the image and, through an overly conventional approach to choreography, the very intelligent conclusions of his premise and unquestionable originality of his intellectual message. But who are we to complain after seeing brilliant direction coupled with the barest of scripts. As it stands, *Smiles of a Summer Night* is a very satisfying film. ■

Jean-José Richer, *Cahiers du cinéma*, July 1956

Le Sang des bêtes (Georges Franju, 1949)

THE FILM IN DUS TRY

Hôtel des Invalides (Georges Franju, 1952)

During the Vichy government, around 1943, a serious attempt was made to "purify" the film industry. This was not a new idea though, for a similar attempt had been made by the Popular Front. The thirties was a golden age for bad checks, and nearly one in every five film contracts was either broken or ignored. The profession, which was infested with dishonest producers and more or less full-time swindlers, had become extremely vulnerable. The Popular Front decided it would clean house. For eight years government bureaucrats worked on, and refined, a set of industry regulations. But between 1936 and 1943 the political motivations of the government changed. Having gotten rid of much of the corruption, the Popular Front was now determined to cleanse a system that was far too easygoing to promote the greater good of French cinema. The Pétain government, implementing an Aryan policy, decided to rid the profession of Jews. Though by this time any film assets belonging to them had been confiscated by the Nazis to form Continental Films, which held a near monopoly on film production during the Occupation.

The regulations developed over these years, however, were so well drafted that, aside from minor modifications, they remain in force today. Two important organizations were created: the Comité d'Organisation de l'Industrie Cinématographique[1] (COIC), which changed its name at the time of the Liberation to become the Centre National de la Cinématographie[2] (CNC), and the Institut des Hautes Études Cinématographiques (IDHEC), which trained professionals, now replaced by the Fédération Européenne des Métiers de l'Image et du Son[3] (FEMIS). The important point is that the CNC established the ground rules for the industry and brought them within the umbrella of government control and its bureaucratic mechanisms.

Night and Fog (Alain Resnais, 1955)

As for the regulations themselves, first you needed a card. Only those judged competent by other film professionals had the right to work in the industry. A hierarchy was thus constructed, roughly modeled on the elitist journeyman system, which enabled candidates—editors, camera operators, sound engineers, set designers, and directors—to obtain a work card authorizing them to exercise their profession. The card system became an important asset for people in the industry, and they felt better protected. Anyone who broke a contract was practically banished from the profession and found it impossible to work. The regulations thus served as a kind of cleansing operation for the profession. After the war the CNC continued to resolve industry problems, but it was primarily involved in developing a financial and economic structure for monitoring box office sales. Of course from the sale of each ticket a small amount was deducted and turned over to the CNC, and this amount was then reinvested in the French film industry. Foreign films, including American films, had to pay a tax. A portion of their receipts was deducted up front as well, and used to finance French films. This tax has now become problematic, however, and is one of the reasons for current disagreements over the regulation of the international film market.

The benefits of this legislation for regulating the professional and commercial aspects of the film industry are obvious. But on artistic levels it had unwanted consequences. The system, especially, the work card, quickly became a constraint, for it restricted creativity by promoting academic repetitiveness and a sense of imitation that would conform to professional standards of ability. (The government, aware of the danger of stagnation, had initially intended to issue licenses.) To become a director, the category that obviously had the greatest interest for the future New Wave, there were only two ways available. (The two official schools—IDHEC and École Louis Lumière—certainly accelerated the process of getting people into the profession, but the government still required former students to follow one of the two tracks offered.)

The job track most recognized by the profession, and at the time the most common, was a system of apprenticeships. The candidate began as an assistant-intern (that is, an intern to the assistant director), then rose to become a third assistant, then second, and finally, first assistant director. After a number of jobs as first assistant (at around 40 years of age), candidates had the possibility of making their first film. The process was fairly common but antithetical to the desires of any young, impatient, and inventive filmmaker, who refused, by instinct, a position of practical servitude that enslaved him to an aesthetic that was at best popular, and at worst reactionary. The process produced neither rev-olutionaries nor resistance fighters, simply artisans, occasionally good ones, but rarely artists.

In anticipation of this the CNC created another track and provided talented independents with a "short-film track." The creation of several short films approved by the CNC—which eliminated amateurs and subjected the short to professional standards—was equivalent to a number of assistant positions and, in the end, enabled the candidate to obtain the work card needed to make features. A number of applicants who were willing to take risks, including some talented artists, chose this option.

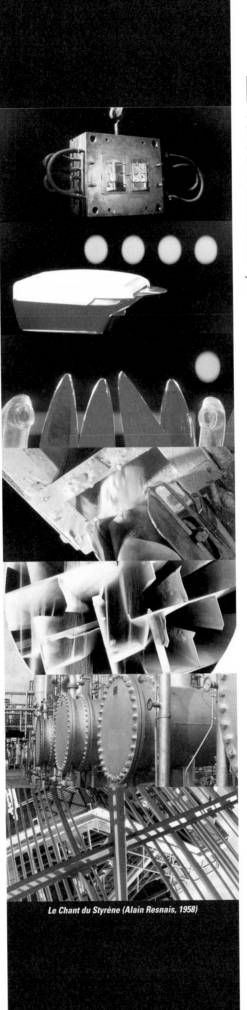

Le Chant du Styrène (Alain Resnais, 1958)

Beginning in 1945 the short film was not only protected but promoted. Anyone who produced a feature film, and wanted to screen it, was required to buy a short that ran before it. This explains why, unlike today, the short film rarely dealt with fiction. Although unlikely, it might have competed with the feature film rather than simply serving as an introduction. Jacques Tati's sketches, for instance, were intended as short fictional pieces. *Jour de fête* is a short (*L'École des facteurs*) that was extended. During the fifties, an evening's film program consisted of a short film (usually educational) and a current events trailer (information), followed by a ten-minute intermission with candy, ice cream, and some advertising (or amusement), followed at last by the main film (the feature entertainment). This was the patriotic approach to a wholesome night at the movies.

The situation quite naturally led directors of short films to follow a documentary format. Many of these short films (*Tour au large* by Jean Grémillon, *Jean Taris* and *À propos de Nice* by Jean Vigo, *Nogent* and *Eldorado du dimanche* by Marcel Carné, *Land Without Bread* by Luis Buñuel) have retained as much prestige as their author's feature films. Reinforcing the esteem in which shorts were held, in 1946 three documentary medium-length and feature films achieved considerable public and critical success: *La Bataille du rail* by René Clément, *Le Six Juin à l'aube* by Jean Grémillon, and *Farrebique* by Georges Rouquier. The best directors of the first generation of the New Wave immersed themselves in the documentary: Georges Franju (*Les Sang des bêtes, Hôtel des Invalides*), Alain Resnais (*Night and Fog, Toute la mémoire du monde, Le Chant du styrène*), Chris Marker (*Les Statues meurent aussi, Dimanche à Pékin, Lettre de Sibérie*), Pierre Kast, and even Agnès Varda and Louis Malle. Jacques Demy, who belonged to both poles of the New Wave, also participated in the documentary movement and filmed *Le Sabotier du Val de Loire*, which was produced and co-directed by Georges Rouquier.

中文参议
娃尔达

conseil sinologique: **AGNES VARDA**

Dimanche à Pékin (Chris Marker, 1956)

The young writers associated with *Cahiers du cinéma* rejected documentary, however. They anticipated the traps laid by the system and the artistic risks involved in any "professional" career path. The high production costs, and the weight of the entire " professional" system complicated not only the shooting of the film but the design of the project. Films were often surreptitiously undermined by the lure of "French quality," haunted by the irrepressible clichés of poetic realism. Too often it was only the picturesque that mattered, the unusual, the exotic (the many films about Paris, the Seine, lovers and their public benches). Too often the ambition of the project was content-oriented, with the aestheticism of a beautifully composed and finished image. With the exception of those directors like Marker, Resnais, and Franju for whom film was both political *and* artistic, this attitude, although political or artistic in spirit, failed to provide a genuine vision of reality, according to the young generation of filmmakers. Only Jean-Luc Godard with *Opération béton* (1954) made an attempt at the genre and filmed, at his own expense and as an amateur, the construction of a dam in Switzerland. Even when the producer Pierre Braunberger convinced François Truffaut to film the flooding around Paris in 1957, Truffaut managed to introduce a fictional story line into the film. He ran into difficulty with the project, however, and had to pass its direction over to Godard, who subsequently broke every narrative and cinematic rule in *Une histoire d'eau,* in a foreshadowing of his work to come.

Bernadette Lafont and Gérard Blain,
Les Mistons (François Truffaut, 1958)

The New Wave of *Cahiers du cinéma* rejected the documentary in the name of life and thus in the name of reality. The review's young Turks felt that the short fictional film, imbued with a sense of real life and subject to the randomness of existence, offered greater potential for grasping the world's truth. Reality for them was in lived experience, immediacy. It burst forth accidentally from the filmed event as it did in real life, revealed itself in Jean Rouch's ethnographic approach as a document that is allowed to speak. In short, it privileged notions of immediate reporting, and a spur-of-the-moment, impromptu, and improvised reality in contrast to the definitive, static, and mummified aspect typical of so many documentaries.

Silvia Monfort and Philippe Noiret, *La Pointe courte*
(Agnès Varda, 1956)

The writers for *Cahiers du cinéma* had no intention of deifying the short film. "Down with the Short" was the title of a report by Godard on the Festival de Tours in February 1959. In it he wrote, "Is the short film really the aesthetic future of the cinema? I'll go further, Is it even cinema? . . . Truth requires me to state that none of us [those associated with the *Cahiers*] believes in the short film as such." In their eyes there was nothing unique about the short: it was one way of making cinema. It was one way of confronting the very real problems of directing and, in particular, of directing actors. Rohmer (*Journal d'un scélérat, Charlotte et son steak*) in 1950–1951 and Astruc (*Le Rideau cramoisi*, which won the Prix Delluc in 1953) were the first to try their hand at the short, but with the exception of Claude Chabrol, they all made short fictional pieces: Truffaut filmed *Les Mistons*; Rivette, working with a screenplay by Chabrol, directed *Coup du berger*; Rohmer made *Véronique et son cancre*, Godard, as part of the *Charlotte et Véronique* series made *Tous les garçons s'appellent Patrick* in 1957 with Jean-Claude Brialy and, in 1958, *Charlotte et son jules*, his first film with Jean-Paul Belmondo (the two heroines of this series were no more than a pretext created by the staff of the *Cahiers* to enable them to introduce the amorous adventures of two young girls, "modern and Parisian," into their short films). Godard was equally interested in films like *Blue Jeans* (Jacques Rozier), *Pourvu qu'on ait l'ivresse* (Jean-Daniel Pollet), or *Opéra-Mouffe* (Agnès Varda), which were presented as fictionalized reporting or fictions in journalistic form.

But at no time were these shorts undertaken as part of the CNC program. While the other wing of the future New Wave, inspired by the "documentary" ethic, took advantage of the CNC approach, which opened the way to a career in film and longer features (*Le Sang des bêtes* and *Night and Fog* are as stylistically self-contained as feature films by Franju and Resnais), those who were part of the *Cahiers du cinéma* had no intention of wasting their time making four or five shorts just to prove that they could direct. At the age of twenty, these young cinephiles had made their choice. They refused to enter IDHEC (Resnais and Malle did, however, and managed to stay a few months). The cinephiles knew that they would have to confront the rules of the system directly if they wanted to penetrate it. So they devised a strategy and organized a takeover. Their proposed victory was worked out in advance and continuously refined.

Between 1952 and 1953 the awareness that they would have to act which in their case meant direct, without going through the restrictive process imposed by the CNC, forced them to confront the problem of money and how to get it. They drew up their own strategies, retaining the lesson they learned from the success of Italian neorealism. It had shown, during the post-War period, that when the system on which a cinema is based is itself in ruins, directors are free to accept the laws of a cinema of poverty and reject the ponderous apparatus typical of fictional and even documentary productions. In the years 1957–1958, the documentary had become extremely difficult to manage and, thus, very expensive, and the short news film was by then a kind of institution. In order to live their dream, the young generations of the New Wave decided to enter the profession (ie. begin soliciting backers and making feature-length films) without becoming members of the "profession." They understood that as filmmakers their "license," as Godard so aptly put it, was a lot like the one prostitutes had been issued in 1946.

1   Cinematographic Industry Organizing
      Committee.
2   National Center for Cinematography.
3   European Federation of the Image and
      Sound Professions.

Le Mystère de l'atelier 15 (Alain Resnais, 1957)

Jean-Claude Brialy, *Tous les garçons s'appellent Patrick* (Jean-Luc Godard, 1957)

1957

AND GOD
CREATED WOMAN

UN CONDAMNÉ À
MORT S'EST
ÉCHAPPÉ

BABY DOLL

ASSASSINS ET
VOLEURS

WRITTEN ON THE
WIND

LES AVENTURES
D'ARSÈNE LUPIN

THE GIRL CAN'T
HELP IT

AN AFFAIR TO
REMEMBER

AND GOD
CREATED WOMAN

Roger Vadim

TRIVIAL AMORALITY

Although critics and the public are generally willing to treat a young director's first film with a degree of tolerance, I felt only a vague curiosity for Vadim's film before viewing it. His run-ins with the censorship committee and the suggestive anecdotes and trivial amorality of the situations created by this same author for recent films by Marc Allégret (*Effeuillons la Marguerite*, among others) led me to expect no more than another of those insipid pieces of racy fluff that French cinema produces with such regularity. This helps explain my enthusiasm for one of the most pleasant cinematic surprises of the year: *And God Created Woman* is more than just good film, it's an auteurish film by a young, serious, and gifted director.

I have to mention the film's eroticism, since it is generally assumed that this is the film's sole purpose. Vadim goes pretty far in this film, but he is fortunate enough to know how to make the film's more daring scenes appear absolutely necessary to the

production and has directed them with talent. Bardot is always unclothed with intelligence and in this film pornography takes second place to cinematic invention.

And God Created Woman makes me think of Françoise Sagan's novels. Vadim borrows her framing devices and many of her characters, but his work is never cynical; his protagonists are devoid of merely ordinary intelligence. They are well mannered, however (something Sagan would appreciate), with a disarming honesty that is often similar to a kind of wholesome stupidity and keeps them from being petty or cruel. ■

Michel Perez, *Cinéma 57*, January 1957

UN CONDAMNÉ À
MORT S'EST
ÉCHAPPÉ

Robert Bresson

BRESSON IS UNCLASSIFIABLE

This film magnificently confirms Bresson's best qualities and the components of his personal universe: a concern with interiority, a lack of ornamentation, an emphasis on psychological analysis in his

description of the world, a set that functions as counterpoint to his characters' feelings. Bresson isn't a realist, but he achieves realism through excess and always from within. For Bresson realism is primarily a question of psychological and moral truth rather than material resemblance, which is the only truly authentic conception of realism.

Indeed, Bresson defies classification. It's been said that his work is austere, that he finds his inspiration in Racine. But he is, above all, a passionate analyst of human nature. His camera is a microscope. It introduces us into a world where beings never before seen live out their strange existence according to a rhythm that differs from our own. ■

Marcel Martin, *Cinéma 57*, January 1957

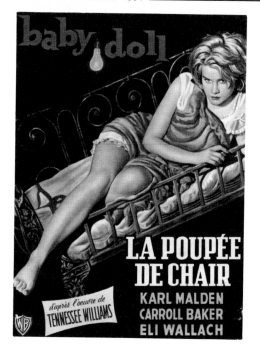

BABY DOLL

Elia Kazan

POETRY AND REALISM

Elia Kazan has set this bitter tale of the South in a fascinating environment. Never has the cinema so closely approximated the unique atmosphere found in the strain of American literature that ranges from Faulkner and Caldwell to Truman Capote. Kazan's strength is his ability to create a poetic ambience while maintaining the appearance of realism. For example, the empty and desolate house where the astonishing ballet between Baby Doll and Vacarro takes place would be nothing more than an abstract and gratuitous set if the beginning of the story hadn't shown us how and why the movers had carted off the furniture.

Avoiding color and a large-screen format, Kazan has developed and maintained a consistent directing and acting style of uncommon energy and effectiveness, which not everyone may appreciate. Everything works in this film, with all its ambiguous detail and harshness, every scene is right.

Kazan has changed something about the way American actors are directed. The director of an acting school in New York and with many years of experience in the theater, Kazan obviously knows what he's doing. But he has been able to impose "his" actors and his method of acting on the film. Together with Orson Welles, he is probably the best director of actors that Hollywood has known in the last twenty years. ■

Jacques Doniol-Valcroze, *France-Observateur*, January 3, 1957

SPIRITUALLY SCANDALOUS

Baby Doll is Elia Kazan's adaptation of the last play by Tennessee Williams, author of *The Rose Tattoo*, *A Streetcar Named Desire*, and *Cat on a Hot Tin Roof*. The film was subject to the wrath of Cardinal Spellman, America's primate and in all fairness, the Cardinal had reason to be upset.

In *Baby Doll* unconsummated marriages, adultery, and grown women who dress like little girls are openly encouraged. Virtue, morality, marital fidelity, the need to "grow and multiply," the obedience of a wife to her husband, the quasi-divine authority previously exercised by husbands—all have been eliminated. The most innocent games (horseplay is devil's play) are used for purposes that are far from innocent. Cribs and beds are profaned, mental illness, sexual infantilism, and American impotence, have now been proclaimed "urbi et orbi." Pyromania has been raised to the level of ersatz, a symbol of frustration. It's too much.

A husband who is a cretin and pyromaniac, a seductive sadist, a vicious wife, a crazy, greedy old aunt who visits patients in the old-age home nearby to steal their sweets, and grinning, do-nothing negroes provide a representative cross-section of American culture. Spiritually, *Baby Doll* is a scandalous film, scandalous enough to make a college of cardinals blush. From a literary point of view, it's both Zola and Félicien Champsaur, with more of the second than the first. Cinematically, however, the film is excellent.

The best scene in the movie is the one in which Eli Wallach's Sicilian seducer chases a bewitched Carroll Baker through the house. The atmosphere is typical of Tennessee Williams's South: ruined, poor, shameless, unhealthy, and sad. It's all admirably brought to the screen in the film. All in all, it's an important document, a kind of Kinsey report on America and Americans, as seen by themselves. ■

Simone Dubreuilh, *Les Lettres Françaises*, January 3, 1957

MASTERFULL DIRECTION

There is obviously a great deal of complacency in this fabricated cruelty, a lot of exhibitionistic eccentricity. It would be easy to criticize *Baby Doll* as unwholesome and decadent, if we weren't always captivated by its charm and extraordinary sensuality. Kazan directs his actors superbly and has what is probably the surest, most creative touch in film.

What bothers Kazan and what he is incapable of handling well are the transition scenes involving several characters. Here, he's managed to eliminate them—except at the beginning of the film—and as soon as the Sicilian begins his courtship, it's clear that every gesture, every glance counts. These details are rendered with precision and it soon becomes obvious that we're looking at a film masterfully dominated by a single man, unquestionably a man of genius.

Kazan's talent, which is essentially decorative in nature, is better suited to subjects of this type—what we could call the Broadway genre—than tedious social commentaries, which are inevitably dishonest since the dice they use are loaded. ■

François Truffaut, *Arts*, January 2, 1957

WORN-OUT TECHNIQUES

All the worn out techniques used by the authors of *Streetcar* can be found in *Baby Doll.* The frantic energy of a country fair, the repressed sexuality, the pale, delirious showgirls—all are found in this story of a ruined and pyromaniac cotton carder who has promised to take revenge on a Sicilian played by Eli Wallach. The sets are deliberately sordid. The ruined house, the inedible food, and an old car overgrown with weeds compose one of those falsely poetic environments whose prefabricated wonder is one example among many of Cocteau's fatal influence (on those willing to accept it, of course, which limits the damage). The heroes, the abject whites, and the lazy, grinning negroes are marked by a sense of morality that, because it is racist lacks all conviction and could only arise from a tormented love. ∎

Louis Seguin, *Positif,* January 1957

ASSASSINS ET VOLEURS

Sacha Guitry

THE HUMOR SPARKLES THROUGHOUT

Assassins et Voleurs was conceived, written, and directed by Guitry. The characters murder and steal; they commit the kinds of acts that morality condemns and justice doesn't always succeed in punishing. It's a bleak and terrible story, but Guitry tells it in such a way that it's impossible to take it seriously. If we cry, we do so from laughter, as in the scene when Darry Cowl testifies before the court. If we tremble, we do so with desire, as the sensual Magali Noël emerges from the water. The dialogue is spirited and sparkles with humor. One of the victims lives on "Boulevard John Cocteau," a satirical anachronism that gives the film clarity. It will undoubtedly be a great success. This band of outlaws (captured on film) isn't quite ready to be locked up yet. ∎

Paul Giannoli, *Paris-Presse,* February 9, 1957

AN IMMORAL FILM

Assassins et Voleurs is a supposedly immoral film—the immorality of a cynical screenplay that glorifies adultery, theft, injustice, and murder, the immorality of combined financial and artistic success, which defies all the rules of common sense and experience, a paradoxical, nearly scandalous success. *Assassins et Voleurs,* unlike most of the films we support at *Cahiers du cinéma,* is devoid of any aesthetic ambition. The film doesn't show the least sign of professional conscience. A scene in a boat that is supposed to take place on the open sea was obviously shot on sand. And the hotel's elevator doesn't go up any more than the boat advances over water. The same set is used several times. The long scene between Poiret and Serrault, broken into ten or twelve fragments, has obviously been filmed in one afternoon with two cameras, and it was done so badly that by listening closely we can hear the buses that pass in front of the studio and the mechanics on the next set happily discussing their lunch.

Because they arrive at a particular time and combine certain specific features, some films become—not always with the director's intentions—symbols, emblems for the critic. Arriving after a number of well-made (perhaps too well-made) and overly expensive French films that were

ambitious failures, *Assassins et Voleurs* nevertheless possesses a certain charm in spite of the cynicism behind it, its imperfections, both in its conception and realization. It manages this in spite of the lack of a big budget, and not because it has one, as in the failures referred to above. ∎

François Truffaut, *Cahiers du cinéma,*
   April 1957

THE ACTOR'S REVENGE

Assassins et Voleurs will do nothing to improve Sacha Guitry's reputation. The screenplay is nonexistent, the direction is haphazard, and the actors, left to their own devices, are stuck with a hopeless screenplay: "She entered the ocean the way you throw yourself in the water." "Though no longer a cuckold, he was already a dupe." Although, by some miracle, Magali Noël is stunningly beautiful, Poiret and Serrault look drained. It's worth seeing *Assassins et Voleurs,* however, for the brilliant performance by Darry Cowl, who manages to parade his rhetorical skills throughout the film and, as a misleading witness, declares to the judge, "Beat it, kid!" Actors do sometimes get their revenge after all. ∎

Positif, March 1957

WRITTEN ON THE WIND

Douglas Sirk

THE POETICS OF WEALTH

Douglas Sirk has made wealth poetic, ennobled new and shiny, colored and lacquered things. From the small yellow car Bob drives through the forest of oil rigs to the dead leaves that sweep across the perfect beauty of the black and white tiles in the perfectly beautiful house, from the pink and mauve hotel in Miami to the run-down little bar where Dorothy lies in wait in her pink dress—everything is visually shocking. But it's pleasure without heat.

Like François Reichenbach, Sirk knows color and how to get it on screen. The French documentary filmmaker has been able to elevate ordinary things; the American director, however, has demeaned, humiliated, and humanized his beautiful sets. The impeccable kitchen, the sumptuous bedroom, and the dream airport are all fake. Even the Cadillacs, the pastel visions, and Winston's cufflinks can't provide protection against human misery and poverty. Obviously, the rich are corrupt; but what do they get out of it?

Sirk has managed to turn this compromise, this story without any real interest, into nothing more than a very good film, which is more than can be said for most. ∎

Jean Loth, *Cinéma 57*, May 1957

LES AVENTURES D'ARSÈNE LUPIN

Jacques Becker

THE MEDIOCRITY OF AN EXCELLENT TECHNICIAN

Several reviews of Jacques Becker's work have appeared in *Positif*. His latest film does nothing more than confirm the

mediocrity of this excellent technician, who with remarkable regularity, has managed to make the marvelous character of Arsène Lupin dull and uninteresting. Lamoreux looks about as comfortable in the role of a gentleman-thief as a nun at a strip show. Let's hope the film doesn't prevent the younger crowd from reading Maurice Leblanc, the epitome of warmth, humor, and romanticism. ∎

Positif, April 1957

CHARMING, DISTINGUISHED AND ELEGANT

Arsène Lupin is not a masterpiece. It doesn't captivate the audience or engage them in any profound way; it never stirs up a whirlpool of emotion or allows viewers to temporarily forget who or where they are. It is, however, a charming, distinguished, and elegant film, polished in its smallest detail, even aristocratic in a way. It will, however, never achieve the heights that *Casque d'Or* managed without even trying. But, in spite of the slow pace of this film, audiences will enjoy it. ∎

Albert Decamps, *Cinéma 57*, May 1957

THE GIRL CAN'T HELP IT

Frank Tashlin

CONSISTENTLY FUNNY

I won't say too much about this film other than that I like it very much. *The Girl Can't Help It* is not just a good film, it's a witty film and an excellent parody. In a way, it's a kind of masterpiece of the genre.

What's it about? Basically, the film is a variation, or variations, on the theme of Pygmalion. The sculptor in this case falls in love with a model whom he gives up trying to sculpt. In Tashlin's film the happy-go-lucky hero of *The Seven Year Itch* is an impresario who drowns himself in alcohol because of his unrequited love for a well-built heroine protected by an ex-gangster. The heroine in question, unlike the character in *Baby Doll*, and contrary to all appearances, dreams of nothing but making dinner for an ordinary husband who will provide her with a brood of kids. And she cannot, or will not, sing. In fact, she's so bad that, when she sings a high note, the lightbulbs burst. Everything turns out for the best, however. This is fortunate because Tashlin is so competent that an unhappy ending in one of his films would probably lead to a spate of suicides.

Consistently funny, *The Girl Can't Help It*, is also beautiful to watch. The picnic on the beach where Jayne Mansfield, dressed in a swimsuit, talks about her criminal father and terrible childhood, with the ocean behind her, is simply wonderful.

Having had the chance to see *The Girl Can't Help It* three times before preparing these comments, I discovered that this film, like many great films, gets better with repeated viewings. Seeing it again, you laugh less but enjoy it more, and it's easy to be moved by the film. Of all the American films now being shown, it happens to be the best. ∎

François Truffaut, *Arts*, April 10, 1957

VIRULENT CRITIQUE

Not long ago, Mr. Chepilov, former commissar for foreign affairs of the

USSR, made an interesting comment about entertainment in the West. Among other things, he claimed that rock and roll was a form of leisure "worthy of the caveman" and that it expressed, perhaps even more so than "non-figurative" painting, the degeneracy and dissolution of bourgeois civilization. Would Mr. Chepilov see in Frank Tashlin's *The Girl Can't Help It* a glowing confirmation of his claims? I'm not sure. But I do know that the film is one of the most virulent criticisms made by intelligent Americans about their own civilization.

The Girl Can't Help It is presented as a musical comedy. Tashlin more or less respects the basic rules of the genre, but adds a new dimension: realism, in the truest sense of the word. Not only does he describe social types with humor, but he establishes the existence of a form of collective madness based on fraud. The irresistible attraction that the most vulgar byproducts of literary, musical, or cinematic culture exercise on people, haunts Tashlin, and he is a tireless observer of the phenomenon. There is a unity of intent that may surprise someone concentrating only on the surface of his films, but which is, finally, not that unusual considering the American film-maker's penchant for examining the cruelest truths that lie behind the flimsiest pretexts. The deliberately offbeat approach Tashlin takes in this film comes more from the intrusion of realism than any narrative techniques borrowed (for the most part) from his experience as a cartoonist. Purists—and I exclude myself from the group—may be surprised to find that, under cover of reviving the musical comedy, Tashlin has actually destroyed it, offering viewers scenes that are both charming and seductive. We would be making a serious error about Tashlin's intentions, however, if we were to assume that his only goal was demystification. His approach is more subtle. Based on the atrophied notion of jazz "for the millions," Tashlin wants to ridicule the orgy of musical contortions, the stammering, hip swinging litanies chanted to a would-be obsessive tempo that the public

eats up. Tashlin's target is the discount excitement, the ersatz collective hysteria that reveals an immeasurable emptiness within. There is little need for Tashlin to point the finger at capitalist society directly, with tremolos from the stage of the Vélodrome d'Hiver in the background, since sex, and its more or less scandalous and obscene derivatives, provides an excellent starting point. He pays tribute to Abbey Lincoln, the black singer, because it helps him tear down rock's impostures, Eddie Cochran and the others whose names you'll forgive me for forgetting. In this sense he's a bit like Gene Kelly in the second sketch from *Round Around the Rosie*, but with more bite. ■

Jean Domarchi, *Cahiers du cinéma*, June 1957

A REAL AMERICAN SCREWBALL

Tashlin is excellent at rendering color and line, form and volume. A loony intellectual, he "eats" with relish, loves private jokes and burlesque gags, employs obscenity and is a careful and thoughtful observer. A documentarian of contemporary life, advertising, and film, Tashlin is at the same time—which is his way of making his audience swallow the bitterest of sociological pills—a real American screwball. "You know what? He *is* crazy." ■

Roger Tailleur, *Positif*, April 1957

SUPREME SILLINESS

Tashlin has made a series of films that are funny and far out, but they do have an undeniable uniformity of intellect in common. They denote his concern for exposing some of the obsessions that characterize the average *Homo americanus*—who is cowardly, domestic, frightened, and stupid—played successively by Bob Hope (*Son of Pale Face*), Jerry Lewis (*Artists and Models*), and, here, Tom Ewell. Atomic pin-ups, embodied by Jane Russell, Anita Ekberg, and Jayne Mansfield have replaced the customary psychiatrist, and through the clever use of allusion, or more direct contact, they help their very middle-class partner create an artificial paradise for himself. Tom Ewell, a remarkable actor trained at the Actor's Studio, embodies both Bob Hope's cowardice and Jerry Lewis's vicious innocence.

It would be easy to conceive a farce based on Jayne Mansfield's curves, but Frank Tashlin shows no deep affection for his characters or any of the raciness that might have saved them. A former cartoonist, he has created a two-dimensional world on film, without elegance, without love, as depressingly brash and empty as the advertising for the film. A screenwriter before he was a director, Tashlin has retained a taste for detail and the ability to exploit a scene for all it's worth (for example, the gag in which

Jayne Mansfield breaks a light bulb is repeated three times as is Edmond O'Brien's attempt to sing rock and roll). The profound truth of these characters, however, can't overcome the poverty of the script. At most we can enjoy the silliness of the on-screen action and the smirk of the narrator whose job it is to amuse us.

The Girl Can't Help It does make you laugh at times. Tom Ewell is a fine actor and Jayne Mansfield certainly offers plenty to look at. But should cinema do nothing more than treat its audience merely as passive viewers, like a bunch of cows watching a passing train? ■

Louis Marcorelles, *Cinéma 57*, May 1957

AN AFFAIR TO REMEMBER

Leo McCarey

NOTHING SHORT OF SUBLIME

It's been said that "American comedy" is a dead-end. Did it ever exist in the first place or was it the product of critics in need of generalizations? Such a claim would not only overlook the masters of the genre, such as Frank Capra and Leo McCarey, and their brilliant followers, Tay Garnett and George Stevens, it would also ignore accomplished filmmakers like Norman MacLeod, Elliott Nugent, and Mark Sandrich. Such an attitude implies a misunderstanding of the moral climate of the pre-War period and a vision of the world that was broad enough to support the great revolutionary Soviet films, the French cinema of the Popular Front, and the Italian neorealism of the post-War period. Today, prematurely undermined by Sturges and then by the detective films of 1944–1945, American film can do no more than reflect the breakdown of a society in the grip of the absurd: Nicholas Ray and Frank Tashlin bear eloquent witness to this phenomenon. Under these conditions, the return of Leo McCarey is nothing short of sublime, for he is always faithful to himself, unconcerned with modes and moods, and capable of a seemingly effortless adaptation of the fugal technique of American comedy to CinemaScope. McCarey is more than a technician, however, even though he is a brilliant one. In his films the absolute mastery of form results in an original vision of the world. ■

Louis Marcorelles, *Cahiers du cinéma*, November 1957

TWENTY YEARS BEHIND THE TIMES

The pre-War American comedy is dead. It died with Lubitsch. Capra reduced it to silence. Now Leo McCarey returns to the big screen and his old love after five years in television with a remake of his 1939 *Love Affair*.

Not even the use of color, CinemaScope in this case, or an aging Cary Grant can convince us that this dated comedy is from 1957; the film is conventional in so many ways that it feels twenty years old. During the first ten minutes, the audience hopes it will be able to experience at least some emotion in watching this souvenir album of a movie, but McCarey prematurely runs out of steam and the few gags that manage to shake us from our torpor are no more than the last gasps of a dying man.

Although McCarey neglects realism, he hasn't forgotten noble sentiments, and he tries to drag the apparatus of maudlin comedy into the film: well-behaved children, an understanding pastor, a doting grandmother with common sense who wills her lace shawl to her adored grandson's exquisite companion, the tact of the disabled heroine who abandons her love so she won't be a burden on her husband, etc. However, it's not the tears we've spilled that cause our bitterness, but regret for a lost genre, which this saraband of broken hearts, uninterestingly filmed, does little to restore. ■

Charles Bitsch, *Arts*, October 19, 1957

The intellectual excitement that drove the various film club movements at the end of the forties, the profound influence of the Cinémathèque français, and the change in attitude toward the history of the medium brought about by its screenings—these were a cruel reminder of the lack of a suitable vehicle for theoretical and critical writing about the cinema. The disappearance of *La Revue du cinéma* (and its founder Jean-Georges Auriol) and *L'Écran français* simply exacerbated the situation. The euphoria of the film-club movement awakened and concretized the need for a film journal.

At the time, the Latin Quarter film club published a newsletter and under the directorship of Éric Rohmer it managed to transform itself into a small magazine, similar to what is now called a fanzine, entitled *La Gazette du cinéma*. It was eight pages long, badly printed on mediocre paper, but full of ambition. The publication became a venue for those who would later form the future *Cahiers du cinéma* and eventually the New Wave itself. The *Gazette* included articles by well-known

Adieu Philippine makes the cover of *Cahiers du cinéma*, December 1962

writers such as Sartre and Alexandre Astruc, but there were unknowns as well: Éric Rohmer, Jean-Luc Godard (using the pseudonym Hans Lucas), Jacques Rivette, and many others. François Truffaut, who was having problems with the military for desertion, never wrote for the magazine. Claude Chabrol didn't join the group until a year later. *La Gazette du cinéma* was the logical result of the group that formed around the Festival du Film Maudit in Biarritz in 1949 and 1950. Their attitude toward the cinema frequently coincided with that of André Bazin and the new criticism that developed after the war. But they were more emotionally involved in their work and their aesthetic sense was sharper (they were already defending Hitchcock). With its small readership, however, *La Gazette du cinéma* lasted no more than five

ERS

CAHIERS
DU CINÉMA

N° 1 • REVUE DU CINÉMA ET DU TÉLÉCINÉMA • AVRIL 1951

Gloria Swanson in *Sunset Boulevard* (Billy Wilder, 1950)

MA

issues, and at the beginning of 1951, there was still no journal capable of accommodating the different strains of critical opinion.

It was within this context that André Bazin and Jacques Doniol-Valcroze, gathering together the former writers of *La Revue du cinéma*, decided to create a new review. Because Gallimard refused to give the rights to the title to Auriol, they finally decided to call it *Les Cahiers du cinéma*. The first issues of the review with the yellow cover brought together some of the finest critics from a wide variety of backgrounds—honest and worldly men who had written some of the best post-War criticism. They were literary gentlemen capable of studying cinema and evaluating films, but not sufficiently passionate about film to take sides or fight for its success. The arrival of François Truffaut as a member of the editorial team caused a violent break with the journal's sober and well-intentioned tone. Supported by Bazin (who helped him straighten out his affairs with the military and gave him a place to stay), Truffaut, in March 1953, rejoined his friends Rohmer, Rivette, Chabrol, and Godard, all of whom contributed articles to the publication. Bazin and Doniol-Valcroze devoted a certain amount of column space to these insolent, rebellious, but ultimately sympathetic, young filmmakers. Rohmer, the oldest and most respected of them, was treated with greater respect.

Although these "young Turks" weren't writing feature articles for the review, they began to receive increased exposure in the *Cahiers*. The first action in their takeover of cinema was a polemic, "A Certain Tendency of the French Cinema," a pamphlet Truffaut wrote against "the tradition of quality." Based on notes he had written in prison, the twenty-two year old critic virulently denounced the tradition of literary adaptation that undermined films made by the major representatives of the French cinema. The article wasn't published in *Cahiers du cinéma* until nearly a year later, in January of 1954. In 1953 Bazin and Doniol feared they would lose readers and anger the filmmakers mentioned by the article, some of whom were personal friends (René Clément had been president of Objectif 49). When it was finally published its strident tone came as a sudden shock to the polite character of the review and the world of film, which was both offended and gratified by its publication. The article was devastating and received a great deal of notoriety. Seduced by the riotous effects of "A Certain Tendency of the French Cinema," the owners of the

cultural weekly *Arts* turned their film page over to Truffaut. The claims of the young Turks thus began to be heard and were beginning to be taken seriously by Bazin and Doniol, in spite of their disagreements with those claims. Their status within *Cahiers* rose.

Starting in 1954, Truffaut, Rohmer, Godard, Rivette, and Chabrol began to promote their favorite directors within the review and establish the *auteur* concept. Their unrestrained love of film also expressed itself in recorded interviews with their favorite directors. These interviews

107 ★ REVUE MENSUELLE DE **85** ★ REVUE MENSUELLE DE CINÉMA ● JUILLET 1958

Covers of *Cahiers du cinéma*: *Party Girl* (Ray), *Monika* (Bergman), *A Woman is a Woman* (Godard), and *Le Beau Serge* (Chabrol)

CAHIERS
DU CINÉMA

★ REVUE MENSUELLE DE CINÉMA ● AOUT 1961 ★ 122

REVUE MENSUELLE DE CINÉMA ● MARS 1959 ★ 93

were carefully prepared by men who knew every detail of the films being discussed and had thought at length about the directors' works. And in spite of an occasional naiveté and excess, these interview with contemporary directors helped shape the film-makers of the future.

The directors interviewed (especially the Americans, who were little accustomed to people discussing their work with such accuracy and depth) were dumbfounded and deeply impressed by these young writers' ideas, not only about the craft, but the art of cinema. The reputation of *Cahiers du cinéma* began to grow. In Hollywood the review became essential reading and Fritz Lang, Joseph Mankiewicz, Samuel Fuller, and Nicholas Ray often posed for photographs with a copy of the magazine in their hand. The magazine's success spread to Tokyo, Berlin, and Moscow. The growing fame of *Cahiers du cinéma* was obvious and enabled it to reduce its debt and eventually turn a profit.

Slowly the review changed and reorganized. The articles on individual films were guided by very specific biases: a writer provided criticism of a specific film, that he or she promoted and insisted on defending. The principal articles (unlike those in *Positif*, its literary opposite) were always favorable. There were shorter pieces (about ten to thirty lines each) and capsule reviews designed to cover the rest of the month's films (sometimes in excoriating prose). Negative reviews weren't excluded, but there was a policy of discussing only films that the *Cahiers* felt worthy of attention. This prejudice enabled the review to avoid becoming too closely allied with current films, but left them still free to discuss them and their influence. They also published technical details about all the films that appeared during the month.

The review devoted increasing coverage to less popular films. It not only took an interest in filmmakers it wished to defend, but also in new filmmakers it discovered. Slowly, new names began appearing in the pages of the *Cahiers*. The review's aesthetic judgment became more confident with time, and fewer mistakes were made. Of course, there were some, but these often resulted from considerations that had little to do with a specific film, such as the omission of John Ford, which resulted from the polemic launched by Roger Leenhardt (who preferred Wyler). The same was true for Buñuel; although supported by Bazin, he was rejected by the entire younger staff (with the exception of *The Criminal Life of Archibaldo de la Cruz*), who saw the Spanish filmmaker as the champion of the competing review, *Positif*, which was said to be "leftist" and surrealist, but at bottom more dogmatic than doctrinaire. As with Ford, the deliberate rejection of Buñuel eventually became unpopular with the filmmakers of the New Wave, and both of them were given a reserved seat on filmmaking's Mount Olympus.

The austere tone of the review, based on the tradition of seriousness associated with the former *Revue du cinéma*, was soon discarded. Now more impertinent and lively, the journal's young writers conveyed a sense of satisfaction that was in complete harmony with their love of cinema. Under Truffaut's leadership the section entitled "Le Petit journal intime du cinéma" provided an opportunity for a more whimsical approach by someone completely dedicated to film. At the same time, Truffaut could report on productions by his favorite filmmakers, launch new polemics, pan certain producers and praise others. Unlike *Positif*, *Cahiers du cinéma* was a review by, about, and for the young. It is strange today to see the review attacked for being recondite, intellectual, and boring.

The journal's seriousness, on the other hand, arose from the fact that this

Carl Theodor Dreyer (left)

UNE CERTAINE TENDANCE DU CINEMA FRANÇAIS

par François Truffaut

« On peut aimer que le sens du mot art so tenté de donner conscience à des homm de la grandeur qu'ils ignorent en eux.

ANDRÉ MALRAUX
(Le Temps du Mépris, préface).

Ces notes n'ont pas d'autre objet qu'essayer de définir une certaine tendanc du cinéma français — tendance dite du réalisme psychologique — et d'e esquisser les limites.

DIX OU DOUZE FILMS...

Si le cinéma français existe par une centaine de films chaque année, il e bien entendu que dix ou douze seulement méritent de retenir l'attention de critiques et des cinéphiles, l'attention donc de ces CAHIERS.

Ces dix ou douze films constituent ce que l'on a joliment appelé la *Traditio de la Qualité*, ils forcent par leur ambition l'admiration de la presse étrangèr défendent deux fois l'an les couleurs de la France à Cannes et à Venise où, depu 1946, ils râflent assez régulièrement médailles, lions d'or et grands prix.

Au début du parlant, le cinéma français fut l'honnête démarquage du ciném américain. Sous l'influence de *Scarface* nous faisions l'amusant *Pépé le Mok* Puis le scénario français dut à Prévert le plus clair de son évolution, *Quai de Brumes* reste le chef-d'œuvre de l'école dite du *réalisme poétique*.

La guerre et l'après-guerre ont renouvelé notre cinéma. Il a évolué sou l'effet d'une pression interne et au réalisme poétique — dont on peut dir qu'il mourut en refermant derrière lui *Les Portes de la Nuit* — s'est substitu le *réalisme psychologique*, illustré par Claude Autant-Lara, Jean Delannoy René Clément, Yves Allégret et Marcel Pagliero.

Cahiers du cinéma, no 31, January 1954

Claude Chabrol and Jean-Luc Godard in the offices of *Cahiers du cinéma,* summer 1959

Joseph Leo Mankiewicz (right)

Fritz Lang (right)

ludic spirit was better equipped to reveal the fundamental values that were expected of, demanded of cinema. Specifically, the value of Truth, which was positioned morally above the Good and aesthetically above the Beautiful. The common thread that united all the members of the *Cahiers du cinéma* was based on the postulate that a film must necessarily speak the truth about the world. The quarrel, which was internal to the review, revolved around the question: should we refer to "truth" (broadly), "the truth" (as it is conceived in Bazin's theory), "a truth," or "a true fact"? The *Cahiers'* dominant point of view turned out to be that of Bazin, whom Godard exposed in *Le Petit Soldat* in 1960: "Photography is the truth. Cinema is the truth twenty-four times a second." This theoretical position was quickly abandoned by Godard ("it's not a true image, just an image") but it did become, and remains, the foundation of Rohmer's entire oeuvre.

Slowly, the spirit of *Cahiers du cinéma* spread and soon occupied two or three publishing strongholds: *Arts,* the weekly arts and entertainment magazine for which Truffaut and his friends at the *Cahiers* wrote the film page from 1955 to 1963; *l'Observateur* and *Le Parisien libéré,* for which Bazin and Doniol wrote regularly. The ideas the magazine represented became better known

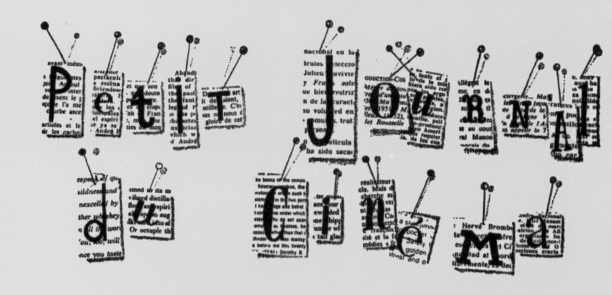

O SAISONS ! O CHATEAUX !

Plus je vois ce court-métrage d'Agnès Varda plus je l'aime. A Cannes, il fut acclamé par le public et c'est justice. On y trouve fantaisie, goût, intelligence, intuition et sensibilité, cinq vertus dont aucune ne devrait jamais faire défaut dans les films. Grâce à Agnès Varda, on peut mesurer quel serait l'apport au cinéma de quelques femmes dotées de certaines qualités qu'un homme ne saurait posséder sans rougir. Plus simplement, je veux dire que le bon goût, masculin, d'un Becker ou d'un Vadim ne résiste pas à la comparaison vardesque. Le seul homme qui puisse selon moi rivaliser de raffinement, de légèreté et d'insolence ésotérique avec Agnès Varda est Norman McLaren lequel précisément, en tant que juré des courts-métrages, milita bruyamment contre *O Saisons! O Châteaux!*

Je n'ignore pas que l'aisance d'Agnès Varda rencontre bien d'autres adversaires; ceux-là, je crois, n'ont que le tort de ne pas deviner que la préciosité et la désinvolture sont ici une forme de la pudeur. Ce qui, dans le cinéma français du moment m'irrite le plus, c'est de sentir l'effort, le labeur, l'obstination poussive, la peur de filmer. Rien de tel chez Agnès Varda qui s'amuse en tournant ses films, afin que nous puissions nous amuser en les voyant. — F. T.

DEJEUNER DES CAHIERS

Au cours du dernier Festival de Cannes, nombreuse et brillante assistance au traditionnel déjeuner des CAHIERS. Parmi les convives, on reconnait plusieurs membres des jurys : Cesare Zavattini, Serge Youtkevitch, Norman McLaren, Helmut Käutner, Jacques de Baroncelli ; et aussi Nicole Berger, Roger Leenhardt, Jacques Baratier, Claude Chabrol, les deux vedettes suédoises, Ingrid Thulin et Bibi Andersson.

Les questions sur Ingmar Bergman, décidément très à la mode, pleuvent. On s'inquiète de sa santé, car, selon les bruits qui courent, Bergman est au plus mal. Ses interprètes nous rassurent : souffrant d'une sorte d'ulcère à l'estomac, il fait de fréquents séjours en clinique où il trouve le calme propice à l'éclosion de ses scénarios. De la conversation se dégage peu à peu le « cycle du Bergman » : chaque automne, lassé du cinéma, il se consacre au théâtre et monte des pièces à Malmoe (les dernières ? « Peer Gynt » et « Faust »), mais dès les premiers beaux jours, il est pris d'une furieuse envie de faire du cinéma, entre en clinique, écrit d'un seul jet un ou deux scénarios auxquels il n'apporte ensuite presque aucune retouche, puis se met à tourner jusqu'à la fin de l'été ; et ainsi de suite.

Les questions s'orientent plus précisément sur *Au Seuil de la vie* ; six semaines de tournage, 30 millions. Les films suédois sont très bon marché, l'équipe de tournage étant là-bas réduite à son strict minimum. Le devis de *Sourires d'une nuit d'été*, film cher, atteignait à peine les 80 millions. On apprend encore qu'une scène du film a été coupée par Berg-

La scène coupée par Ingmar Bergman dans Au seuil de la vie.

42

Double-page spread from *Cahiers du cinéma*, no. 84, June 1958

Le déjeuner des « Cahiers ». On reconnaît de gauche à droite : Jean de Baroncelli, Bibi Andersson, Georges Sadoul (de dos), Serge Youtkevitch, Nicole Berger, André Bazin, Mme G. Sadoul.

man lui-même : on y voyait la doctoresse et un jeune docteur conversant en présence de Hjördis (Bibi Andersson), devant une tasse de café et un gâteau couronné d'une cigogne en sucre portant un bébé. A la fin de cette scène, Hjördis, avant de quitter la pièce, du doigt noyait le bébé dans la crème.

On s'étonne également de la liberté dont jouit Bergman, car aussi bien *Le Septième Sceau* qu'*Au Seuil de la vie* ne semblent guère tenir compte des goûts du public tant ils se refusent à tout compromis. Mais l'un comme l'autre, le second surtout, sont de gros succés commerciaux. — Ch. B.

LES FRERES D'INGMAR

Les cinéphiles parisiens vont avoir, au cours des mois prochains, la bonne fortune de découvrir plusieurs des douze films d'Ingmar Bergman encore inédits en France. C'est parfait, mais n'oublions pas non plus les autres grands cinéastes suédois.

1° Des quinze films mis en scène par Sjöberg, les distributeurs français n'ont diffusé que *Le Chemin du Ciel* (1942), *Tourments* (1944; scénario : Bergman) et *Mademoiselle Julie* (1950). Réclamons donc, à cor et à cri, *La Chasse Royale* (1944), *Voyage au loin* (1945), *Iris et le cœur d'un lieutenant* (1946), *Rien qu'une mère* (1949), *Oiseaux sauvages* (1955), et *Le Dernier Couple qui court* (1957).

2° Nous ne connaissons le grand metteur en scène Hasse Ekman que comme acteur pour l'avoir vu séduire Harriett Andersson dans *La Nuit des Forains*. Pourquoi ne pas nous montrer à Paris quelques-uns des trente-deux films qu'il a mis en scène? Signalons essentiellement : *Changement de train, Une Dynastie de cabotins, Promenade sous la lune,*

Les Agapes, La Fille aux jacinthes, Le Chat blanc, Le Loup noir, Gabrielle et *Entrée privée!*

3° Ingmar Bergman est en tête du peloton, cela est vrai, mais le peloton existe et je connais d'excellents films suédois signés : Gummar Hellstrom, Alf Kjellin, Hampe Faustman, Gosta Werner, Kjellgren, Gosta Folke et Kenne Fant.

Il appartient aux « Cinémas d'Arts et d'Essai » de faire venir des copies de ces films et d'organiser, peut-être, une sorte de panorama qui satisferait notre curiosité suédoise. — J.B.

HITCH : VERTIGO

Comme dans tous ses autres films, Hitchcock apparaît brièvement dans *Vertigo*. Tout d'abord il envisageait de traverser l'écran en portant une maquette de paquebot entre ses bras. Craignant ensuite de prendre trop d'importance et de « voler la scène » à ses interprètes, il décida plus simplement de déambuler prestement au milieu d'un chantier naval. Les plus fidèles hitchcockiens de nos fidèles lecteurs auront d'eux-mêmes interprété la signification de cette apparition : Alfred nous annonce qu'il va enfin concrétiser un vieux rêve, filmer le naufrage d'un paquebot en mer, pour la M.G.M. — F.T.

Nous avons omis de signaler à nos lecteurs que les photographies illustrant l'article d'Eisenstein, publié dans le numéro 82 des CAHIERS, sont inédites et proviennent, non pas du film lui-même, mais de chutes négatives ou positives, remises à Georges Sadoul par Mme Eisenstein.

Ce petit journal a été rédigé par JEAN BÉRANGER, CHARLES BITSCH et FRANÇOIS TRUFFAUT.

43

and this resulted in a backlash: the aggressiveness of the review and its writers was felt to be excessive by some. Truffaut was the primary target (especially his ability to hit where it hurt most), for his virulence was held to be disruptive, unfair, and scandalous. It resulted in barely concealed hatreds within the profession. Between 1954 and 1958 two camps were at war. The young critics of the *Cahiers* felt the battle was necessary and they increased their declarations of war against French filmmakers "of quality" with a violence similar to that exhibited by Jesus in chasing the moneylenders from the Temple. The Philistines were hardly appreciative, nor were the gentiles for that matter.

Michel Subor and Anna Karina, *Le Petit Soldat* (Jean-Luc Godard, 1960–1963)

The small group of writers, who came to be regarded as terrorists, did not fight exclusively with their pens. They considered criticism only to be a transitional phase. Their ultimate goal was directing. The only thing that mattered was to make films and to do this they had to quickly infiltrate the traditional bastions of the profession and destroy them. They became a kind of light infantry, forming (with colleagues at the review or personal friends) a small core of filmmakers and technicians, prepared to perform any job that came their way (Rivette and Charles Bitsch, for example, both worked as chief cameramen before becoming assistant directors). Their band increased in number and was joined by several young actors who appeared in their short films (Jean-Claude Brialy, Jean-Paul Belmondo, Bernadette Lafont, Gérard Blain). By 1958 they were ready to go on the offensive.

Paris vu par . . . (the sketch by Jean Douchet: *Saint-Germain-des-Prés*, 1965)

This presented a problem for the *Cahiers*. Within a year, Truffaut, Rivette, Chabrol, Godard, Rohmer, Kast, and Doniol, had made their first features. But the *Cahiers du cinéma* had to continue, if only to support the new filmmakers and perpetuate the spirit

Le Petit Soldat

of the review. André Bazin's death, which took place, rather symbolically, during the night of the first day's shooting of *The 400 Blows*, signaled the end of the golden age of the "yellow" *Cahiers*. From 1959 to 1963–1964, a second generation of young cinephiles replaced the first group at the *Cahiers*. This new group did not share the tastes or opinions of their predecessors, and the transition was not without its casualties. In fact, it resulted in what may have been the most violent conflict ever to take place at the review. Supported by the new group of writers, Jacques Rivette, out of work after the failure of *Paris nous appartient*, took over as head of the *Cahiers* and replaced Rohmer, who was then editor in chief. The apparent sense of community at the review suddenly fractured and the New Wave broke with it. Produced a few months later, *Paris vu par ...* (1964), the New Wave's collective film, did not escape unscathed from the conflict. Both Rivette and Truffaut, who had managed to hold onto control of *Cahiers*, were

LES DIX MEILLEURS FILMS DE L'ANNÉE

Michel Subor, *Le Petit Soldat*

symbolically excluded from the film. The split had begun. Each of the filmmakers associated with the *Cahiers* went their own way, and their ways began to diverge more and more.

Henri Agel. — (Par ordre alphabétique) Les Contes de la lune vague; Deux hommes dans Manhattan; La Forêt interdite; Hiroshima mon amour; L'Impératrice Yang Kwei Fei; Moi un noir; La Mort aux trousses; Pickpocket; Rio Bravo; Le Tigre d'Eschnapur.

Jean de Baroncelli. — 1. Ivan le Terrible; 2. Hiroshima mon amour; 3. Les Quatre cents coups; 4. Les Fraises sauvages; 5. Les Contes de la lune vague; 6. Pickpocket; 7. Le Général della Rovere; 8. La Corrida interdite; 9. Orfeu Negro; 10. La Tête contre les murs.

Charles Bitsch. — 1. Les Contes de la lune vague, Ivan le Terrible; 3. Autopsie d'un meurtre, Le Déjeuner sur l'herbe, Hiroshima mon amour, Pickpocket; 7. Les Quatre cents coups; 8. Rio Bravo, Le Tigre d'Eschnapur, Vertigo.

Pierre Braunberger. — 1. Hiroshima mon amour, Les Quatre cents coups, Ivan le Terrible, Les Fraises sauvages; 5. Le Pigeon; 6. Vertigo; 7. Les Contes de la lune vague; 8. Le Déjeuner sur l'herbe; 9. Les Cousins; 10. Moi un noir.

Claude Chabrol. — 1. Le Tigre d'Eschnapur, Les Contes de la lune vague, Ivan le Terrible; 4. Vertigo, Les Quatre cents coups; 6. Hiroshima mon amour, Rio Bravo; 8. L'Impératrice Yang Kwei Fei; 9. La Tête contre les murs; 10. Le Journal d'Anne Frank.

Philippe Demonsablon. — 1. Les Contes de la lune vague; 2. L'Impératrice Yang Kwei Fei; 3. Ivan le Terrible; 4. Le Général della Rovere; 5. Autopsie d'un meurtre; 6. Vertigo; 7. Hiroshima mon amour; 8. Rio Bravo; 9. Le Tigre d'Eschnapur; 10. Moi un noir.

Jacques Demy. — 1. Pickpocket; 2. Les Contes de la lune vague, Du côté de la Côte. Hiroshima mon amour, Ivan le Terrible, Ossessione, Les Quatre cents coups, Rio Bravo, La Tête contre les murs, Vertigo.

Jean Domarchi. — 1. Ivan le Terrible; 2. Rio Bravo, Vertigo; 4. La Brune brûlante, Autopsie d'un meurtre; 6. Hiroshima mon amour, Pickpocket, Deux hommes dans Manhattan; 9. Le Jugement des flèches; 10. La Tête contre les murs.

Jacques Doniol-Valcroze. — 1. Pickpocket; 2. Hiroshima mon amour; 3. Ivan le Terrible; 4. Les Contes de la lune vague; 5. Vertigo; 6. Les Fraises sauvages; 7. Les Quatre cents coups; 8. La Tête contre les murs; 9. Moi un noir; 10. Les Enfants perdus.

Jean Douchet. — 1. Le Tigre d'Eschnapur; 2. L'Impératrice Yang Kwei Fei; 3. La Forêt interdite; 4. Rio Bravo; 5. Autopsie d'un meurtre, Le Général della Rovere, Vertigo; 8. Qu'est-ce que maman comprend à l'amour?; 9. La Brune brûlante; 10. Les Contes de la lune vague.

Jean-Luc Godard. — 1. Pickpocket; 2. Deux hommes dans Manhattan; 3. Les Rendez-vous du diable; 4. Moi un noir; 5. La Tête contre les murs, Le Déjeuner sur l'herbe; 7. Hiroshima mon amour; 8. Les Quatre cents coups; 9. Les Cousins; 10. Du côté de la Côte.

Fereydoun Hoveyda. — 1. Le Tigre d'Eschnapur; 2. Les Fraises sauvages; 3. Rio Bravo; 4. Le Jugement des flèches; 5. A Double tour; 6. L'Impératrice Yang Kwei Fei; 7. Les Quatre cents coups; 8. Autopsie d'un meurtre; 9. Hiroshima mon amour; 10. Les Proies du vampire.

Cahiers du cinéma, no. 104, February 1960

THE CONCEPT OF THE AUTEUR

For the young writers at the *Cahiers*, the critical reflection that followed from viewing films at the Cinémathèque, the movies, or the film clubs, the elaboration of a sense of aesthetics that could be tested against experience, the familiarity with film theory, and the development of exciting and original points of view—all led quite naturally to the introduction of what came to be known as the "concept of the auteur."

It became increasingly obvious that a director could be identified not simply by the similarity of the themes he worked into his films but primarily by his own unique style. Truffaut and Chabrol described this concept in terms of embroidered fabric or tapestry and used it to describe Hitchcock's work in their first interview with him: "Can you describe the pattern in your tapestry?" (*Cahiers*, no. 39, October 1954). From this moment on, Hitchcock abandoned his traditional approach of making mass-market suspense films, which had aroused the disdain of the sophisticated snobs of the film press. Suddenly, he began to speak seriously of his work and confirmed another obvious point about the concept of the auteur, namely, that the so-called subject of the plot didn't matter much at all; it was only superficially important. On the contrary, the auteur's true subject, the truth of his creation, lay in his style,

the way he "wrote" the screen. This was confirmed by Hitchcock, who admitted to Chabrol and Truffaut "You see, for me the screenplay is almost secondary. I make the film before I know the story. It provides the form, an impression of the whole. It's only afterward that I look for the screenplay and bring it into line with what I have in my head."

This attitude toward the cinema came at a time when the screenwriter was the most important figure in contemporary film. He served, often unwillingly, as a form of insurance for, and objective ally of the producer. In France, for example, Henri Jeanson, along with Prévert, the most celebrated screenwriter of the years 1935–1960, could claim that he was the real author of a film and that the directors were mere technicians carrying out his ideas. In the United States the system was such that producers and studios imprinted their own style on their films. The style of a film was associated with their logo; directors were forced to follow it. There was an MGM style, a Paramount style, a Universal style, etc.

Interestingly, after the sixties, a post- and anti-New Wave cinephilia developed that would defend this approach to style and introduce the *studio concept*, an approach that soon turned sterile. Given the number of partisans of the studio approach who invaded the media and voiced their attitudes, it can even be said that they were responsible for a lowering of film standards and a profoundly negative effect on film. Aside from the promotion of a handful of minor filmmakers, this lack of aesthetic reflection resulted in a point of view similar to one of a fetishistic collector—films were "good" only if they conformed to a specific style or look. It produced a jumble of confused values, whereas the concept of the auteur, by encouraging viewers to choose between unlike styles, established a historical classification on the basis of artistic criteria.

We have only to compare the so-called B-film directors discovered by the New Wave with those elevated to the cinematic Pantheon by succeeding generations. On one side we have Samuel Fuller and Jacques Tourneur, whom the New Wave admired and took their inspiration from. On the other we have Cottafavi, Duvivier, Curtiz, Thorpe, and a number of other minor masters of well-crafted films, occasionally marked by aesthetic stylization, but tragically lacking in creative force or any sense of imagination.

Initially, the notion of the auteur made slow progress. Around 1953–1954 the idea of seriously defending someone like Hitchcock was so shocking and farfetched that it was necessary to use tact, and flatter the critical expectations of the time. These expectations were based on fairly widespread humanist attitudes (found in filmmakers such as John Huston and Vittorio De Sica), attitudes reflected in screenplays and readily apparent in films. Critics catalogued these attitudes and convinced themselves that they demonstrated the quality of the films in which they occurred. The future New Wave focused instead on thematic issues. It was necessary to show that Hitchcock, who had been denied the status of auteur, had a lot more than general attitudes going for him. His themes were personal, complex, and multilayered. And a special issue of the *Cahiers*, number 39, was devoted to his work and his defense.

Alfred Hitchcock and François Truffaut in 1972

ALFRED
HITCHCOCK
PAR JEAN DOUCHET

Frontispiece of *Alfred Hitchcock* by Jean Douchet (Éditions de l'Herne, 1967)

CAHIERS
DU CINÉMA

62 ★ REVUE MENSUELLE DU CINÉMA ● AOUT - SEPTEMBRE 1956 ★ **62**

Alfred Hitchcock on the set of *The Man Who Knew Too Much*

In spite of Bazin's doubts, Rohmer, Chabrol, Domarchi, and Rivette attempted to identify the themes that characterized Hitchcock's work. Truffaut analyzed *Shadow of a Doubt* to test his hypothesis of a Christian author tormented by the idea of sin and redemption, a theme that had been clearly present in *Under Capricorn*. To convince their readers of Hitchcock's genius, the *Cahiers*' authors made use of contemporary critical methods and approached Hitchcock thematically, not stylistically. Rohmer opened his article on Hitchcock with the following words: "This issue, devoted to the most brilliant of technicians (something no one would dispute), will have little to do with technique. Hopefully, our readers won't be too surprised to find that words like traveling, framing, or lens, the entire mess of hideous studio jargon, have been replaced by nobler and more pretentious words such as soul, God, devil, disturbance, and sin."

But it was Alexandre Astruc who clearly defined what the future New Wave meant by an auteur; he did so in a short editorial entitled "When a Man . . . ,"

which opened the issue: "When, over the course of thirty years and fifty films, a man tells more or less the same story—that of a soul at war with evil—and maintains the same style throughout this single trajectory, based essentially on stripping his characters bare and plunging them into the abstract universe of their passions, I have a hard time not admitting that we are confronting something that is, after all, extremely rare in this industry: a film *author*."

"After watching these films over and over again, at times I have the impression—which we often get from reading authors such as Dostoyevsky or Faulkner—of being in a universe that is at once aesthetic and moral, where black and white, shadow and light, everything in fact that is shared by film and the novel, and which we refer to as *mise-en-scène*, express, far better than the story itself, the explosive secret that the characters harbor within themselves."

In 1954 it would have required an unusual degree of obtuseness not to recognize in Hitchcock the mark of a filmmaker and auteur. But to elevate a director like Howard Hawks to the same level presented a problem. Hawks was the prototype of the skilled Hollywood craftsman, but he had set himself the goal of creating masterpieces, that is to say, films that were perfect, finished, unequaled "models" of filmmaking in every genre of American film. Auteur wasn't the first word to spring to mind, however. In 1953 (a year and a half before the special issue on Hitchcock appeared) Jacques Rivette scathingly remarked in issue 23 of *Cahiers*, "Obviousness is the mark of Hawks's genius."

Page from the first edition of *Cinéma selon Hitchcock* by François Truffaut, 1966

MES RÊVES SONT TRÈS RAISONNABLES ■ LES IDÉES DE LA NUIT ■ ■ ■ UN EXEMPLE DE PUR EXHIBITIONNISME ■ NE JAMAIS GACHER L'ESPACE ■ FAIRE VOYAGER LE GROS PLAN ■ PSYCHO ■ LE SOUTIEN-GORGE DE JANET LEIGH ■ UN « HARENG ROUGE » ■ LE MEURTRE D'AR-BOGAST ■ LE TRANSPORT DE LA VIEILLE MÈRE ■ LE POIGNARDAGE DE JANET LEIGH ■ LES OISEAUX EMPAILLÉS ■ J'AI CRÉÉ UNE ÉMOTION DE MASSE ■ PSYCHO NOUS APPARTIENT, A NOUS CINÉASTES ■ 13.000.000 DE DOLLARS DE BÉNÉFICE ■ EN THAILANDE, UN HOMME DEBOUT...

13

FRANÇOIS TRUFFAUT   M. Hitchcock, vous m'avez dit ce matin que cela vous troublait un peu d'avoir remué tant de souvenirs ces derniers jours et que vous aviez eu le sommeil agité. Par ailleurs, nous avons vu que certains films, comme *Notorious, Vertigo, Psycho*, ressemblent à des rêves. Je voudrais vous demander si vous rêvez beaucoup?

ALFRED HITCHCOCK   Pas beaucoup... quelquefois... et mes rêves sont très raisonnables. Dans l'un d'eux, je me trouvais sur Sunset Boulevard, sous des arbres, et j'attendais un taxi jaune (Yellow Cab) pour m'emmener déjeuner. Il n'y avait pas de taxi jaune, car toutes les voitures qui passaient étaient de 1916. Et je me suis dit : « C'est inutile de poireauter ici à attendre un taxi jaune puisque je suis en train de faire un rêve de 1916. » Alors j'ai marché jusqu'au restaurant.

F.T.   C'est vraiment un rêve ou un gag?

A.H.   Non, pas un gag, un rêve.

F.T.   Alors c'est presque un rêve d'époque! Vous admettez qu'il y a vraiment tout un côté onirique dans vos films?

A.H.   Ce sont des rêveries du jour.

F.T.   C'est peut-être inconscient chez vous et cela nous ramène encore aux contes de fées. En filmant l'homme seul, entouré de choses hostiles, même sans le vouloir, vous débouchez automatiquement dans le domaine du rêve, qui est aussi celui de la solitude et des périls.

A.H.   C'est probablement moi au-dedans de moi-même.

F.T.   Certainement, parce que la logique de vos films — dont on a vu qu'elle ne satisfait pas toujours les critiques — c'est un peu la logique des rêves. Des films comme *Strangers on a Train* ou *North by Northwest* sont des successions de formes étranges, comme dans un cauchemar.

Through his writing the young critic broke new ground not only in the way we understand a film or work of art, but cinema itself. With *Monkey Business*, which had just come out, as his springboard, Rivette noted a Hawksian constant: "His work is divided equally between dramas and comedies; there is a remarkable sense of ambivalence. But what is more remarkable is the frequent fusion of two elements that affirm rather than deny each other, and are mutually enhanced." This dangerous equilibrium, close to vertigo, meant that "although comedy provides tragedy with its effectiveness, it is dependent on ... a harsh attitude toward existence, in which no action can be isolated from the web of responsibilities." Rivette referred to *Monkey Business* as "a fable that, with a lighthearted logic and spiteful wit, recounts the fatal steps that lead to the mindlessness of superior intellects.... Hawks is only interested in intellectual adventure.... It's easy to recognize in this a classical notion of man, who can only achieve greatness through experience and maturity: at the end of his life, he will be judged by his old age." Truffaut, Rivette's close friend, was struck by these

words and illustrated them in *L'Enfant sauvage*. Further on, Rivette wrote "Hawks, a filmmaker of intelligence and rigor ... films *actions*, while speculating on the power of their exterior form alone."

Rivette continued, in a paragraph that at the time appeared sacrilegious, provocative, unthinkable:

"Hawks summarizes the highest virtues of the American cinema, the only one capable of providing us with a sense of moral value, of which this is a perfect example, an admirable synthesis that possibly contains the secret of its genius. The fascination we find in him is not that of an idea, but its efficacy; the act holds our interest less by its beauty than by its very action within its universe. . . . This art demands a fundamental honesty, characterized by the use of time and space. There are no flashbacks, no shortcuts. Continuity is the rule. When a character moves, we follow. There are no surprises that the hero doesn't share with us. The place and interrelation of each gesture have the force of law, but a biological law whose most decisive proof

James Stewart and Kim Novak in *Vertigo* (Alfred Hitchcock, 1958)

Cahiers du cinéma, no. 23, May 1953

Psycho (Hitchcock, 1954)

Dial M for Murder (Hitchcock)

is found in the creature's existence. Every shot contains the efficient beauty of a neck or an ankle. Their succession, smooth and rigorous, recalls the pulsing of the blood. The entire film, this glorious body, is *animated* by a supple and profound breath."

For the first time, a film critic didn't limit himself to the surface of the film but attempted to grasp its internal organization and penetrate its organic life. We can imagine the effect this produced on the review's professional readership. *Cahiers*' reputation for unreadability stems from this, not from the words and phrases being obscure. Today, they are striking in their clarity. It was the thing itself ("the thing from another world" as Hawks would have called it) that seemed incomprehensible. This wasn't what a film was supposed to be like or the way it was supposed to be interpreted.

The article on Hawks appeared in issue 23, that on Hitchcock in issue 39. Gradually the idea of the auteur was refined. The band of "Hitchcocko-Hawksians" irritated, exasperated, and in one sense terrorized the film community. Mediocre, clever, and established members of the profession feared being unmasked or losing their prestige. They were wrong to fear auteurism though; their fall took place quite naturally. It was enough for the writers of the *Cahiers* to defend good filmmakers and show what film was all about to ensure that. The occasional teasing and prodding by the Hitchcocko-Hawksians was perceived, however, by their more conservative colleagues as a sign of outright aggression.

The importance of the auteur was too obvious to ignore; it shook the world of cinema, and its shock wave was felt all the way to Hollywood. From the closed world of Hollywood's ivory tower, the *Cahiers du cinéma* appeared to be run by a bunch of lunatics. But their way of writing about film and talking about it in interviews intrigued and fascinated their Hollywood readers. After the years 1956–1957, to be called an auteur by *Cahiers* became, in this reticent, gossipy, and snobbish American village, a *must*. The filmmakers named (at the time you weren't "nominated"), admired, and analyzed in the pages

CAHIERS
DU CINÉMA

143 ★ REVUE MENSUELLE DE CINÉMA ★ MAI 1963 ★ 143

CAHIERS
DU CINÉMA

139 HOWARD HAWKS 139

The Birds and *Hatari*: triumph of the "Hitchcocko-Hawksiens"

of the review, understood the originality and value of a new approach to their work, one that was purely artistic rather than commercial, even if they didn't always understand the substance of what was written. The others, those excluded from the journal, were resentful and jealous, and experienced their rejection as personal injury.

Such injury resulted in the increasingly overt attempts to minimize and ridicule the discourse that had struck a chord among filmmakers the world over. Ever since its introduction, the auteur concept had been attacked. It was often parodied and an attempt was even made to replace it with the studio concept or, worse, the *film concept*, which privileged only the "greatest moments from the world's most beautiful films." Luc Mollet introduced the *actor concept*[1], which was a justifiable approach to film. A great actor, he claimed, is a universe, opening a world before our eyes. This is evident in a number of film actors: Charlie Chaplin, Buster Keaton, Erich von Stroheim, Orson Welles, Jerry Lewis, Clint Eastwood. The concept, of course, is derivative of the auteur concept, a logical extension in a way.

The auteur concept was vigorously attacked because on a superficial level it appeared to snub those unable to comprehend, either as directors or critics, the essence of mise-en-scène (the concretization and spatialization—spatial, temporal, aural, and visual—of thought and imagination in motion). The idea itself was disquieting because it was, for the most part, simply misunderstood.

The choice of the word "auteur," the source of which was Astruc's famous editorial, was not very fortunate. It would have been better to introduce not only the concept of the auteur (as recently suggested by Jean-Claude Biette),[2] but also the concept of the *metteur-en-scène* and especially the *cinéaste*. Distinguishing among them would have provided a way of comparing them and a way to better understand the idea of the auteur. For example, Fritz Lang, who was held in contempt by critics during the fifties, is at the same time auteur (by the richness of his obsessional themes), metteur-en-scène (he is a director's director the way Cézanne is a painter's painter), and cinéaste.

But Dreyer, an indisputable auteur and metteur-en-scène, was primarily a cinéaste. Which of the two is greater? The problem can't be resolved because it depends on one's point of view. The three categories, which allow us to better describe questions of art, are at odds with the concept of the filmmaker, or *réalisateur*, which can only be applied to film*makers*, professionals of the trade, who, as craftsmen, can be good or bad from film to film.

But in its isolation, the auteur concept became vulnerable because it was quickly adopted by filmmakers of varying ability. In equating it with writing their own screenplays or dialogue, they trivialized it, claiming that the directors of the New Wave had done the same thing. But writing one's screenplays or dialogue was neither a requirement nor a habit for the French New Wave auteurs. Although Rohmer wrote all of his screenplays (with the exception of *Perceval le Gallois* and the *Marquise d'O*, which are scrupulously faithful to the texts of Chrétien de Troyes and Kleist), Resnais worked with writers, novelists, and playwrights. Directors sometimes wrote their films alone, sometimes in collaboration with others. The New Wave's incompetent and untalented followers unfairly accused it of navel gazing. The proof lies in the films, which were made by people who embodied the auteur concept in all its complexity and served as witnesses of their time. As Chabrol recently stated,

"The auteur concept is powerful, but on condition that we know what it is. People imagine that an auteur is a filmmaker who writes his own screenplays. Yet the two directors so often used to typify the auteur, Hitchcock and Hawks, never touched a screenplay. The idea was that the director, if he had enough will, personality, and a world of his own, was the auteur of the film. Cinema wasn't the screenplay but the film. Which seems obvious."

1   Luc Mollet, "Politique des acteurs," *Cahiers du cinéma*, 1993.
2   Jean-Claude Biette, *"Qu'est qu'un cinéaste?" Trafic*, no. 18, Spring 1997.

Posters in the background of the set of *Contempt*: *Hatari, My Life to Live, Vanina Vanini,* and *Psycho*

1958

THE KILLING

BONJOUR TRISTESSE

THE SEVENTH SEAL

LES GIRLS

THE OUTCRY

MONTPARNASSE 19

TOUCH OF EVIL

LES AMANTS

LETTRE DE SIBÉRIE

UNE VIE

THE KILLING

Stanley Kubrick

A SECOND-RATE GANGSTER FILM

The Killing is no more than the work of a perceptive student. An admirer of Max Ophuls, Robert Aldrich, and John Huston, Stanley Kubrick is far from being everything the publicity surrounding this film makes him out to be. Compared to this second-rate gangster movie, even the *Asphalt Jungle* looks like a masterpiece, much less *Kiss Me Deadly*. I wouldn't even mention Ophuls if it weren't for the fact that Kubrick mimics him with his tedious camera movements, the kind generally preferred by the director of *Le Plaisir*. But what can be seen as a particular vision of the world in Ophuls amounts to nothing more than gratuitous hot air in Kubrick.

Still, the film has its good points. An independent production, *The Killing* was shot quickly and with a small budget. Although the screenplay isn't very original (an attack occurs on a Los Angeles racetrack) and the final episode not much better (like *The Treasure of the Sierra Madre*, the money is blown away by the wind after an unfortunate accident that is badly filmed), we have to credit the ingenious adaptation, which, by systematically rearranging the chronology of the action, makes an otherwise commonplace story interesting. But aside from the film's "journalistic" shooting style and Sterling Hayden, we'll have to content ourselves with waiting for Kubrick's next feature, *Paths of Glory*, whose praises the American press is already singing. ■

Jean-Luc Godard, *Cahiers du cinéma*, February 1958

A NEW AUTEUR IS BORN

Before you do anything else, write this name down if you don't already know it: Stanley Kubrick. The name of the film is *The Killing*. It's the story of a hold-up. *Kiss Me Deadly* was also based on an uninteresting unoriginal story by Mickey Spillane, and we know what Aldrich did with that story. Although temperamentally very different from the director of *Attack*, but equally gifted, determined, and combative, a new American *auteur* has been born. ■

René Gilson, *Cinéma 58*, March 1958

BONJOUR TRISTESSE

Otto Preminger

A TOTAL LACK OF ORIGINALITY

The novel by Françoise Sagan, often confused with the life of the author, has become something of a social phenomenon and the subject of much speculation. The producers of this film are obviously counting on this, forgetting that this is a literary work whose characters, with their unforseeable reactions, and intense interior life, can't simply be transposed to a prefabricated set. Is it possible to assume, however, that one could ever extract this book's substance, its sensibility, its slightly acidic taste of shellfish, the nuances of a quick but precise intellect, its astonishing psychological acumen, and especially the tone—half cynical, half passionate—through which the "I" of the novel, the Cecile who forms the book's capricious heart, expresses her feelings?

This confession, which owes everything to its style, subtlety, and delicacy, has been turned into a hopelessly tedious and clichéd soap opera, a comedy no longer situated in a city but on the shore of a pastel Mediterranean run riot with color. Otto Preminger has so slavishly copied the story that forms the basis of this film, adding so little that is original, that he has managed to radically denature, sterilize, and chloroform it. He has produced a cold, stiff corpse, made-up in Hollywood style and ready to be propped up in a display window.

An intolerable gap exists between what the characters should be (seen in the cruel but truthful light with which Françoise Sagan illuminates them) and what we see on screen—pale and insipid doubles whose very words sound false. The screenplay follows the track of the novel (which continues to escape it) with characters who, through their lack of conviction and the boredom they exude, aggravate the defects of an adaptation intent on destroying everything that made the book worthwhile. Is there any point in alternating black-and-white and Technicolor scenes in an attempt to lend an air of authenticity to the story? The color scenes are so ugly that Preminger would have done better to leave the film in restful shades of gray, with a few shadows thrown in for good measure. ∎

Michel Capdenal, *Les Lettres Françaises,*
March 13, 1958

THE SEVENTH SEAL

Ingmar Bergman

THE NAÏVETÉ OF GREAT PERIODS OF ART

This film's greatest merit is that it is above all a film—and one of the most beautiful—in spite of the abstract and theoretical nature of the story. There is nothing in *The Seventh Seal* that might resemble a clearly defined premise. The director informs us (and I have little difficulty believing him) that the starting point for his meditation wasn't an idea but an *image*. The different motivations he touches on were inspired by themes shared by painters and sculptors of the Middle Ages.

There is certainly some naiveté in this allegory, but there is in any fable. It's the naiveté characteristic of great periods of art—here the Middle Ages—whose flavor Bergman has been able to capture without adulterating it with pedantry. This can be attributed to the incomparable skill with which he transposes into cinematic terms the motifs provided by the iconography that inspired him. The figures and forms he presents are never simply a one-dimensional stencil, but the fruit of a consistently original work of art. The art here is so fresh, so new, that we forget the art for the "problem" and its infinite chain of corollaries. Rarely have the cinema's ambitions been so exalted or so fully realized. ∎

Éric Rohmer, *Arts,* May 23, 1958

THE PRECARIOUSNESS OF THE HUMAN CONDITION

Bergman, a true existentialist, demystifies Christian mythology, strips it of its mystical elements, and affirms the primacy of the real. His is a world of continuous renewal, even when through its own stupidity mankind risks destroying its inhabitants. The anxiety caused by the atom demands an overwhelming affirmation of faith in humanity. *The Seventh Seal* is the product of Bergman's reflection on the precariousness of the human condition in the twentieth century.

Bergman's method is similar to that of classic Swedish cinema, especially Sjöström, whom he greatly admires, and incorporates the continual intrusion of the fantastic into everyday life. Yet he does so without any of the techniques that were so renowned during the era of the silent film and which now appear dated (the weight and presence of the actor, the refinement of plastic composition, an emphasis on visual symbolism). Bergman's work is ambiguous, however, to the extent that the director fragments the real and asks questions instead of focusing on pure continuity. In this he represents the theatrical ascendancy of one of the most complex figures of contemporary cinema, a well-rounded artist whose previous work, such as *Smiles of a Summer Night* and *Sawdust and Tinsel,*

provides ample evidence that the Marivaux, Mussets, and Shakespeares of our time will record their fantasies directly on film. ∎

Louis Marcorelles, *France-Observateur,*
April 17, 1958

LES GIRLS

George Cukor

TRUTH AND ARTIFICE

Anyone who likes Cukor's work will no doubt be a bit put off at first by his new film, *Les Girls.* The film is cold and doesn't try to make us laugh (it even sidetracks our laughter), relying more on the power of dialogue than the cinematic gag. Such impassivity is surprising in an author who is so capable of making audiences howl with laughter. No doubt Cukor wants to provide audiences with a film that's easy to watch, and he exerts more effort than any previous director in this complete and systematic examination of the musical comedy. In its artificiality, the screenplay provides the springboard for the film. Cukor presents three different versions of the same event from the point of view of three narrators: Sybil (Kay Kendall), a former showgirl with an itch for memoir writing; Angel (Taina Elg), her ex-girlfriend, who is suing Sybil for

libel; and Barry Nichols (Gene Kelly), the ballet master, who claims to be too in love with his current wife (Mitzi Gaynor) to pay any attention to the other two. A man carrying a sandwich board on which the words "Where is truth?" are written appears three times during the film, expressing the moral of Cukor's tale. Rather than trying to reconstruct this puzzle, Cukor limits himself to painting three sketches, or, if you prefer, three "movements," each with its own individual tonality.

What difference does the plot make? As in Mozart's operas, I'm not convinced that the lyrics are as important as the music. In a film that tries to present us with the essence of the musical comedy, the theme of sincerity is clearly privileged since the very essence of the genre lies in its blend of truth and artifice. Here Cukor—by instinct I assume, rather than intent—has hit the bull's eye: "Where is truth?" We've heard the refrain before, and not only in Pirandello. Recall Camilla's inspired variant of the question, "Where does comedy begin and where does life end?" Upon the theme of the interplay of personality and appearance, a fundamental cinematic motif, Cukor improvises a rich fabric whose patterns resemble the arabesque of late Renoir. *French Cancan* and *Elena* are also referred to as musical comedy or fantasy, and in both cases we are presented with the same work of synthesis and re-creation, the same rejection of psychology and comic suspense. ■

Éric Rohmer, *Cahiers du cinéma*, May 1958

A BIRTHDAY CAKE

It's pretty, creamy, and pastel-colored, like a birthday cake. And, like a birthday cake, it sits in your stomach. We'd ask for more if we didn't suddenly realize that we're nauseous. The ballet scenes are exactly what we would expect of ballet in film: they're novel enough to interest the audience and traditional enough not to tire it out. And the story is exactly what you would expect in a musical comedy: it's clever enough to make you smile, conventional enough that you don't have to think. But it goes on too long. George Cukor has given us Pirandello in rhymed couplets and pirouettes. ■

F. R. *France-Soir,* April 12, 1958

THE OUTCRY
Michelangelo Antonioni

ANEMIA AND REFINEMENT

One story is as good as another, but in his attempt to faithfully follow the hesitant and uncertain thread of life, Antonioni keeps forgetting to tell the tale; by trying to give his characters the ambiguity of reality, he forgets to give them depth of character.

We never feel love or despair in Steve Cochran, who acts more like an aspiring bum on the edge of a nervous breakdown than a desperate lover. Antonioni is more interested in capturing the opalescent light of a rainy and desperate spring than in revealing its soul. His talent is like that of a diaphanous infanta who is preciously dying of anemia and refinement. It would be nice if Antonioni were to discover a robust Muse filled with red blood cells. She would no doubt lead him to the success he deserves. ■

France Roche, *France-Soir,* December 19, 1958

ONE OF THE GREATEST LIVING FILM DIRECTORS

It might be said that Antonioni is a stylist, that his art is cold, precious, refined, that he is obsessed with composition, that he systematically rejects the scene being shot or the effect, that he lingers too long on his characters, as if he were unwilling to take sides, letting them wander around these snowy river banks. Yet it's impossible to say for sure. But what do we call, and how do we explain, the emotion that grabs hold of us, this secret warmth, this anguish that gradually builds up inside? Certainly Antonioni is one of the greatest directors alive. ■

Alexandre Astruc, *L'Express,* December 11, 1958

LOVE'S ASHES

Antonioni is the Pavese of cinema. Both director and writer share the same taste for premonition and the same love of fog and rain. They both share a desperate fascination with suicide. It should come as no surprise then that, after adapting *Tra donne sole* for the screen, Antonioni conceived and directed *The Outcry*, the most Pavesian of all his films.

Abandoned by his mistres who runs off with a younger man, Aldo leaves in the dead of winter to wander along the plains of the Pô. No one, not Betsy Blair, Gabriella Pallotta, Dorian Gray, or Lyn Shaw can make him forget Alida Valli. His life ended and, far from the woman he loves, he can only taste the ashes of love in his mouth. He leads a kind of fuzzy, schizophrenic existence until the day he returns to his village and, with a gesture of farewell that is beyond despair, throws himself from a metal tower. The film is ambiguous, however. The change of scenery, the substitution of poverty, cold, and mud, for the warm brilliance of modernity might lead us to believe in Antonioni's belated conversion to a phantom "neorealism," but he displays none of De Sica's single-minded optimism, none of Rossellini's awareness of sin, shows no tenderness for the poetry of rags or the brotherhood of the working class. Antonioni's ambitions are unique, as are his passions. He reveals that poverty is always damp and cold, that the world can seem empty when someone close to us is missing, and that no miracle can mend a broken heart. *The Outcry* is an anti-*Viaggio in Italia*. Whether hitchhiking on a gasoline truck or driving a Maserati, love and despair look very much the same. ■

Louis Seguin, *Positif,* July 1959

MONTPARNASSE 19
Jacques Becker

IS THIS A FILM?

The passionate life of Amedeo Modigliani? You may as well go to see the Van Gogh. Is it a chronicle of Paris after the First World War? You may as well read Maurice Sachs. Is it the journal of an illuminated painter? You may as well read or see the *Journal d'un Curé de Campagne*. Is it the story of some poor soul, a madman, degenerate, or

genius? Is it an adventure film or a love story? But first of all, is it a film? To this last question *Montparnasse 19* is silent. It answers, rather, by asking a question in return: Yes, but what is cinema?

If, as the ads suggest, *Montparnasse 19* is the most moving of Jacques Becker's films, it's because every twenty-fourth of a second, close-ups, continuity shots, boom shots, zooms, and swish pans dare to ask, what is cinema? And rather than answering, each scene again asks the same incisive question, What is cinema?

The only thing that makes *Montparnasse 19* great is the fact that not only is it a film in reverse, but in a sense it's cinema in reverse, just as a photographic negative is the reverse of the positive print. In general a great film is great because it demonstrates beauty through its very existence, and renders any question about the subject pointless by providing a response from the outset. Welles, Eisenstein, Murnau—they proceed through a process of affirmation. They don't say, this should be filmed because it's beautiful, but it's beautiful because I've filmed it this way.

Montparnasse 19, on the contrary, is without question the first film whose premise is wholly negative. It matters little that this may be due in part to the many risks involved in both the preparation and shooting of the film (Ophuls's death,

supervision by Modigliani's daughter, arguments with Jeanson, etc.). The fact is that *Montparnasse 19* doesn't prove that Modigliani loved Jeanne, or that Béatrice loved Modigliani, or that Paris is a great city, or that women are beautiful, or men cowards, or that love is wonderful, or that painting is fun or exhausting, or art more important than anything else, or that anything else is more important than art. No. *Montparnasse 19* doesn't prove that 2 + 2 = 4. That's not the intent of the film. Its premise is the absence of a premise, its truth, the absence of truth. *Montparnasse 19* only proves that 2 − 2 = 0.

It would be wrong, however, to believe that this is the most Bressonian film by the director of the excellent *Rue de l'Estrapade*. For, by agreeing to shoot *Montparnasse 19*, Becker did not yield to the temptation of the absolute, he yielded to the attraction of the void. *Montparnasse 19* is a dizzying film. And, when all is said and done, although the project wasn't devoid of cowardice at the start, it wasn't necessarily devoid of courage at the end.

Montparnasse 19 is a film about fear. In this sense, it could be subtitled, *The Mysterious Director*. By incorporating his own fear as a component of Modigliani's unhinged mind, Becker allows us to penetrate (clumsily, perhaps, but with great feeling) the secret of artistic creation far better than Clouzot when he filmed Picasso at work. After all, if a modern novel is the fear of the blank page, a modern painting, the fear of the empty canvas, a modern sculpture, the fear of stone, then a modern film has a right to be the fear of the camera, the actors, dialogue, editing. I would give all of post-War French cinema for the single scene, badly acted and poorly framed, but so sublime, in which Modigliani tries to sell his drawings for five francs on the terrace of La Coupole.

Everything, therefore, in this disagreeable film draws the viewer in. Everything rings true in this highly artificial film. Everything about this obscure film is perfectly clear. For he who leaps into the void owes nothing to those who remain behind. ∎

Jean-Luc Godard, *Cahiers du cinéma*, May 1958

TOUCH OF EVIL
Orson Welles

A MAGICAL FILM

There's a certain type of cinema practiced by imbeciles who are also cynics (*The Bridge Over the River Kwai*, *The Young Lions*), intended to flatter the public into thinking it is better or more intelligent than before. There is an intimate and proud cinema practiced by a handful of sincere and intelligent artists who, since they do not belittle the public, prefer to disturb than to reassure, to awaken audiences rather than put them to sleep. Leaving Alain Resnais' *Night and Fog*, we don't feel "better," we feel worse. When leaving *Le Notti bianche* or *Touch of Evil*, we feel less intelligent than when we entered the movie, but are overcome with a sense of poetry and art. These are the films that remind us what film is about and make us feel ashamed of our indulgence toward films based on so little talent and so many concessions.

Touch of Evil awakens its audience. It reminds us that men like Méliès and Feuillade were among the pioneers of cinema. This is a magical film that brings to mind fairy tales such as Beauty and the Beast or Tom Thumb, and the fables of La Fontaine. It's a film that is slightly humiliating because it is made by a man who thinks a lot faster than we do, and

more clearly, and throws one marvelous image at us after another. This sense of acceleration that is a kind of intoxication results in a sense of vertigo.

I hope we have enough taste, sensibility, and intuition to acknowledge that this film is great and beautiful. The fact that some critics have tried to find fault with the film, which is a work of art purely and simply, is like the grotesque spectacle of the Lilliputians criticizing Gulliver. ■
François Truffaut, *Arts*, June 4, 1958

LES AMANTS
Louis Malle
A NEW GENERATION

Les Amants is a very important film. It marks the rise of a new generation within a French cinema that, since the war, has resembled a closed shop for fifty years. The public and the jury weren't wrong in Venice. They preferred Louis Malle's youthfulness to Autant-Lara's maturity.

Finally, we are presented with a film that can sustain a comparison with the best that literature has produced throughout the ages. But this time, it's not the young who are going to blanch with envy but their elders, from whom they have so quickly snatched the baton. Film is a bizarre art form, which can accommodate the most humble subjects at times. But as soon as it makes itself shine in a particular area—emotions, mores, psychology, call it what you will—where literature has achieved renown, its focus comes to the attention of the specialists of the genre, the true writers rather than those literary pariahs who have, until recently, divided up the pathetic wasteland of French cinema.

Les Amants shocks us the same way that *L'Eau vive* did in the past. It is the revelation that a filmmaker has everything to gain in working with someone who knows how to write and writes about what they know. In Giono's dialogue, as in that of Louise de Vilmorin (why couldn't she also have written the dialogue for *The Earrings of Madame de*), elegance and truth are wonderfully married, and this wonder is attributable to talent alone. The excellence of the screenplay never

detracts from the film's naturalness, nor do its bold non-sequiturs or gratuitous dialogue. The only pedants left are half-wits, and when we possess the science of speaking well, we are capable of making the most outlandish expression ring true. There are no revelatory words because behind each word we feel the presence of an author worthy of the name. But words are true only because they are spoken by real characters. Those characters who, fleshed out by a less expert hand, would have resulted in conventional types (the sulking husband, the impertinent provincial or Parisian woman, the young stud, the grumpy mechanic), disregard the tawdry finery inherited from Clair, Prévert, Capra, and other less assured artists. We would have to list everything to do the film justice, the courtship in the car, the dinner, and especially the afternoon in the library, the high point in this fireworks display of a film.

Unlike Arenche and Bost, who chop their screenplays into playlets, the director of this film has provided this precious jewel with a setting of extreme refinement, while providing the flow of his story with the freedom of written narrative. As in *Ascenseur pour l'échafaud*, Malle has drawn inspiration from the best sources, primarily Bresson. But the clear superiority of his second film in large part comes from the fact that the "suspense" relies on the characters' emotions and behavior rather than chance. In his first film, Malle's

flirtation with anecdote resulted in satire, which is not exactly his strong point. Nor do I believe that lyricism is something he does well, in spite of the beauty of the night scenes and the quality of Henri Decae's cinematography. Decae is the glory of the new school of cameramen, the destroyer of the thousand taboos that prevented his elders from accepting the imperatives of modern filmmaking. ■
Éric Rohmer, *Arts*, November 12, 1958

WHAT SCANDAL?

The only thing left to talk about is the "scandal." But what scandal? We are no longer scandalized by the almost pornographic vulgarity of detective and love stories, any more than we are by the stupidity and conformity of three-quarters of today's films. But as soon as a sincere and highly talented author attempts a frank portrait of love, without obscuring the physical component, our respected citizens are up in arms crying obscenity. Of course, love is obscene for such people. This film wasn't made for them but for those "sensitive souls" so dear to Stendhal, for whom the sexual act wasn't obscene but magic. We are told that some things shouldn't be shown on screen. And why not? If the fascinating beauty of pleasure isn't the purest, the most moving image in the world, then nothing is pure, nothing is moving. ■
Jacques Doniol-Valcroze, *France-Observateur*, November 13, 1958

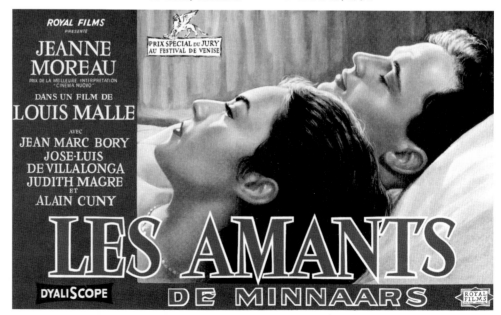

A GREAT LOVE POEM

The Champs-Élysées finds *Les Amants* scandalous because it portrays an ideal couple in which the man and woman are from somewhat different social backgrounds. This is a film in which the wife leaves home after love brings her the sudden realization of the extraordinary vanity of "her world."

Although social criticism is certainly not the primary intention of this love poem, it would lose its meaning and depth if it weren't clearly expressed. The conflict and subsequent rapture would also be meaningless if they didn't take place within a social environment that is as clearly determined as the unforgettable decoration of the château, which the highly talented Bernard Evein built in the studio. ∎

Georges Sadoul, *Les Lettres Françaises*,
November 14, 1958

LETTRE DE SIBÉRIE

Chris Marker

A DOCUMENTARY ESSAY

Strictly speaking, *Lettre de Sibérie* is the filmed report made by a Frenchman who was allowed to travel freely over several thousand miles of Siberia. In the past three years several documentaries by French travelers in Russia have appeared, and *Lettre de Sibérie* doesn't resemble any of them. Let's take a closer look at the reality of the film. I'll offer the following tentative description: *Lettre de Sibérie* is an essay, which takes the form of a filmed report, on the reality of contemporary Siberia. Or, to borrow Jean Vigo's description of *À propos de Nice* ("a documented point of view"), we could say it's an essay documented by the film. The key word here is "essay," understood in the same sense as it is in literature, an essay that is both historical and political, though written by a poet.

Generally, and even in the "engagé" or thematic documentary, the image, the specifically cinematic element, constitutes the film's raw material. The orientation is provided through a process of selection and editing, the text completing the organization of meaning conferred on the document. Marker goes about this quite differently. In his case, I would say that his raw material is intelligence, its immediate expression speech, and that the image only intervenes afterward, through reference to the filmmaker's verbal intelligence. The process is reversed. ∎

André Bazin, *Les Nouvelles Littéraires*,
October 1958

UNE VIE

Alexandre Astruc

EXELLENT JUST THE WAY IT IS

No one gives a damn about the Walt Disney carousel, the picnic on the plastic table cloth, the chewing gum green of the ball of yarn. The accumulated bad taste shown by Astruc, Claude Renoir, and Mayo are immaterial. And so is Roman Vlad's saxophone as well. Besides, he's not bad. No, we need to look elsewhere to find the real beauty in *Une vie*. It exists in Pascale Petit's yellow dress as she shivers in the Velasquez gray dunes of Normandy. Hey! Wait! That's not Velasquez gray. That's not even Delacroix gray, the "connoisseurs" would shout.

It doesn't matter that the version currently being shown in theaters no longer corresponds to the shooting script. Nor does it matter that each scene is systematically arrested in full swing. *Une vie* is excellent just the way it is. And, as such, *Une vie* is presented as the opposite of an inspired film. The madness behind realism, Astruc commented on in an interview, but he was misunderstood. Julien's madness was to have married Jeanne, and Jeanne's to have married Julien. Nothing more. There was no point in remaking *La Folie du Docteur Tube* when it made more sense to show that the love between a dull man and an introverted woman is madness. In reality, *Une vie* makes Astruc's most ardent supporters uncomfortable, just as *Le Plaisir* made those who thought they knew Maupassant uncomfortable. Although we were expecting a lyrical Astruc, it was Astruc the architect who turned up.

Like *Bitter Victory*, *Une vie* is a very simple film. Simple, not stylized. Astruc is nothing at all like Visconti, and it would be idiotic to compare them. In *Le Notti bianche*, Maria Schell was certainly used to better effect. But in *Une vie*, her performance rings true and has greater depth. During his time, Maupassant was no doubt considered a modern author. Paradoxically, the best way to discover the nineteenth century's true flavor was to make the story feel like 1958. No better proof can be found than Christian Marquand's wonderful reply to the woman who offers him her dowry and château, "Because of you, I've ruined my life."

On the Threshold of the Unknown would be an appropriate subtitle for *Une vie*. For *Une vie* forces cinema to look beyond. ∎

Jean-Luc Godard, *Cahiers du cinéma*,
November 1958

A GREAT CLASSIC FILM

Une vie is neither a psychological film, nor a social film, nor a historical film, nor a costume drama. It is a great classic, that gives a profoundly personal twist to an eternal theme: the drama of loneliness. Obviously, it's not a faithful literary adaptation. Maupassant is used simply for security, and the visual equivalents of his wonderful descriptions possess rare beauty. There is something more important than photography here, however, and that is the characters, who are not presented for themselves, but as part of the unfolding of a life. What is most important about this film is that in rejecting cheap effects, conventional techniques, conspiratorial winks, and gratuitous picturesqueness, Astruc succeeds in using a language all his own to recreate a powerful work of great beauty. Under his direction not only does Maria Schell not frown, she even manages to arouse our sympathy from time to time. Christian Marquand is appropriately boorish and Pascale Petit a genuine discovery. Antonella Lualdi burns up the screen—to our delight and torment. ∎

Albert Descamp, *Cinéma 58*, November 1958

The STUDIO

In the beginning was the street.

In the beginning was life.

In the beginning was Lumière (August and especially Louis).

Soon Méliès appeared. And the studio (1898) was born.

La Lutte pour la vie (René Leprince and Ferdinand Zecca, 1914) by Pathé studios
Georges Méliès's studio in Montreuil just after the war and shortly before its destruction

Is the first film in the history of cinema a metaphor? As if *La Sortie des usines Lumière* emptied the studio and placed the cinema squarely in the street, where it belonged. Three years later Georges Méliès hastened to get it off the street and re-install it, like a mistress, in the studio—cinema's lifelong refuge.

Lumière/Méliès. They came to represent two great movements that contradicted as much as they complemented one another. For the past century they have been fighting each other in the theoretical space of cinematic art. The conflict that resulted from their opposition resurfaced with renewed vigor with the appearance of the New Wave. And the choice of one and rejection of the other had aesthetic, economic, and political repercussions for the film industry.

In the beginning the studio was a tool.
It soon became an instrument of control.

The studio was able to organize and eliminate the unpredictable and accomplish within its walls what was disturbing, costly, uncontrollable, or even impossible outside them. With the transition of the studio from artist's tool to instrument of production, a sense of distortion arose that often led to contradictions: "The cinema is an art, but it is also an industry." The comment by André Malraux aptly summarizes the history and problem of the studio.

Originally Méliès created the studio as a convenience. He conceived an enclosed space, much like a sculptor's or photographer's studio. Between four walls, one of which was broken by a large opening that facilitated the coming and going of actors, technicians, and sets, a relatively large space was lit by a skylight that served as both a ceiling and a roof.

From the outset Méliès turned the studio into a place where he could manufacture illusion and fantasy, made it the center of a magical universe, both artificial and dreamlike, which represented in the popular imagination the very essence of

cinema. This rectangular building was the architectural symbol of the ambitions of the artist, craftsman, and poet, but it structurally imposed upon him its own industrial truth: it was a factory, a dream factory.

And it quickly destroyed its creator. Méliès was effectively out of business by 1910, when the first monopolies—Pathé and Gaumont—took over cinema, organizing their industrial and sales activities around their own "block" of properties. This happened even though, at the time, the studio was basically nothing more than a tool.

All this changed around 1920, when electricity was introduced, and the skylight disappeared. Choked with catwalks and spots, the ceiling became a fifth wall, more inviolable than the others. Now a fortress, the studio turned its attention inward. It invented its own lighting. In the German expressionist manner, some studios used projectors to punch holes of light in the studio's gloom, magnifying its occult powers and accentuating the terrifying darkness that encircled and

threatened the fragile column of light. The Hollywood approach, however, displayed its power and brilliance through an exhibitionistic excess of sparkling and magical electric lights, their brilliance designed to attract, fascinate, and hypnotize the millions of human fireflies who would see them. In 1925 Erich von Stroheim pushed this method to its extreme, indeed beyond its limits. In a kind of radical critique, von Stroheim captured and exploited this brilliant delirium of seduction, temptation, and trickery, visually demonstrating the artificiality of Hollywood lighting. Josef von Sternberg, another Viennese director, though somewhat more complacent (he stayed in Hollywood ten years longer than von Stroheim but also ended up its victim), magnified the effect of Hollywood lighting and provided the visual style that the studios were looking for. For von Sternberg, light was something erotic, he used it like a fabric that clothed the bodies of his stars and caressed their faces.

As a functional apparatus the studio dictated a rhetoric, style, and aesthetic that could better control and extend an ideology. A number of skilled trades were created, became specialized, and developed into a body of knowledge and trade secrets. The studio became the heart of cinematographic activity, to the point that the major American houses were no longer referred to by what they do but where they do it. A film is produced at MGM, Fox, Paramount, or Warner.

With the arrival of sound and the talkie, the financial investment required to produce them strengthened the presence and omnipotence of money. The point man, or producer, was responsible for applying the fundamental principles of industrialization to film. He Taylorized the industry by a careful division of labor, which he compartmentalized into discrete specializations. In this way the producer had complete control over the most insignificant activity. He controlled everything, decided everything, from what subject was chosen all the way through to the final cut.

The economic power and commercial efficiency of this cinema, its imperialist function (conquering markets, hitching up countries like wagons to the American dream) managed to impart a real sense of dynamism to the creative abilities of its artists—provided, however, that they had sufficient talent and character to turn the dictatorial studio system to their advantage. In short, for a director to rise above the restrictions of a house style, he had to conquer it and create his own directorial style, which carried through and reinforced the true subject of his films. This was the basis of the intense interest with which *Cahiers du cinéma* followed the developments of American cinema during the fifties. They countered the studio concept and apparatus with the notion of the auteur, and were able to do so with the studio's own artists. They chose two of the greatest studio directors, Howard Hawks and Alfred Hitchcock, as emblematic of the artist able to transgress the artificial vision of the world offered by Hollywood and impose a point of view about the truth of that world.

In France, however, the studio never played the same role that it did in Hollywood. It had always been more discreet. No one would dream of referring to Gaumont or Pathé as studios; these honorable centenarians are referred to as the Maison Gaumont or Maison Pathé, as in a story by Balzac. Their presence, however, has had an effect on film's history. Through the twenties, the French studio remained only a tool. Two successive waves of émigrés gave it a stylistic coloration that did, however, have significant influence on French cinema. The first, following the October revolution, saw the arrival of representatives of czarist cinema, known, since 1915, for the avant-garde sophistication of its aesthetic and architectural innovations. Its lighting, sets, costumes, and makeup, as well as its physical gestures, obeyed the formalist rules of what claimed to be a highly modernist architecture. Under the patronage of Pathé, these White Russians founded Albatross, whose studios (like those of the Méliès before them) were located in Montreuil. Before the talkie, Albatross also produced work by young French filmmakers such as Marcel L'Herbier, Jacques Feyder, and René Clair. Clair, a consummate studio filmmaker, refined a so-called realist vision of Paris, a poetic vision that stereotyped its characters and sets. The representation of the world, the French, and Paris that René Clair achieved was internationally renowned for a period of twenty years, even though today it appears old fashioned, charming, fantastic, and lacking in realism.

After Hitler's rise to power in 1933, a second wave of emigrants fled to Paris, filmmakers from central Europe. They brought with them an expressionist approach to film, the bias of a working class socialist realism, and a highly stylized dramatization of the everyday. The refined elegance of the White Russians vanished from the studios, giving way to the heavy atmosphere of a disordered and tragic passion. After 1936, Marcel Carné, who was deeply impressed by German cinema, pushed the studio approach to its extreme by constructing an identical copy of the Barbès subway station in *Les Portes de la nuit* (1946). Carné became the leading proponent of this approach. For twenty years German cinema infiltrated French film, contaminating it to the point where what came to be known as French quality cinema, was actually the expression of German melancholy.

But this cinema quickly lost the creativity of its German counterpart. After 1945 the French studio system grew increasingly rigid, eventually becoming mannered and

Architectural designs for the Albatros studios in Montreuil, 1925
Entrance to the Paramount studios in Hollywood, circa 1920

La Sonnette d'alarme (Christian-Jaque, 1935), a film produced for Paramount-France

academic. Its attitude toward the world was patently false, since it could only be conceived of or imagined in the studio. Until 1960 the dictatorship of the studio hid, like any other dictatorship, behind a kind of false positivism, referred to as "professionalism." To help bring down the citadel, the New Wave had to attack the "professionals of the profession." The young, future filmmakers of the New Wave also challenged the representatives of the studio attitude, notably Clair and Carné, but also their successors, Henri-Georges Clouzot, René Clément, Claude Autant-Lara, Jean Delannoy, and Yves Allégret. They were reproached primarily for not having the courage to adopt a neorealist approach in France and for having accepted—either through complacency or opportunism—the artificiality, conventionality, and falsity of the studio. Because of the financial resources available to these "professionals," their aesthetics served as a vehicle for the retrograde ideological discourse of a middle class accustomed to the privileges, attitudes, and habits of the pre-War period. Thus they fabricated a cinema that no longer corresponded to the lived reality of the post-War citizen, a cinema that no longer offered the French public an image of its identity.

Obviously, this is a moral point of view (the studio, like the tracking shot, is a moral issue). In the eyes of the new generation, the studio film was dishonest. The most commonly heard expression on sets of the period was "we can fake it," which they did with camera placement, lighting, sound, facial expression, acting, sets, costume, and editing. They falsified feelings, scripts, and dialogue. And behind a multitude of minor scams, sat the master meddler, the producer, who used the studio to triple or quadruple the cost of a film and pocket a significant amount of money that would never make its way to the screen.

Traveling shot in Cinecittá from *Contempt* (Jean-Luc Godard, 1963)

The young filmmakers of the future New Wave were not hostile to the idea of the studio. They remembered Jean Renoir's lesson: if a studio set recreates the authenticity of a real location, as, for example, the interior of the château de La Colinière in *Rules of the Game*, why not use it? The difference, though, was to maintain the journalistic or documentary tone that introduced the film from its first scene. Once they had become filmmakers, Rohmer, Godard, Chabrol, and Truffaut all used the studio in this way from time to time (for example, Chabrol's *Les Cousins*, Rohmer's *My Night at Maud's*). It was also used overtly, ostentatiously, to draw attention to the reality of the studio. It was used in a quasi-documentary manner as a place of work (Godard in *Contempt* and *Passion*, Truffaut in *Day for Night*), even as a specific space (in *Perceval Le Gallois*, Rohmer used the architectural layout, the ogival structure of the studio as a physical representation of medieval thought). This was the reason for the admiration shown to Cocteau, Ophuls and their successors by *Cahiers du cinéma*. Artifice and ruse, filmed directly, can turn falsity into the ultimate reality (*Orpheus* and *Lola Montès*). The height of this aesthetic was achieved by Jacques Demy, who moved his camera into the street, changing the street into a studio and coloring it to resemble the sunlight, walls, facades, and store windows of a port (Cherbourg, Rochefort, Nantes, Marseilles, Los Angeles, etc.). The New Wave didn't kill the studio. It simply destroyed the spirit of lucre that had taken possession of it.

The Barbès metro station recreated by Alexandre Trauner (*Les Portes de la nuit*, Marcel Carné, 1946)
Nino Castelnuovo, *The Umbrellas of Cherbourg* (Jacques Demy, 1964)

THE

ST

"Well, at bottom film's greatest enemy is the studio. I only use it when I have no other alternative. But as soon as I'm inside its enormous machinery, I'm forced to dress in a certain way . . . wear this pair of pants, that shirt, etc. The film uniform in other words. Then the great parade of machinery and technology begins. It's essential to assume the right attitude. Which means I have to start being intelligent. But as soon as I feel I'm becoming intelligent, I'm screwed.... You know there's something I'd like them to tell Carné. I consider him to be the greatest European director along with Clouzot, but I wish he'd free himself of the studio's leash. I wish he'd get out more, take a closer look at the street."
—Roberto Rossellini[1]

We can go out into the street or take to the streets; get a change of air or get some air. The distinction can be applied to film as well as to everyday life (our day-to-day activities) or politics (revolt or revolution). Ever since the Lumière brothers, the history of film has been riddled by incessant comings and goings between the studio and the street, the street and the studio. Each ebb and flow has its logic, its distinguishing features.

Take, for example, the phenomenon of Italian neorealism, which is interesting because it not only preceded the New Wave, it presaged it. Neorealism came into being at the end of the Second World War. The physical and economic devastation as well as the condition of the great studios at Cinecittà, which lacked the material and financial wherewithal to operate, were its immediate cause. The street was the only place left where it was possible to make a film. But film exposed the street's wounds, displayed its miseries so visibly that it was impossible to conceal them. They had to be dealt with, made a part of the story, treated as the film's true subject. Shooting outside against real backgrounds was not a choice, but simply a necessity.

At the same time, cinema responded to a theoretical intention. When Italy entered the war in 1940, there was a relaxation of police control in terms of the strict application of fascist ideology. In fact, the move to liberalize ideas was promoted from within the highest levels of the party. In October 1941, in the magazine *Cinema* (under the direction of Vittorio Mussolini, the Duce's son), Luchino Visconti wrote about Giovanni Verga, one of the creators of verism in literature and referred to his "revolutionary art inspired by a suffering and hopeful humanity." The sentence defined what would later become Italian

neorealism. A disciple of Jean Renoir (he was an assistant on *Toni* [1934], a film that served as a model for neorealism), Visconti directed *Osses-sione* in 1942, a screen adaptation of the James Cain novel *The Postman Always Rings Twice*. In it he captured the new spirit of open-mindedness, and although the film immediately ran afoul of the censors, a page in the history of cinema had been turned.

Neorealism was conceived as a reaction against Mussolinian cinema, which, for twenty years, had fled the representation of real life and pro-vided a falsified vision of the world, that of the "telefeno bianco." This was the sarcastic name given to the films made at Cinecittà. Dramas of "intense emotion" or light comedies, the films took place in sumptuous, marble-laden townhouses, immacu-lately decorated. In the virginal bedroom was a gigantic bed covered with white furs, and next to it, on the night stand, sat the famous white telephone, which was essential to the emotional gusts that wracked a sobbing yet guileless heroine. The reality of the war had made these films tiresome and obscene. Poverty was everywhere. It was the cinema's responsibility to show it.

But looking isn't a neutral act. "Suffering and hope" Visconti had written, giving a Christian (Christian Democrat, some might say) interpretation to the reality of the Ita-lian situation. Filming the reality of the outside world meant putting one-self in the position of a journalist to relate, as honestly as possible, the lived history of those who were really homeless. The camera abandoned its aristocrats to focus on the people and poverty's victims: mothers, children, women, old men, young lovers. Soon, generally through ideological conviction, filmmakers began to use non-actors in their films. Their commonplace attitude would ensure

their truthfulness. The true actors would have to adapt and bend to the naturalness with which they were confronted. This was the first time in the history of the cinema that stars (Anna Magnani, Ingrid Bergman) and unknowns played opposite one another almost as equals. This approach was quickly dropped though, and only Rossellini and Visconti continued to use it (they remained loyal to it until 1952). The public grew tired of verist subjects, but the technique itself stuck. It was used to illustrate the two tried and true genres into which neorealism now slipped, almost without resistance: melodrama (suffering) and comedy (hope). Just like the old days of the white telephone.

The New Wave followed a different tack. Although it also took to the streets, it went in a different direction. Initially, it attempted to destroy the citadel that French cinema had erected in the studios and which protected the profession and its bureaucratic structure. The attack was directly aimed at industry and commerce, which were undisputed allies of the film unions. There were two ways of going about this. The first meant a frontal assault (which quickly proved to be impossible because it was both too costly and strategically unthinkable). The second involved calmly ignoring them. The New Wave turned its back on the system and although treated as a bunch of miscreants, took to the streets to make its films. And, as if by magic, the cost of making a film dropped from 4 million to 400,000 francs. Film crews were reduced in size. Mobility and action were the watchwords of the day. Holed up in their Bastille, the industry's "true" professionals resembled the knights at the battle of Crécy, shrouded in armor, immobile, rigid. By 1960, less than one year after the New Wave's assault, the traditional French cinema collapsed (for a while).

Yveline Cery and Stefania Sabatini in *Adieu Philippine* (Jacques Rozier, 1960–1963)

Johanna Shimkus in *Paris vu par* … (sketch by Godard, *"Montparnasse–Lavallois,"* 1965)

At the same time one of the most formidable unions in the history of the profession, the extras, disappeared (although only momentarily), as if by magic and much to the delight of cinephiles. Extras dominated film sets throughout the world. As a trade union they took advantage of the corporatism of the other film unions to obtain jobs. Extras were everywhere and no one was spared their presence. What was most typical of the extras of the time (they could still be seen in films by Mizoguchi and even in Bresson's *Pickpocket* of 1959), was their total and well-known lack of naturalness. Motionless, they posed, "expressed" themselves, and had no other ambition than to be seen. They got in the way of the modern filmmaker and interfered with the audience's involvement in the film. By shooting on location, which overturned the rules of the studio, they were thrust outside the camera's field of view. And as in the films of Lumière and Griffith, the great silent films or the first talkies (1930–1933), Renoir (*Boudu* or *La Chienne*), Vigo, Barnet, the impression of life once again swept across the screen. When people were needed for a scene (a café, newsstand, bus stop), friends were used, or friends of friends, or even passersby who were willing to give an hour or two of their time. It not only lent an air of truth to the film, it was fun as well.

This use of unknowns is more than mere anecdote, however. There was a deliberate attempt on the part of filmmakers of the New Wave to assume the role of amateur. Not an amateur in the sense that the unions and technicians used the term, however. It was important to regain the spontaneity and impression of innocence found, for example, in Griffith. Far from a sign of incompetence, their attitude required increased skill—the ability to adapt one's

Anna Karina, *My Life to Live* (Jean-Luc Godard, 1962)

My Life to Live (Jean-Luc Godard, 1962)

technique to the subject. The practical conditions imposed by shooting in the street or in a natural setting responded to the question that the New Wave had been asking for ten years and now attempted to resolve: What is the street? What purpose does it serve aside from saving money? How can we use it and give it meaning?

Obviously, this was no longer the street found in neorealism. The streets of Paris 1958 had more cars and less poverty. People had no problem with signs of prosperity. The stories that resulted—and for which this prosperity provided a neutral field of operations—involved money, which had an annoying habit of being in short supply, and the sentiment, sometimes coupled with love, of being free and living life fully. Just as with neorealism, the street reflected the status quo, Italy's poor were succeeded by a generation that was eager to share in the pleasures offered by a society on the brink of an economic boom. This led to accusations that the New Wave was neo-bourgeois. The accusation is both true and false. It's true in the sense that it acknowledges a visible phenomenon— the furious desire to enjoy the material side of life. It's false because it adhered to a moral point of view—its vision was objective and unflinching. In any event it never supported the insidious ideological propaganda of happiness, which Lelouche (who directed *Scopitones* in the beginning of his career) embraced, as do so many of today's young filmmakers who have their sights set on advertising. The street, as seen by the New Wave, reflected the aspirations of the young people who made it theirs. It embodied their dominant fantasy of riding around in a sporty convertible (there is no New Wave film, good or bad, without this mythic device). Paris was at their feet. It was a place of unlimited possibility.

Jean-Luc Godard in Paris nous appartient (Jacques Rivette, 1958–1961)

It was Jean Rouch in "Gare du Nord," his segment of *Paris vu par . . .* (1964), that best exemplified the New Wave's philosophy of the street. A young, lower-middle class woman, living in a very modest apartment, argues with her husband about the mediocrity of their life. She slams the door, goes downstairs (end of the first sequence), out into the street (beginning of second and last sequence), and immediately meets a kind of prince charming, who offers to take her away and provide her with all the things (including a convertible) she had previously itemized in the scene with her husband. The sudden possibility of realizing them terrifies her and she refuses. The young man throws himself on the tracks at the Gare du Nord.

The New Wave refused to acknowledge the determinism of the set typical of films influenced by expressionism. The most famous examples of which remain the set, dripping with fatality, of *Quai des brumes* and the tragic street in *Le Jour se lève*. Here, destiny had been inscribed for all eternity, no one could escape. Many filmmakers, of which René Clair was the most brilliant representative, also had an annoying tendency to poeticize Paris. They looked for unusual locations, original and picturesque, or tried to make ordinary locations uncommon by means of cinematic effects. They saw Paris from the point of view of a tourist and its most celebrated monuments were turned into filmic post cards without dramatic relevance for the film. The marketers (producers, distributors, directors) thought such inclusions would make films more salable, and the city was turned into a fantasy that had to be maintained. It was no longer a question of photography, the city had become a cliché.

The New Wave was horrified by this. Their contempt was greatest for what they referred to as the *Red*

Gianni Esposito and Betty Schneider in Paris nous appartient

Balloon (1956) syndrome, whether typified by Albert Lamorisse, who won a number of awards (including the Louis Delluc prize in Cannes for best feature) or the glass of red wine that workers belted down, elbows on the bar, in so-called popular films of the time (which claimed to show what the people were really like). The Paris that the New Wave directors wanted to represent was the Paris of everyday life. The city that was laid out before them as a kind of immense background, the city that no one paid attention to. People went about their business with indifference. And since the majority of the young were from the provinces, they affected the behavior of the blasé Parisian. On the other hand they acknowledged that the street was indiscriminate in its indifference to individual fate. Out of this stubborn indifference Rohmer extracted the drama of *Le Signe du Lion*, Rivette that of *Paris nous appartient*, Varda, *Cleo from 5 to 7*, Chabrol *Les Bonnes Femmes*.

The absolute neutrality of the outside world provided an infinite field of opportunity for the meetings, surprises, incidents and accidents of the New Wave. Space opened out in all directions. Stripped of any features that would attract our attention, the street became both concrete—the reality of the set—and abstract, through its deliberate reduction of this same set to its principal lines. Thus we see the Champs Élysées in *Breathless*, place Clichy in *The 400 Blows*, Saint-Germain-des-Prés in *Le Signe du Lion*, or the Sarah Bernhardt theater as a lived space in *Paris nous appartient*.

The city offered the viewer a clear field that emphasized the interplay of movements, trajectories, and meanderings to which form was subject and against which the action took place. Walking, strolling,

flirting, and relaxing were all part of the landscape. The street again became a vector of undirected motion and was no longer a goal. It was no longer a place where one went toward (someone), for (something), from (the previous scene), or to (the next scene). It no longer defined a single, implacable path toward a unique destiny. Now everyone followed his own path, even, especially, in unusual circumstances: Cleo's cancer, the gradual marginalization in *Le Signe du Lion*, the student Doinel's ramblings in the woods, Poiccard hunted for killing a biker (*Breathless*), the Algerian war and vacations in Corsica (*Adieu Philippine*), etc.

A catalog of New Wave locations would be informative. They would be radically different from those frequented by traditional cinema: the railway station, for example would be absent. Once it occupied a central, indeed climactic, location in a film's dramatic structure since the fate of its characters was often decided there. Any destination was transformed into an inexorable destiny. With the New Wave, arrivals and departures lost their emotional power. They were no more than variations on an encounter. For this reason they didn't merit any special treatment, much less the wet handkerchiefs that waved up and down the platform. Strictly speaking the railway station never makes an appearance in the films of the New Wave. It has disappeared. There are two or three airports, which serve as connecting points or backgrounds for interviewing a celebrity (Jean-Pierre Melville in *Breathless*). Even ports are only present through the city. The boats in Demy's films remain off camera. They're waiting in the wings. There's no point to their visible presence because their mental presence is so great. They must be

banished from physical space because they offer an escape to an imagination inflamed by the thirst for an encounter that is constantly intersected, perceived, missed, frustrated, but so intensely desired that it finally occurs. Only Jacques Rozier, at the end of *Adieu Philippine*, provides us the with the sight of a ship steaming out of port. But after two hours of idleness, of taking advantage of a life remote from military service, it was necessary to end with a departure in order to make the audience feel the criminal absurdity of the Algerian war.

The New Wave eliminated a number of such locations and settings from its films and chose to explore new ones. Sometimes they are the same, but they are always treated differently. The New Wave was interested in the way of life that its young filmmakers had known since 1950. The maid's rooms—so-called student's quarters—and even smaller hotel rooms; the minimalist apartments lent or shared with friends; the cafés in the Latin Quarter or near Saint-Germain, preferably with a terrace where conversations went on for hours on end, where books were read, sometimes stolen, or dropped negligently onto a table top (providing an opportunity for the viewer to discover the director's favorite authors), where scams for making money or techniques for picking up women were tried out. There were concert halls, theaters, movie houses. But no restaurants (except in Chabrol, obviously), and only occasionally a self-service restaurant or school canteen. The New Wave supplied the truth of everyday life that earlier cinema had falsified, hid, and generally ignored. From this arose the impression of novelty and freshness that immediately seduced the public.

At the same time the New Wave introduced a Balzacian

element of accuracy into film and the desire to create a truthful image of society at the end of the fifties. The result was an unspoken, but frequently applied rule to respect the topography and configuration of place. There was no screen image that didn't correspond to its real-life double. The real took precedence over fiction, prevented any sense of facileness or trickery, ensured that characters harmonized with their environment. This was Chabrol's method. He always worked in a natural setting. His scenes of country life, and sometimes Paris, demanded it. Not for financial, but for moral and aesthetic reasons. The banality of the real brushes against, breeds, and gives birth to the monstrous. The transition from one to the other occurs in obscurity, through a series of small, barely perceptible shocks. There is no psychological explanation because it is the banality of the world that is monstrous and the monstrous is banal. To attempt to film this in the studio falsifies the true subject visually and aurally. Over the course of fifty films, Chabrol filmed only his second (*Les Cousins*) and third (*À double tour*) in the studio, and he did so because it was convenient. *Landru*, a character with a reputation as a legendary monster, justified Chabrol's use of a highly stylized approach.

This strict adherence to the real did not mean that French filmmakers simply copied the principles of neorealism. In fact, the contrary was true. The ethos of neorealism was no longer consistent with the sociological truth of France during the Fifth Republic. It would be difficult to imagine a New Wave director picking unknowns from the street to play characters in a film. Roles were given to young, unknown, but talented actors (Bernadette Lafonte, Jean-Paul Belmondo, Gérard

Jean-Pierre Léaud and François Lebrun in *The Mother and the Whore* (Jean Eustache, 1973)

Barbet Schroeder and Michèle Girardon in *La Boulangère de Monceau* (Eric Rohmer, 1963)

Du côté de Robinson (Jean Eustache, 1964)

Blain, Jean-Claude Brialy, etc.), who were perfectly in synch mentally, physically, and verbally, with the new crop of directors. The accuracy of their portrayal was not based on an authentic representation of an impoverished existence but their ability to simulate the easygoing attitude and the *look* of a young and aspiring middle-class. The New Wave, however, managed to grab hold of a reality that was becoming increasingly obvious on the streets of Paris—the internationalization of human relations. Its films are populated with Japanese, Africans, Americans, and Danes, who through some chance meeting, become the principal heroes in a story they charm with their accents. For once the audience is spared the horrific Parisian accents that became the norm in France's "quality" films.

The New Wave was itself like a change of scene. People could breathe again. They could fill their lungs with air. The impressionist refinement of the old guard was abandoned for a more physical confrontation with the outside world. Truffaut theorized and put into practice this sense of respiratory urgency. He believed that the public would tire of interior scenes and experience an almost physiological urge to head for the exits. Consequently all his films had to end in the open air. What use was the street? The New Wave responded: to breathe. To live fully. There was the danger, however, of becoming its victim. The world of sensations is precarious. Movement is controlled, harnessed, frustrated. It was inevitable that the joyous spontaneity of 1958 would one day have to confront politics. And this is exactly what occurred ten years later, when the streets were again full.

1   Interview with Roger Régent in *L'Écran français*, November 2, 1948.

Jean-Pierre Léaud, Patrick Auffay, and Claire Maurier in *The 400 Blows* (François Truffaut, 1959)

1959

LES MISTONS

LE BEAU SERGE

LES COUSINS

HIROSHIMA, MON AMOUR

THE 400 BLOWS

RIO BRAVO

LA TÊTE CONTRE LES MURS

DEUX HOMMES DANS MANHATTAN

SOME LIKE IT HOT

LE DÉJEUNER SUR L'HERBE

LES MISTONS

François Truffaut

THE REINVENTION OF CINEMA

Little kids become big kids. One day they'll be able to deliver their four-hundred blows. For now, they travel in a compact group, with their chubby thighs and sly smiles, following the lovers across the sun-drenched plains of Nîmes, and the tennis courts, attracted by the whiteness of a girl's skirt. They are drawn to the scent of her skin, the odor that clings to a saddle or spreads like a tail behind her as she, a comet cyclist, flies by. The camera of the man who was once their equal, has tamed them, just as the animal documentarian has tamed the wild beavers near the river. The camera follows their steps, their most secret intimacy, slips into their games, answers their silly jokes, surreptitiously points out a poster for destruction as soon as the crippled guard has turned his back.

I love this superficial sincerity, which follows them like the gaze of someone who hasn't forgotten his own childhood, this luminous sensuality they track (and the camera with them) without being entirely conscious of it, this unrestrained eroticism filtered through a demanding purity. It's *La Partie de compagne* as Jean Vigo might direct it, the blushing maiden, the intrusion of burlesque into a love story, the lost time found in a fluttering heart. "For me," someone once said, "they're like little bits of wood." With little bits of wood and immense talent, Truffaut has reinvented cinema. ∎

Claude Beylie, *Cahiers du cinéma*, January 1959

LE BEAU SERGE

Claude Chabrol

A FAIRY TALE

Chabrol's story feels like a fairy tale. He took his inheritance and decided to devote it to his love of film by producing, at his

own expense, a film he wrote and shot entirely in Sardent, a small village in the Creuse, where his family's summer home is located. There were some problems, of course, but relatively few when we consider the audacity of Chabrol's project and the fact that he had no classical training, never went to film school, never served as anyone's assistant, never even made a short. Nothing at all.

This is where the fairly tale continues. When the film was finished, it was presented to the committee on feature-film quality and awarded an advance of 350,000 francs. The producer J. Bauvy referred to the grant as "an impudent challenge to our film industry." But the film had cost 350,000 to make. ∎

Jacques Doniol-Valcroze, *France-Observateur*, October 9, 1959

BEYOND APPEARANCES

Here's the story: Two young men, very dissimilar but nevertheless friends, live within the very carefully described framework of a poor country village. Although I rejected the artificiality of physical difference, I attempted to emphasize their moral and social differences. Pictorially, Serge's universe is characterized by dark colors, that of François by bright colors. But while Serge is clearly visible against this dark background,

François is most often dark and somber. This illustrates an aspect of the film that seemed very important to me: the element of appearances. During the first sequences of the film, it appears as if Serge is unstable, tormented, complex, and neurotic, whereas François seems rather stable, somewhat linear in fact. Thus the film's drama could be graphed as follows: a straight line, corresponding to François' character, onto which the sudden intrusions of Serge's personality are superimposed.

Yet the events in the film, to which I added the colors (which I happen to like) of melodrama, tend to modify the structure of this dramatic line, as if, once the problem were stated, the search for a solution would radically alter the underlying data. For once you get beyond appearances, a truth should slowly reveal itself to the viewer: the unstable, neurotic, mad character isn't Serge after all, but François. Serge understands himself. He knows the reasons for his behavior; he knows where he's going. François, however, only understands himself on the level of appearances. His inner nature is buried in his unconscious and only bursts through intermittently. He tries to escape himself, and his illness has resulted in psychosis; in the fear of dying. Like many young men haunted by the fear of death, his psychosis translates into a typical Christ complex. I've made François, without his acknowledging it and without its being expressed (other than by subtle aspects of his behavior), a latent homosexual with a tendency to regress to childhood. The film's denouement is two-fold. In an environment in which these two contradictory elements are combined, a snowy night, it appears as if François has saved Serge from destruction, and this is true in one sense. But François is at the same time saved from madness by Serge, who has taught him to beat the truth out of things. ∎

Claude Chabrol, *Cahiers du cinéma*, May 1958

A RETURN TO THE EARTH

One of the novelties of this film is the way it situates the action in the most ordinary countryside of one of the most ordinary regions of France, Creuse, but I don't want to blow this out of proportion. Until now we have seen a number—although a limited number—of French films shot in the countryside. None of these films were really remarkable. This may have been because we didn't take these settings seriously; they were treated as a kind of safe haven or backdrop required by a concern for faithfulness to a literary model. With Chabrol, on the contrary, we return to the earth, just as Italy took to the streets in *Open City*.

At the same time there is no attempt to create picturesque backgrounds. For the French countryside in the twentieth century, as varied and relatively unknown as it is, is hardly picturesque. This film doesn't trot out peasants and villagers, concepts from a bygone age. These are people who, whether high-school or grammar school graduates, turn out to be very similar to their forty million countrymen.

The region suffers from a very common illness, boredom, and the photography expresses this brilliantly throughout the film. But this is not the same as literary ennui. A handful of sober comments underline the fact, enlarging the issue by giving it social or, if you prefer, geographic significance. The rest of the film revolves around the interaction between two men and the shock of juxtaposing two very different personalities. This treatment would be fairly commonplace if *Le Beau Serge* weren't a French film. But in French cinema, even the most recent, the same story is told over and over—the misfortunes of a couple struggling with destiny, envy, prejudice, etc. No matter how grand the scope of these films appears to be, it is a hundred times more restricted than that of a single American western. ∎

Éric Rohmer, *Arts*, February 11, 1959

LES COUSINS

Claude Chabrol

THE INVENTION OF THE PANNING SHOT

The story told in Chabrol's *Les Cousins*, his second film, is wonderfully simple, or, if you prefer, simply beautiful. It begins like a story straight out of Balzac, for it presents the Rastignac of *Père Goriot* living with the Rastignac of *Une étude de femme*. But *Les Cousins* could also be a fable by La Fontaine, presenting as it does, a city rat (Jean-Claude Brialy) showing off for his country cousin (Gérard Blain), while a cricket (Juliette Mayniel) jumps from one to the other with typically Parisian disgust. In short, *Les Cousins* is the story of a contest between crying Jean and laughing Jean. Chabrol's originality lies in his ability to make laughing Jean come out the winner despite his flashy appearance.

For the first time in years, perhaps since *The Rules of the Game*, we find a French director who pushes his characters as far as they can go by transforming their evolution into the Ariadne's thread that unravels the story. This was one of the principal attractions of *Le Beau Serge*. But the process is even more apparent in *Les Cousins*. We're interested in the characters not so much because they work hard, sleep with "the right women," or get drunk, but because their actions show them in a continuously different light throughout the film. This turns out to be a crucial element. For Chabrol has successfully managed to make the transition from the theoretical beauty of a screenplay written

by Paul Gegauff to a kind of practical beauty, the film's representation on screen. Chabrol's success is significant because it's extremely difficult to get it right. Antonioni, for example, was unable to pull it off when he directed *Il Grido*.

The difference between *Le Beau Serge* and *Les Cousins* is equivalent to that between a Cameflex and a Super Parvo. Throughout nearly the entire film, Chabrol's heavy camera pursues his characters, with tenderness and cruelty, to all four corners of the astonishing set designed by Bernard Evein. Like a large animal, it *suspends* an invisible threat above Juliette Mayniel's pretty head, forces Jean-Claude Brialy to reveal his hand, encloses Gérard Blain within the camera's amazing circling movement. I can offer no finer praise of Chabrol's work than by saying that he has *invented* the panning shot, the same way Alain Resnais invented the dolly shot, Griffith the close-up, or Ophuls the use of framing. ∎

Jean-Luc Godard, *Arts*, March 17, 1959

HEAVIER THAN A FRUITCAKE

A former PR officer for Fox, with good friends on the editorial staffs of some of the Fifth Republic's best newspapers, as well as in television, Chabrol, who is far from naive, has been careful in orchestrating his publicity. "Those miraculous 300,000 francs make room for the new generation of the New Wave; freedom of expression; film can't be taught; my production company AJYM was named after my wife and children; censorship doesn't exist; I shoot in the countryside; my discovery, Juliette Mayniel, has eyes as clear as water. . . ." These have been some of Chabrol's favorite themes. He has managed to succeed in doing what, traditionally, only movie starlets can do through their charm and beauty: get the press all worked up before so much as a scrap of film has been screened.

Now, it's water under the bridge. *Le Beau Serge* and *Les Cousins* have appeared on movie screens in Paris within a few weeks of one another. But pretension does not a work of art make. Why excuse a film of such glaring defects of continuity, just because it's the director's first? Would we justify a book that ignores the most elementary rules of syntax and is devoid of style for the same reason? Stringing together in-jokes and references to directors one admires is not enough. The struggle to win over the viewer and the ambition to integrate nature with the action of the film are less convincing here than they are in Rossellini. The painful calvary of a second, tubercular Christ in *Le Beau Serge* is as interminable as Bresson's original. Bernadette Lafont's blouse and the way her foot plays with the lamp, and Juliette Mayniel's sun bath in *Les Cousins*, are taken straight out of Vadim. Someone must have told Gérard Blain too many times that he resembles James Dean, for his hysterical outburst is a direct nod to the Actor's Studio. The vertigo (hmm), the framing, the suggestive close-ups, the heavy narrative pace could only have come from Hitchcock. The implausible tenderness and the sex scenes are a direct nod to Becker's *Rendez-vous de Juillet*, etc., etc. ∎

Michèle Firk, *Positif*, July 1959

HIROSHIMA MON AMOUR

Alain Resnais

THE TONE OF A TRAGEDY

Alain Resnais has orchestrated a strange *danse macabre* in which atomic skeletons lead the joined bodies of the two lovers. The film's tone is that of a tragedy. The dialogue is sung like a dirge, while the camera wanders through horror and ruin, demonstrations and railroad stations, present and past, nevers and Hiroshima, here and eternity. A great love is born that will endure a lifetime but can't last more than twenty-four hours. ∎

Georges Sadoul, *Les Lettres Françaises*, May 14, 1959

MODERN

In *Hiroshima, mon amour*, Alain Resnais presents the aesthetic concerns of the other modern arts in cinematic terms. He breaks the framework of the narrative story line and introduces the novelistic technique so often found in Faulkner, in which the past bubbles to the surface of the present and in so doing, poisons that present. The film's subject is also modern. It is the tragedy of the impossibility of the self's union and plenitude, the victory of division, dissociation, and fragmentation. Like two elements that combine to form an explosive mixture, like Picasso (recall his short film on Guernica), Resnais simultaneously reveals the face of horror and the profile of tenderness. Recall the film's horrible scenes of the wounded accompanied by the lyrical and bucolic commentary on Spring and the return of flowers to Hiroshima. ∎

Jean Douchet, *Arts*, June 17, 1959

TERRIBLE CONFUSION

If we are to believe Louis Malle, *Hiroshima, mon amour* is a hundred years ahead of today's cinema. Claude Chabrol considers the film a work of genius, sublime. François Truffaut, overwhelmed by the film, has repented and acknowledged the error of his ways. I have the misfortune of being less enthusiastic. *Hiroshima, mon amour* reminds me of the work of Pieyre de Mandiargues or Klossowski, which delight literary hacks and critics but leave the rest of us in a state of terrible confusion. This is a film for film lovers, paved with clever innuendoes, a film for those terribly in the know, capable of grasping subtle references, a work composed with an edgy intelligence, startling refinement, and based on extremely subtle equivalences. But it flies a bit too high. Perhaps it will be the beginning of a cinema of great virtuosi.

Mad love? Passionate love? In spite of the surrealist references, the love here is glacial. It lacks any sign of heat. It's an abstract love. And Resnais' film, which is so dense, so intelligent, so lucid, hovers inaccessible at some vague and cloud-filled distance. *Hiroshima, mon amour* is an admirable film in many respects. But at no time do we sense the gentle caress of a wing upon our skin. ■

Michel Aubriant, *Paris-Presse*, June 12, 1959

A FILM THAT PIERCES THE DARKNESS

This film is sharp and fluid, precise and vague; it pierces the darkness to reveal the dry, melancholy clarity of remembrance beyond the shadows of oblivion. Harmony and counterpoint: the harmony of this woman ravaged by her first love, the harmony of the city ravaged in the fullness of its being: The counterpoint is this concert for several voices around a unique act of devastation, the gray silence of Nevers and the lights of Hiroshima. This ruined woman, assassinated in her youth, and this ruined city, its teeming life assassinated, are won over by existence, and conquered by forgetfulness. The same desolation, the same decay, the same power to forget—this film depicts not internal will so much as an irresistible force that pulls us along, and against which we struggle—the same stigmata in the flesh of this city and the flesh of this woman, the same memory of parting, of rupture. What once was will return, obscurely perhaps, but with points of extreme clarity. What exists no longer belongs to the same skin,

but to another being, in another city.

With tenderness and humility Alain Resnais and Marguerite Duras have managed to recreate these feelings, made them accessible to our emotions. Critics will complain that the film is literary and artificial. They'll say that the dialogue isn't always up to the precision and tenderness of the imagery. They're right. Yet, once we relax a bit, once we ease into the film, these two forms of writing blend, the voice of Alain Resnais extending that of Marguerite Duras, adding his own perspective, balancing the landscape to the sonority of her language, the film's editing to the rhythm of her speech, so that in the end we are unable to distinguish them. *Hiroshima, mon amour* is miraculous because we are unable to determine where the image begins and the word ends. ■

Pierre Marcabru, *Combat*, June 13, 1959

CONFUSED AND DANGEROUS RHETORIC

The second reproach I would make to *Hiroshima, mon amour* is political. Without going so far as to claim that Resnais is a Nazi or a fascist, the parallel between the liberation of Nevers and the bombing of Hiroshima, which brings to mind the slogans in *Rivarol*, is unfortunate. I realize that Resnais doesn't use these elements the way the neo-Pétainists do, and that he wanted to compare the triviality of individual tragedy with the collective destruction of a city, but the opposition between them is a bit fuzzy here. *Hiroshima, mon amour*'s theme appears to borrow the confused and dangerous rhetoric of the "partisans of peace at any price," those who condemn all war (even though peace is sometimes worse than any war). These were the same people who stood by as the concentration camps flourished and Japanese militarism spread. Resnais seems to have aligned himself with a group that strongly resembles the partisans of non-intervention in '37, who, more or less consciously, and whether out of a puerile sense of anarchism or because they were pro-Franco, played into the hands of their future aggressors. ■

Louis Seguin, *Positif*, November 1959

THE 400 BLOWS

François Truffaut

BETTER THAN A MASTERPIECE

The 400 Blows is not a masterpiece. So much the better for François Truffaut. More often than not that overused word generally ends up signifying everything and nothing. And then, at 27 and with a masterpiece under his belt, Truffaut would find himself at something of a disadvantage. He would spend his career trying to get over a work that had become an impediment. *The 400 Blows* is better than a masterpiece. Together with *Hiroshima, mon amour*, it's one of the two most original films to have appeared in post-War France.

Truffaut has no problem mixing genres. The film begins as a typical narrative, and ends up a chronicle. It returns to being a story, evolves into a morality tale, then wanders off into a comic interlude. Truffaut inserts a tragic episode, relates a full-fledged adventure story, and ends the film with a beautiful image. All the while he remains a detailed observer of reality, an investigator, a poet, with an excellent directorial touch.

Having watched *The 400 Blows* several times, I wonder what miracle enabled Truffaut to avoid complication and confusion and produce a work that is moving and coherent. That miracle is François Truffaut's talent. His ideas and creativity are bursting through every scene in the film. In *Les Mistons* the story line was mixed up with the whirlwind events taking place on screen, yet we were able to experience the enchantment of this film, which managed to recompose itself into a uniform and endearing whole rather than a formless mass.

Truffaut's films remind me of magic. "Nothing in the hands, nothing up my sleeves." One high-wire act follows another, and the unexpected pops out of a hat. But if he's a magician, Truffaut is an illusionist that doesn't create out of thin air. The raw material he employs is among the richest and most enduring: Reality. That's the secret of his success. Turning his back on that "certain tendency" he virulently denounced because it destroyed realism "by enclosing beings in a world barricaded by formulas, wordplay, maxims," Truffaut allows his characters to "reveal themselves to us just as they are."[1] Here, as elsewhere, he has remained faithful to himself.

What is Truffaut trying to tell us? He's trying to make sense of one of the most difficult periods in our lives, which adults with short memories often cloak in hypocritical beauty. *The 400 Blows* is an episode in the difficulty of simply being, the confusion of the individual who has been thrust into the world without asking, and who is denied any means to adapt to it. It is a faithful report on the inability of parents and educators to understand the problems faced by a child contemplating adulthood. It is a second birth, but one whose pain no one is willing to assume. It is the child's responsibility to create an acceptable world with the means at hand. But how can one escape the tragedy of everyday life when he remains torn between his parents, fallen idols, and an indifferent, often hostile, universe? ■

Fereydoun Hoveyda, *Cahiers du cinéma*, July 1959

1   *Cahiers du cinéma*, no. 31.

A FILM WITH FEELING

The first thing that strikes me about this film is its humanity. The hero is a child living in Paris, looking for a little affection. Neither his parents nor his teachers care much for him. He runs away. He lies. He commits one or two petty crimes, and gets locked up. He's nothing more than a desperate and solitary prisoner. That's the crux of the story, which is told in a simple, direct style, without affectation. It's a film with feeling, and it continues to haunt you hours after you've left the theater.

As happened in the past, this film pins an invisible yellow star to the chest of these young boys. The film accuses. It doesn't hate. Aside from the adults and the boy's vile mother, this film implicates not mankind but a world, whether the director intended it to or not. A great talent has been born. I greet Truffaut with admiration and respectful friendship, only regretting that the demands of journalism prevent me from speaking of his art at greater length. ■

Georges Sadoul, *Les Lettres Françaises*, May 7, 1959

A TRIUMPH OF SIMPLICITY

I regret speaking so pompously about a film so devoid of rhetoric, for *The 400 Blows* is a triumph of simplicity. This film is neither insipid nor uninventive. The most precious element in cinema, the most fragile, is that which gradually disappears in the hands of skillful technicians: a certain purity of vision and a cinematic innocence, both of which are abundantly present in this film. Perhaps it's sufficient to believe that things are what they seem, and to see them on screen the way they are in reality. Could this belief exist outside film? Yet, this vision, this thought, is exposed to the center of the world's being. This is the filmmaker's state of grace: to be inside film, master of a domain whose borders may extend to infinity. It is an approach typified by Renoir.

I could dwell on the extraordinary tenderness with which Truffaut represents cruelty, which calls to mind the extraordinary gentleness with which Franju represents madness. In both cases a nearly unbearable force arises from the continuous use of understatement. The refusal of eloquence and violence, of explanation, makes each image beat from within, gives it a pulse, which bursts out suddenly in a few brief flashes, brilliant as a knife blade. The inevitable comparisons to Vigo, Rossellini, or, more appropriately, *Les Mistons* or *Une visite* come to mind. In the end, however, none of these references amount to much. I only want to say, as simply as I can, that we now have in our midst a man who is no longer a gifted and promising newcomer, but a real French director, equal to the greatest. His name is François Truffaut. ■

Jacques Rivette, *Cahiers du cinéma*, May 1959

RIO BRAVO

Howard Hawks

A WESTERN WITHOUT INDIANS

I hate westerns. That's why I adore *Rio Bravo*. The genre annoys me because, although the sentiments it portrays are admirable, they are almost always based on principle rather than fact. What little directing exists is concerned with something other than itself—personal problems, politics, technique. It denies the spirit of the true western and presents its opposite: emphasis, decorum, lyricism. Yet, *Rio Bravo* is pretty much the opposite of *Johnny Guitar*. There's nothing intrinsically poetic about the film, although the end result is a kind of poetry. As always with Hawks the rules of the game are respected, at least until that moment when the director has had enough. *Rio Bravo* is an extremely original film in that it's a western about confinement in which there are no Indians, landscapes, or chase scenes. It does something rare in rediscovering the essence of the genre, but it does so in this rather remarkable way (whereas *Red River* and *Big Sky* arrive at the same result without breaking with tradition). *Rio Bravo* brings to mind a thriller like *To Have and Have Not* or a melodrama, like *Barbary Coast*. So why did Hawks make this western? Because it enabled him to present actions that are not ordinarily seen in our everyday world, by beings outside of nature. I'm not a sheriff, or Angie Dickinson, or a pharaoh; neither are you. Yet Hawks shows us that the appeal of such individuals is unrelated to what we might expect (the world of adventure, the extraordinary). Hawks the classicist has always rejected these values, satirized them, ridiculed them, even ignored them in *The Thing*. Yet he also accepts the everyday: a man is a sheriff the same way he's a laborer or a subway conductor. There are plenty of gunshots in *Rio Bravo*, but none of them are real, none of them have any true dramatic

value. The incessant gunfights end up only becoming monotonous, and they eliminate all suspense. Each repeated gesture cancels its predecessor. And Wayne's blasé intelligence, far from contemplating the act, somehow immediately grasps the range of possible consequences. How Wayne does this is a question of telepathy, similar to the way Hawks' previous heroes had eyes in the back of their head. ■

Luc Moullet, *Cahiers du cinéma*, July 1959

LA TÊTE CONTRE LES MURS

Georges Franju

CINÉMA FOU

Like amour-fou, Franju's first feature film could be called cinéma-fou. *La Tête contre les murs* is a madman's film about the insane. The film is, therefore, insanely beautiful. *La Tête contre les murs* is an *inspired* film. For Franju, going as far as he could here consisted not in surprising the madness behind realism but the realism behind madness. Unlike *Sang des bêtes* and *Hôtel des Invalides*, where the length of the films may have

forced Franju to systematically use provocative effects, the direction of *La Tête contre les murs* is carefully restrained. This film is beautiful because it is logical. Franju may not know how to direct his actors, but Jean-Pierre Mocky, Anouk Aimée, Paul Meurisse, and Pierre Brasseur have never been better and their dialogue never more appropriate. They don't act, they *tremble*.

A motorcycle rider heads for a ravine at breakneck speed. A girl in a bathing suit climbs up the ladder of a swimming pool in the suburbs. Headlights follow a traveling shot across the walls of an asylum. An electric train winds through a garden. A car bursts from a phantasmagoric grove of trees (cinematography by Shuftan). The lights of Paris overwhelm a madman on the loose. Large white pigeons make Aznavour dream. Unlike Hitchcock, and like Lang, what we remember from Franju are his scenes, not individual shots, a characteristic of this Dionysiac director. ■

Jean-Luc Godard, *Cahiers du cinéma*, special Christmas issue 1958

SOCIAL CINEMA

Franju could be criticized for his perpetual concern with bizarre landscapes: the fence spiked with twisted iron and the stuffed birds, where Gérane and Stéphanie, his future lover, speak with one another for the first time; the white tree that pierces the night; the incongruous grove of trees alongside a straight road; the cage full of doves behind which two doctors speak. We could just as easily criticize Franju for his apparent lack of concern with plot, his disregard for the articulations, explanations and other secondary matters that ordinarily signal the clumsy formulas and overrated skill of the typical French screenwriter. What is important in this film is that the sound track replaces what would be illuminating bits of dialogue with noise or weary accents. Franju's goal is not to unravel a clever plot—little or nothing of the original novel remains in the film—but to mark the extent to which the characters have become mired in an inextricable trap.

At bottom, the director of *Saumon d'Atlantique* has little taste for pure aesthetics, and no sustained interest in the Beautiful. The headlights in the night, the oblique traveling shots, the always inventive flexibility of the screenplay, the brilliant use of sound—nothing in this sustained piece of bravado prevents Franju from boldly affirming that he is one of those people who wants to change our life. But to hell with simplistic objections. Franju strenuously, and justifiably, defends his right to make "social cinema." He's willing to concede harebrained neorealism, picturesqueness, humanity, and neurosis to Fellini. ■

Louis Séguin, *Positif*, July 1959

DEUX HOMMES DANS MANHATTAN

Jean-Pierre Melville

AMERICA THROUGH THE EYES OF A FRENCHMAN

Deux hommes dans Manhattan contains an aborted detective film and several successful documentaries. One documentary, unfortunately too short, takes place in the corridors of the UN. Another contains a brilliantly caustic comment on the habits of the media, and another on a New York woman's nightlife. Seen through the eyes of a Frenchman, this America is not Reichenbach's version. The picturesque has been left in the coat room. Instead, we're shown a bustling city that bubbles with energy and captivates viewers with its undoctored black-and-white imagery. In the end, this is a documentary about Jean-Pierre Melville, all-around filmmaker (he was screenwriter, director, and actor in *Deux hommes dans Manhattan*). I still have a hard time understanding how, after *Le Silence de la mer* and *Bob le flambeur*, so much awkwardness and accumulated sloppiness manage to yield such unquestionable

charm. Melville's charm is the charm of imperfect things otherwise known as "sincerity." ■

Pierre Billard, *France-Observateur*, October 22, 1959

A STORY FOR BIG KIDS

Melville is a great amateur, but only an amateur. This is the source of his films' undeniable charm as well as their irritation. *Deux hommes dans Manhattan* is a succession of scenes, one more astonishing than the next, but the film lacks continuity and is bizzarely joined together. The scenes form a kind of grownup fairytale, which I found myself liking, in spite of its naiveté and childishness.

The influence of Orson Welles is deliberately obvious, not only in the personality of the characters—such as the opposition of a fundamentally abject individual with an honest, although not particularly brilliant, man—but especially in certain scenes, such as the extraordinary scene in the hospital or the car chase with the reporter and the victim's daughter. The latter inevitably brings to mind certain scenes from *Mr. Arkadin*. Melville, like Welles, likes to frame his plots as fables, with all the influence of the marvelous they imply. For this reason it makes sense to point out the film's weaknesses. Melville, if he were a bit less of a dilettante, could easily have made several very great films in his career. Why did he choose actors who are so awful together that some otherwise excellent scenes are inadvertently funny? Why did he insist on a chase car that so completely frustrates the viewer's expectations? These are the kind of mistakes that no gifted director can afford to make after three or four films.

The cinematography by Nicolas Hayer is extraordinarily beautiful. It proves that this great chief cameraman is as capable as Decae, and perhaps better, in filming location shots without losing his sense of poetry. ■

Jean Douchet, *Arts*, October 21, 1959

SOME LIKE IT HOT

Billy Wilder

CLEVER, EFFECTIVE, VULGAR, AND TRIVIAL

Billy Wilder's film bears no trace of nobility. *Some Like It Hot* is clever, effective, and very intelligent, but it is intentionally vulgar and trivial. The film revolves around two principal ideas, one based on the screenplay, the other on the directing. The screenplay is based on the idea that no man can resist Marilyn Monroe. Their lives at stake, two men (Jack Lemmon and Tony Curtis) are forced to dress up as women and treat Monroe as if they were just one of the girls. Under these circumstances how will one of them ever win the girl without giving himself away? This variation on the myth of Tantalus inevitably leads to innumerable situations where ambiguity is the essential spice. By locating the action in the 1930s, the era of prohibition and gangsters, Wilder has ample opportunity for cinematic parody, something he effectively employed in *The Seven Year Itch* and *Sunset Boulevard*.

All in all the film doesn't appear to surpass the director's intentions, which are modestly low. Consequently, there are two ways to respond to *Some Like It Hot*. We can sit back and enjoy the film because the director has adequately fulfilled his intentions, or we can acknowledge that the subject isn't very interesting to begin with, in which case we have plenty of time to dislike the ugliness of the cinematography and lack of conviction in Wilder's directing. There is, however, plenty to admire in the ever marvelous Marilyn Monroe, and Jack Lemmon's performance is astonishing. ■

Jean Douchet, *Arts*, October 7, 1959

AN AMBIGUOUS BUT INTELLIGENT FILM

I'm not convinced that Wilder's ultimate aim is to make us laugh. Wilder is clever, too clever not to deliver the goods we expect of him. That's why *Some Like It Hot* has been such a hit in New York, London, and Paris, and Wilder has spared no expense to ensure it. He used the best recipes in this film and used them well enough to make it a success around the world. Once success was assured, he decided to make the film *he* wanted to make: an ambiguous, often bitter, sometimes terrible, but always intelligent film that is subtle and moving at times.

The film is also an homage to Marilyn Monroe. Playing a minor, passive role in the film, she is always acted upon, never providing any personal impetus to the story, except in the scene with the phony billionaire. Yet, in every scene in which she appears, she's treated like a queen. Although she's not as good here as she was in *Bus Stop* or *The Seven Year Itch*, she is no less incomparable in her heart-rending optimism, her tortured sensibility, and look of hopelessness.

This essay on the confusion of the sexes is anything but homosexual, but it's not an anti-homosexual film either. It's just that Wilder states his problem in other terms and on another level. The only real weak point in the film is that Curtis himself is ambiguous. (I'm referring to his character in the film, not the actor's private life, which doesn't concern me and about which I know nothing.) But the result is there to see: his character seems to have a penchant for wiggling his hips and speaking in a falsetto. Jack Lemmon's strength in this picture comes from the fact that he always looks like a man playing the part of a woman. Wilder's genius is that he's able to show Lemmon's character taking himself seriously as a woman. This is one of the most fascinating demonstrations of the actor's paradox. Like Bergman in *The Magician*, Wilder is careful to reveal only bits and pieces of his characters, and it is at this moment, and this moment alone, that truth and authenticity are born. Wilder smiles when he asks the question (but he asks it just the same): Isn't being a man or a woman a matter of getting up in the morning and convincing ourselves, I'm a man or I'm a woman? Once upon a time we used to burn people in public for much less than that. ∎

Jacques-Doniol Valcroze, *Cahiers du cinéma*, November 1959

LE DÉJEUNER SUR L'HERBE

Jean Renoir

ENDLESS BEAUTY

Renoir is wonderful. The older he gets, the more youthful, bold, and innovative his work becomes. He's taken a new approach to film here, although he is fully aware of the difficulties, potential pitfalls and mistakes that such attempts invite. Approaching this as the culmination of his earlier work, Renoir plunges forward with all the enthusiasm of a hound on a fox hunt. *Le Déjeuner sur l'herbe* gives the impression of a unified whole and the film is wonderful in spite of its defects. It is an endless source of beauty and has all the richness of ripe fruit, whose taste is that of life itself. ∎

Jean Douchet, *Arts*, November 18, 1959

A TESTAMENT

Le Déjeuner sur l'herbe has all the clarity, sincerity, and significance of a testament—the testament of an artist with a very sound mind. Yes, the landscapes remind you of his father, and his father's lifelong love of trees, the body, and life. But the film reminds me most of Courbet. Not so much the Courbet of *Déjeuner sur l'herbe* but of *l'Atelier*, where, by means of a marvelous nude, he separated the characters charged with representing what he hates and loves. Jean Renoir the pantheist hates falsifiers, prigs, schemers, insolent servants, and Valkyries. He loves what Virgil, Horace, and Rabelais loved. Yet he is not a womanizer, for look how he handled the squall, those lightweight skirts, Nénette's bath, and the extraordinarily intense transposition of the "reproductive act" into a series of undulating and tormented images of supposedly impassive vegetation. ∎

Paul Guyot, *France-Soir*, November 14, 1959

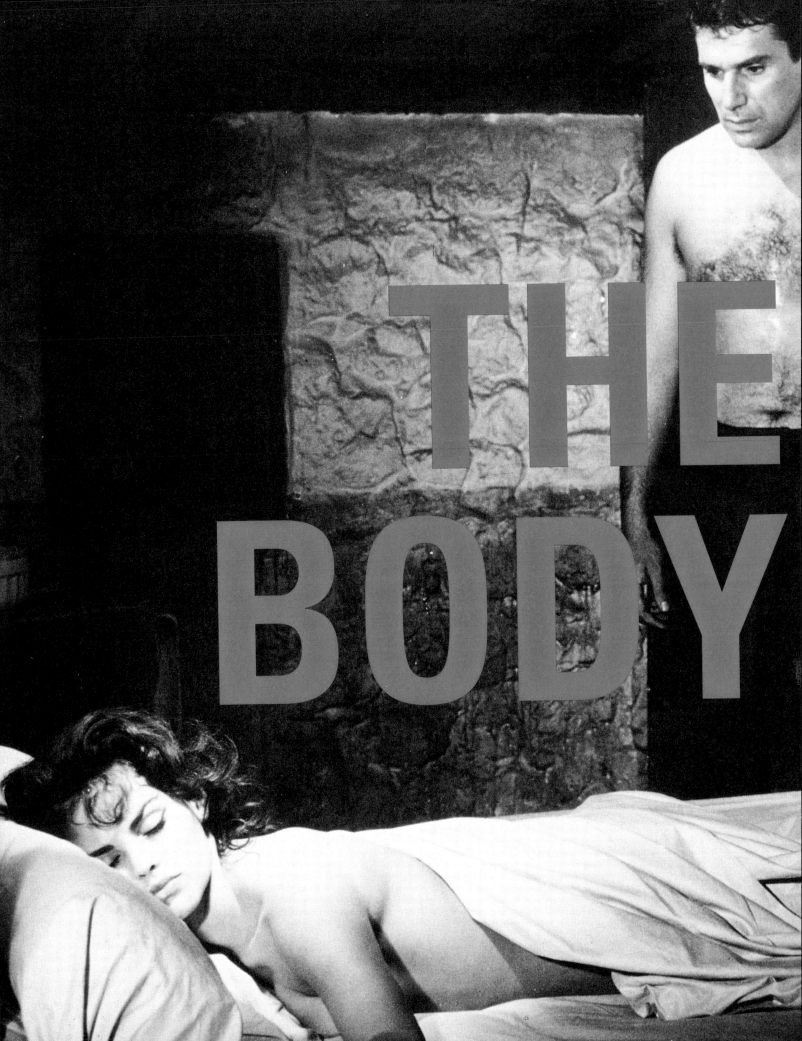

THE
BODY

1
The Body Without Truth

The traditional French filmmakers who preceded the New Wave had paid scant attention to the truth or evolution of society, and even less to the changes in physical comportment and behaviour that were taking place in the world around them. They continued to portray an intellectually retrograde bourgeois society, mired in nineteenth-century morality, and seemed determined to maintain outdated values of sacrifice and frustration. Although they occasionally acknowledged the desire for pleasure that was animating a new generation tired of the deprivation experienced during the Occupation and post-War period, their acknowledgment served merely as a pretext on which to judge, condemn, and punish (Henri-Georges Clouzot's *Manon*, Yves Allégret's *Manèges*, Julien Duvivier's *Voici le temps des assassins*). The world they represented was a closed one, a mediocre and rancid *huis clos*, characterized by cowardice and

Catherine Rouvel and Robert Hossein in *Chair de poule* (Julien Duvivier, 1963)

petty rivalries. It was a vision of pessimistic bleakness, which was captured by Claude Autant-Lara in *l'Auberge rouge* and *La Traversée de Paris*.

Their characters, with their feigned suffering and conventional, outdated intrigues, offered nothing concrete or genuine for the camera's eye. The truth of the body's language and the characters' dramatic confrontation evaporated behind the actors' stage mannerisms, which were based on conventional facial expressions and a tired repertoire of academic poses, attitudes, and gestures. Lackluster characters served as nothing more than flashy props for actors, who themselves served as a pretext and mouthpiece for purportedly brilliant dia-logues that were completely out of touch with the reality of the time. "Elegance"— an appearance without substance—flashed across the screen. The bourgeois moral order corseted the body in the same way it

Raymond Rouleau, *Falbalas* (Jacques Becker, 1945)

Danielle Darrieux and Vittorio de Sica, *Madame de ...* (Max Ophuls, 1953)

femme, Le Plaisir, La Poison, etc.) or absence (*Falbalas, Madame de ... , Éléna et les Hommes*), its refusal, rejection, and repulsion (*Le Testament du docteur Cordelier*) drove the story and guided the mise-en-scène. The new post-War directors—Bresson, Melville, Tati—radicalized this effort. They refined dialogue, neutralized it, and in Tati's case, reduced it to noise. Their only language was the *body*: treated as a pale and impassive mask by Melville; examined with maniacal attention by Bresson; broken and dislocated by Tati to draw from it a sense of gymnastic comedy. Similar concerns are found in more conservative filmmakers of the same generation such as René Clément and Clouzot, though, unfortunately, without accompanying screenplays that would support the effort. It is no accident that Clouzot's best film is *Le Mystère Picasso* (1956). The director examines the body—and what a body!—of the artist as he

Mon oncle (Jacques Tati, 1958)

demanded short hair, tight collars, and three-piece suits. Naturally, the story of a body that dared transgress these codes, even slightly, became the principal subject of films that ultimately sought to control such transgression; scandal justified the sublime courage of conventional directors, though in fact this proved to be little more than pathetic audacity. Claiming to have broken the bonds of censorship, directors did nothing more than fetter their inspiration, intelligence, and freedom. The stereotyped representation of reality triumphed, and the cliché was king.

At the opposite end of the spectrum were the directors admired by the future film-makers of the New Wave. These included Renoir, Grémillon, Becker, and to some extent Pagnol, Ophuls, and Guitry, all of whom made the body's existence the principal object of their films. The body's presence (*French Cancan, L'Amour d'une*

138

Françoise Arnoul in *French-Cancan* (Jean Renoir, 1954)

continues to preoccupy filmmakers. Superficially, *Lola Montès* is a product of the traditional French film industry, part of the tradition of "quality" cinema. It oscillates between the noble version of *Le Rouge et le Noir* (1954) and the risqué popular version embodied in *Caroline Chérie* (1951), which launched Martine Carol's career. Casting an ex-starlet in the title role, whose qualities as an actress were inversely proportional to the physical measurements that had made her a star, inspired Ophuls rather than discouraged him. He stuck to his subject: Martine Carol wouldn't interpret Lola Montès, instead, the historical character would play Martine Carol. In this way Lola would be what she had been during her life, and the character is completely credible in representing the cinematic adventure of a courageous young woman metamorphosed into a sex symbol. A body that was the subject of scandal (the bourgeois scandal of French "quality" cinema) becomes purely

Jean Gabin and Françoise Arnoul in *French-Cancan*

instrumentalizes the painterly gesture, obeys the creative act, and slowly reveals the obvious necessity of both the painting and the act of painting taking shape before our eyes.

Naturally, the film was defended by the *Cahiers*, just as they had championed films based on physical exploits such as *Les Étoiles de midi* by the mountain climber Marcel Ichac (1960), *Volcano* by the volcanologist Haroun Tazieff (1959), *Le Monde du silence* (1955) by Louis Malle and captain Jacques-Yves Cousteau, or concrete descriptions of peasant life like *Farrebique* (1946) by Georges Rouquier. This attention to physical movement recalls the early pre-cinematic works of Muybridge and Marey, with their breakdown of motion.

It was even more natural for the *Cahiers* to support Ophuls's *Lola Montès* (1955). Its subject "fictionalized" the conflict that

scandalous, slowly detaches itself from its convention and leads it toward its destruction. It was a theme that Godard would later use for *My Life to Live* (1962).

It was through auteurist cinema, which focused on the concrete nature of facts, the materiality of things, and the truth of the body, that Ophuls was able to respond to the demands of his producers and, due to the film's commercial failure, ultimately ruin them. Truffaut quickly saw through this stratagem and used it as the basis of his critique of *Lola Montès* in the January 1956 issue of *Cahiers du cinéma*. Truffaut writes, "Martine Carol, like Marilyn Monroe, is simply a courageous and coquettish young woman who, through the mysterious laws of the box office and the demands of producers, finds herself playing roles that would be perfect for Ingrid Bergman, Greta Garbo, or Joan Crawford. Max Ophuls, who quickly realized that Martine Carol had as

Martine Carol, *Lola Montès* (Max Ophuls, 1955)

Martine Carol, *Lola Montès*

much in common with Lola Montès as he had with the Pope, decided to turn Lola into a plaster statue endowed with the capacity for suffering. . . . Like Balzac, Max Ophuls 'pushes' our emotions to their extreme physical consequences. In the end the fevers and sweats get the better of the abandoned woman, who dies in the manner of Ursule Mirouet and Madame de Mortsauf."

Truffaut later adds, "The dialogue in the shooting script was good, but that in the final film is extraordinary because the actors were unable to recite it verbatim and because of changes on the set. . . . Ophuls deliberately kept many of the outtakes in his final cut rather than the successful takes." Truffaut gives several examples of this: "The king of Bavaria at the theater, 'I was coming to visit you, Madame . . . No, that's not right.' (He walks around the room and continues.) 'I was coming to visit you, Madame . . . to spare you the trouble.' This sublime notion of 'that's not right' was obviously a mistake made by Anton Walbrook [the actor who plays the king] when the scene was being shot. It is this process of continuous improvisation and improvement, directed toward a *truer truth* that puts Max Ophuls on a par with Jean Renoir." Truffaut's message was acknowledged, retained, and frequently used by the New Wave.

Truffaut also skewers the traditional actor's method, insisting on its bodily incarnation. "The worst mistake of the modern actor consists in showing that he possesses 'the intelligence of the text.' It's only necessary to have heard Gérard Philipe recite poetry to imagine the pleasure one might feel in strangling an actor. The multiple displacement that occurs constantly in *Lola Montès* between the personality of the actors and their diction, between their diction and their text, creates a sense of enchantment. . . .

Simone Signoret, *Manèges* (Yves Allegret, 1949)

Le Mystère Picasso (Henri-Georges Clouzot, 1956)

Lola Montès is the first film to stammer, a film in which the beauty of a word (the voluptuous texture Walbrook gives to the word 'audience') constantly takes precedence over the meaning of the sentence."

After *Lola Montès*, suddenly, the New Wave is everywhere. From Godard to Rozier, from Resnais to Demy, from Chabrol to Rivette, from Truffaut or Rohmer to Eustache. Though the films of the New Wave came into being only a few years after *Lola Montès*, they are films that we have, in a way, already heard and seen.

2
Brigitte Bardot

Michel Piccoli and Brigitte Bardot in *Contempt* (Jean-Luc Godard, 1963)

Contempt

No more than a few months separated *Lola Montès* from *And God Created Woman* (1956). Suddenly Martine Carol's charm seemed stale and old fashioned. A wild, liberated, animal presence burst across the screen. It undermined and revolutionized social customs, not just in France but around the world. Brigitte Bardot—or B.B. as she was familiarly known—created a new wave all her own and the swell was felt across the globe.

The explosion took some time to ignite. After posing for a number of fashion magazines, the young Bardot launched herself as a "starlet" in what turned out to be a modest yet productive career. Between 1952 and 1956 she appeared in fifteen films. It was Roger Vadim who broke the mold in which she had been confined, that of a middle-class child-woman of obvious erotic appeal, protected by a pouting, mischievous expression and a falsely modest veil of innocence that was only too easily stripped

143

became the darling of the Parisian jet set, and took his first steps in filmmaking. He was part of an avant-garde that used amorality as a means of weakening the corrupt and calcified morality of the bourgeois world.

Bardot, however, was satisfied with the slow, obscure, yet radical transformations of popular opinion. Slowly, surely, she made her way forward. She had received an excellent middle-class education, came from a fairly well-to-do family, and grew up in a fashionable part of the city (Paris's 16th arrondissement). All in all, she led a kind of charmed youth. But her sense of independence, her attraction to bohemian life, along with years of training in classical dance, pushed her toward the more "carefree" world inhabited by the friends of her future husband.

She evolved in symbiosis with the new way of life to which the young generation unconsciously aspired. Bourgeois society was

away. Vadim knew that the old formula of equating beauty with guilt didn't apply to Bardot. He had known Bardot since she was fourteen and eventually married her. As far as Vadim was concerned, she deserved an image more appropriate to her nature and to the social changes taking place around them. She was comfortable with her own body, and this is what he wanted to convey.

Vadim was often the more adventurous of the two. After the war he led a bohemian existence in Saint-Germain-des-Prés. His life was one of improvisation, and he frequented the neighborhood basement jazz clubs (jazz was still considered "negro" music by many reactionaries), which provided the musical background for his first film. Eager for success and able to take advantage of the aging social structures that were beginning to crack at the seams, he tried his hand at journalism, rubbed elbows with the hip and highly professional playboys of *Paris-Match*,

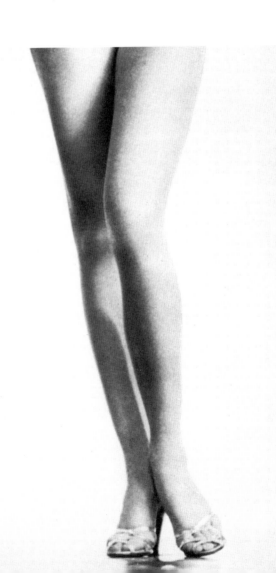

who was able to portray her desire on screen, free of psychological complications or guilt. And men, mesmerized, submitted. Bardot gave birth to a new state of mind, or rather a whole new moral attitude, one of ease with one's physical self.

Both in her private life and on screen, Bardot had no use for the public's opinion or their judgment. Her body was hers to do with as she pleased. In this sense she was representative of the needs of her time, and she introduced an era of liberalization that, over a twenty year period (1956–1975), managed to break down every social and cinematic taboo.

Her impact on the media surpassed that of the most successful American stars; even Marilyn Monroe never challenged Bardot's uniqueness. But she wasn't as fortunate as Monroe, who was directed by some of Hollywood's greatest filmmakers—Lang,

sloughing off its old skin and had to confront its own censorship. In establishing a new set of values—consumption, money, and pleasure—as the goal of existence, it undermined its own morality. Bourgeois society's punitive morality, ultimately based on frustration, began to crumble; propriety, in both dress and behavior, was cast aside. People were again learning to be comfortable with their bodies and carried themselves accordingly.

And God Created Woman was very much about being comfortable with a physical presence. The film penetrated the small, closed world of Saint-Tropez. At its center was a superb, wildly exciting female animal. But Bardot's character was neither a vamp nor a criminal. She was simply a "nice" young woman, comfortable with who she was and how she looked, and devoid of any notion of sin. She had poise and was a phenomenal dancer. Here was a woman

Hawks, Mankiewicz, Cukor, Huston, Preminger, Wilder, and others. The filmmakers, steeped in the "tradition of French quality," who cast her after Vadim's film—along with Vadim himself in subsequent films—didn't know how to direct Bardot; her body was always a problem for them. Either they attempted to sanitize her, like Boisrond, Christian-Jaque, René Clair, and the rest, by casting her as the courageous little French girl: comical, harebrained yet positive, sensual but reasonable. Others, like Autant-Lara, Duvivier, and Clouzot, were of a more naturalist bent; they saw in her a way to scandalize the middle class. She was the slut—this was the way *they* viewed her—who could provoke others through her lack of self-consciousness, her freedom and egotism.

There was only one filmmaker who didn't consider B.B. "bad luck." It was Godard who offered Bardot a masterpiece, the vehicle for her finest role. *Contempt* (1963) begins

Contempt

with a man who is deeply and hopelessly in love, and the film explores his attitude toward the woman's body he both desires and fears. She in turn feels contempt for the man who observes her body and feels unworthy of it even when she offers it to him "totally, tenderly, tragically." Godard was the only filmmaker truely to tackle Bardot as a subject and the body as moral attitude. For Godard, Bardot was no slut and her behavior wasn't scandalous. She was an ordinary young woman, a secretary—someone simple, honest, and untouched by the sickness of the age, and its great tragedy, money. This isn't made explicit in the film but it is visible in the body that Godard observes, follows in its movements, its poses, its way of speaking, of saying "words," and in the animal truth of its being. Like Ophuls with Martine Carol, Godard didn't want Bardot to interpret Camille, he wanted Camille to be Bardot.

3
Gesture, Space, Movement

Françoise Fabian and Jean-Louis Trintignant in *My Night at Maud's* (Éric Rohmer, 1969)

American film of the rich period 1945–1960 had provided some answers to the question posed by the young writers of the *Cahiers du cinéma*, "What is Cinema?" The question had been asked by André Bazin and was one Godard would ask throughout his career. Éric Rohmer, in an article written under his real name, Maurice Schérer, sketched a response in an article that appeared in the June 1948 issue of *La Revue du cinéma*.[1] Cinema, he claimed, is the art of space.

In this seminal article Rohmer minimizes the importance of time, which is too theatrical in his eyes, and emphasizes instead the physical phenomenon involved in apprehending and manipulating space. To further his argument, he also minimizes the importance of editing, for while editing does indeed manipulate the relationship between two spaces, it is too closely associated with issues of temporality. Rohmer prefers to focus on the *stationary shot*, which, within the unity of its frame, respects the integrity of the filmed space. This space serves two purposes: dramatic, since its existence necessarily provokes action; and plastic, not through pictorial composition, but rather through "the expressive value of the relationships of dimension and the movement of lines within the area of the screen."

There is a slight edge of perversity in the way that Rohmer activates the spiraling movement of his argument, turning it like a gear. First, although it may seem paradoxical, the screen space has always been, even before the systematic use of depth of field, a three-dimensional space, whereas the stage has most often been two-dimensional, its height above at least part of the audience negating the sense of movement between the front and back of the stage. The greatest directors have been those who have worked to suggest this depth. And it is perhaps only simple coin-cidence that the visual theme of the spiral is found in works such as *The Cabinet of Dr.*

Blue Jeans (Jacques Rozier, 1958)

Henri Serre and Oscar Werner in *Jules et Jim* (François Truffaut, 1962)

Caligari, Nosferatu, Old and New, and *The Lady from Shanghai*.

Ten years later Rohmer further developed this theme of the spiral when he noted that it was the key motif in Alfred Hitchcock's *Vertigo*. He showed that from this point on, the lines of force that drove the story forward would be found within the heart of film space. Physical respect for the reality of this space was to become one of the precepts of the New Wave.

Rohmer came to an important conclusion from this general reflection. "The very nature of the screen—a completely filled rectangular space that occupies a relatively narrow portion of the visual field—conditions a gestural plasticity that is very different from the one the theater has accustomed us to. . . . The film actor's gesture has not only gradually become more discreet but more 'self-contained,' distorted so to speak by the proximity of the screen's edge." This idea of gesture, attitude, and the position of the body was to become crucial. A number of the short films made between 1955 and 1958 by Rivette, Truffaut, Godard, and Rohmer show distinct signs of mannerism and affectation—the New Wave's admiration for Griffith has not been exaggerated—even as they attempted accurately to delineate a gesture or posture; but this mannerism was a youthful error that they didn't repeat in their feature films. Still, it's hard to think of Godard without thinking of the way his female characters are always combing their hair or of the incessant yet sensual movements of their heads. Though best exemplified by Godard, a search for truth in and through the body extends to all the New Wave directors: Resnais, Marker, Demy, Rozier, Eustache, and Straub.

It was American cinema that had turned gesture and space into a necessity. The psychologism that dominated European cinema at

Claude Brasseur in *Band of Outsiders* (Jean-Luc Godard, 1964)

Anna Karina in *My Life to Live*

the time could no longer accepted. What mattered instead was the concept of behavior that quite naturally and effectively served as the impetus for American film of the time. Here too, Rohmer was able to describe the sentiments of those who had fallen in love with the cinema of the fifties. "Works as popular as *Broken Blossoms*, *Cimarron*, and even the films of Douglas Fairbanks, reveal to us a sense of space that many avant-garde filmmakers would envy. The modern spectator . . . has become too accustomed to interpreting the visual sign, understanding the reason for the presence of each image to take an interest in the actual *reality* of its appearance. The cinematographic spectacle is presented to him more as an act of decoding than a vision; his eye is no longer sufficiently naive to linger in fascination for minutes at a time over the sinuous curves of two bodies engaged in the typical 'fight,' or the galloping rider cutting across the surface of the screen."

But in 1948 a model as pure as that of the great comics of the silent era (Keaton, Chaplin, Langdon) intersected the evolution of the cinema: new and different ways of visualizing space appeared and these were European. First was the neoexpressionism of Robert Bresson's *Dames du bois de Boulogne:* "The fact that stylization in the expression of time has received greater attention than spatial construction is an indication of the distance that separates modern cinema from that of the 'great age' of the silent film." Second was the neorealism of Rossellini's *Paisan*, which "required . . . a certain richness of spatial expression, but in a very different sense than that of plastic distortion. Here the very choice of subject is fundamental: the themes of the black soldier led by the little shoeshine boy, the crossing of the Arno, the partisans wandering in the plain of the Pô river, correspond to an obsession whose very presence gives the anecdote the effectiveness of a myth."

Brigitte Bardot, Jack Palance, and Michel Piccoli in *Contempt*

The strength of the article obviously arises from the fact that Rohmer relies on the different uses of space that found their way into the first fifty years of the cinema: the use of space in Griffith and the Scandinavian directors (Sjöström and Stiller), the spatial distortion of German expressionism and its reinvention by Murnau, the development of Eisenstein's "operatic" convention. But it found the strongest evidence for its argument in a vaudeville comic, Buster Keaton. In Keaton's films, what serves as the source of laughter and the very rationale of the drama is simply the body's constant confrontations with its own spatial presence. Rohmer was able to articulate what would remain the secret invocation, the ideal of the New Wave, a secret that American cinema had innocently, but thoroughly, conveyed: the treatment of space, efficiency, and economy are intimately related.

The concept of movement as an act in itself breaks with the notion of action as seen in the Hollywood film. This new concept of movement characterizes the style of the New Wave in general, and is what finally distinguishes it from the American approach. The New Wave is a physical cinema where movement becomes the center of interest (*The 400 Blows*, *Le Signe du Lion*, *Breathless*, *Hiroshima, mon amour*, *Blue Jeans*, *Adieu Philippine*, etc.), and a moral cinema as well (Rohmer's *Moral Tales*, Resnais's *Muriel*, Demy's *Lola*, Godard's *Contempt*, Chabrol's *À double tour* and *Les Bonnes Femmes*), rather than a moralizing cinema.

This new cinema affected not only the form of the film but also its content. The famous expression "The tracking shot is a moral issue" should be understood on the basis of this notion of movement (whether of the camera, sound, a character, etc.). In

What Rohmer didn't yet understand at the time, and what Rossellini's subsequent films up to *Viaggio in Italia* would make glaringly obvious, was that Rossellinian cinema changed the very nature of space. Space was no longer something to be conquered as it was in the American cinema. In Rossellini, all recourse to the future was cut off; space was handed over to the present as an event that a news camera records, the characters submit to, and the spectator, the witness to the accident, observes. It is exposed to danger, imprisoned, and arouses uncertainty. Transformed into a field of view, space metaphorically becomes a firing range. Characters no longer have physical control over their conduct; they lose track of their goal and begin to wander. Forced to become aware of their status, to gauge the condition of their existence, and judge their behavior, characters are led toward a moral position. Rossellini filmed displaced persons, following the lead of their movements.

Breathless, whether or not Poiccard-Belmondo is stopped by the police has far less importance than his movements along the Champs-Élysées with Jean Seberg. The choreographic pleasure of watching their life together is more important than the necessarily stereotyped behavior of the police. In *The 400 Blows*, the movement of the child and the camera as they run toward the sea can't conclude with the word "End." It has to continue, accompany the young Doinel as he turns, freezes with the image, stares at the lens and looks us straight in the eye, forcing us, like Bergman's *Monika*, to react morally. In *Last Year at Marienbad*, movement is presented as a game, opening onto a complex and labyrinthine system.

Even if we look at them apart from the New Wave, it seems clear that Rohmer, Demy, Rivette, Rozier, Straub, Eustache, and even Pialet were interested in a concept of movement freed from an obsolete sense of

Jean-Paul Belmondo, *Breathless*

Claude Chabrol, *Brigitte et Brigitte* (Luc Moullet, 1966)

finality. The journey is richer through the encounters and unforeseen events that occur along the way than in its actual details. Movement altered the behavior of the characters and thus the way the actors portrayed them. (It is difficult to imagine an actor like Jean-Pierre Léaud outside the framework of the New Wave, be it French or foreign. The same is true of Belmondo, the quintessential New Wave actor.) The New Wave invented a new type of gesture that didn't operate according to traditional cinematic rules, offering the body a sense of freedom that, except by Renoir, had rarely been seen before, one which consisted not in becoming but in being.

1 "Le cinéma, art de l'espace" appeared in *Le Goût de la beauté*, a collection of Éric Rohmer's criticism. Paris: Éditions de l'Étoile and Flammarion, 1989.

Jean-Pierre Léaud, Françoise Lebrun, and Bernadette Lafont in
The Mother and the Whore

1960

- **L'EAU À LA BOUCHE**
- **PLEIN SOLEIL**
- **BREATHLESS**
- **EYES WITHOUT A FACE**
- **PARTY GIRL**
- **À DOUBLE TOUR**
- **LA DOLCE VITA**
- **LES BONNES FEMMES**
- **L'AVVENTURA**
- **SANSHO THE BAILIFF**
- **PSYCHO**
- **SHOOT THE PIANO PLAYER**

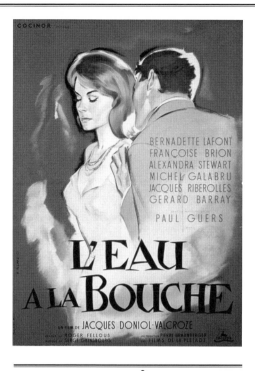

L'EAU À LA BOUCHE

Jacques Doniol-Valcroze

A CINAMATIC POINT OF VIEW

The originality of *L'Eau à la bouche*, the first important film from writer Jacques Doniol-Valcroze, can be attributed to the fact that cinema has betrayed literature to reveal the beauty of the world and characters who are accurately portrayed, in spite of the director and the clearly novelistic structure of the film. Doniol-Valcroze puts the written word on the back burner here and his vegetal camera focuses more on location than atmosphere. The osmosis between verb and image, fiction and reality, achieves a dialectical intensity that is infinitely more advanced than his predecessors and models. The primary reason is that Doniol-Valcroze has confidence in the cinema. In spite of his extremely literary background and his natural talent for being chic, like Rivette or Domarchi, like *L'Après-midi d'un faune* or the beginning of *The Stranger*, this disciple of Renoir and Visconti—the Renoir of *The River*, the Visconti of *Le Notti bianche*—looks, contemplates, then recreates. Words are not taken for granted, and the image doesn't maintain a respectful distance. We sense that the director always began from a purely cinematic point of view. ∎

Louis Marcorelles, *Cahiers du cinéma*, March 1960

PLEIN SOLEIL

René Clément

THE WORST CLICHÉS OF THE THEATER

Plein Soleil is a well-made film. There are interesting complications, and suspense, but the film is completely devoid of sensitivity, tenderness, or humor. René Clément doesn't like his heroes and isn't interested in them. For him, they aren't beings of flesh and blood, with weaknesses, anguish, and manias, but mathematical variables in a problem that needs to be solved. This inevitably results in unpleasant consequences.

The actors in *Plein Soleil* are badly directed and the director continuously falls back on the worst clichés of the theater. Although she is beautiful and endearing, Marie Laforêt's acting is a veritable anthology of hackneyed gestures: fear (fingers spread across her face), anguish (she wrings her hands nervously), etc.

Alain Delon is on the lookout. He glances slowly from right to left and left to right. The only actor who is direct, natural, and convincing is Maurice Ronet, who has obviously come a long way.

In spite of its ambiguous characters, who might have been fascinating, its love story, which might have been touching, and the overall feeling of the film, which could have been as suspenseful as *Vertigo*, René Clément has managed to come up with nothing more than a detective thriller that ends on a dramatic note. Clément has no doubt forgotten that Hitchcock's greatness lies not in his mastery of suspense but his concern for his characters. ■

Claude Choublier, *France-Observateur*, March 17, 1960

BREATHLESS

Jean-Luc Godard

A WILLINGNESS TO TAKE RISKS

Breathless was made in four weeks, without sound, using actual interior and exterior sets in Paris and Marseilles. Production costs were 4,500,000 francs, which is minimal when you realize that the producer had to pay the internationally well-known star Jean Seberg. The camera was generally handheld, operated mostly by the chief cameraman, and kept hidden in the storage compartment of a delivery bicycle driven by Godard to minimize the effect of camera and crew.

Michel Poiccard, the anarchist car thief, kills a policeman who is chasing him. In Paris he meets his American friend Patricia Franchini, and they become lovers again. He convinces her to go to Italy with him, but the police have discovered the identity of the murderer and hunt him down. Patricia betrays Michel, who is accidentally shot by the police.

There you have the plot of a perfect thriller. Godard initially wanted to make a commercial film along conventional lines. But in the end, due to laziness and a willingness to take risks, Godard disgarded everything except the overall framework

and the use of physical action.

Godard succeeds in convincing the viewer that this modern universe is a marvelous world full of beauty, even though it is as metallic and terrifying as science fiction. Jean Seberg is less "energetic" than she is in Preminger's films and more remote in the fragmentation of her being. ■

Luc Moullet, *Cahiers du cinéma*, April 1960

ARTIFICIAL AND MANIPULATIVE

A bunch of friends, with a bit of outside help, got together to make this film. Remember what Georges Sadoul said, "What talent!" "What energy!" "What skill!" Just as *Breathless* contains predestined murderers and professional informers, Jean-Luc Godard is a born filmmaker. The actual work, the apprenticeship, he's left to others. Gifted, special, he is the young hero of the cinematic elite.

Having said this, *Breathless* is one of the most artificial, most manipulative films around, and its structure is among the most banal. Godard has his hero say one thing one moment and its opposite a moment later, and presents this paradox as life's ultimate ambiguity. The film's style is similar. Godard "objectively" follows his characters using "dizzying" camera movements, being careful to eliminate any continuity between the various stages of

their journey. The film has a chaotic feel to it that is, presumably, indicative of the vitality of genius.

You can be certain, as the director and the "communist" critic quoted above noted, that the film's hero, once cleaned up and modernized, like the criminal in *Quai des Brumes*, is simply an aberration. The deserter of the thirties was part of a synthetic mythology but acceptable because he was perceived to be a leftist. The thug of the 1960s, who says he likes the police, and his girlfriend, who, according to Godard, fulfills her character by denouncing him to the cops, share a different mythology, at least as artificial but here abhorrent because it is right wing. The anarchist Gabin was made of the same mettle as the combatants in the International Brigades. The anarchist Belmondo is part of the same group that writes "Death to the Jews!" in the corridors of the subway, and makes spelling mistakes in doing so. ■

Louis Séguin, *Positif*, April 1960

REBEL WITHOUT A CAUSE?

No experienced editor could watch *Breathless* without trepidation: every other continuity shot is wrong. Like the use of dialog in literature, the spelling mistakes are not what's important. It's a question of style.

This is reflected in the film's own dialogues and plot, where tension is reinforced by cutting out the traditional effects used to create suspense. We sympathize more with the criminal being chased because he doesn't care that he's being hunted down. The dialogues themselves make use of everyday expressions; they avoid all "literary" allusions. The film appears to break completely with the brilliant dialogues of the thirties, where the actors' replies flew back and forth like a tennis ball in the Davis Cup match. In *Breathless* the characters move from one subject to another and do more talking than listening.

Truffaut and Chabrol provided some insurance for Godard, the former as screenwriter, the latter as "artistic and technical consultant." Their support was purely amicable, intended to reassure the film's backers. Godard could teach his friends something about energy and verve. Their first films were clumsy first steps compared to *Breathless*. Still, I prefer the sincerity of *Le Beau Serge* or *The 400 Blows* to this stupefying success, whose hero and plot fail to move me.

In *Breathless*, a sympathetic murderer hunted by the police wanders around a big city and meets the love of his life. He's preparing to take off for the happiness of parts unknown when he meets his maker. You can't escape destiny. I'm sure you're familiar with the story line. It's been used in American, French, Italian, and British cinema for the past twenty years. One more remake of our own *Quai des Brumes*. Godard would be the first to admit this. Still, I can't bring myself to like his two heroes. Unlike Prévert, who contrasted good and bad, Godard tries to show that better and worse are within us all. The actors he chose to make his point are very well cast. Belmondo, who is excellent here, plays the same character (including his name) that he played in Chabrol's *À double tour*. And it must have been no small feat to transform the cold fish Seberg plays in *Bonjour tristesse* into this lively, electrifying, and supple creature carried away by the torrent of events. As seductive as she may be, however, her character is no less "despicable" in the end. Some critics tried to find excuses for her character's behavior, but Godard discouraged them when he stated (to a film club audience) that, by ratting to the police, she had "emancipated" herself. As for his hero, he's right when he says "I like the cops," because conformity would require him to criticize them, as does the media in general. Someone near Godard stated that he hated Buñuel's conformism, which amounted to nothing more than attacking the police and the clergy. But what's good for the goose is good for the gander. This anti-conformism is worse than the worst conformity.

It would be wrong to say that Godard, in his first film, has simply managed to repackage old wine in a new bottle. He's gotten good mileage out of the dramatic situation. But, whether we like them or not, the characters are unconventional

and possess a rare gift: life. Godard has stated "I made the anarchist film I dreamed about." Fine. But this rebel is far from being a leftist. ∎

Georges Sadoul, *Les Lettres Françaises*, March 31, 1960

IMPROVISATION AND HASTE

Breathless is an extremely sophisticated film, and its structure is intentional. Since he's the director, Godard has chosen a car thief as his hero. This gentle young man, traveling from Marseilles to Paris, kills a policeman. He's a despicable yet fascinating character. Relaxed, cynical, slovenly. Uncultured. Without the least shadow of moral sense. He speaks badly and eats sloppily. He is complacent about the cowardice and disorder of his life. He affects the greatest contempt for women. He indiscriminately hates the French, Americans, La Fayette, and Maurice Chevalier. But he likes the cops, mostly out of a sense of bravado, although he has no qualms about killing them. He enjoys Mozart. He's the kind of hero that makes you grit your teeth. Romantic old ladies won't like him. But it would be pointless to grow indignant. Jean-Luc Godard, as often happens with directors at his age, has opted for provocation. His film, for example, contains no opening credits.

Filmed on a small budget with the help of his friends, using a handheld camera, this wonderfully daring film breaks all the pseudo-rules of film technique. The work of an amateur, *Breathless* is uneven, confused in parts where we sense it was improvised and shot quickly. ∎

Michel Aubriant, *Paris-Presse*, March 17, 1960

EYES WITHOUT A FACE

Georges Franju

MORE THAN A HORROR FILM

The publicity surrounding *Eyes Without a Face* has misrepresented it as a horror film. From the book, which is addressed to

individuals with nerves of steel, to the sophisticated weekly column by our gossipy Parisian Michèle Manceaux, all the ads predict miscarriages and mass fainting fits.

In an interview with *Europe I*, Franju responded "It's not just a horror film." When asked if he was worried about the film, he answered "I never laughed so much in my life."

Franju's work is the struggle of poetry against the gray concentration-camp world of comfortable values. In my opinion there is no other way to interpret the entire final sequence of the film. Behind the blank mask, without any perceptible emotion, Christine's eyes without a face are aware of the horror, and the scalpel that was intended for Altariba's face will instead be used to cut the straps on the operating table before being plunged into Alida Valli's neck. Christine, this white shadow in the underground chiaroscuro, frees the dogs, who carry out justice by administering to the eminent and respected surgeon the fate he inflicted on his victims. Franju has more confidence in dogs than in the police, as he noted in his interview with *Europe I*. "I don't like it when the police show up."

Against the darkness of night and the pale silhouettes of trees bent with anguish, highlighted against the black sky like a photographic negative, Poetry slips toward the perilous limits of Madness, accompanied by the flight of doves and the rustle of a white satin gown that is already from another world.

The everyday is in danger. Normalcy is imperiled and the fantastic reigns in this elegy of poetry. It's up to you to discover the heart-rending cries, muffled by the dark subterranean walls, or Juliette Mayniel's operation, or Edith Scob's ravaged face beneath the mask. As Franju himself remarked, "It's not just a horror film." ■
Marcel Oms, *Positif*, May 1960

PARTY GIRL

Nicholas Ray

THE TRIUMPH OF SILENCE

Party Girl is Nicholas Ray's masterpiece. With this film he appears to have reached the end of his search and has been able to flesh out the secret relationships and the silent language that unites beings and things. *Party Girl* is the triumph of silence, meditation, and self-control over noise and fury. This silence is of such importance, when compared to the outbursts of violence that punctuate the film, that *Party Girl* can only be fully appreciated in its original version.

Chicago, 1930. A famous lawyer has

gone to work for a powerful gang and through his clever stratagems succeeds in making them invulnerable to the law. During a party organized by the leader of the gang, he meets a dancer, who has been invited, along with some friends, as a party girl. They fall for one another. Yet these two individuals, degraded by life, conceal a secret wound and attempt to earn back, to regain their lost dignity. Although their fall results from an event in their childhood, for the first time in Nicholas Ray, the two heroes are no longer romantic children but adults, and they react like adults.

The entire film is based on the interplay between these two individuals, who carefully observe one another. What appear to be moments of rest, when the two lovers are alone together, and which occupy nearly half of the film, in reality produce great tension. Will they be able to earn one another's respect, win one another over? In contrast, the moments of physical violence that correspond to the gangsters' activities are seen by the viewer as moments of respite and relaxation. This internal tension explodes in moments of fury, the beauty of which has rarely been equaled on screen. The final scene incorporates elements of both violence and repose, culminating in a note of overall calm that affects the characters, their consciences, and their surroundings.

Like all great films, *Party Girl* is primarily about the search for beauty. Constructed around a sense of internal strife that seems to resolve the external violence, and an admirable use of color, especially the way the director uses purple and gold, *Party Girl* is at the same time a poem, a meditation, and undoubtedly a confession. ■
Jean Douchet, *Arts*, March 9, 1960

À DOUBLE TOUR

Claude Chabrol

ARMCHAIR ANARCHISM

Based on a novel by Stanley Ellin, Chabrol has made what he describes—with typical sardonic provocativeness—as the most

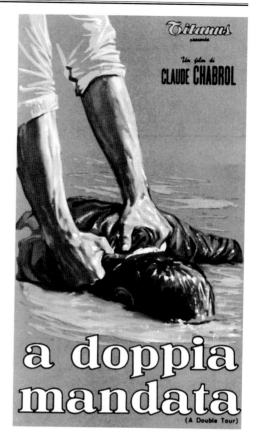

beautiful film he's ever seen. *À double tour* isn't the worst film I've ever seen, far from it. There have been many French films like this, with that French quality that was once in favor at the festivals, with all their psychological devices, overdone colors, and "powerful" dialogue. To fall from Delannoy to Chabrol, Jeanson to Gégauff hardly seems exciting. This armchair anarchism, redeemed by the final injunction to "Get the police right away," evokes a thousand reminiscences from films that Chabrol and his friends have castigated in the past. Audiences will quickly forget about *À double tour*, along with Chabrol's earlier films. Although *Hiroshima, mon amour* and even *The 400 Blows* may be worth seeing, and seeing again, the most committed partisans of *Le Beau Serge* willing to sit through this film a second time are in for a number of surprises. Remember, you heard it here first. ■
Paul-Louis Thirard, *Positif*, April 1960

LA DOLCE VITA

Federico Fellini

A WORLD OF DEAD SOULS

La Dolce Vita is a film that has been designed to thwart the viewer's expectations. The apparent lack of structure allows our interest to wander. Many of the sequences only take on meaning during the latter part of the film and seem to drag on forever (for example, the dinner party at Steiner's makes sense only after his death). The film makes no attempt to excite, distract, or even move viewers, but makes them feel uncomfortable, provokes a conscious sense of malaise intended to conclude in lucid and fruitful reflection.

Fellini presents some difficult questions to the viewer about the meaning of life, the impossibility of purity, the difficulty of communication (this theme is well developed in the film: the silent telephones, the conversations drowned out by music or the noise of the sea or the wind, the barrier of foreign languages, excessive restraint, inexhaustible but empty volubility, woman's direct communication with nature, her direct participation in nature so to speak, sexual love as the only means of communication and understanding between men and women, etc.). Fellini doesn't

provide us with an answer, doesn't even suggest one. He reveals our solitude to us and delivers us to a world of dead, desperate, and liberated souls. ■

Pierre Billard, *Cinéma 60,* June 1960

MISSING A SCRIPT

To my mind the greatest, the most outstanding merit of this film lies in its lack of a screenplay. Fellini and two assistants for a three hour film isn't much; in Italy it's nothing at all. Normally four people work to produce one and a quarter hours of script. Four screenwriters for every director. Now that's what the cinema needs. In physics the people involved are all laboratory researchers. Only cinema prostitutes its instruments, its research equipment, to the lowest form of literature. Making a film generally consists in fabricating a "story" that will please a backer. Once this has been taken care of, the only thing left is to waste some film. We end up where we should have begun; we start with something that should never have existed in the first place. Fellini must have gone through this. His earlier films, commercial films full of "ideas," prove this point, with a few (bankrupt) exceptions. What's surprising is that he managed to succeed and, once he obtained his first blank check from the bankers, immediately went back to being

the director of *The White Sheik* and *Variety Lights*. ■

Jean-Louis Laugier, *Cahiers du cinéma,* June 1960

LES BONNES FEMMES

Claude Chabrol

PURITY OF VISION

Chabrol's latest film is not only his masterpiece but the culmination of the new French cinema. I don't want to belittle the supporters of *Breathless* (of which I'm one) but was Godard's film really the culmination of the New Wave? An auteurist film, yes, but are auteurist directors the only ones responsible for advances in film? It seems that while they benefit from the progress that has been made, they don't determine its direction or, if they do, only to a very limited extent. *Breathless* is more about Godard than it is a modern film, while *Les Bonnes Femmes* is obviously modern. Godard uses cinema while Chabrol promotes it. Chabrol may have "nothing to say," but having a message isn't, after all, a necessary basis for being a filmmaker. He may be driven instead by the simple need to observe the

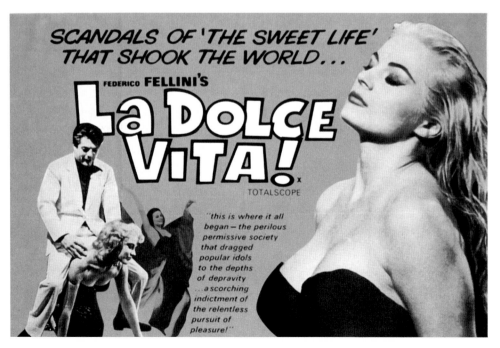

world around him. Chabrol's mise-en-scène is nothing other than this act of looking. A director's greatest skill is his ability to bring his purity of vision to the screen. Chabrol's entire career can be summed up as the history of this purification. ∎

André-S. Labarthe, *Cahiers du cinéma*, June 1960

AMUSING BUT NOT CONVINCING

You may recall the characters in *Les Cousins*. They were indolent and seemed to have little on their mind. They daydreamed, and the viewer followed these spoiled children and their dreams. It was charming and relaxing, since no one bothered to find out if Chabrol actually had any ideas. But the cousins in this film are a bizarre pair of young women, who dream, get bored, chase happiness while gossiping in their empty store, and, to distract themselves, spend their evenings flirting with strangers: dancing, fancy cars, music halls, pools, small restaurants, and walks in the park. Chabrol follows the two friends around Paris and lets loose a pack of poor toothless animals on their trail, the kind who hang around nightclubs trying to figure out how to get these attractive young women into bed—or possibly a bed of ferns to strangle them. None of it is very serious, and while Chabrol's film is certainly amusing, it's hardly convincing. ∎

Bruno Gay-Lussac, *L'Express*, April 28, 1960

THE NASTY SOAP OPERA CONTINUES

There's not much to like in *Les Bonnes Femmes*, a film that pretty much misses the mark. The nasty little soap opera continues. I expected more of Claude Chabrol. His only excuse is the poor screenplay. The script is ridiculous, pretentious; the artificial dialogues are grating, and make the worst writers of an earlier generation of filmmakers look good by comparison.

Chabrol is free to prefer this style and stick to it of course. But criticizing viewers who dislike the film is hardly a sign of moral refinement. The young director has

forgotten his debt to the public, whom he pretends to despise, although he desperately needs them in his audience.

But let's take a look at the film. Even though the plot is thrown off balance by the exhausting bravado of the dialogue and is seriously inconsistent, you can vaguely make out the author's intention. Intentions, rather. Chabrol tries to portray four young Parisian women of modest means selected at random. At the same time he wants to portray the desperate monotony of their lives. They are always waiting for something to happen—for work to end, for a successful romance.

It's hardly a new idea, but an acceptable one. What is strange about this film, however, is that the four heroines work in a store on the Boulevard Beaumarchais (selling electrical appliances) under the supervision of a miserly boss, who, in spite of his miserliness, seems to have hired them to do absolutely nothing. No customer ever shows up in this store, with the exception of an elderly gentleman who has come to buy a battery. Out of the nine protagonists in the film, six of them are either contemptible or mediocre. This is the currently fashionable percentage among our young amoral "moralists." I'm sure Chabrol would respond, "What! We're just showing you society as it really

is." Excuse me? We're shown an aspect of humanity that no doubt exists, but so does its opposite. And this opposite apparently holds no interest for new French film, nor its statistics. To paint the reality of the world, it makes sense to paint it in its entirety. The repeated insistence on the world's worst elements eventually turns the criticism into a kind of indifference, or worse. The way in which auteurist directors describe boredom is relatively successful in the following sense: viewers are soon fed up with the boredom they experience in watching their films. ∎

Louis Chauvet, *Le Figaro*, April 28, 1960

L'AVVENTURA

Michelangelo Antonioni

A HYMN TO WOMAN

Finally Michelangelo Antonioni has found his true place in Parisian film: he's one of the best. By the end of the year, we'll be talking about *L'Avventura* the way we talked about Ingmar Bergman in 1958 and Fellini and *La Strada* in 1955. Everyone is talking about this film. Some see it as a revelation, a shock, a painful wound. Others grow indignant, speak of its mystification, boredom, incoherence, and coldness. The discussions are always passionate. Proof that the work is of considerable importance.

L'Avventura has been "dedramatized" in the sense that in trying to represent man in the grip of modern drama, the director refuses to let himself ever show this. Here "an enormous drama hovers over contemporary man, terrifying normal beings with its endless perspectives, against which our intimate and private dramas appear meaningless." This results in the director's tendency to "dedramatize," "without even being aware of it" (Antonioni).

Like Bergman, but with a style that is completely different and more substantial, Antonioni has turned nearly all of his films into a hymn to woman. In *L'Avventura* the blonde Monica Viti is always captivating when on screen, and the character she portrays is not easily forgotten. But she is a passive creature (unlike her character in *Le Amiche*, for example) and she experiences life passively rather than living it for herself. All the dramatic action, every new direction in this spiritual and physical adventure is determined by Him, not Her, through his actions and his speech.

About this couple Antonioni has said, "I understand the man, with his vices and virtues, since they are part of many men I've known, including myself no doubt, but I especially love the woman. Maybe because I understand her better. I was raised by women." ∎

Georges Sadoul, *Les Lettres Françaises*, September 23, 1960

SANSHO THE BAILIFF

Kenji Mizoguchi (1954)

A DESCENDENT OF HOKUSAI AND HIROSHIGE

The coastal horizon is streaked with pink. The fog-covered lakes are tinged with misfortune. Sunlight flickers between two steamy pools of water. Mizoguchi treats the region around Kyoto the way Ford treats Monument Valley, or Sternberg a China that has been fabricated in the studio. These shades of gray, this flat luminosity illuminates the image from within and marks the director, a would-be painter, as a descendant of Hokusai and Hiroshige. Throughout his career Mizoguchi has always managed to cleverly "expose" reality. Plastic splendor is well rendered by his subtle editing, which cuts his scenes with regret, blends his soft colors into the background. His stationary camera stretches the image as it pans, and imposes a frame that is more attentive to surface than depth.

This simplicity of vision is reflected in Mizoguchi's way of telling a story, which is both highly mannered and extremely refined. He discounts the horrifying detail

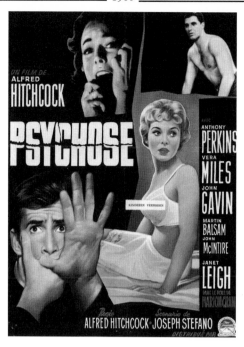

with an off-screen camera movement at the last second, as though excusing himself for making a suicide (Anju walks slowly into the water to drown herself) the climax of the film. As incongruous as this seems, her death becomes the visual focus of a scene in which the water's surface, closing around the victim in slow, concentric circles, brings peace and repose. Mizoguchi's simplicity is also found in his themes, where a good sentiment signifies a great sentiment, providing it condemns violence, reflects love—whether passionate, filial, or fraternal—and fills itself with pity, generosity, and sacrifice. ∎

Roger Tailleur, *Positif*, January 1961

PSYCHO

Alfred Hitchcock

A FEW GOOD SCENES

For the benefit of those viewers who haven't yet been exposed to this new form of media rape, I'll reveal a few secrets about this film: Anthony Perkins has murdered his aged mother and stuffed her. Apparently not very well, since she looks like a mummy and scares the hell out of people. This clever young man's split

personality pushes him to identify with the deceased and, out of jealousy, murder any young woman who sexually excites him.

This stylish horror film contains several good scenes, and if you don't figure out the plot during the first half hour, your enjoyment may parallel that of the director who, from a sidewalk in the film, follows Janet Leigh with an appreciative glance. ∎

Louis Séguin, *Positif*, January 1961

A VOYAGE TOWARD DEATH

Hitchcock's work, in one way or another, always reflects the duel between Light and Dark, Unity and Duality. The very first scene of *Psycho*, which follows an abstract title sequence by Saul Bass, reveals an immense expanse of land surrounding an ordinary city, lit by scorching sunlight. Subtitles indicate the location, time, and date. This light is contrasted in the second scene with an absolute blackness, in which we immerse ourselves along with the camera, before a room, a bed, and two lovers slowly come into view. In two scenes Hitchcock has expressed his theme: *Psycho* is about the eternal and the finite, existence and nothingness, life and death, seen in their naked truth. There is nothing

pleasing in *Psycho*, which is the opposite of *Vertigo*. Hitchcock's earlier film was constructed around seduction, artifice, the surface of appearances, and attraction. Here, everything is based on crudeness (no detail has been spared in portraying this), unadorned faces, sharp editing (it cuts like a knife). This voyage toward death is terrifying, and it terrifies because of its harshness. ∎

Jean Douchet, *Cahiers du cinéma*, November 1960

SHOOT THE PIANO PLAYER

François Truffaut

A MORAL AUTOBIOGRAPHY

Truffaut is a remarkable scriptwriter, perhaps the best we have. The screenplay for *Shoot the Piano Player* is irreproachable, in spite of its casual air. It is structured around a very touching central character, played brilliantly by Charles Aznavour. There are three colorful and appealing brothers, three women (a servant with a big heart, a selfless whore, and a wife of irreproachable moral character), and a handful of funny (Claude Mansart), sublime, or remarkable minor characters (Serge Davy as the bistro owner). The exquisite dialogues are lifelike (the soliloquy by Daniel Boulanger, the bumbling gangster, is wonderful); there's some very original music; and a handful of admirable sequences shot in a snow-covered landscape are worthy of the best of Nicholas Ray (*On Dangerous Ground*). There is one scene, the shot of the dead Marie Dubois, her face flecked with snow, that is sublime. Her face, shown upside down, presents the terrifying tranquillity of death, a calm that points to the irremediable loss that follows.

Shoot the Piano Player is the story of a gangster, a bourgeois drama. The fact that the director has mixed genres in the film is of little importance once we realize that, behind the cleverly structured plot, Truffaut has engaged the audience in a dialogue that speaks to his true interests: timidity, friendship, the love of women, relationships. In this sense *Shoot the Piano Player* extends the moral autobiography begun with *The 400 Blows*. The reason I prefer the more recent film is its sense of anarchy, which is missing in *The 400 Blows*, noticeably so. ∎

Jean Domarchi, *Arts*, November 30, 1960

UNIVERSE OF INNOCENCE

There's a certain way of looking at people with a mixture of curiosity, perplexity, and sensitivity, the way a child looks at them. A certain way of looking, looking from another point of view, of not giving details the same importance an adult would give them, a way of refusing to be serious, and discovering, beneath the surface of seriousness, the truly grave. A certain way of allowing ourselves to be astonished, or to be moved, to laugh, and to laugh openly.

Innocence. The world of innocence, the world of children, an uncertain world, scornful, farcical, but extremely impressionable, instinctively clairvoyant, and wonderfully lucid. It is the apprehension of another dimension. *Shoot the Piano Player* is a thriller told by a child. Everything is lost in dream. The sordid is obscured by poetry, a poetry that models life to suit its own needs, without cruelty.

Charles Aznavour, wonderfully directed, is a timid soul who wants to lead a wild life. He withdraws, pulls back. He's a fearful man, afraid of others, who are afraid of him. He is unsure of anything and feels threatened, threatened by the world around him. He's a tender soul who feels condemned by his tenderness, who feels like a target, the center of the circle. The circle's closing in on him, and he doesn't know what to do. On top of this Truffaut has written some remarkable dialogue for *Shoot the Piano Player*, probably the best in today's cinema. ∎

Pierre Marcabru, *Combat*, November 29, 1960

LITTLE CONCERN FOR DETAIL

No one can claim that *Shoot the Piano Player* does a very good job at thumbing its nose at traditional cinema. The director does a pretty good job, however, in ridiculing the audience, but I don't think he's chosen the right time to do it.

Truffaut's first film, *The 400 Blows*, was filled with sincerity and tenderness. There's no trace of either in his current film. Nor is there any trace of the poetic charm that was no doubt the result of the soft rhythm of that earlier film's imagery, which made it easier to overlook the clumsiness of a young narrator.

In *Shoot the Piano Player* there's no narrator at all. The story? It exists on paper and is based on a pop thriller. You can piece the story together after the film is over if you have enough patience. Truffaut obviously has little concern for details. He extracts them from the plot and disintegrates them. Why bother even writing a screenplay under such conditions? As for its disintegration, it appears like film today is making progress in reverse. No risk of an atom bomb from this group. *Duck Soup*, we are told, was a masterpiece compared to *Zazie dans le métro*. Now *Zazie* is a masterpiece compared to *Shoot the Piano Player*. To the extent we can make them out, the dialogues are terrible.

Let's talk a bit about "pure" cinema, if you can call it that. The film is mystifying and its secret—assuming it has one—is mysterious. The lighting changes all the time; the style and pacing curtails our emotional involvement and makes it difficult to even take an interest in the story. The hero experiences a tragedy whose bitterness the film goes to great lengths to demonstrate. The gangsters in pursuit of the hero are straight out of the burlesque tradition. But it's the audience that gets shot down. Why? What exactly is Truffaut trying to ridicule? What's he trying to affirm? ∎

Louis Chauvet, *Le Figaro*, November 28, 1960

History of the New Wave

My Life to Live (Jean-Luc Godard, 1962)

The term *New Wave* appeared for the first time in the October 3, 1957, issue of *L'Express*, entitled "Report on Today's Youth." It was used as the title of an article by Françoise Giroud, a journalist for the weekly magazine. In June 1958 she published a book entitled *The New Wave: Portrait of Today's Youth*, which dealt, not with cinema but with the need for change within French society. The book's purpose was primarily political and was intended to foster Pierre Mendès France's platform. With his failure, the expression fell into disuse. In February 1958 Pierre Billard used it in *Cinéma 58*, applying it for the first time to describe the desire for a renewal of French film. But the expression didn't really gain wide acceptance until the 1959 Cannes Film Festival, where it was used to refer to the many young directors present. By 1960 it was known throughout the world.

We can date the birth of the New Wave itself to 1956, the year when *Coup du berger*, a short by Jacques Rivette, produced by Pierre Braunberger, was filmed. The role played by Films de la Pléiade—the small production studio run by Braunberger, a former producer of Renoir, Buñuel, Clair, and others—was central to the renewal of French cinema. Braunberger had been interested in the young staff of *Cahiers du cinéma* ever since the meetings of the Objectif 49 film club and the Festival du Film Maudit in Biarritz. He produced the first films by Rouch, Resnais, Truffaut, Godard, Pialat, Reichenbach, Doniol-Valcroze,

Rivette, Lelouch, and others.[1] Their collaboration, however, didn't really start until 1955. François Reichenbach, his cousin, showed him a short film shot in Morocco under difficult conditions with some fast American film. As an experienced producer, Braunberger sensed the economic and aesthetic potential of the new film stock: location shooting would be easier and expenses reduced. The same film was used by Reichenbach that year to make *Impressions de New York* and this convinced Braunberger to help the young critics he admired become filmmakers.

Rivette was the first to test the water. He shot the twenty-minute *Coup de Berger* in Claude Chabrol's apartment (Chabrol had been delegated producer) for the price of the film stock. The film was the beginning of a series of shorts made by the writers associated with

Tous les garçons s'appellent Patrick (1957), which was based on a screenplay by Rohmer, and *Charlotte et son jules* (1958). Then there was Truffaut.

In 1957 Truffaut married Madeleine Morgenstern, the daughter of Ignace Morgenstern (the wealthy director of Cocinor, a group of film companies). Truffaut asked Marcel Berbert, Morgenstern's vice-president to help him start his own production company, with his father-in-law's company serving as guarantor. Berbert helped him set up Les Films du Carrosse, named in recognition of Jean Renoir's *The Golden Coach*. In the summer of 1957, in Nîmes, he shot his first "true" short film, *Les Mistons*, based on a story by Maurice Pons. Pleased with the success of the film, Braunberger suggested that he make another short. Truffaut would choose the subject. At the time there had been catastrophic flooding in and around Paris, and Truffaut used this as an opportunity to make a short comedy with Jean-Claude Brialy and Caroline Dim. For some reason Truffaut had difficulty following Rossellini's lead in blending journalism and fiction, and he turned the project over to Godard. Godard

René Gilson and Jean-Pierre Léaud in *Le Père Noël a les yeux bleus* (Jean Eustache, 1967)

Du côté de Robinson (Jean Eustache, 1964)

Cahiers du cinéma. Some of them had already made their first films, but with questionable results: Rivette (*Aux quatre coins, Le Quadrille*), Truffaut (*Une visite*), Godard (*Opération Béton, Une femme coquette*). However *Le Sabotier du Val de Loire* (1955) by Jacques Demy (produced by George Rouquier) and the shorts by Éric Rohmer, shot in 16 mm (*Bérénice* in 1954, *La Sonate à Kreuzer* in 1956), are fairly successful. But Rivette's new short, which was made under semi-professional conditions, transformed the situation. He energized the staff of the *Cahiers* and proved to them that it was possible to succeed in film. With the exception of Claude Chabrol, each of them subsequently made one or more shorts of modest interest: Rohmer with *Véronique et son cancre* (1958), Godard with

felt no obligation to follow Truffaut's script, however, and created a discontinuous story, with a commentary that was both lively and innovative. The editing was abrupt and openly broke with contemporary conventions, which were scrupulously followed by the industry at large. The film was *Une historie d'eau*, unquestionably the most original, the most New Wave in spirit of all the short films produced at the time.

There were a number of other short films produced during this period: *Le Bel Indifférent* (1957) by Jacques

Demy, *Pourvu qu'on ait l'ivresse* (1958) by Jean-Daniel Pollet, and Jacques Rozier's fourth short film, *Blue Jeans* (1958). These were followed by first films from Maurice Pialet (*Janine*, 1961), Jean-Marie Straub (*Machorka-Muff*, 1963, which was shot in Germany when Straub was charged with desertion for refusing to fight in the Algerian War), and Jean Eustache (*Du côté de Robinson*, 1964, and *Le Père Noël a les yeux bleus*, 1965, shown together as *Les Mauvaises Fréquentations*). The New Wave also had a documentary side. This was represented by Franju (*Le Théâtre National Populaire*, 1956), Resnais (*Toute la mémoire du monde*, 1956, *Le Chant du Styrène*, 1958), Marker (*Dimanche à Pékin*, 1956, *Lettre de Sibérie*, 1958), Demy (*Ars*, 1959), Pialat (*L'amour existe*, 1960), Varda (*Ô saison,*

cutting production costs. In his office he had two scripts, *Les Cousins* and *Le Beau Serge*; he started with the latter, the less difficult of the two. The film received a prize from the CNC for quality. But Chabrol was dismissed by the profession as an upstart who broke the rules of good filmmaking, and the film was prevented from representing France at Cannes. So Chabrol took the film to rue d'Antibes and screened it on his own. *Le Beau Serge* was well received and rights were sold to two or three foreign distributors. Between his subsidy and the international sales, Chabrol had enough money to finance *Les Cousins*, even before *Le Beau Serge* had found a distributor in France.

Du côté de la côte (Agnès Varda, 1958)

Toute la mémoire du monde
(Alain Resnais, 1956)

ô châteaux, 1957, *Opéra-Mouffe*, 1958, *Du côté de la côte*, 1958), and the small format films by Pierre Kast, which spanned the entire decade (the first, entitled *Les Charmes de l'existence*, 1950, was co-directed by Jean Grémillon).

By 1958 there had been films by Alexandre Astruc, Roger Vadim, Louis Malle (*Ascenseur pour l'échafaud*, 1957, at the time considered practically avant-garde), and Pierre Kast (*Un amour de poche*). But Chabrol was the first of the *Cahiers'* group of young writers to plunge headlong into feature films. Chabrol had married well and had the means to finance his first film on his own, using an inheritance he had received from his wife's grandmother and sharply

Le Joli Mai (Chris Marker, 1962)

Toute la mémoire du monde

The transition from writer to director had all the trappings of a collective activity. (Future detractors of the New Wave were right on this point: it did involve a group of friends storming a fortress. But unlike the many self-serving scoundrels so common in the industry, this group was young and enthusiastic, united in their singular belief that film was an art and in their admiration for the filmmakers who served that art.) Within the small group that formed the core of *Cahiers du cinéma*, they all felt that the moment had arrived and impatiently prepared to enter the arena. This in turn created a strong sense of enthusiasm and solidarity among them. Rivette, the Joan of Arc of the group, who was frustrated at not having led the charge, borrowed eighty thousand francs from the *Cahiers'* account and boldly began filming *Paris nous appartient* in the summer of 1958. Chabrol made his first two films back to back, and Godard finished *Charlotte et son jules*. When the credits for these films rolled by, the same names appeared on screen: actors (Jean-Paul Belmondo, Gérard Blain, Bernadette Lafont,

Gérard Blain, Les Cousins (Claude Chabrol, 1959)

Paris nous appartient (Jacques Rivette, 1958-1961)

Jean-Claude Brialy), screenwriters (Paul Gegauff, Jean Gruault), assistants and camera operators (Charles Bitsch, Claude de Givry).

Truffaut later wrote "The young directors who were able to get the money from their families—this was the case with Louis Malle, Chabrol, and me—made the first films of the New Wave. The success of these first films enabled those who weren't able to capitalize their films right away to obtain funding from small, opportunistic producers. Within two years those at the *Cahiers* who

wanted to make films did so. These films were made under the same conditions as *Hiroshima, mon amour*, which is to say they anticipated the worst. They were made for so little money, generally three or four hundred thousand francs, that even a limited number of screenings paid for their production costs."

Truffaut was right to abandon criticism, and for his first attempt he shot *The 400 Blows*, which was based on his own adolescence. Ignace Morgenstern produced his son-in-law's film for four-hundred thousand francs, a small amount of money compared to the cost of a conventional French feature. In his film Truffaut entered the world of childhood and grasped its truth. In one sense, *The 400 Blows* owes as much to the films the young director admired (*Zero for Conduct*, *Germany Year Zero*) as those he disliked. The child is not supplanted by an adult

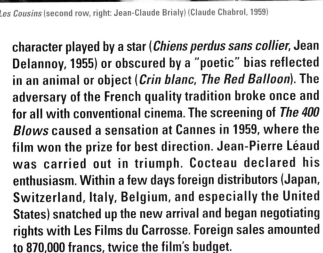

Les Cousins (second row, right: Jean-Claude Brialy) (Claude Chabrol, 1959)

character played by a star (*Chiens perdus sans collier*, Jean Delannoy, 1955) or obscured by a "poetic" bias reflected in an animal or object (*Crin blanc*, *The Red Balloon*). The adversary of the French quality tradition broke once and for all with conventional cinema. The screening of *The 400 Blows* caused a sensation at Cannes in 1959, where the film won the prize for best direction. Jean-Pierre Léaud was carried out in triumph. Cocteau declared his enthusiasm. Within a few days foreign distributors (Japan, Switzerland, Italy, Belgium, and especially the United States) snatched up the new arrival and began negotiating rights with Les Films du Carrosse. Foreign sales amounted to 870,000 francs, twice the film's budget.

In *Paris-Match* and big circulation American magazines, the media spread the word about the bomb

Truffaut had dropped on Cannes. At the Cannes film festival in 1959, the "New Wave" became a sensation. The whole world was talking about it. The "youth" phenomenon carried everything in its wake. The "real" professionals in the industry were suddenly in the position of has-beens. Doniol-Valcroze wrote in *Cahiers du cinéma*, "The door that had been split by blows from Chabrol, Franju, Rouch, Reichenbach, and other like-minded souls ... suddenly

the phenomenon, and the primary targets were the New Wave's best and only true representatives.

In Cannes, Truffaut met Georges de Beauregard, a bold, interesting producer on the verge of bankruptcy. Like his colleagues he had come to Cannes to find that rare gem that would put him back in the black. Truffaut had told him about Jean-Luc Godard, who, sensing the importance of what was taking place in Cannes, quickly

Patrick Auffay and Jean-Pierre Léaud in *The 400 Blows*

Jean-Pierre Léaud, Albert Rémy, and Claire Maurier in *The 400 Blows*

Jean-Pierre Léaud, *The 400 Blows*

gave way and a future began." Conventional producers began to question the system and frantically began searching for anything that resembled, even remotely, a young director. Within four years nearly 170 new directors had made their first film, but that was as far as most of them went. Their numbers, however, had a negative effect on the New Wave, and by the end of 1960 tradition had reestablished itself. It became fashionable to denigrate

came down from Paris, borrowing the money for the ticket from the *Cahiers'* petty cash fund. Godard proposed several projects, including one Truffaut had come up with that was based on a story he had seen in a newspaper and from which he had prepared a four page synopsis. It was called *Breathless*. Beauregard liked the idea. To reduce the film's cost, Truffaut sold the rights for 100,000 francs. Godard was an unknown, however, and as a guaranty, Beauregard demanded that Godard's friends, now well-known, appear in the credits.

Truffaut was credited with the screenplay and Chabrol was "artistic advisor," although he had practically never set foot on the set. *Breathless* was to be the only film by Godard that was really successful on its own, without the support of major stars.

Because it was modern and innovative, the film served as a kind of manifesto, illustrating the theory and practice of the New Wave. At the same time it maintained a link to a classical film heritage. Godard wanted to recreate a well-established and much loved tradition (that

is reflected in the film's direction, which overturned nearly all the principles of good filmmaking. Godard's film revolutionized cinematic style, and forever changed the history of cinema, dividing it into two epochs: before and after *Breathless*.

At this time Chabrol, with the success of his first film behind him, came to the assistance of his less fortunate friends. With Truffaut he helped Jacques Rivette finish *Paris nous appartient*. Begun in 1958 under difficult conditions, the film was still unfinished a year later.

Jess Hahn, *Le Signe du Lion* (Éric Rohmer, 1959-1962)

Jean Seberg, *Breathless*

Jean-Paul Belmondo, Jean-Luc Godard, and Georges de Beauregard around 1960 in Saint-Germain-des-Prés

Jean Seberg and Jean-Paul Belmondo, *Breathless*

of Preminger and Walsh), using a French–American couple with little in common. The man is obsessed with death, reads Lenin, listens to Mozart's concerto for clarinets, (which he composed shortly before his death), sees a man die on the street, and has a presentiment of his own impending end. The woman never thinks of death at all. Her approach to life is psychological, his poetic. They use the same words but give them different meanings. This artificial moral connection between Michel and Patricia

Rivette was able to shoot the remaining scenes in 1959, then began the long process of editing and synching, which lasted until 1961. Chabrol also helped Rohmer make *Le Signe du Lion*, but both films were commercial failures and the accountant ran off with the remaining funds. Chabrol found himself without a production company and was forced to turn elsewhere. He developed a strategy of financing that turned out to be highly successful. Drawing as little attention to himself as possible when directing his films, he made it a point of honor to control his budget in such a way that he would never cause problems for a producer. In return, he expected his producers to completely finance his films, which freed Chabrol from wasting time and energy looking for funding. Chabrol's strategy, which was modeled after that used in the traditional film industry, enabled him to make some 50 films in a period of 38 years, beginning in 1960. He was as prolific as Hitchcock, Ford, and others working with large studios.

Truffaut, who had been eager to turn Les Films du Carrosse into a kind of New Wave studio, lowered his ambitions considerably. After the success of *The 400 Blows* (450,000 tickets sold), the first films he produced (by Claude de Givray and other friends) were failures and his own second film, *Shoot the Piano Player* (1960, 70,000 tickets sold), never caught on. The company's financial

directors but of all contemporary artists, in using and manipulating the media, as a man of instinct and spontaneity he displayed an aversion for long-term management. He worked stroke by stroke, film by film. Initially, however, like Truffaut and Chabrol, he attempted to develop a close knit community around himself. With *Breathless*, he was able to save Georges de Beauregard from bankruptcy; Beauregard, impressed and grateful, not only produced Godard's next six films but gave him complete artistic freedom in producing his friends' work. Godard quickly transformed de Beauregard's company into

Shoot the Piano Player (François Truffaut, 1960) with Boby Lapointe in the cen

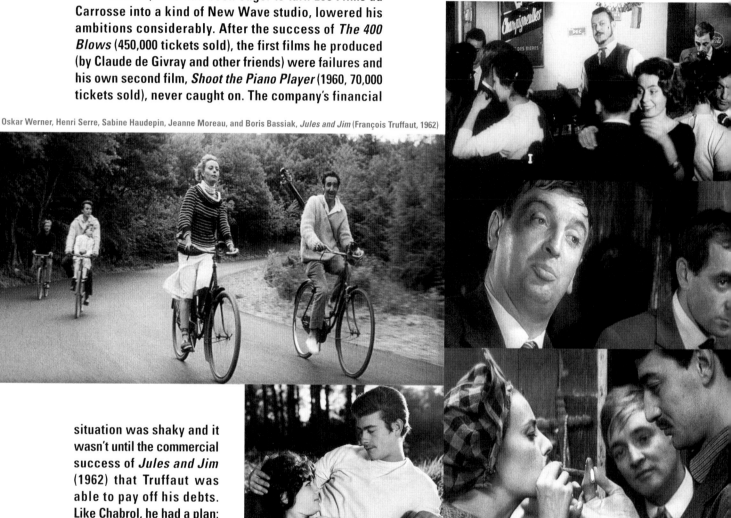

Oskar Werner, Henri Serre, Sabine Haudepin, Jeanne Moreau, and Boris Bassiak, *Jules and Jim* (François Truffaut, 1962)

Stefania Sabatini and Jean-Claude Aimini, *Adieu Philippine* (Jacques Rozier, 1960–1963)

Albert Remy and Charles Aznevour, *Shoot the Piano Player*
Jeanne Moreau, Oscar Werner, and Henri Serre, *Jules and Jim*

situation was shaky and it wasn't until the commercial success of *Jules and Jim* (1962) that Truffaut was able to pay off his debts. Like Chabrol, he had a plan: he made it a rule to produce only his own films and referred any projects sent to him to other producers (Pierre Braunberger, Anatole Dauman, Mag Bodard, and Georges de Beauregard). Truffaut managed Les Films du Carrosse with intelligence, caution, and skill. He was careful to keep all his own films in the catalog (including those financed with American capital, with the exception of *Fahrenheit 451*) and got by with a small administrative structure, which, free of outside interference, assured him total independence.

Godard's situation was somewhat different. Though he was the most astute, not only of the New Wave

a receptive environment for the New Wave. He produced the first films by Jacques Demy (*Lola*) and Jacques Rozier (*Adieu Philippine*), two of the most typical films of the New Wave. A few years later, however, de Beauregard's company again, and not surprisingly, ran into financial difficulties.

The decline of the New Wave's media success began in 1960. The successive failures of *Shoot the Piano Player*, *A Woman is a Woman* (65,000 tickets), *Godelureaux* (53,000), and *Lola* (35,000) turned the young directors into ideal scapegoats, guilty of the public's disaffection with the New Wave. The press reproached them for their "intellectual and boring" films. Even the weekly magazine *Arts*, with the arrival of the cosmopolitan Jacques Lanzmann, swung to the other side. At the same time the old guard believed it was exacting revenge with a string of successful films and Michel Audiard's incisive scripts. Truffaut resumed the defense of his friends Godard, Rivette, and Rozier. Trying to explain this change in attitude toward the New Wave, Truffaut wrote in a 1967 issue of *Cahiers du cinéma,*

to make your first film, based on your own life, by the time you're 35—we see that it was tremendously rich. It unexpectedly delivered everything it promised and inspired similar movements in nearly every country of the world. The New Wave was born in 1959 and by 1960 was despised. It had a certain prestige with the public for about a year. The turning point, the transition from praise to denigration, came with the release of *Rue des prairies*,[2] which the press described as an 'anti-New Wave' film. 'Jean Gabin settles his account with the New Wave.' It was then that the demagogy began. The journalists who

Anouk Aimée, *Lola* (Jacques Demy, 1961)

"The other evening on television I listened to a vague polemic between Claude Mauriac and Melville. The only time they agreed, it was to tell the audience, 'Of course, the New Wave was disappointing.' They then went on to other things, as if they had presented us with some self-evident truth. I was shocked by their behavior. If we take a closer look at what the New Wave meant at its origin—

had launched the movement decided to provide the public with the clichés they wanted to hear and nothing else. Before *Rue des prairies*, when we were interviewed—Jean-Luc, Resnais, Malle, myself and others—we said, 'The New Wave doesn't exist, it doesn't mean anything.' But later, we had to change, and ever since that moment I've affirmed my participation in the movement. Now, in

1967, we are proud to have been and to remain part of the New Wave, just as one is proud to have been a Jew during the Occupation."

While the directors joined ranks, they continued to work individually to maintain their financial independence. In 1961–1962 a new production company was founded by a young man of twenty, Barbet Schroeder, called Les Films du Losange. Like other young men of the period, he frequented the Cinémathèque française. Schroeder wanted to experiment with production before directing, so that he could understand how the system worked. Strongly influenced by Rohmer, whom he greatly admired, Schroeder would eventually aid

Barbet Schroeder in *La Boulangère de Monceau* (Éric Rohmer, 1963)

To obtain financing and get the company on its feet, Schroeder mortgaged one of his mother's paintings, a Nolde. Rohmer joined him, contributing *La Boulangère de Monceau* and *La Carrière de Suzanne*, becoming one of the principal shareholders. For a long time, the films provided no returns—other than complete creative freedom. But eventually, they were successful and with them Les Films du Losange, which soon became the most important independent production company in France. In his own way Rohmer became even better at financing than Truffaut.

The first two Moral Tales, however, weren't financially profitable. As a short and medium-length film, they were too long to accompany a standard feature. As

La Carrière de Suzanne
(Éric Rohmer, 1963)

La Carrière de Suzanne

the director. After the failure of the remarkable *Le Signe du Lion*, Rohmer was in financial difficulty and unable to shoot his next film. He had returned to *Cahiers du cinéma*, where he received a salary as editor in chief, running the magazine during the day and in his spare time shooting his first Moral Tale, *La Boulangère de Monceau*. Schroeder decided to help him, and Rohmer offered him the principal role.

In spite of his age, Schroeder knew this was an opportunity for him to make a start as a producer. He supported Rohmer and enabled him to finish the first two Moral Tales, both in 16 mm. The first was shot on location, the second mostly in the apartment of Schroeder's mother. His own bedroom provides the main set for *La Carrière de Suzanne*, and between takes, it was used as an office for Les Films du Losange. Everyone was part of one big family.

features, they were too amateurish to sell as a commercial package. Something was needed that would provide this young and fragile production company with a more comfortable base. Schroeder thought there would be a possibility with a series of sketches. These became *Paris vu par . . .* (1964). He assembled the financial backing for the film in two stages. First, six short films would be made. The directors would apply for grant money and enter the films in competitions where awards were based on merit. Then, the shorts would be assembled into a single feature-length film. No one was fooled, but the Centre National de la Cinématographie played along with the ruse, and in the end the entire film was made for almost nothing (barely 400,000 francs).

In exchange the film imposed strict guidelines on itself: it would push the New Wave principle of subordinating aesthetics to economy as far as it could. However, in the years 1963–1964, when the film was being made, a technological revolution had taken place. With the development of television, lighter cameras and lenses, new sound equipment, faster films, and the widespread use of color had appeared. Schroeder took advantage of all the new technologies. He began by taking his 16 mm stock to a lab and having it blown up to 35 mm, with

director treated with a kind of fictionalized verisimilitude, careful to maintain its spirit, essential features, "village" atmosphere, etc. Other requirements weren't so easily adhered to, however, including the use of non-professional actors (a neorealist rather than a New Wave precept). Today, *Paris vu par...* appears as both the New Wave's manifesto and testament, for it marked the end of the movement.

To borrow a cinematic comparison from Truffaut, the situation came to resemble the end of Rossellini's *The Flowers of St. Francis*: the monks, in a circle, spin around until, exhausted, they fall to the ground in the shape of a compass rose. Then, each of them gets up and leaves in the direction of his fall, to the four corners of the world. The same was true of the New Wave. As Truffaut commented, "Each remained faithful to himself, but in doing so distanced himself from the others."

Micheline Dax and Claude Melki, *Paris vu par ...* , 1965 (sketch by Jean-Daniel Poillet, "Rue Saint-Denis")

satisfactory results. The goal was to prove that films could be made under amateur conditions but yield a product in a professional format, which could be commercially distributed. There were other requirements, but these had been imposed by the New Wave itself. They included the use of location shots, real exterior and interior settings, small crews of three or four—a cameraman, assistant, sound engineer, sometimes an electrician for a fill light (often nothing more than a redhead connected to the mains)—a single neighborhood in Paris, which each

1   Braunberger directed two films of his own: *Paris 1900* (with Nicole Védrès) in 1947 and *La Course de taureaux* in 1951.

2   *Rue des prairies*, Denys de la Patellière, 1959.

1961

ROCCO AND HIS BROTHERS

LOLA

SHADOWS

LA PROIE POUR L'OMBRE

DESCRIPTION D'UN COMBAT

LAST YEAR AT MARIENBAD

CE SOIR OU JAMAIS

A WOMAN IS A WOMAN

ROCCO AND HIS BROTHERS

Lucchino Visconti

NOT A MORALIST

An aristocrat by birth, an aesthete by definition, but a Marxist by conviction, Lucchino Visconti can't escape his own contradictions. Although *La Terra trema* would seem to imply that social documentary is his primary ambition, the fatality of passion and melodrama (in the best sense of the word) are the subjects at which Visconti excels. Is *Senso* anything other than a superb opera, a film that hesitates between theater and life?

But Visconti would be unable to acknowledge whether he's a psychologist or an aesthete, and I'm sure that if we were to call him a moralist he'd say the label was too bourgeois. To compensate for his remorse at being a *grand seigneur*, he's incorporated social concerns into his films, but not always convincingly. I'm not trying to impugn Visconti's intentions. His "bad faith" irritates leftist intellectuals but delights those who love film. ∎
Henry Chapier, *Combat*, March 11, 1961

COMPLEX ARCHITECTURE

Le Notti bianche was a story about the emotional conflict between two persons separated by a third, who could be said to represent Fate. *Rocco and his Brothers* is an extremely subtle film that blends eight intercrossed lives, affected less by destiny than what's often described as a Brechtian amalgam of contingency and fatality. This complex architecture is brilliantly reflected in Visconti's direction. Visconti is the impassive viewer of time as it unfolds before us. Time isn't the principal character in this film, but it sweeps events along in its current as if it were a river. *Rocco and his Brothers* is a modern film because it revolves around the idea of duration. The film relies on the notion of duration rather than trying to destroy it from within (as in Antonioni). This sense of time enables Visconti to use the well-

established technique of parallel editing to good effect at the end of the film. And it is at this point that the film's real structure becomes clear, articulated around the five brothers who function like the five fingers of unequal length on a hand. I wouldn't hesitate to classify Visconti as a builder. ∎
François Weyergans, *Cahiers du cinéma*, 1961

LOLA

Jacques Demy

DEDICATED TO MAX OPHULS

With *Lola* I wanted to make a film about the search for happiness, for love in the modern world. It's difficult to summarize the story: the themes crisscross one another and the film, set in the countryside in June 1960, is constructed around chance meetings and coincidence. That's why I chose three different moments in the life of three characters: Lola, the young cabaret singer and dancer, and a little girl and her mother, who represent her when she's 14 and 38 years old.

I also wanted to describe Lola's faithfulness. She waits patiently for seven years for her son's father to return. Like the Crusades of the past, the war has separated them. Their sentiments may seem romantic and a bit dated, but I feel they exist. My intention wasn't to make a realistic film, however, but a story that constantly wavers between comedy and tragedy. I prefer to transform, to idealize reality. I remember Jean Renoir said something like "If I see people slouching in their chairs in a café, I'll idealize them on film. Otherwise, why go the movies rather than the café?"

I tried to describe a world that's beautiful, and I tried to find this beauty in the actors and the sets. That's why I conceived the character of Lola for Anouk Aimée, while trying to reveal another aspect of her personality and charm. We're so accustomed to seeing her in tragic roles that her desire here runs the risk of upsetting viewers.

I was thinking of Max Ophuls's *Le Plaisir* when I wrote *Lola* and dedicated the film to him. Maybe this fable belongs to the same tradition as the work of Prévert and Queneau. Not that I wanted to plagiarize them or adopt their style, but I'm sensitive to the distance they place between themselves and existence, which they express with delicacy, humor, and often an element of bitterness. I would hope that anyone feeling depressed or glum, who goes to see *Lola*, leaves with a smile on their face and that the film manages to change their state of mind and outlook on life—at least temporarily. ■

Interview with Jacques Demy conducted by **Yvonne Baby**, *Le Monde*, March 4, 1961

LOLA, OR WOMAN

It is likely that Ophuls's detractors will hate this falsely naive film, which is cleverly constructed, almost haphazardly put together. It presents a series of variations on the face of a woman, a provincial replica of *Lola Montès*. But Ophuls doesn't explain everything about this film. Jean-Luc Godard's influence is also apparent in the handsome rush of black and white images, the note of sincerity and insolence. *Lola* contains a similar insistent reserve, the same disdain for the mechanics of film.

The true subject of Demy's film is Lola. Her cleverness, her kindness, her loneliness, her distress. Lola, or woman. Open your heart and you'll find Lola's

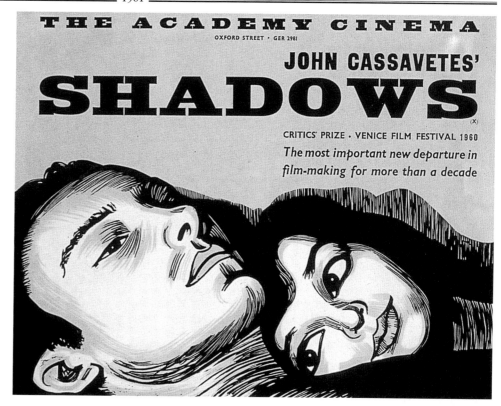

young sister. As disconcerting as it is at times, this film isn't easily forgotten. It exudes a kind of charm, like a heady perfume, and it's a film you'll remember long after you've left the theater. Call it what you like. Personally, I feel that Jacques Demy has tamed poetry. ■

Michel Aubriant, *Paris-Press*, March 8, 1961

SHADOWS

John Cassavetes

A FASCINATING NEW YORK

Shadows may mark an important step in American (and international) cinema. A number of new directors are attracted by the idea of a form of cinéma vérité that provides access to an (apparently) unvarnished reality. This is one of the reasons for their interest in Jean Rouch. And although Godard's influence is unlikely, Cassavetes's work resembles his in several ways. Godard was hobbled by a very conventional script and is overly fond of "quotation." After seeing *Breathless* several times, it's clear that his break with the good old tradition of *Pépé le Moko* and

Quai des Brumes was especially obvious. The film's novelty consisted in a certain style of cinematography, a vision of Paris.

In *Shadows*, New York is fascinating. How often have we seen this city in the ten thousand odd films made in America over the past 35 years? Not many, aside from a handful of films like *The Crowd* (King Vidor) and *Naked City* (Dassin). And like Godard, Cassavetes used high-speed stock, although I think he shot the film in 16 millimeter (successfully enlarged to 35). But he shows us more than the city itself. He allows us to enter its homes, apartments, and bars, and brings everyday life to the screen, its problems too. For his characters are alone with their preoccupations and uncertainties. ■

Georges Sadoul, *Les Lettres Françaises*, May 4, 1961

FOR MOVIE LOVERS

From a purely artistic point of view *Shadows* is not all that original. Its release comes a long time after the celebrated *The Quiet One*, which was made under the same conditions and whose qualities are a good deal more obvious. It follows Truffaut's *Le Petit Fugitif*, a miraculous story by comparison (because of the small miracles that result from improvisation). It is less "accomplished" than *Breathless*.

Still, the film isn't at all bad. *Shadows* is, in many respects, a lot like a secret poem. Its climate of sad intimacy, the human regret it portrays—all of this is shown with feeling. The director's amateurism, the muted noises, vague dialogue, and muffled voices (recorded with a tape recorder) provide the customary compensation: in the end the film's defects manage to add up to something positive. If you're a film enthusiast, you'll probably like *Shadows*. If you're not, well, you won't. ∎

Louis Chauvet, *Le Figaro*, April 25, 1961

LA PROIE POUR L'OMBRE

Alexandre Astruc

SHOT IN SIX WEEKS

La Proie pour l'ombre is my fourth film. I wrote the story and the adaptation, and Claude Brûle helped me with the dialogue. It's about a married woman who works and wants to be independent, until the day she meets another man and realizes that with him she will only become poor and dependent. The woman (Anna) is played by Annie Girardot, the lover (Bruno) by Christian Marquand, and the husband (Eric) by Daniel Gélin. To maintain her independence she renounces both of them and finds herself alone. This isn't an "issue" film, I detest that, but a very real subject, one I take quite seriously. I've tried to show that although women today have the same freedom as men, they are not made for this freedom; they're different. I find the heroine's situation absolutely fascinating, because like many women today, she spends her time trying to regain her independence. Then when she has it, she doesn't know what to do with it.

I shot the film in six weeks, entirely on location, using real interiors, but I hope I've succeeded in giving the film a "polished" look. Not that I believe in "well-made" films, but I think that the formal qualities of a film, its style, are very important. To my mind, however, the story is what counts. I simply hope that my directing fully expresses that story at every moment of the film. Basically, I allowed my camera to follow a woman, watch her, analyze her, walk behind her, track her. The film consists of a series of very long takes, for, although it's a "psychological" film, I've tried to express this woman's feelings and state of mind through her physical movements. I think it's always beautiful to watch the way people move. ∎

Alexandre Astruc, *Les Lettres Françaises*, September 22, 1961

A CINEMATIC NOVEL

It's been said many times that the real novelty of new French cinema is its ability to accurately describe relationships between contemporary men and women, and love in particular, without taking into account social or moral taboos and prejudices. This liberalization hasn't occurred without a certain amount of excess and we've been a bit hasty in praising films that, for all their apparent novelty, soon felt as dated as the literature of 1925, whose primary themes were the emancipation of women and sexual freedom.

Alexandre Astruc is the first director to successfully address the real relations between the men and women of today. *La Proie pour l'ombre* is a cinematic novel that falls from your hands after the last page, leaving you with ample material for reflection. Astruc has done an excellent job in faithfully adapting the book to the screen. Everything that seemed a bit too dry and theoretical in his earlier works has vanished within the classical purity of his style. ∎

Jacques Siclier, *Cahiers du cinéma*, June 1961

DESCRIPTION D'UN COMBAT

Chris Marker

TAMING THE EVERYDAY

As he crisscrossed the surface of our small planet, somewhere between Korea and Cuba, with a pen in his right hand and a camera in his left, Chris Marker found himself in the Near East. For this French writer-director, ex-American soldier, born in Mongolia, nothing on Earth is foreign. Following his trip to Siberia, Marker's Palestinian film could have been called *Letter from Tel Aviv*, although the optimism of his earlier work has been replaced by a pessimism tempered only—but what a consolation!—by the grace of the young girls who provide what would be an ideal subtitle for the film: *Women of Israel*. The author's pessimism stems from his comparison of the still immature growth of the eastern USSR with the decline in tension of a state, which barely twelve years of existence have relegated to the anarchic, disordered, contradictory, and disappointing status of the nations of the Occident of old. Marker's aesthetic premise is based on his ability to look closely at whatever happens to fall within his field of view. He's not looking for the unusual but takes hold of the everyday, doesn't provoke the exceptional but waits for it patiently. Unlike *Lettre de Sibérie*, whose sound track was brilliant, here the succession of carefully arranged sequences, punctuated by purely visual ideas, balances a commentary that is at first slightly grating but is soon eclipsed by the film's cinematic qualities. Throughout his career Marker's success has been largely based on the visual strength of his films. Formerly, he quoted Michaux. Today, while his text owes something to an as-yet-unknown Merleau-Ponty through the many references to the "signs" it contains, the film's imagery is pure Giraudoux. This author's fascination is reflected in the shot of the solemn young boy slowly licking his ice cream, the scene in which the suburbs of Haifa are revealed one by one like so many veils dropping, and the luminous, giggling young girls. Marker's eye is fertile. He brings us the Moon of the Palestinian desert, appropriately bores us during a meeting at a Kibbutz, forces us to contemplate, as Malraux in the presence of a Caravaggio, the image of a young girl drawing attentively, makes us enter a home of obvious poverty, as poignant (I

apologize to any Buñuel fans) as any scene in *Land without Bread*. *Description d'un combat* is sure to repay our *attention*. ∎
Roger Tailleur, *Positif,* July 1961

LAST YEAR AT MARIENBAD

Alain Resnais

A BOOK IS NOT A FILM

It was the producer's idea that we get together—Terra Film, in this case. They were looking for a writer to work with Resnais. He frequently works with writers but is reluctant to use an existing story. *Night and Fog* like *Hiroshima, mon amour,* by Jean Cayrol and Marguerite Duras respectively, came about as the result of the authors' collaboration with Resnais. Having read my books, the producer gave them to Resnais, and he saw the possibility of making a film from *La Jalousie* or *Dans le labyrinthe.* I find the choice interesting, since these two novels have no real "story," unlike *Gommes* or *Voyeur.* But in any case Resnais didn't want to use an adaptation of a novel that he considered to be a work of art in its own right. Even if the novelist's technique was cinematic, he never considered a book as a film waiting to be made. That's why, when we agreed to work together, he asked me to suggest several subjects. I gave him four. He was interested in them all, but since he had to make a decision, we discussed them and kept the one that we felt, for several reasons, should be filmed first. It was initially called *Last Year* and became *Last Year at Marienbad.* ∎
Interview with Alain Robbe-Grillet conducted by Jacqueline Autrusseau, *Les Lettres Françaises,* August 18, 1960

RECREATING THE CONDITIONS FOR READING

G. G. What's *Last Year at Marienbad* about?

A. R. There's a story, of course, but I'd prefer to suggest several psychological themes: the use of language to persuade, the fear of the unknown, rape as ritual or a form of psychoanalytic union that incorporates elements of our modern mental landscape, the representation of non-causal events, repetition and variation, the material reality of the imagination, the actualization of the past or future and the blurring of time in general. In a nutshell, the story takes place in the luxurious and sterile atmosphere of an international hotel where time stands still. A stranger tells a young woman that they have met before. This woman is with a companion but she pretends to remember. She struggles, yields, fights back. But it's through the association of images and sounds, through their instantaneous form, that these themes have to act on the viewer. I wanted to recreate the conditions of reading, address the viewer as if he were a reader, alone. ∎
Interview with Alain Resnais conducted by **Gilbert Guez,** *Arts,* May 8, 1961

FLASHES OF MEMORY

This film bears all the hallmarks of the malaise that affects today's directors (and writers) when confronted with the thought of telling a story using the framework of the conventional novel, that is, its logical and chronological structure. Now seen as a barrier, the linear story line has been rejected. This malaise is not new in literature, where it's existed a long time, ever since the conventional story structure was broken apart. In film, however, the malaise most likely occurs because cinema is still young and viewers, spoiled by the passivity from which film draws its power of persuasion, are apparently less sophisticated than the readers of novels. Yet *Last Year at Marienbad* demands a new attitude of the public, a new openness. Not passivity but complaisance. Not comprehension but complicity, collaboration. This film demands as much from the viewer as a novel by Faulkner demands of the reader.

Ever since *Hiroshima, mon amour* we've known that Alain Resnais excelled in presenting flashes of memory, passing thoughts. Here, in this film, which reveals how the perception of reality allows itself

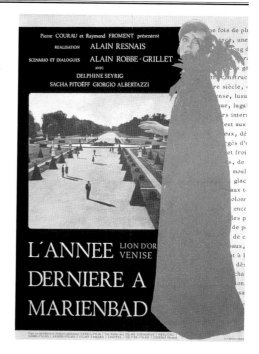

to be contaminated by the imagination, the virtuosity of the editing (hats off to Henri Colpi and Jasmine Chasney) allows mental images to burst through the ceremonial torpor, by weaving back and forth between what is sometimes a ballet of still images and sometimes a series of silent traveling shots, superficially indifferent, which circle insidiously around the characters in the film. ∎
Jean-Louis Bory, *Arts,* October 10, 1961

A SHOCK TO THE IMAGINATION

A few words of advice to viewers of *Last Year at Marienbad*: Don't give in to the temptation to look for a literary explanation. Don't give in to your taste for the romantic. Don't stiffen up. Let yourself glide through this film, accepting the images as they come. Allow yourself to feel rather than understand, as if you were before an abstract painting, as if you were listening to a certain kind of music. What counts is the impression, the emotion, the echo. It's a shock to the imagination. That's all. But that's a lot. ∎
Pierre Marcabru, *Combat,* October 2, 1961

CE SOIR OU JAMAIS

Michel Deville

A GAME OF EMOTIONAL TRUTH

This first attempt is a masterpiece. With his first film Michel Deville has succeeded in composing what was thought to be an impossiblity: a typically French farce based on the style of American comedy. To compare *Ce soir ou jamais* to Marivaux or Musset, Cukor or Minelli, is another way of demonstrating our esteem for the director. Of course, *Ce soir ou jamais* doesn't match up to the work of these masters. The film is not without its weaknesses. But the director's second film, *La Menteuse*, which I saw during a private screening, confirms Deville's talent, and makes Philippe de Broca look a lot less interesting.

Reserve, discretion, intelligence, finesse, vivacity, and elegance are this film's major qualities. It's precious too, in a way, and has a kind of tenderness that belies, as does any good comedy, a subtle touch of cruelty. The lighthearted banter that grates the heart until it bleeds is a very French specialty. And Deville excels in this game of emotional truth.

Because Deville doesn't arbitrarily lock his characters inside some hidden psychology but watches them experience life without interference and is content to capture the movements of the heart, we really feel what's going on inside them. In spite of the conventional, even facile, sides of his story and the traditional plot structure, he reveals himself to be a modern director. He is part of that cinematic trend that wants to make us feel relationships rather than show them to us, an approach masterfully handled by Nicholas Ray and Rossellini. This is the path that the best elements of the New Wave have followed, each in their own way. The elements include Astruc, Rivette, Melville, Rohmer, Godard, and Demy (whose *Lola* appears to me to be the most successful in this sense). A risky approach, where public success is less than certain, it assumes a *dedramatization* of the film. It requires great internal control as well, since the director is no longer able to use structure and genre as a support. ■

Jean Douchet, *Cahiers du cinéma*, November 1961

A WOMAN IS A WOMAN

Jean-Luc Godard

THE ESTHETICS OF THE BABY RATTLE

The shocking incompetence, the hilarious complacency of his bluff, the vulgarity and intellectual vacuum in *Breathless*, surprised contemporary critics, who, oblivious to the world around them, grew increasingly alarmed (at the cost of several monumental mistakes) that they might miss the boat entirely. For a long time I've wanted to write something about Godard. This pretentious idiot, whose comments about torture were obligingly published by *L'Express* (supposedly a leftist publication), should have gotten his face slapped. The only thing that saved him was the touching respect shown by Parisian society for flagrant stupidity. The recent appearance of the aberrant *Le Petit Soldat*, with its mish-mash of outrageous political paradoxes concerning a war that doesn't exactly proceed like clockwork, finally muzzled this mindless imposture. Now we have *A Woman is a Woman*, which plunges the viewer into a bath of lethargy. There's no point in beating a dead horse, however. Godard has given himself away. He's shown that there's nothing inside, that an interior of straw, kapok, feathers, and chicken wire supports his shaky frame. When Orson Welles arrived in Hollywood, he congratulated himself on being given such a nice electric train. Godard's aesthetics are at the rattle stage. A delighted Georges de Beauregard, the devoted nurse, offers his hideous charge a bottle worth a million francs, which the other drains in his cradle, invoking Malraux, Drieu la Rochelle, Zig and Puce, Le Pen and Johann Sebastian Bach. It looks like the "clever plot," which seems to be the unfortunate Godard's obsession (a lot like his idiosyncratic penchant for denunciation), is drowning in this monumental vacuum. The cult of "anything, anyhow"—see how easy it is!—that stunned Messrs. Baroncelli, Sadoul, and A. S. Labarthe, has resulted in such subtleties as "Eva, go fuck yourself[1]," which some readers will find almost Joycean. I once spoke about unfinished cinema, but *A Woman is a Woman* would appear to be a form of pigsty-cinema, an intellectual sump, a glittering bauble, a cheap trick to impress the *pied-noirs*. Anna Karina, as beautiful as she is, should keep quiet, or go to work for Michel Deville. ■

Raymond Borde, *Positif,* January 1962

1 The French "Eva te faire foutre" involves a not so subtle play on words, where the customary "Et va ..." has been replaced by "Eva," one of the main characters in the film.

THE CHINKS MORE THAN THE ARMOR

At bottom Godard recognizes that film fulfills a function that is both simple and fundamental. Film is essentially documentary. *Breathless* and *Le Petit Soldat* were

both documentaries. The first concerned Paris; the second concerned Geneva. *A Woman is a Woman* is one of the most beautiful documentaries I know of devoted to a woman (and incidentally to Porte Saint-Denis). Both document and homage, the key to the film is contained in a scene from *Le Petit Soldat*: when Subor turns around Anna Karina, machine-gunning her with his Leica.

A Woman is a Woman is a documentary from start to finish.

1. It is a documentary in terms of the way Godard directs his actors. The actress Anna Karina only interests him to the extent that her talent enables her to escape her profession. Unlike other directors, Godard keeps only the weakest of her scenes. His intuition is remarkable, for these are by their very nature the most revealing of all. Doesn't the man who betrays himself also reveal himself? (An interesting elegy of treason could be made based on this idea.) Godard's effort consists, quite logically, in increasing the number of obstacles to obtain an improvised gesture, an uncontrolled mimicry, an involuntary intonation in all his scenes—extraordinary moments of truth. The chinks are more interesting to him than the armor. And he goes so far as

to prefer a bad take to a good one, and in fact juxtaposes one against the other.

2. The dialogue that Godard provides his actors with gives some indication of what he's looking for. His dialogues have been called absurd, vulgar, meaningless. Exactly. Words aren't used to express something but to express the characters. Their function is in one sense oblique to the story. When Karina says to Brialy, "You poor jerk," and says it several times, she reveals that the scene's importance has less to do with the meaning of those words than the way she pronounces them. The only things that count here are the *accidents* of speech: accent, modulation, intonation, *form*. I know of only one other film in which spoken language is systematically used for its form, *Les Bonnes Femmes* by Claude Chabrol.

3. The jokes that punctuate the film belie the director's preoccupation with documentary. The jokes aren't there to make us laugh, however. Like the words in this film, their effectiveness is destroyed one way or another (either by dragging them out or through their banality) to emphasize the truth of the characters. Recall the scene in the bistro between Karina and Belmondo.

A Woman is a Woman represents an important milestone in modern cinema. It's cinema in its pure state. It's both spectacle and the charm of the spectacle. It's cinema returning to cinema. It's Lumière in 1961. ∎

André-S. Labarthe, *Cahiers du cinéma*,
November 1961

Truffaut's well-known article, "A Certain Tendency of the French Cinema" (*Cahiers* 31), was essentially concerned with narrative and attacked contemporary screenwriters. Although it may be inaccurate to view the article as the New Wave's manifesto, it did celebrate the appearance of a like-minded group of individuals, overflowing with ideas. These men and women basically rewrote the history, economics, and techniques of the industry, and developed a new morality, and thus a new aesthetic, which situated film art within the current of modern life.

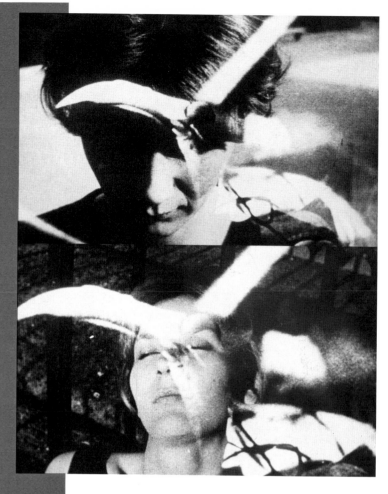

La Jetée (Chris Marker, 1962)

NARRATIVE

Truffaut argued that a film is based on a story and thus the story must be the first part of the film to be examined. Given Truffaut's painstaking attention to the screenplays of his films, there is nothing surprising in his criticism. Yet his ostensibly one-sided criticism remained incomplete. For it limited itself to the question of adapting a literary work. It condemned the then current process known as *equivalence*. "This process," Truffaut wrote, "assumes that the novel contains scenes that can be shot and those that can't, and rather than eliminating those that can't ... *equivalent* scenes must be created, as the novel's author would have written them for the film." The screenwriters of the time demanded "invention without betrayal." Truffaut, then only 21 years old, had a rare talent as a pamphleteer, which immediately secured his reputation. He was able to show that the process of equivalence inevitably resulted in artistic betrayal. The changes and additions involved denatured the literary work that directors claimed to honor.

Citizen Kane (Orson Welles, 1941)

In 1953, the year he was preparing the article, which was read and discussed by other members of the *Cahiers* staff, Truffaut and his group of friends had only a vague estimate of the task at hand. More or less consciously, through the example of equivalence, the article illustrated the need to rethink the very concept of cinematic narrative.

The work was made easier by the upheaval that affected the art world between the end of the war and the sixties. The plastic arts abandoned figuration for abstraction, music abandoned melody, the theater plunged into the absurd, the novel repudiated the linearity of the story, basing its "newness" on the absolute objectivity of a maniacal description of facts, gestures, place, and time. In short, anything that related (or contained) a story or announced a subject was censured. The new art fabricated or integrated an object, whose presence (or destruction) alone determined the narrative.

Cinema, subject to the laws of industry and commerce, didn't embrace the tumultuous current of modernity with open arms. Quite the contrary—between 1945 and 1960 film reached an apogee in which classicism flourished. Film scripts continued to draw inspiration from a long narrative tradition that had culminated in the nineteenth century. The cinema prolonged this tradition, which determined the importance of the question of equivalence for screenwriters. Cinema adopted narrative methods in the form of genres, which it then erected into a system. Genres, however, adhered to sets of codes, laws, and conventions, which filmmakers had to struggle to get beyond. It was imperative, for instance, that the action be perfectly comprehensible and easy to follow, which made it the overriding element in film construction, and everything else was sacrificed to it. Clarity was essential and thus expository scenes, as in Shakespeare or Molière no more than a few minutes in length, served to introduce the characters, explain situations, and orient the action.

Cracks soon began to appear in this uniform surface. The baroque, as it was interpreted by Orson Welles, made a noisy entrance. *Citizen Kane* (1940) revolutionized narrative by adopting techniques of American literature and the new narrative structures of Faulkner and Dos Passos. But his method was too shocking for conventional film, and in the short term it had no direct influence on the screenplay. It did have a long-term effect, however, especially in the United States. Welles's manner of breaking narrative linearity and plunging the viewer into a state of confusion full of noise and fury was widely used in Hollywood after the seventies, when the limpid clarity of the classical era was finally over. Typically American, but increasingly mannered, such modern cinema required that the viewer immerse himself in the first part of the film before attempting to disentangle the details of the action, which the film's intentional obscurity ultimately reinforced. This approach had little influence on the New Wave, however.

Last Year at Marienbad (Alain Resnais, 1960)

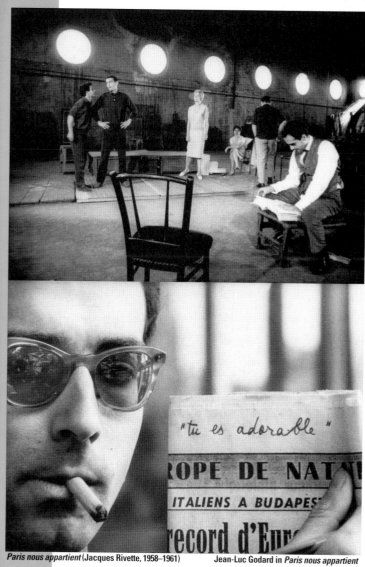

Paris nous appartient (Jacques Rivette, 1958–1961)   Jean-Luc Godard in *Paris nous appartient*

This was not true of all Welles's techniques such as the introduction of voice-over and narration. Their use by Sacha Guitry in *Roman d'un tricheur* had intrigued Welles, who was experimenting with vocal and sound effects in his radio broadcasts. He immediately recognized the narrative possibilities for *Citizen Kane*, embodied in the contrast between the official story told objectively by the reporter and the personal voices of the other characters, who disclose their version of events to the journalist responsible for discovering the hidden meaning behind "Rosebud." This intrusion of texts, like foreign bodies, refracted the story. It amplified ambiguity and complexity. The effect offered so many possibilities that it was quickly adopted and reworked by others, notably by Joseph Mankiewicz, whose brother Herman was responsible, in large part, for the originality of *Citizen Kane's* screenplay. The New Wave greatly admired Mankiewicz, the author of *The Quiet American*, *All About Eve*, and especially *The Barefoot Contessa*.

Quite naturally the New Wave adopted the process. Narration and voice-overs became standard and even necessary elements in the construction of narrative. This made sense to the New Wave, and they added something to the way the process was used. They introduced it into the dramatic, theatrical side of film, where until then it had been used only to advance film's fictional possibilities. Here we recognize the New Wave's Balzacian origins. Narration no longer whispers confidences; it comments for real. It describes (places, journeys, characters), analyzes the action, judges and measures conduct. It sees different things and sees them differently than the image. The New Wave based its dramaturgy, its sense of action, on this duality. Action was displaced, and no longer resided in the sequence of events unfolding on screen but in the reality of their unfolding, the "how" of their development. All of Rohmer's Moral Tales, for instance, are based on this principle. Narration introduced criticism—an environment most of the New Wave directors were familiar with—as a means of driving the narrative forward.

The approach embodied the basic principle of Brechtian alienation, which was much in favor in Parisian intellectual circles of the time. Some, like Marker and Resnais, who had used it in their documentaries, retained its political message. Others, like Truffaut, Rohmer, and Eustache (Demy's situation is somewhat more complex since he treated his songs as narrational elements) made use of its aesthetics. Varda turned it into something precious. Rivette, rather perversely, eliminated it in favor of another technique: the creation of a story within the fiction that could be used to develop the plot. It was Godard who made it one of the fundamental elements of his style. In Godard voice-overs have affective force—they serve as vehicles for our emotions, impressions, and sentiments, and deliver moral, political, and aesthetic judgments. They question, ignore, and respond to one another, like so many interjections, interrogations, or

Anna Karina, *A Woman is a Woman* (Jean-Luc Godard, 1961)

Jean-Paul Belmondo and Anna Karina, *Pierrot le fou* (Jean-Luc Godard, 1965)

182

reflections in search of a soul or mind. They populate the solitude of a microcosm of pathetic anecdotes with the tragic immensity of the universe.

Another aspect of Welles's style was also adopted by the New Wave; this involved the transgression of genre. Welles's scope was too broad and too forceful to be contained within a given genre (the film noir, for example, as handled by Welles in *The Lady from Shanghai, Mr. Arkadin*, or *Touch of Evil*). His personality devoured codes and conventions as it attempted to bend to the rules of the genre. Even what was for Welles the supreme genre, Shakespearean theater, wasn't exempt from his need to remold the genial Elizabethan to the dimensions of his inspiration. It is this creative supremacy in Welles that fascinated the New Wave's young directors.

With the exception of Chabrol, who (apparently) played policeman, they themselves were wary of genres. In the tradition of the filmmakers they admired, they assumed complete freedom over their work. They used different genres as a starting point, took inspiration from them, arranged and rearranged them, reinvented them with a sense of joyful transgression. Genres were no more than a frame, a simple reference: the crime story in the hands of Godard (*Breathless, Pierrot le fou, Détective*), the musical comedy in Demy, the comedy as interpreted by Rohmer, imaginative science fiction in Resnais, the love story—sorrow and joy combined—in Truffaut, who became less interesting whenever he attempted to remain faithful to a genre (*Fahrenheit 451, Mississippi Mermaid, Vivement dimanche!*). Yet, the exception that confirms the rule is Godard's *Alphaville*, which remains one of the best science-fiction films ever made. Except in this case, the rule invalidates the exception. In one sense the film was conceived as a kind of journalism, using the reality and background of Paris in 1965, without any decorative elements or any of the special effects customary in this type of production and which, in fact, defined the genre (*Metropolis, 2001: A Space Odyssey, Blade Runner*, etc.). Yet, *Alphaville*, which made politics and philosophy the fundamental elements of science fiction, was the quintessential expression of a genre. Because science fiction is rarely taken seriously in the cinema, where far too often peripheral matters take precedence over the subject, Godard also, and quite unconsciously, made a film outside the genre.

Even here the New Wave followed an auteurist policy: it was the work itself, its conception, that became the genre. We refer to a Rohmer, a Resnais, a Rivette, a Eustache, a Demy, etc., and the name suffices. The name serves as a kind of brand and indicates the type of film we can expect. Succeeding directors, who lacked the scope of the New Wave, confiscated the concept of the auteur and so, in the same way, we refer to a Lelouch, a Besson, a Beinex, even though, beneath a spuriously modern coat of varnish, their films adhere to the conventions of well-worn genres. The

Jean-Paul Belmondo, *Pierrot le fou* (Jean-Luc Godard, 1965)

exception is Bertrand Tavernier. Because of his fondness for American culture, Tavernier has always, in good conscience, accepted the role of an artisan too enamored with genres not to respect them. Nevertheless, the split between French and American cinema is based on this question of genre. Even the post-New Wave directors who were most strongly influenced by it—Coppola, De Palma, Eastwood, Ferrara—and deserve the title of auteur, are forced to continue to work within genres. A number of these genres have exhausted themselves or are disappearing (the western, musical comedy, etc.), and these directors have again returned to them. In true auteur fashion, they make use of their remains, treating them as ghosts, and in this context bring them back to life as the true subject, the real story of the film: *The Godfather*, *One from the Heart*, *Dracula*, *Carlito's Way*, *Mission Impossible*, *Unforgiven*, *The Funeral*, etc.

The American cinema made genre into the artistic basis of its financial enterprise. Because genres are constructed from solid foundations, because they describe clear and precise contours within larger amorphous forms (tragedy, drama, melodrama, comedy), shareholders and managers could make "forecasts" and thus control the returns from a film and speculate on its profitability. In Hollywood the genre beat a triumphant path to capitalism's door, exposed its ideology. Did it reinforce the dramatic structures that have remained unchanged for millennia? Or did a *past* block the present?

To captivate (and make captive) a paying public, the American cinema overdramatized and overvalued the action in which it concentrated all its energies—the action of the production and the actors, the rhythm of the film, the public's mental and affective action. In pretending to take pleasure in the moment, it puritanically denied the true conditions of the *present* for the false reality offered by fiction. The only thing that mattered was the breathless race toward the future. This justifies the mythic credo of the American way of life: success, happiness, achievement. The narrative was conceived as an incessant and insatiable "to be continued." Its construction was entirely focused on the final scene of the film, which was of "capital" importance (in the capitalist sense of hoarding wealth) and had to have a formulaic happy ending where all is resolved. *Ideologie oblige.*

In this sense the use of genre by Hollywood more or less consciously reflected a political attitude. It was the instrument of an idealized and equivocal representation of capitalism. By refusing to take advantage of it, Welles and Chaplin (beginning with *Monsieur Verdoux*), the New Wave, many European, Asian, third- and fourth-world directors, even American directors like Cassavetes (who worked to undermine it from within), became part of a *resistance* movement. In the case of directors like Rohmer, Demy, and Eustache, this was reflected in a simple aesthetic morality. This resistance often turned into a form

Jean-Paul Belmondo, Jean Seberg, and Daniel Boulanger, *Breathless* (Jean-Luc Godard, 1960)

of cinema engagé for New Wave directors such as Resnais, Godard, Garrel, and the most radical among them, Jean-Marie Straub and Danièle Huillet. This helps explain why the virulent attacks against the New Wave were often based on the screenplay it was supposed to have done away with, just as it was supposed to have destroyed the studio. The sterile admiration for conventional cinema so prevalent during the sixties and the decade's fascination with dandies (genre hacks for the most part) was extremely detrimental to film as a whole. Contrasted with the concept of the auteur, it constantly advanced the notion of the studio or, worse, assigned the title of auteur almost at random (Richard Thorpe, Michael Curtiz). Now, forty years after the birth of the New Wave, the conflict is as sharp as ever. From the crowd (of collaborators) to resistance, the choice is as current as ever: Kiarostami or Spielberg.

In Europe, after 1945, the narrative underwent considerable change. Already, the narrative structure and especially the dramaturgy of *Rules of the Game* (1939) were a portent of things to come. But after the war, auteurs such as Bresson, Bergman, Tati, Cocteau, Ophuls, and Melville made efforts to escape categorization and alter film's relation to the story and its characters, and refused to work with well-established screenwriters. Around 1960 the stage was set for revolution. It is worth noting in passing that, with or without the New Wave, change would have occurred. Ingmar Bergman with *Wild Strawberries* (1957), Renoir with *Le Testament du docteur Cordelier* (1959), Robert Bresson with *Pickpocket* (1959, Jacques Tati with *Mon oncle* (1958) and especially *Playtime* (1967), Michelangelo Antonioni with *L'Avventura* (1960), Federico Fellini with *8 1/2* (1963), and Buñuel during his French period, beginning with *The Milky Way* (1969)—all broke with the traditional rules that had provided guidelines for storytelling until then. They entered the modern period. Film concerned itself with the present and the past slipped away. The future was no longer something to be conquered, but accepted. The sense of uncertainty ("what's going to happen?") lost its urgency, and thus its importance, and was replaced by a concern for the here and now. The incredible thing is that this narrative upheaval was received favorably by the public. These films had genuine, although relative, commercial success. The same was true (with the exception of Rohmer and Rivette) of the first films of the New Wave.

The situation was somewhat different for Rossellini, who was the first director to truly revolutionize cinematic narration. Beginning with *Paisan* (1946), and in spite of his professional and personal relationship with Ingrid Bergman, perhaps the biggest star of the period, he met with nothing but setbacks and failure. Rossellini was too far ahead of his time, his films were, quite literally, misunderstood. They didn't operate according to the dramatic and narrative conventions the contemporary viewer was accustomed to, and these held no interest for Rossellini. His genius was to have reset the cinematic clock—back to zero. He dismissed fifty years of theatrical and romantic dramaturgy. In Rossellini's cinema we return to film's origins, to the Lumière brothers, that is, back to current events and journalism when the dramatic force of real events was sufficient to drive a story forward.

To film fiction within this framework disturbed the foundations of narrative. The viewer no longer projected himself into a film that magically changed into reality before his eyes. He lost the impression of security, the sensation of power provided by the possibility of dominating the totality of a field of view that stretched from past to future: the manipulation and arrangement of another's destiny was over. The public tha]t viewed Rossellini's films was no longer invited to participate mentally and magically in the story, to enter into the action, anticipate it, wish for it, lead it, and in the end become its master. The viewer was abruptly turned into merely a witness. He was forced to observe the incident—or accident—that the character—or victims—experienced at the same moment on screen. The viewer's interest, previously focused on the plot, now depended solely on his ability to feel what someone else felt.

In other words, the narrative changed direction. Instead of moving from left to right (an absurd metaphor inspired by the act of reading) from past to future, Rossellini in a sense reversed direction, caused the narrative to move from right to left. The event "to come" suddenly burst in upon the present, and cinema no longer mimicked life. In Rossellini life mimicked cinema. The viewer was deprived of the sense of distance provided by the old system, and was subject to the randomness of existence. Before, the past had blocked the present. In Rossellinian cinema, it is the future that blocks the present. No longer able to predict where the characters were going in the story, viewers were forced to rely on miracles, belief, faith, and hope to escape from a space that time had turned into a prison. They were forced to experience the febrile uncertainty of the characters and observe, with sadism or compassion, their incessant movements, like laboratory rats caught in their own labyrinth.

Rossellini established a new set of rules with the audience. Unlike Hitchcock, who encouraged the viewer to enter the screen and mentally intervene in the story, Rossellini nailed him to the witness stand. This was the opposite of suspense. The story, and eventually History (*Paisan*, *Viva l'Italia*, *The Rise of Louis XIV*), unfolded before the viewer. He had no control over it. The story was based on objectivity, the inexorable truth of the event, and the synchronous emotional shock experienced by the viewer. The viewer interacted with the film in terms of echoes, resonances, reverberations, physical sensations, the unspoken impressions of a given place, environment or circumstance that reveal the silent language of experience. In Rossellini, the site precedes the situation and serves as an echo chamber. From this moment on the viewer is fixed

Paisan (Roberto Rossellini, 1946)

186

in place, forced to experience, to suffer (people characteristically burst into tears, spasmodically, unbearably, in Rossellini). The viewer's sensitivity is exacerbated. The purpose is to create awareness. We are there to fulfill our role as viewer: to look, hear, examine, grasp, comprehend. In short, to understand and learn. This was cinema, as defined, desired, and conceived by the New Wave.

The New Wave accepted and absorbed the lessons of their Italian master: make the present *present*. Based on its concept of narrative, the New Wave retained the most important elements that followed from the desire not to film a story but to record an event. Screenplays emphasized surprise and chance, insisted on the meeting that would become the focal point of the construction, revealing the absurdity and failure of scenes, plots, and intrigues. This was the typical framework for a New Wave script, although directors individualized it. Rohmer, for example, reinterpreted the classical scenario: a character determines his future and, consequently, his behavior, then ascribes to a morality more conducive to life's dissolute stream. Life in its capriciousness, will succeed where calculation failed. In Truffaut, meetings between characters are the product of an intrigue fomented by a seducer who is as insolent as he is timid. When the meeting finally occurs, as in *La Femme d'à côté*, it ends in intrigue, fatality, drama, and tragedy. Demy's films involve nothing but encounters that are missed, intersect, and are missed again, until a final moment of fruition occurs. Resnais, who was more inclined to follow the modernism of the *nouveau roman* than Rossellini, worked within an internal temporality where a future nourished on the memory of the past shapes a hypothetical present in which every encounter is part of the infinite play of possibilities, and becomes a simple element of chance that moves the pawns on the board. Straub and Huillet gave the present such density that they established the weight of its duration, and rarefied, to the point of asphyxiation, encounter and chance. A similar analysis could be made of Chabrol, Rivette (the plot as source of life's risks), Pollet, Eustache, and especially Godard, the most Rossellinian of all, for whom life is so free that it constantly evades our attempt to control it. Characters have almost no past in Godard, even less of a future. They have nothing but the uncertainty, intoxication, and tragedy of the moment. They are nomads, owning neither time, nor space (characters don't live anywhere in Godard, they occupy a bare dwelling). Since they are incapable of possessing anything, they attain the only property worth having: the property of being. The construction of a story that is continually disrupted becomes the source of encounters and accidents, a collage that follows the rules of its own necessity.

Alphaville (Jean-Luc Godard, 1965)

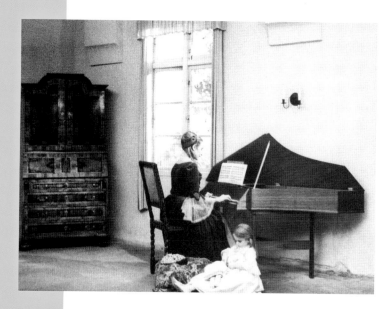

Chronique d'Anna Magdalena Bach (Jean-Marie Straub, 1967)

Anémone (Philippe Garrel, 1966)

Tu vois mes pieds dans la glace? - Oui. - Tu les trouves jolis

A syllable is a monosyllable
if it ends in a polysyllable

Truth
DIALOGUE
and lies

Theater *is* text. Cinema *uses* dialogue. It is only one of the elements of film language, together with, but less important than, image and sound. It provides a kind of insurance, functions as a discreet echo, a complement. Good dialogue resonates. Bad dialogue rationalizes; it shows off, makes itself the center of attention, obliterates everything in its path. It even claims to lead the action and reduce the film to its words.

Dialogue was largely responsible for the success of French quality cinema. What follows is a telling excerpt from a criticism of *Cette nuit-là* by Maurice Cazeneuve, the only feature film by the well-known television director. The film is interesting because, as F. Bonnaud notes, "this film, made in 1958, is a caricature of French pre-New Wave cinema. To stay with it until the end, you've got to sit through the leaden dialogue. 'How do I look? Barely . . . ' How about 'Look, a man! Let's not exaggerate.' These and other inanities are rattled off in a conspiratorial manner, between silences laden with meaning. They serve as an adornment to a banal story of adultery."

Even when the writer was talented, the emphasis on dialogue by directors such as Henri Jeanson, Marcel Achard, and Michel Audiard, remained a stain on the cinema, French or otherwise. In France it perpetuated the long tradition that developed at court and in the literary salons of the ultra-Parisian nineteenth century, which made intellect, or what passed for it, preeminent in social and human relations. To be a man of wit was considered a means to success and fortune. These directors turned it into their stock in trade, and they boasted of it. Primarily dialogue writers, and only incidentally screenwriters, directors like Henri Jeanson claimed to be the only true authors of the film. The worst part is that in Jeanson's case he's right. His dialogues destroyed any hint of directorial continuity, beginning with the physical interaction among the characters. Disembodied, turned into an effigy, the actor could no longer keep up with his role. He was reduced to providing replies.

Auteurs, on the other hand, *work* the character's dialogue, that is, they demand the reply that logically follows from the situation and reveals the character's truth. The character's dialogue is often funnier than the author's since it is not artificial. Everyone remembers the wonderful Arletty with her "atmosphere, atmosphere" in *Hôtel du Nord* but most have forgotten the circumstances. The reply was written specifically for the actress but had little do with her character in the film. (In reality, it was part of a private joke by Henri Jeanson, who was irritated by Marcel Carné's repeated demands to consider the film's "atmosphere," the French translation of German *Stimmung*, which had been made fashionable through German expressionism.) The expression hung in the air, useless and sterile. While it may have engraved itself in the mind of the viewer, it did so autonomously, like some vain and comic pleasure. It's not hard to imagine Louis Jouvet, for example, saying "I need a change of perimeter." "Perimeter! Perimeter!" Arletty would have responded. "Do I look like a goddamn perimeter?" It would have been less tidy, less musical, heavier. But, ultimately, it would have changed nothing. These are the kinds of reply that leave the character without a response. They are used to pin a character in place, with a touch of superiority and condescension. Worse than that—they turn the character into a target. Arletty thus became the pugnacious and comical little Parisian we see on screen, but an uneducated one, which triggers our laughter.

The dialogue spoken by the poacher Marceau in *Rules of the Game*—"Do you want my rabbit, Schumacher?" or "Me? I don't have an old mother"—belong only to this character, even though we know they are being masterfully interpreted by the great Carette. The difference between these two types of dialogue is that in the case of the author's dialogue, we only remember the reply, whereas the actor's dialogue forces us to recall the visual scene itself and the elements of the situation. In the former approach we are "outside the film," in the latter we are not only in the film, we *are* the film.

The New Wave's admiration for *Rules of the Game* was based in part on the film's masterful dialogue (considered the best in French cinema if not the world), which it used as a model for its own productions. Both simple and wise, apparently natural but highly sophisticated, it speaks the characters, leads the action, builds the plot. But most importantly, it perfectly mimics the words of a real conversation, binding the scene together. We get a good idea of Renoir's approach during the celebrated exchange between the Marquis and Marceau during the ball at the château. "Well, the first thing I try to do, whether I want to win a woman, or leave her, or keep her, is make her laugh. When a woman laughs, she is disarmed, you can do what you want with her." A conventional scriptwriter would have stuck to this incisive formula and have been satisfied with its effect.

Renoir, however, dampens its brilliance by allowing Marceau to continue as follows: "But you, Sir, why don't you try to do the same?" "My poor Marceau, because you need talent!" "Of course." The letdown suddenly voids the formula and allows the strangeness of the situation to resonate: this surprising, friendly complicity between two men who are socially worlds apart but humanly close through their part-childish, part-infantile and playful nature. And it enables the wily Marceau to use this complicity to his advantage by asking (practically ordering) the Marquis to find out if Schumacher has been wandering around the grounds.

In reality, point of view determined the distinction between the dialogues the New Wave rejected and the ones it accepted—Cocteau's, primarily, and especially the dialogue he wrote for Bresson's *Les Dames du bois de Boulogne*, the dialogues contracted and supervised by Becker and Ophuls, Melville's taciturn dialogues, Tati's absent, faded dialogues, the theatrical dialogues modeled on Pagnol and based on everyday Provençal speech, or Guitry's, composed as a bouquet of fireworks in search of paradoxical truths. It wasn't a question of style. After all, Audiard has a definite and recognizable style, which claimed to be part of the Rabelaisian or post-Celinian tradition established by the creators of the language. Dialogue, like the traveling shot, is a question of morality. The young directors of the New Wave wanted to provide a voice for the people they were filming. It was a matter of life, truth, and incidentally, and therefore fundamentally, democracy. Real people didn't speak like they did in French films of the period, and they certainly had no desire to speak like them. The writers of the *Cahiers* used to say that "It's 1958. Young people don't talk to one another the way they do in a Duvivier film." The words and expressions are different. And consequently, their attitudes, gestures, and even the sparkle in their eyes are different.

From this point on dialogue, even more than the screenplay, became one of the New Wave's most important critical issues. It wasn't perceived in the same way, however, by the two generations that formed the New Wave. The first generation had been deeply influenced by literature. Far from trying to free themselves from it, they accentuated this influence. Alain Resnais is the perfect example of this approach. Not only did he refuse to write narration (short documentaries) or dialogues (fictional feature films) but he turned the work over to a well-known writer. Resnais pretended to obliterate himself behind this writer and requested that he create a narrative object

es cuisses? - Aussi... - Tu vois mon derrière dans la glace?

3
4

- Oui... - Tu les trouves jolies mes fesses ? - Oui, très... - Tu veu

that he could explore with his camera. This need to objectify what he filmed explains an approach to film that was based on authors more or less closely associated with the nouveau roman (Duras, Robbe-Grillet, Cayrol, Semprun, even Queneau).

Dialogue thus lost its informational function. It no longer guided the plot or served as the engine of the action. It was heard and spoken as if it belonged to another, parallel world, the world of cinema, and it operated in a closed circuit, mechanically, as if it had been stored permanently in memory. Resembling the mechanism of information technology, it was repetitive and yet uniquely singular (the lines from *Hiroshima, mon amour*, "You're killing me, you're good for me" and "You're completely Japanese or not completely Japanese"). This dialogue, even when terribly dated, as it was in Henri Bernstein's *Mélo*, became an object of study (How did "it" control the affect of an era?) and broke with the way dialogue had been used before Resnais. It became a vehicle for Brechtian alienation, but it no longer stunned the viewer; it forced him to reflect. Once active, stimulating, and provocative, it now introduced a grisaille of neutrality and indifference. Much later, in his last films he tried to recover and integrate the faceted dialogue of traditional French cinema.

Other directors were less audacious. Chris Marker, a writer as well as filmmaker, blended word and image in a continuous interplay of mirrors that reflected one another. This same method was used by Agnès Varda, who turned dialogue into a form of impulsive preciosity displayed in many of her films. Alexandre Astruc assumed a slightly faded, flamboyant tone, in the tradition of Chateaubriand and Malraux. Pierre Kast played the role of a libertine in his drypoint dialogues, modeled on Laclos, Stendhal, and especially Roger Vailland. Jacques Doniol-Valcroze cultivated an amused, though disillusioned, style that oscillated between Maurois and Valéry-Larbaud. Georges Franju directed Hervé Bazin's novel *La Tête contre les murs* for the screen, based on Jean-Pierre Mocky's adaptation. (Because of his lack of experience, producers were hesitant to use Mocky for the film and forced him to sell the story. He did, however, obtain the principal role in the film and the promise that he would direct his next project, *Les Dragueurs*, in 1959.) There was nothing innovative about Franju's dialogue, however. It is simple, functional, and has been surreptitiously turned into a vehicle for the birth of a strange fantasy world.

Rohmer, although he belonged to this generation, participated, cinematically speaking, in the next.

Although his dialogues are a model of the genre—considered sufficiently literary to be published (which is uncommon)—their primary purpose was to grasp, in an almost sociological sense, the nature of contemporary speech. The way he worked is well known: Rohmer spent from six months to a year with his actors before filming, and, from among the constant stream of lighthearted conversation, kept anything that seemed interesting or witty, the idiosyncrasies and words common to his actors and actresses. He inserted them in a carefully written dialogue, which thus assumed a casual air and produced an illusion of impulsiveness and spontaneity. This grammatical rigor was consistent with the behavior of his characters. And it was needed to introduce a certain amount of play—perverse play—within the rectitude of their behavior. By shifting the use of words and phrases, it instilled a kind of license into their sense of morality. In this way Rohmer crafted a form of speech that would be the French of today if we were still capable of using our language properly, that is correctly and simply. It was an attempt to fuse the "written speech" of the eighteenth century with the "spoken speech" of the twentieth. The result is an impression of strangeness and fascination, expressed by the feeling of suspense that a now captive and attentive audience associates with long, *intentionally* anti-cinematic discussions.

Truffaut—more childish, liberated, and insolent ("We want to liberate dialogue")—adopted the tone of the second generation of the New Wave. One that was more accurate. Exit the outmoded dialogue that unfolds over time, follows an idea, modulates its effects, leads the scene, calculates its fall—in short, is based on a solid logic of construction. Enter the discontinuous, the cerebral, the unplanned and impromptu, the dialogue that obeys the mood of the moment. Rupture becomes the rule in dialogue. It oscillates between the non sequitur of the Marx Brothers, the stylistic exercises of Queneau, and the suddenness—the gravity—of the brilliant word or phrase in Blanchot. A dialogue that rides around in a convertible, moving down the highway in fourth gear just like in the films of Robert Aldrich and Howard Hawks. It was dialogue for a generation that planned to take maximum advantage of consumer society.

Paul Gegauff would become the master initiator of this approach and a source of inspiration, even—especially—when he turned this dialogue against the characters who spoke it. His elitist dandyism rejected the hedonism associated with consumer society. For Gegauff hedonism was the source of the vulgarity and

7
8

aimes? -Oui. Énormément. - Doucement, Paul. Pas si for

Pardon Camille. – Qu'est-ce que tu préfères ? Mes seins ou la

lack of culture, the crass materialism that was inevitably detrimental for those who went along with it. From this point of view, the film he put together for and with Chabrol, *Les Bonnes Femmes* (1960), remains one of his masterpieces, a cult film of the New Wave and a model for its new dialogue. A talented writer, though precious, brilliant, and cynical, he had a volatile personality that cultivated and cherished a kind of affected wickedness. This fascinated Rohmer, who became friends with him at the end of the forties. It was the direct source of inspiration for two of his films, *Le Signe du Lion* and *La Carrière de Suzanne*. It also had a profound influence on the young writers at *Cahiers du cinéma*, to whom Rohmer had introduced Gegauff, in particular Godard and Chabrol. Chabrol, starting with *Les Cousins*, used Gegauff as his scriptwriter on nearly a dozen films. This lent a kind of *Gegauffian* tonality to all the first New Wave–*Cahiers* films, with the exception of Truffaut. Perceptible in the character of Poiccard (Belmondo) in *Breathless*, it is characterized by a handful of distinctive traits.

Wit, authorial dialogue, even the character's dialogue gave way to facile bits of wordplay ("Get in your Alfa, Romeo," Godard), hackneyed puns ("I'm going to be perm-in-Nantes," Demy; "Satan's in me," Mocky), shopworn vagaries ("In Mexico you can say I never saw such a Mex-i-cun," Godard), or the latest joke ("What's the difference between Florence and Bécon les Bruyère?" Answer: You may find a woman named Florence in Bécon les Bruyère, but you'll never find a woman named Bécon les Bruyère in Florence.). In short, the shared foundations—some might call them the dregs—of the collective language that furnishes the vacuity of everyday conversation.

But this shared background extended to language as a whole and covered the entire field of a civilization that was now seen to be mortal. Godard claimed that dialogue, like film in general, had been thrown on the scrap heap. It functioned only by and through its references. A dubious joke was succeeded by a poem of Lautréamont, a philosophical reflection, a line from a novel, a reply from a film, and so forth. The quote, the private joke, the collage of an entire song by Fréhel (Eustache) or Boby Lapointe (Truffaut), a sketch by Devos (Godard), the maniacal respect, down to the comma, shown to an original text by Kleist or Chrétien de Troyes (Rohmer)—these were now paramount. The limit of such intertextuality was reached by Godard in a film appropriately entitled, *New Wave*. There wasn't a line of dialogue in the film

that wasn't borrowed. As Godard enjoys pointing out, the only word in the film by him is "hello."

Unlike previous generations, New Wave characters no longer felt as if they were the owners of their words or the artisans of forged repartees, honed to the fine edge of a dueling sword. The word was no longer certain and secure. It no longer belonged to them; they were only users, borrowing their words from the remains of a decadent civilization. Jacques Demy, for example, knew that paradise was lost, the paradise of a defunct genre known as melodrama. His dialogue could thus be treated by an audience as "between quotes" so to speak, ironically. His job was to subvert this tendency, to get the public to accept his dialogue, to again experience dialogue directly, without irony. Demy ran a considerable risk in doing so, and this risk was further increased by the use of sung dialogue. In the end, he provoked a response from audiences that fell somewhere between extreme irritation, anger, ridicule, and amazement.

Similar effects could be ascribed to Truffaut. Nothing irritated him more than the brilliant, precise dialogue that characters hurled at one another machine-gun fashion in "quality" cinema. There were exceptions, of course: Guitry, Hawks, Lubitsch. But they belonged to another era. Truffaut knew the common man always makes the best he can of language; he spends three days mulling over the reply that was on the tip of his tongue. Or he spends three days preparing a reply that he blurts out inappropriately at the moment of utterance. Truffaut's entire body of work falls within these poles. Each character is approached from the point of view of language, the character's problem with language, with others, and with himself. This is why language occupies such a central place in his work (*L'Enfant sauvage*). In Truffaut speech and cinema blur together. Their relationship to the verb, the word, to language, becomes the true essence of his characters, the deep subject of his films. In Truffaut speech is not used for an exchange of repartees, like a tennis match, but tries, feverishly, passionately, to construct a dialogue. The physical urge is so strong, so violent, as in *La Femme d'à côté*, that failure can only result in tragedy. The word, like love in *The Last Metro*, is both joy and suffering.

The interiorization of dialogue as a fundamental and constitutive element of film structure was a characteristic New Wave innovation. It marked the preference of directors for such an approach in spite of their diversity (the return to deliberate exteriorization, as in Bertrand Tavernier, Bertrand

paules ? Tu les aimes ? - Oui. - Moi j'trouve qu'elles sont pas

13

assez rondes. - Non, ça va. - Et mes bras? - Mh, oui. - Et mon visage

14

Aussi. - Tout ? Ma bouche, mes yeux, mon nez, mes oreilles ?

17

18

– Oui. Tout. – Donc, tu m'aimes totalement. – Oui. Je t'aime tot

Blier, and other less talented directors, was the sign of an anti-New Wave reaction). Individual directors approached dialogue differently, of course. In Rivette, for example, the dialogue was external to the narrative situation. Having lost its sense of finality, it continued without end. It occupied a space, a terrain that assumed the appearance, whether concrete or virtual, of a scene. Dialogue thus became the theater that his camera recorded. The process of creation was now reversed. Dialogue was no longer dependent on the situation but rather created it through improvisation—created and recreated it. Rozier, Pollet, Pialat, and Eustache—all start out with a shared concept, but the everyday language they employ in their films diverges increasingly. Rozier uses dialogue like a choreographer; Pollet employs it like an obsessional leitmotiv; Pialat treats it as a form of spectator combat; and Eustache immerses it in the film to further its escape. The post-New Wave, based on the attitudes of its predecessor, followed suit: Philippe Garrel and André Téchiné, for example, or clever outsiders such as Jean-Pierre Mocky or humorists like Luc Mollet.

In Godard dialogue no longer develops continuously, along a gradual dramatic curve. The characters' responses are no longer confrontational, thus eliminating any sense of conflict. Conflict can occur, of course, but it happens suddenly, without warning. It is simply another source of environmental noise. Dialogue is reduced to a succession of monologues or soliloquies, a series of reflections and commentaries that a character utters, depending on the response a given state or situation triggers in him. Following Rossellini and pushing his insights to their extreme consequences, Godard restores to dialogue its primary function: resonance.

To accomplish this, he plays with the mechanics of film. Godard understands that on the editing table, the film track moves in synch and in parallel with each of the two sound tracks. For most directors, these sound tracks should converge and blend to support and strengthen the dramatic power of the image. Godard approaches the tracks not only as independent elements, but also as elements with equal value, and moreover a value equal to that of the film track. Mentally, he superimposes them on one another, like a cross-section of different layers of consciousness. While each continues to play an independent role, he establishes between them a kind of echo or reverberation, an exchange, a dialogue that no longer originates in narrative but in poetics. At the end of *Every Man for Himself,* there is a scene in which the husband lies on the ground dying after being hit by a car. His ex-wife and their daughter view the accident but don't get involved. The woman says to the daughter, "Come Cécile, this doesn't concern us," and as they leave, they walk in front of the orchestra for the film. The bottommost sound track now rises to the surface (in the sense that the music track is the last to be finished and added during editing). Its sudden visualization, through the introduction of the physical reality of the orchestra, liberates and unleashes an emotion and affect that the film and its characters had, until then, gone out of their way to contain, to hold in check. The dialogue, obstinately refused throughout the film, finally bursts forth, but too late.

The work of Jean-Marie Straub and Danièle Huillet is different, and even more radical. The dialogue (the dialogues of Corneille, Sophocles, Hölderlin, Kafka, or the music of Bach, Schönberg, etc.) is no longer interiorized, nor even enclosed. It is simply closed. Signifying nothing, illuminating nothing it certainly doesn't distract with its brilliance. It exists only as a unit: compact, dense, impenetrable. Based on an absolutist Marxist conception, which makes Resnais's approach appear lighthearted and pleasant, the Straubs reject the use of frivolous intelligence and futile comprehension. The film is conceived as a hard, unyielding object that demands an intense effort of understanding. This is the very goal the New Wave had set for cinema: to learn again how to recognize the truth of the real. This asceticism wasn't without humor or joy, however. The Straubs wrote a cantata on film: "Cinema Remains My Joy."

* Excerpts from *Contempt* (Jean-Luc Godard, 1963)

captions

1. *Cleo from 5 to 7* (Agnès Varda, 1962)
2. *Brigitte et Brigitte* (Luc Moullet, 1966)
3. *Hiroshima, mon amour* (Alain Resnais, 1959)
4. Emmanuèle Riva and Eiji Okada in *Hiroshima, mon amour*
5. Delphine Seyrig, *Last Year at Marienbad* (Alain Resnais, 1961)
6. *Last Year at Marienbad*
7. Emmanuèle Riva in *Hiroshima, mon amour*
8. Emmanuèle Riva and Eiji Okada in *Hiroshima, mon amour*
9. Charles Aznavour and Jacques Charrier in *Les Dragueurs* (Jean-Pierre Mocky, 1959)
10. Bourvil and Jean Poiret, *Un drôle de paroissien* (Jean-Pierre Mocky, 1963)
11. Gianni Esposito and Françoise Prévost in *Paris nous appartient* (Jacques Rivette, 1958–1961)
12. Jean Seberg, *Breathless* (Jean-Luc Godard, 1960)
13. Juliette Mayniel, Jean-Claude Brialy, and Gérard Blain, *Les Cousins* (Claude Chabrol, 1959)
14. Michèle Meritz and Gérard Blain in *Le Beau Serge* (Claude Chabrol, 1959)
15. Claude Mann and Jeanne Moreau in *La Baie des anges* (Jacques Demy, 1963)
16. On the left, Corinne Marchand, *Cleo from 5 to 7*
17. Anouk Aimée in *Les Mauvaises Rencontres* (Alexandre Astruc, 1955)
18. Martin Loeb in *Mes Petites Amoureuses* (Jean Eustache, 1974)

During the 1950s, a number of advances in film technology affected optics, film stock, processing, photography, and especially lighting. The primary reason for these advances was the growing popularity of television.

The historical background to these innovations is worth examining. One of the reasons for the sudden use of sound in film was the rapid spread of radio and the easily used portable phonograph. It became obvious that the film industry could no longer expect audiences to watch silent films when at home the radio brought them music and news of the world. Enormous amounts of money was spent researching how to add sound to film, and by 1931 the film industry's financial backers were assured of success. Like the *Titanic*, proud of its unrivaled supremacy, cinema considered itself invincible.

But the film industry failed to account for technological advances in radio broadcasting. Laboratories had succeeded in transmitting not only sound but images. Between 1945 and 1952 the film industry struggled to win back the loyalty of the consumer who could now watch images at home. The industry's first reaction was simply to ridicule its rival by pointing out the obvious disadvantage of a small screen. To do so, it unearthed a technical invention that had been discovered in 1927 and fallen into oblivion: CinemaScope, invented by Henri-Jacques Chrétien, enabled filmmakers to double the size of the screen. In 1952, with stupefying audacity, the film industry produced yet another version of the passion of Christ, entitled *The Robe*. The film, however, was a flop.

This was followed by a deregulation of film formats. The earliest format ratio used was 1.33:1 (1.33 meters wide by 1 meter high). This format, which had remained nearly unchanged since the beginning of the cinema, was used throughout the classic film period for both silent films and talkies. Nearly square in size, it resulted in a pleasing and subtle composition, with good balance among vertical, horizontal, perpendicular, and oblique planes. It gradually disappeared, so that it is now impossible, aside from a handful of specialized screening rooms, to view an accurate projection of a Chaplin film whether from the twenties or fifties. The format left a lasting impression on the imagination of cinephiles of the period, including the New Wave. The New Wave directors, however, were forced to use one of several expanded formats (1.66:1 for CinemaScope) that had come into use.

More often than not, CinemaScope was a requirement rather than a matter of choice. When it was introduced,

Anna Karina and Jean-Paul Belmondo in *Pierrot le fou* (Jean-Luc Godard, 1965)

Pierrot le fou

Nicholas Ray and Anthony Mann were the only directors who voluntarily, and quite naturally, embraced CinemaScope (in *Contempt*, Fritz Lang remarks that it had been invented to film snakes and burials), using the horizontal frame to express a personal poetics. The older 1.33:1 format continued to be used for a while but was soon abandoned entirely. Its spirit lingered throughout the sixties, however, and haunted the films of Rohmer, Eustache, Straub, Marker, and others. They consented to the use of 1.66:1 format films simply because it was the closest format offered to them. Some New Wave directors took an interest in CinemaScope. Resnais, for example, in *Le Chant du Styrène* (his last short documentary feature), willingly embraced its artificiality. Truffaut, in his first four features, preferred black and white to wide-screen color, which had become common. Godard infused his use of the wide-screen format with a poetics of space redolent of Nicholas Ray. Demy, beginning with *Lola*, always conceived his films for wide screen projection.

But CinemaScope and its various derivatives wasn't enough to prevent the inevitable rise of television. Television wasn't perceived as a form of defense or competition, but as a necessity, and it thus had to affirm its existence. Consequently, it attempted to quickly eliminate a cinematographic technology that was both costly and inadequate, and invested in research on new methods of production and distribution. Television, for example, turned from 35 mm to 16 mm, and eventually eliminated film stock altogether for video and digital processing techniques. These advances nevertheless had positive effects on the film industry that would alter its style and ultimately contribute to the growth of the New Wave revolution. These advances affected cameras, optics, film, and the use of light.

Until the fifties the cameras used for non-documentary films were heavy, hard to operate, and required several people simply to set them up and move them. Cameras could be made lighter by removing their noise insulation and synch systems. This was what the Italian neorealists did; they shot film without sound and post-synchronized. Television's need for lightweight and easily portable equipment, however, led to the development of 16-mm cameras like the Coutant.

The desire to break with heavyweight hardware and achieve a freedom of movement that enabled filmmakers to move in step with the life around them also affected non-documentary film. Lightweight cameras like the Arriflex and Cameflex became very popular. The 35-mm Arriflex was invented by the Nazis during the Second World War to film news and current events, and it developed an effective weapon for disseminating information. The Cameflex was French. It was Jean-Pierre Melville's favorite camera. Both of the Arriflex and the Cameflex cameras were lightweight and portable and could be easily synched. Carried around on the operator's shoulder, it could closely follow the actors' every movement. A new intimacy developed between the camera and its subjects. The act of filming became a close physical encounter.

An effective filming technique was created and developed by the news cameraman (a considerable amount of physical training was required to obtain control over the operator's body movement), and it was soon applied to journalism, which it thus helped free from the confines of traditional, static documentary. Jean Rouch, a disciple of Rossellini, made use of the portable filming technique in his ethnographic work. Intent on revealing the rites, customs, and imagination of a people, Rouch was able to meet his subjects on an equal footing. A film like *Les Maîtres Fous*, made in 1954, incurred the wrath of traditional ethnographers, however, who felt they were objective observers (an attitude that implied the superiority of the observer, protected behind a mask of "scientific" neutrality) and did not appreciate an intimate approach that invited the audience to *participate* in the trance of the other. The film, however, had a profound impact on both documentary filmmakers (Marker, Resnais) and the *Cahiers du cinéma* of the future New Wave. Rouch reinvented and concretized the myth visualized by Dziga Vertov in *Man with a Movie Camera,* in which a lone individual sees, hears, and films the world through a movie camera that has become the direct instrument of a mind constantly on the alert.

Contempt (Jean-Luc Godard, 1963)

Pierrot le fou

By the end of the fifties, the hand-held camera had become commonplace. Alongside ethnologists, the portable camera became popular with journalists such as Drew Associates in the United States (Mekas, Leacock, Pennebaker, the Maysles brothers), who were looking for a new means of expression, and John Cassavetes and Shirley Clarke applied the method to fiction. In France the lightweight camera was quickly adopted by the New Wave. With *Breathless*, Godard best demonstrated its physical and aesthetic advantages (his preference for paradox led him to "pit" the lightweight Cameflex against the heavy Mitchell in the same film). In terms of craft, the camera enabled filmmakers to abandon the use of heavy equipment (and its operators) and provided rapidity of movement and execution (with less time required during filming). It gave them the ability to film from a variety of vehicles (the camera operator could work in anything from a car to a baby carriage), which allowed the use of camera movements that were not only unthinkable but impossible with dolly tracks. And it introduced the camera into actual spaces whose cramped quarters reinforced the impression of real life. Aesthetically, a new and unexpected style exploded across the screen and added a sense of buoyancy to otherwise serious issues. It was as if the law of gravity had been temporarily suspended.

The handheld camera became one of the distinctive features of the New Wave, which employed it well during location shooting, generally avoiding the waltzing movements which Lelouch was so fond of, (which quickly turned into an annoying mannerism). An intentional technique of making the camera shake to convey veracity was introduced shortly after. No longer placed in a vehicle to reduce camera movement and prevent the frame from shaking, the cameraman was asked to walk either behind or in front of the actor, which, in spite of the operator's efforts, inevitably caused the film image to jump around. When used with care, as in Jean-Marie Straub's *Othon*, it resulted in a brutal realism, a strong sense of concreteness. But during the seventies, the technique became so commonplace, and was so frequently praised by critics who extolled its sublimity, that it soon fell into aesthetic disrepute. With the arrival of the steadycam, it disappeared from the screen.

OPTICS

For many years technological innovations in camera optics were rare. There were, however, a number of gradual improvements as lenses became sharper and allowed more light to pass through to the film. New optics were designed for special uses (undersea photography, astronomy, scientific research, etc.), yet each individual lens was unique. A camera operator generally carried around a complete set of the principal lenses, which he carefully tested before a shoot, one at a time.

This changed with the introduction of variable-focal length lenses. Invented after the war, they didn't become widely used, however, until after 1950 (first in 16 mm, then, by the end of the decade, in 35 mm). Such lenses are now generally referred to as zoom lenses. They enable the operator to make a continuous transition between short and long focal lengths. These lenses covered an extremely wide field and, within the field of view, provided a constant change in perspective. This had a very distinct effect on the viewer's perception of the image and the incessant modulation gave the impression of movement, the illusion of moving toward or away from the subject.

The impact on the industry was immediate, although its effect was first felt in television. When filming news events, zoom lenses provided the cameraman with an opportunity to remain physically stationary and maintain his distance from the filmed subject, while moving in for a close-up or pulling back for a long shot by simply turning a small lever. He had the ability to isolate the subject from the surroundings or immerse the subject in his environment. He could introduce an element of abstraction into the image by pushing the subject out of the frame or making him immediately present, placing him concretely in his world at will. The traditional approach to news reporting was revolutionized and the zoom lens became an essential component of journalism; it provided the ability to film, to capture, the immediacy of an event (the assassination of Lee Harvey Oswald for instance). At the same time its use raised a number of ethical and political questions. Did filmmakers have the right to film a subject surreptitiously or should filmmakers clearly indicate the distance from which they would film (and stick to it)? The issue still remains an open question, which cinematographers such as Pierre Lhomme and Yann Le Masson have been debating since the zoom's introduction.

Film directors reacted quickly to the new technology, especially Rossellini. Throughout his career Rossellini had linked the framework of his subjects' lives with the film frame, which he made entirely subject to the events that unfolded

Pierrot le fou

Pierrot le fou

within it. In the tradition of Griffith, this frame (or frames) imprisoned the individual otherwise capable of flight. It circumscribed the unfolding of the world, of history, of the character's personal history, subjecting him to anxiety and fear (tellingly the title of his last film with Ingrid Bergman). Like a scientist observing the reactions of a guinea pig in a maze, Rossellini filmed the disquieting febrility of characters no longer in harmony with the world around them.

Rossellini made a number of technical improvements to zoom technology, and he personally handled zoom shots during shooting. His techniques reinforced the meaning of his style. The uncertainty of a threatening world could now be expressed tangibly. The frame lost its fixed limits and along with them its reassuring status as a reference. The edges of the frame became fluid and relentlessly tracked their prey, and the impression of anguish was reinforced. The characters had only one desire: flee or fight (one often succeeded the other, for combat was the final solution to flight). Beginning in 1960 with *General Della Rovere* and *Era Notte a Roma*, Rossellini's style became increasingly, and sometimes violently, dependent on the zoom lens. His technique reached its apogee in *The Rise of Louis XIV* (1966), a film made for French television. The incessant change in the edges of the screen contradicted the young king's foolhardy attempt to design a framework (Versailles) that would fix his sense of absolute power like the sun in the sky, immobilize it like death. With twentieth-century irony Rossellini captured, recorded, and painted a sense of seventeenth-century vanity: the vanity of trying to turn the self—or its alter ego, the royal "we"—into the only event worthy of centering everyone else's existence.

Luchino Visconti was another director who made superb use of zoom techniques, but gave them a different meaning. Visconti was interested in filming splendor at its zenith, the moment when decadence begins. He wanted to capture the magnificent brilliance of the majestic flower that masks the beginning of the inexorable process of its decay. Visconti used zoom for the insidious, secret, nearly invisible task of manifesting death's hand at work. It is important to realize that although Hitchcock juxtaposed zoom and traditional fixed focus techniques to obtain effects that were visually disturbing (*Vertigo*), the technique was rarely used for genuinely artistic ends at this time.

Sometimes it was used to purely negative effect. During the sixties, television and film succumbed to a highly contagious disease known as *acute zoomitis*. The camera danced from angle to angle and twisted in every direction.

Les Carabiniers (Jean-Luc Godard, 1963)

Filmmakers peppered the audience with a flurry of high-speed zoom shots, usually resulting in an audience knock out. At best, faced with this unsettling pitching and tossing, the audience merely became seasick. Directors acted like children with a new toy, and they convinced themselves that this was the mark of their "style," that they were being modern. The sympathetic desire of a director like Lelouch to infantilize cinema easily succumbed to the zoom craze, and just as easily went out of fashion.

With the exception of Jacques Doniol-Valcroze, whose own attack of zoomitis led to *L' Eau à la bouche* (1960), the New Wave in general appears to have approached the technique with some reserve. It is important to remember that, the New Wave retained its fascination with classic cinema and, in spite of the temptations of the large screen, showed a marked preference for the 1.33:1 format. The idea of the movement of the frame shocked the New Wave; yet, it was pragmatic to take advantage of zoom as a technical innovation. Used cautiously, without trying to draw attention to disagreeable changes in perspective, the zoom was able to replace the dolly shot. This resulted in a considerable savings in production costs and set-up time. Far from rejecting zoom techniques, the New Wave was quick to make use of them, since they eliminated the need to keep changing fixed-focus lenses. The proper focal length for an individual shot could now be obtained by a simple movement of the hand, but the selected focal length remained fixed for the duration of the shot.

Aesthetically, the New Wave felt a certain reticence over perceptible changes in the spatial relationships between shots, but at the same time, such visual changes to the image were felt to be interesting. Purists such as Rohmer and Straub used zoom techniques infrequently, and then only under special circumstances. Rohmer, for example, used it exclusively for his 16-mm films. In his 35-mm productions he used zoom rarely and like a dolly in, considering it optically false. In general the New Wave simply took advantage of the convenience of the new tool.

Les Carabiniers

FILM

During the fifties film underwent a technical revolution. Faced with the number of serious accidents caused by the use of nitrate-based films, an international moratorium on their use was introduced. In spite of a loss in brightness, they were replaced by cellulose acetate film (often called safety film), whose mechanical qualities were similar but which provided stability and non-flammability. This change in film stock had no effect on the aesthetics of the cinema.

The situation changed, however, with the introduction of high-speed film: XX in 1950, Tri X in 1954, and 4X in 1964. Derived from color negative film and intended for 35-mm black and white use, these supersensitive film stocks could be used for natural-light photography in low-light conditions. In particular they offered the possibility of filming outdoors at night using nothing more than existing lighting. The disadvantage was that they provided less definition and that the lack of sharpness made the grain more visible.

Traditional camera operators rejected the "dirty" images these films produced. They used them only when forced to or for economic reasons. The New Wave, on the other hand, understood the aesthetic advantage they offered and saw that the so-called ugliness of high-speed film contained the kind of beauty it had been looking for: a documentary look, an impression of veracity, a realist truth. In 1957, Louis Malle in *Ascenseur pour l'échafaud* was the first to take such a realist approach. It played a significant part in the interest surrounding the film. Other filmmakers followed Malle's lead. But it was in *Les Carabiniers* that Godard maximized the use of contrast. He worked with it as a form of Art Brut, the way Dubuffet treated paint and canvas. He extracted from it a chalk-colored world of immense sorrow, the end of a civilization that has known only war, destruction, and the emptiness of thought as its goal and rationale. Sensitive to the theater of the absurd, his film documented the theater of cruelty of our modern society.

The film, however, was harshly received by the critics and ignored by the public (one evening, a theater on the Champs Élysées simply closed its doors when it discovered there was no one in the audience). In response to the violent attacks on the film, Godard responded, point by point, in *Cahiers du cinéma* no. 146, particularly to those who criticized the film as being "overexposed," "poorly photographed," "amateurish," "badly done, badly lit, just bad." As a craftsman Godard was careful to correct their incompetence in judging

Les Carabiniers

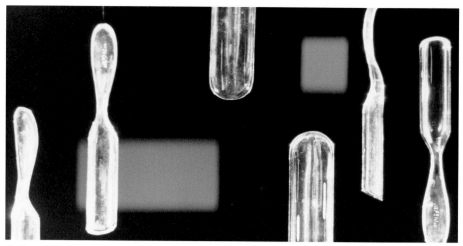

Le Chant du Styrène (Alain Resnais, 1958)

technical matters: "*Les Carabiniers* was filmed on Kodak XX negative film, which is currently the best film on the market, the densest, as smooth as the old Plus X, as fast as Tri X, but with better definition. It is the best film overall, the one with the widest gray scale, as any technician will tell you as he displays its response curve." Godard added that the lab had developed the film for its highest gamma value and that the print "was made without manipulation on special high-contrast Kodak stock. A similar process had been used, rightly or wrongly, to obtain the photographic density of the first Chaplin films, which mimicked the black and white of earlier orthochromatic film stock. Some shots, which were too gray under normal light, were then duped several times to achieve the highest possible gamma level. This was done so they would contrast with the news footage, which was also duped more than is customary."

This was the first time in the history of cinema that a filmmaker had openly displayed an intimate knowledge and understanding of technique and the effects that can be gotten with it, the effects that one can and should obtain, effects which, in expressing an art, determine the viewer's thoughts. The director wryly concluded, "As for Raoul Coutard, after

making five films altogether, he's already on his third award for cinematography." Unfortunately Godard's challenge fell on deaf ears.

After 1960 French cinema was faced with another problem: the introduction of color. Until then, color films had been too expensive and thus uncommon (outside Hollywood at least). It was used almost exclusively for major film productions. But color became increasingly common throughout the industry, and by the end of the decade black and white films disappeared entirely. There was an interim period during which individual filmmakers wavered between the two. Obviously, the New Wave's first films had to be in black and white. But soon it became a question of personal choice. Truffaut deliberately refused to work with color stock until *Fahrenheit 451* (1966), his sixth feature film. Chabrol, however, was the first of the New Wave to use color for a feature when he shot *À double tour* (1959), his third film. But he returned to black and white for his next two films, *Les Bonnes Femmes* (1960) and *Les Godelureaux* (1960). Rohmer didn't use it until he directed *La Collectionneuse* (1967), but he conceived *My Night at Maud's* (1959) as a black and white film. Until 1967 Godard used both color and black and white.

Le Chant du Styrène

Éric Rohmer (on the left, in the car) shooting Le *Signe du Lion*, 1959

His vacillation between the two had as much to do with questions of cost and production as it did with the resistance of someone trained in the classic tradition of superb composition based on rich blacks, brilliant whites, and an infinite range of grays. The idea of abandoning the black and white of their youth affected many New Wave directors almost as deeply as the decision to abandon the silent film for the talkie had affected their predecessors.

But once they accepted the inevitability of color, the New Wave was prepared to tackle it head on. Both Resnais and Demy had been eager to film in color from their first short films. Resnais's *Le Chant du Styrène* (1958) is an abstract painting awash in the violent acidity of industrial color. Demy's *Le Bel Indifférent* (1957) was shot entirely indoors, on a set bathed with an intense red light that reinforced the feeling of claustrophobia and asphyxiation. Both directors made two black and white features before shooting their first color film. Color was never handled naturalistically by Resnais but always imposed on the world—from the apparently dull realism of *Muriel* (1963) to the gradual introduction in his last films of an artificial color scheme that is manifestly theatrical. Color was used to startling (some would say unbearable) effect

by Demy, beginning with *The Umbrellas of Cherbourg* (1964). He splashed color across every surface in the film, blending extremes of tone that are constantly on the verge of harmonic rupture; he let it ripple across the strident thread of laughter and tears, joy and pain, that weaves its way through the film. Color was such an integral part of his universe that he continued to use it for the remainder of his films.

More reserved, Rohmer's pictorial vision remained modest and seemed to bend before the subject at hand. Still, color plays a crucial role in his films, each of which is inspired by a specific painter (Matisse, Mondrian) and is subject to a dominant hue. Unlike Rohmer, Godard's tastes are modern and ostentatiously displayed in his films. During the early part of his career, he took his inspiration from abstract painting and worked with primary colors against a uniform background and, to the extent possible in cinema, without perspective. Beginning with *Every Man for Himself*, he abandoned this cold, objective, external use of color and interiorized it. Godard sought a kind of chiaroscuro effect in which light itself became the primary element in play (recall the director's anguished search for light in *Passion*). Other directors—including Eustache (who clearly displayed a suspicion

Filming *The 400 Blows*

Jacques Rozier (left) shooting *Adieu Philippine* (1960–1963)

toward color and a predilection for black and white), Straub, Rozier, Pollet, and later Téchiné and Garrel—were all somewhat circumspect in its use. The New Wave, with the exception of Jean Rouch, rejected the idea of realistic color, the color the camera mechanically recorded. It remained preoccupied with the idea of not disrupting the viewer's impression of reality and rejected the painter's ability to choose his colors at will. It attempted, within the limits allowed by cinema, not to master color but simply to maintain a certain control over it.

Jacques Rozier (behind the camera) on the set of *Paris nous appartient* in 1958. On the left is chief cameraman, Raoul Coutard.

LIGHTING

André S. Labarthe once made the insightful observation that French quality cinema was concerned only with lighting, the New Wave with light. The New Wave attempted to break the lead shell that studio lighting imposed on film. Throughout the fifties and sixties, not only did the chief cameraman assume a dictatorial role on the set, he tried to impose his own style on the film. This was true not only of Hollywood productions but of films around the world. The well-known cameraman Leon Shamroy claimed, "for me, contrast has become a kind of signature. People used to say to me, 'use more light.' But I liked shadows. Lots of people were able to distinguish my work at first glance regardless of the director." Another cameraman made a similar comment, "I would light significant details more strongly and I was able to do it even though I worked with a large number of directors." Another added, "I think that in this film I've achieved my own style: harsh shadows, brilliant highlights, and lots of reflections on the furniture."

The independence of the chief cameramen of the time was based on the photographic conventions that governed film practice. An image had to be lit from three separate sources, which could be adjusted individually but were all carefully fused into a unified whole. This left the cameraman with ample room to add his personal touch and create what came to be an increasingly academic image. The technique was referred to as "three-point lighting." "The main, or key, light, generally set up like a three-quarter shot on the actor, is used to model the scene and project the actor's principal shadow. The back light is used to highlight objects and delineate them from the background. It adds volume. A fill light is then used to fill in any areas that the main lights missed and open up the shadows."

The theory and practice of film lighting was considered sacrosanct. But the chief cameramen of the New Wave, like their directors, developed a radically different, if not antagonistic, conception of how to light a film. "The main idea," writes Charlie Van Damme in his remarkable book *Lumière actrice*, "was to construct the lighting from naturalistic elements rather than some preconceived idea ... whether it be Glamour, Film Noir, the convention of nighttime shooting ... The key idea was 'What lighting is going to be closest to reality?' We achieved a kind of 'functional' photography that promoted the independence of the camera, the actors, and the director."

The New Wave quickly began to view natural light as the only legitimate source of light. It systematically refused to use

Breathless (Jean-Luc Godard, 1960)

213

Nino Castelnuovo, *The Umbrellas of Cherbourg*

backlighting, except when the real light source was located behind the character. The result—an abomination from the academic point of view—was overexposed scenes, flare, and close ups where the character's eyes are plunged in shadow or his features deformed by direct light. As Charlie Van Damme remarks, the use of a single light source "should, in terms of its intensity, quality, and spatial orientation, translate the reality of the assumed source of natural light. We use a great deal of ambient light, the physical environment being materialized by reflection in place of traditional fill light. This is generally accomplished by using a light source, opposite the camera. This light, which is of very-low power, has the advantage of not casting a shadow." The scene was arranged so that a single shadow was projected by a single light source, unlike the three shadows created by three-point lighting.

The revolution brought about by the New Wave's use of light was largely based on the *single source* of light and the use of *ambient* lighting. This is amply demonstrated in the way the New Wave approached the studio. As indicated earlier, the studio was characterized by the use of a "fifth wall," or ceiling, from which a battery of spot lights was suspended. Direct light fell from the flies and catwalks on to the set, where the absence of a physical ceiling enabled the light to wash over the stage,

pick out the scene, and sculpt space. As Van Damme wrote, "It's impossible to create ambient lighting, except by using so-called 'soft' lighting." The New Wave broke with this tradition. For the New Wave, the use of soft lighting had nothing to do with ambient light. To create a more naturalistic environment, it put a physical ceiling on the stage, something that was felt to be an aberration at the time. Now light no longer came from above but from below. Light was directed toward this ceiling, which served as a reflector and reflected light throughout the scene. This helped restore a sense of truth to the natural environment.

Under these conditions it was easy to create a smooth transition to any location shots in a film. As noted, the willingness to shoot in a natural environment was the natural response not only to economic need but to an aesthetic and moral choice. Light had to be used in a certain way: it implied the use of natural interior light as well as the light implied by "the spatial constraints determined by the architecture of the location." It was impossible to remove walls or hide ceilings, to shift doors and windows the way one could in a studio: everything filmed was real. "The position of the lights and camera [were] dependent on this architecture," which was often quite cramped. This limitation "bore within itself a harmony

Anne Vernon, *The Umbrellas of Cherbourg*

Anne Vernon and Catherine Deneuve in *The Umbrellas of Cherbourg*

that arose from the space and the way it was lit," and resulted in a beauty that was no longer arbitrarily manufactured by the chief cameraman who moves light sources around at will, but from the need to accept the very limited possibilities offered by the location. It emerged from the vibrant light captured directly by the camera. The lighting no longer captured the frozen beauty of a magnificent mausoleum, but the beauty of life.

"New Wave cinematography was never the result of a technical formula, like three-point lighting, but closer to an analysis of the natural light whose technical implications we tried to understand."[1] It was dramatic as well, and forced a confrontation with a realistic context. Thus dramaturgy was subject to the laws that governed the real world. Sound itself reinforced this requirement and gave off its own illumination; it accentuated the physicality of a natural location and, by opening up the scene to voice-overs, plunged the viewer into a universe that was no longer illusionary but absolutely certain. Even a director like Demy saw this relationship. The paradox of his work is that no film is more realistic than *Peau d'âne*.

1   All quotes are from Van Damme, *Lumière actrice.*

1962

JULES AND JIM

VIE PRIVÉE

ADORABLE MENTEUSE

ACCATONE

CLEO FROM 5 TO 7

ADIEU PHILIPPINE

BONNE CHANCE, CHARLIE!

L'AMOUR À VINGT ANS

JULES AND JIM

François Truffaut

TENDER AND SAD

F. T. Henri-Pierre Roché's story relates the trials and tribulations of two friends who love the same woman for a period of more than twenty years. The true subject of the film is the way in which they adapt to this situation. I feel it's a moral film, without any sense of provocation, very tender and extremely sad. I was crazy about Roché's book and circumstances alone made it impossible for me to adapt it for my first film. In fact, I was so crazy about it that the narration is based entirely on sentences taken directly from the book. When a book is as good as this, there's no point in trying to find cinematic equivalences. You've got to read the book out loud, the same way Melville did for *Les Enfants terribles*, and make sure the direction is as straightforward as possible.

M. M. Do you see directing as a language, a kind of cerebral exercise, similar to the "camera-as-pen" concept?

F. T. No. My directing is always very empirical. If I have a style, it's the style used by the majority of directors who produce their own films, a style deter-

mined by the need to stay within budget. For example, if the actors who are speaking are good, there's no point in complicating things: long take. If they're uneven, use an angle/reverse angle shot. For a bad actor alone on screen, use a succession of very short takes with a very mobile camera and soft lighting. For scenes that include violence, fast-paced editing. It's the method used by Samuel Fuller, Otto Preminger, and every other director who doesn't want to waste time or money, and wants to avoid the usual mess associated with making films. ■

Interview with François Truffaut conducted by Michel Mardore, *Les Lettres Françaises*, January 31, 1962

A TENDER HEARTED CARICATURE

I'd like to thank Truffaut for having a world to himself, a tone all his own: his way of framing his actors, for example, which suggests their relationship to those around them, or the way he suddenly intercuts a background shot the way you might open a window. Truffaut's style, or "tone," which finds its perfect expression in *Jules and Jim*, is one largely based on tenderness. I'm thinking of the scenes in which Truffaut's camera follows, with subtly allusive emotion, Catherine and Jules's young daughter. A sense of modesty too, which is expressed through humor and which leads here to a tenderhearted caricature of the belle-époque of the twenties. It is expressed as well in a kind of overall sense of discretion: the discretion of the text and musical score that do more than merely mimic the image. Truffaut doesn't insist, he indicates, glides, especially during the film's dramatic scenes. I can't imagine what another director would have done with the scene in which Catherine, burning her love letters, sets fire to her slip. ■

Jean-Louis Bory "Un fête de tendresse et d'intelligence." *Arts*, February 6, 1962

SENTIMENTAL ROMANTICISM

I reproach Truffaut for having taken this philosophical and somewhat pagan novel, with its frank hedonism (almost indifference at times), and giving it a veneer of gray and sentimental romanticism, which in no way corresponds to the emotional or intellectual choices made by Henri-Pierre Roché. It would have required more humor, more firmness in the characterizations, and a bit less concern for romantic emotions, a sensibility less receptive to affected and exaggerated emotionalism, and less fondness for sing-song poetry.

In comparing the novel to the film, I'm cognizant of the fact that Truffaut wanted to remain faithful to the book, to provide us with a literary film. The story of *Jules and Jim* is the story of a friendship between Jules and Jim and their love for the same woman, Kathe. But none of the essential violence, which arises from the happiness that returns in memory, a kind of disembodied happiness, an insolent, dangerous, and cruel happiness, remains. This is one of the risks in making a film adaptation of a literary work. The more we try to be faithful, the more the camera betrays. It's an artificial genre, and that's why *Jules and Jim* isn't as good a film as *Shoot the Piano Player*, where Truffaut took other liberties. ■

Pierre Marcabru, *Combat*, January 27, 1962

VIE PRIVÉE

Louis Malle

THE B. B. WE EXPECT

It's clear that Louis Malle hasn't for a second tried to clear up the Bardot mystery. Once upon a time there was a very unhappy princess.... From the very first images, the documentary breaks off to become an uplifting fairly tale. Young girls, young girls, beware of sunlight and journalists. Not for a second does *Vie Privée* try to demystify. Just the opposite. La Bardot, as the Italians say, is exactly what *France-Dimanche* and *Ici-Paris* have turned her in to. It's always B. B. Here, B. B. tries to show us how much B. B. suffers by playing B. B., who spends her time showing us B. B. acting, etc. We experience the same sense of vertigo as we do standing in front of a succession of mirrors

or the ad for the Laughing Cow. A laughing B. B. A B. B. who says shit. B. B.'s eyelashes. B. B.'s cheek. And, of course, B. B.'s underwear. Once upon a time we made fun of Jill. But Jill doesn't exist. It's B. B. we want, and it's B. B. we've got. And Louis Malle gives her to us in spades. The only serious criticism we can level at the film is that Malle has given us the B. B. we expect. He plays B. B. exactly as her predecessors played her. B. B. naked in a man's pajama top. B. B. in the morning, rubbing her eyes with her fists like a little girl. It's the same old song. And everyone knows the refrain. ■

Jean-Louis Bory, *Arts*, February 8, 1962

A FILM OF RARE INSIGNIFICANCE

Louis Malle has made a film about Bardot. He's taken advantage of the Bardot myth and, by assuming a critical distance with respect to that myth, has, at the same time also tried to analyze it, introducing into his film—and Malle is careful to let us know it—a touch of fashionable psychodrama.

Is there anything wrong with this? Oh, no! The idea, which could have resulted in a masterpiece, ends up as a film of rare insignificance in Malle's hands. Also it happens to be profoundly boring. Yet, in

spite of Malle's efforts, any camera that stands between Bardot on one side and Decae on the other has got to record a few halfway decent moments. ■

Michel Delahaye, *Cahiers du cinéma*, March 1962

ADORABLE MENTEUSE

Michel Deville

LIKE REAL LIFE

Adorable menteuse (1961) is a masterpiece. This film, perfect in nearly every respect, especially the acting, is dominated by its director. There are a few elements from his earlier films here. For example, Deville continues to include in his scenes several characters, all of whom behave differently and speak simultaneously. His dialogues are still as accurate, and as barely audible, as they are in real life. His male actors, émigrés from the theater, are as irritating as before. But Deville's skill provides a different hue to the same raw materials. In retrospect, *Adorable menteuse* explains what Deville failed to capture in *Ce soir ou jamais*. ■

Luc Moullet, *Cahiers du cinéma*, March 1962

HAPPINESS, PURE, UNADULTERATED

The good humor is never forced, never vulgar. There isn't a trace of anger in this film. It has a kind of dancing movement to it, and radiates a sense of pleasure in simply being alive. Pure, unadulterated happiness. This desire for happiness, which French cinema has long since forgotten, has been rediscovered by Michel Deville with astonishing facility. The film possesses a naturalness and grace all its own. The elegance of the director's style, which was already apparent in *Ce soir ou jamais*, is even more obvious in *Adorable menteuse*. And Deville's elegance has nothing to do with pretense or affectation. ∎

Pierre Marcabru, *Combat*, February 6, 1962

ACCATTONE

Pier Paolo Pasolini

CHAOTIC, IRRITATING, AND AN HOUR TOO LONG

Pier Paolo Pasolini occupies a special place in Italian literature. Poet and novelist of the Roman sub-proletariat (the poorest in Europe), man of the world and polemicist for the far left, apostle of bad manners and occasional gangster (according to the press), Pasolini is preceded by a sordid and lurid past. The Italians refer to him as "their Genêt" and idolize and defile the man behind the initials P.P.P. The comparison is certainly inaccurate. Whenever P.P.P's slang-ridden and sensational stories have been brought to the screen (Mauro Bolognini's *Les Garçons*, for example), they've turned into coproductions diluted with elegant cynicism in which the ragazzi of Trastevere are played by Jean-Claude Brialy in a pinstriped suit. Now, with *Accattone*, Pasolini the director describes his world with ineptitude, insolence, forced solemnity, and a nauseating lack of concern for detail.

The film is chaotic and irritating, and too long by an hour. At least the product is

guaranteed to be original. A series of inimitable faces file past, a bunch of thugs that Pasolini must have recruited from among his friends. Thumbing his nose at the box office, he's tried to make stars out of a bunch of fat and rather pathetic young women who are extremely unphotogenic. Accattone himself, a bargain-basement pimp, is played by a young brute with bulging eyes and a simian gait, who goes by the name of Franco Citti.

The story is overdone and would be unbearable if it weren't interspersed with moments of sudden excess. A procurer, loquacious coryphaeus from the slums, delivers nonstop prophecies to the camera. A starving man devours flowers, grinning from ear to ear. Accattone, dead drunk, lets his wet head loll in the sand, stares like a statue, or rolls his eyes like a madman. The film is a scented elegy to stinking feet, which brings us back (although remotely) to Jean Genêt. Pasolini's displays of extreme bad taste are not frequent enough to distract us from the boredom of the slow-paced, cataleptic action. Today, we've had our share of rambling. What would really be bold in 1962 would be to make a film in which *no one* goes for walks. But the author's pretension explodes on screen in those whiffs of Bach that punctuate the fighting or drinking scenes, or the simplistic dream sequence that adds

absolutely nothing to the film. Yet, his naiveté is astonishing. From one scene to the next, Accattone changes his shoes several times (we're not at Marienbad, however). And the young hero's obvious misogyny makes it impossible to believe in the idyll that seems to set him on the path to "redemption."

Pasolini is playing his own game here. There's no intermediary to interfere with his vision, no doubt authentic, which he attempts in his own way to poeticize. "The world will destroy me, or I'll destroy the world," Accattone cries. His rebelliousness is touching but difficult to understand since P.P.P. doesn't explain it. This baroque commentator is content to express the aggressive disorder of a small marginal world, which society rejects but which fashion may very well reclaim. ∎

Robert Benayoun, *France-Observateur*, April 5, 1962

MEDIOCRE AND FUZZY

Although plausible, the character lacks any real interest or picturesque qualities, and his behavior continuously defies analysis, a defect that in all fairness should be attributed to the director. The other protagonists aren't worth mentioning since they're all more or less associated with the main character. The only thing we know about them for sure is that they're always hungry and passive. Even the story's atmosphere is mediocre and fuzzy, at least throughout the first two "acts." The episode with the four Neapolitan thugs, written in a difficult dialect and no doubt poorly subtitled, is very obscure.

On a poetic and emotional level, the "hero" becomes interesting only at the end of the film; a premonitory dream, a trial run by Accattone in his new career as a thief, a tragic epilogue. The last scenes give the film the energy and poignancy that it lacked all along. The outlines of the true subject begin to emerge: the futility of our attempt to counteract destiny. Accattone assumes a psychological existence; his desperate but fearful melancholy touches us in the end. ∎

Louis Chauvet, *Le Figaro*, April 1, 1962

CLEO FROM 5 TO 7

Agnès Varda

THE STRUGGLE BETWEEN COQUETTISHNESS AND ANGUISH

Y. B. What's the story behind *Cleo from 5 to 7*?

A. V. The encounter of beauty and death expressed as the portrait of a woman over a ninety-minute period. She's a young singer (Cleo), not too well known, spoiled, adulated, who discovers she's sick and suddenly thinks she may die. Nothing has prepared her for this idea, which turns all her relationships with the world upside down. During that hour and a half, she has a chance to gauge the egotism of her close friends. Her need to share with others is so great that she becomes sensitive and attentive to them. This struggle between coquetishness and anguish allows Cleo to be truthful for the first time in her life, at the very moment when that life hangs in the balance.

I tried to make a subjective documentary about a young woman, but also about the people around her, about the Dôme, Parc Montsouris, the way an eye fully conditioned by a sentiment as violent as the fear of death might see them. The time frame and geography are realistic because I wanted to show the subjectivity of mental time and the intermittent importance of place. In the film there are passages that indicate time. They are a lot like a ticking metronome. Whatever happens in the film, they provide a very precise measure of time passing, giving the viewer the opportunity to step back from the action.

Y. B. Cleo's suffering from cancer. Why?

A. V. It's a "popular" fear. Cancer is only one of the forms of generalized anguish. It's also the monster of our era. The struggle with the monster is a classic theme, and the young hero here, who snatches the victim away from the monster, assumes the appearance of a modern hero. He's one of those men whose melancholy courage consists in loving life, in sharing, etc. I also wanted the film to be fixed in time. It takes place on June 21, 1961, and the context of real life assumes the form of a news report that's broadcast on the radio. It's the real news for that summer day and I don't think any fiction exists that isn't connected, directly or otherwise, to a collective situation. ■

Interview conducted by **Yvonne Baby**,
  Le Monde, April 12, 1962

THE PARADOX OF DEATH

Cleo from 5 to 7 relates the unfortunate story of a character who unmasks herself before death, a character who strips herself of her armor and suddenly recognizes her vulnerability. Her revelation doesn't come at once but through a number of petty details, an infinite yet instantaneous sequence of perspectives, which Varda handles as a succession of quick, sharp notes, like a heart skipping a beat. The intelligence of her vision is obvious; the quality of her writing, its precision and intelligence, admirable.

But what's striking beneath this intense white light is the fragility of the heroine's full, rich flesh. It's the paradox of death, the inexplicable degradation of that which appears to be unchangeable. Through the film's excellent cinematography, the accuracy of her portrayal, the refusal of any romantic prejudice (romantic in the most trivial sense), the impassivity of her vision (a violent, almost threatening impassivity, which we experience as a kind of petrified sensibility), Agnès Varda locates the feature, sharp and penetrating, that will enable her heroine to define a life that is astonishingly confirmed at the very moment when it comes undone. At that same moment, through a similar confrontation of two antagonistic forces, as in some luminous dance of death, she grants that life both happiness and despair, the joy of living and the despair of dying. In Varda's film it is time that controls and synchronizes this eternal hesitation. ■

Pierre Marcabru, *Combat*, April 11, 1962

ADIEU PHILIPPINE

Jacques Rozier

THE STRENGTH OF CONVICTION OF A DISCOVERY

I'll say it right away: With *Adieu Philippine* Jacques Rozier has introduced a new attitude and modern characters into French cinema. This is not the first time we've seen young people on screen, or even workers, and the theme of saying good-bye to youth, which is the theme of this film, is nothing new. But it's how you say it that matters. And Jacques Rozier's film has the freshness and strength of conviction of a discovery.

Rozier made a clean break with the past. He forgot everything that had been said and everything that had been filmed about today's youth, from Carné's *Tricheurs* to Godard's *Breathless*, including Chabrol's *Les Cousins*. He rejected established character types once and for all (black leather jackets, the only son, the good worker, bad worker, etc.), also psychology, and even sociology. He chose as his character Michel, a stagehand for television and "typical" Frenchman (he even has a mustache), and followed him throughout his professional and emotional odyssey during the months preceding his departure for the army. And since the film was shot and takes place in 1960, this meant 28 months of service in Algeria.

Rozier is not interested in cinéma vérité here. *Adieu Philippine* is a film with a carefully developed story line, acted by professionals and amateurs (who don't play themselves in the film but roles that Rozier created for them). The only improvisation that took place occurred when the film was being shot. Rozier then rewrote the majority of the script, basing it on the actors' dialogue. ■

Bernard Dort, *France-Observateur*,
  October 3, 1962

"PASS THE SALT" DELIGHTS ME

In one of the very first articles written about *Adieu Philippine*, the author reproached me for having one of my actors say, "Pass the salt." So what's wrong with "Pass the salt?" "Pass the salt" delights me: it's heavenly; it sums up my entire approach to aesthetics. In fact I find that "Pass the salt" is what's missing from film. "Pass the salt" is just as good as "Are you hungry?" "What's it like outside?" "When are you going on vacation?" "What do you think of the new Simca?" "Did you find a spot?" or "When's your next perm?" I think that from now on, critics will understand that I wanted to make a film where the characters are the kind of people you can meet anywhere.

For me these people are the most interesting. Of course they have tiny mustaches, push baby carriages full of kids on Sunday in the Bois de Boulogne, and vacation in St-Brévin-les-Pins or Castelnaudary with the family, and there are probably a handful of aesthetes who will find the film ordinary because it represents ordinary people.

Three crews, each with a photographer and an attractive female reporter, approached young men in the street who looked like they would be good for the film. We asked them a bunch of indiscreet questions on the pretext of doing a survey. The photos taken during the interview were sent to the office along with the reporter's notes. I called the most interesting prospects and from that group, gave the ones that looked best for the part a screen test. There were ten and we kept four: Jean-Claude Aimini, who played Michel, and three others who played his three friends in the film.

I then hired an Italian girl who didn't speak a word of French and began shooting the film. I had the screenplay and the dialogues, but I didn't give them to the actors. I said, "Here's what's going on. This is what you should say. Now say it however you like, in Italian, French, etc." Several takes, several texts, and I selected the best text or created it during editing using the best moments from each take. I worked this way because I wanted them to mumble a bit in the film. Mumbling is really revealing and very moving. Although I like to follow the script (the scene where the family is eating for instance), I used two cameras to maintain the continuity of the acting. This enabled the professional actors to circumvent (if I asked them) the formal elements of the written text. ■

Jacques Rozier, *Arts*, October 16, 1962

BONNE CHANCE, CHARLIE!

Jean-Louis Richard

A MARATHON OF TRAVELING SHOTS

Unlike French quality cinema, which has made the opening and closing of doors a tired cliché, the new cinema shows an unreasonable fondness for walking. *Bonne chance, Charlie!*, a brilliant illustration of a celebrated song by Henri Salvador, is yet another addition to the already long list of athletic thrillers in which the hero systematically logs three or four miles per reel. We're a long way from the casual flaneur we find in Melville's *Bob le Flambeur*. If I had to choose a name, it would be Rohmer, whose film and Richard's are remotely related through their sense of physical exertion. Moullet would say that *Bonne chance, Charlie!* is *The Mysterious Mr. D.* multiplied by *Le Signe du lion*. He would be wrong otherwise, however. Based on certain stylistic quirks, his refusal to use dissolves, and an immoderate affection for still images and other tricks, Jean-Louis Richard seems to be more a disciple of Truffaut. Using an unchanging, and sometimes effective, approach, the camera never leaves the characters, which results in an orgy of camera movements that transform the film into a marathon of traveling shots. When, by some strange accident, Eddie Constantine agrees to stand still, the director feels he has to reframe the scene from 40 feet back—carefully and cautiously.

In spite of this the film isn't bad. The director has managed to retain an important lesson from American cinema: It's less important to have a directorial style than a way of approaching a serious subject, in this case the survival of Nazism, through a well known genre like the western or police thriller. His illustrious predecessors, Richard Brooks in *Deadline U.S.A.* and *The Last Hunt*, and Delmer Daves in *To the Victor* and *Broken Arrow*, were similarly able to create magnificent "objective and synthetic" parables, to borrow Jacques Rivette's wonderful expression.

Jean-Louis Richard sometimes misses his target because of the sluggishness of the narration, but it's hard not to feel sympathetic toward his attempt, which proves once again that in the cinema, any approach to politics, even when it's naive, is extremely engaging. Following on the heels of films as different as *Le Combat dans l'île* and the admirable *Paris nous appartient*, it's clear that *Bonne chance, Charlie!* confirms that, in this field, the French cinema that isn't, will be. ■

Bernard Tavernier, *Cahiers du cinéma*, September 1962

THE UNDENIABLE PLEASURE OF BEING A TOURIST

The story in *Bonne chance, Charlie!*, takes us to Greece, where the sympathetic Eddie Constantine plays a character based on Lemmy Caution, who is looking for a lost friend while unseen enemies watch his every move and threaten him at every moment.

Such poignant solitude! The camera meticulously describes the hero's risky and often gratuitous wandering. Long walks during which he lingers, sticks close to nearby walls, or quickens his pace to cover his tracks, indicate that some sort of incident is hovering nearby. But the expected event rarely happens. It's as if the director had told Constantine to take us through Athens to save time. Although there's an undeniable pleasure in being a tourist, the action languishes, the "suspense" is disappointing. ■

Louis Chauvet, *Le Figaro*, June 17, 1962

A MODEST SUCCESS

Bonne chance, Charlie! reintroduces the character of Eddie Constantine, who has become solemn, bitter, haunted by moral problems. Yet Richard develops a serious theme without equivocating: the search for a Nazi torturer. The clever staging (a pursuit that takes place in an antique Greek theater), noncondescending dialogue, and well-chosen locations, such as the canals of Corinth and Delos, make for a moderately successful film. ■

R. B., *France-Observateur*, July 28, 1962

L'AMOUR À VINGT ANS

François Truffaut

PARISIAN HUMOR AND BARROOM FRENCH

Jean-Pierre Léaud, older but suffering from the same misfortunes, again plays Antoine, this time as an adolescent in love. Parisian humor and barroom French (the heroine, Marie-France Pisier expresses herself with the same unique distinction as Bernadette Lafont), inane conversations attributed, as always, to the "working people," simplistic refrains borrowed from so-called popular songs (Antoine works in the record business), and a report on youth and music—all populate this somewhat forced follow-up of an over-the-top film that had its moment of fame. After *The 400 Blows* is Truffaut now going to give us *Jules and Jim against the Piano Player?* Forgetting that he is a believer in "cinematic individuality," hostile to any form of literature, Truffaut supplies a second commentary in voice-over (Antoine and another actor who recites Henri Serre). Shades of Aurenche and Jeanson, whom he insulted not too long ago.... ■

Robert Benayoun, *France-Observateur*, June 28, 1962

RESTRAINT, DELICACY, AND SENSIBILITY

It's a trivial subject: as a stratagem to seduce a young woman, a young man decides to seduce her parents. The young woman, indifferent, looks for other love affairs. The young man watches television with the family he has won over. There's nothing to it, or practically nothing, but it's directed with restraint, delicacy, and a wonderful sensibility that is both discreet and ironic. Never has Truffaut been more sure of himself, more precise in the details, the accuracy of his portrayal, and the sense of gentle melancholy. All of this gives an ethereal elegance to the film's realism, which is a characteristic of Truffaut's best work. Jean-Pierre Léaud's naturalness and gravity are astonishing. ■

Pierre Marcabru, *Combat*, June 27, 1962

Sound.

Rohmer's *Le Signe du Lion* was shot using a magnetic sound track on sprocketed 35-mm film. Many of the outdoor scenes that required freedom of movement were shot without sound and synched in the studio. Chabrol's first two films, *Le Beau Serge* and *Les Cousins*, were recorded live, whereas *The 400 Blows* (Truffaut), *Breathless* (Godard), and *Paris nous appartient* (Rivette) were all post-synched. It is obvious, for example, that the scene in which the young Doinel is questioned by the psychologist in *The 400 Blows* could only have been recorded live. But the technical requirements—the full rolls of film (900 feet or 10 minutes) that were used to allow Jean-Pierre Léaud complete freedom to improvise his lines—demanded a tight, static shot, which reinforces the jail-like impression the viewer experiences with such emotional force in this famous sequence.

During the fifties, sound recording changed from optical to magnetic: from live, 35-mm sound with three-phase power to battery packs on a sound truck for location shooting. The means evolved, but it still required an armada of equipment. At the time, filmmakers had a choice between this heavy equipment or sound synching in the studio.

The first New Wave films were not immune to these impediments. They lacked access to the new microphones, or the Nagra 3 or Perfectone, which were self-contained and portable recorders. It has often been said that the New Wave had the advantage of new technologies, but this was certainly not true regarding the use of sound. They had to wait several years before they had access to modern equipment, and it still wasn't available in 1959. Most young filmmakers of the time were aware how useful the new hardware would be. They wanted to build a "dense sound" that would produce the effect of accuracy, of naturalness, and especially of the freedom that went along with their imagery. Aesthetically, even ethically, the New Wave anticipated, prefigured, and prepared the technical revolution in sound, the sound that has been so important in documentary films and journalism.

Breathless was shot without sound, using an unsynched guide track. Godard post-synched the background sound but the dialogue was recorded in bits and pieces. To achieve a "live" effect during shooting, he whispered the dialogue so the actors would appear to be lip synching. In the film we rarely see the characters speak directly to the camera.

Godard used a number of editing tricks to add simple sounds, and the actors are often shot at three-quarter angle or from behind. Godard was already creating voice-in and voice-off effects, using angle/reverse angle shots in which the character seen is rarely the one speaking. As flexible sound recording technology was unavailable, Godard sidestepped the problem by recording the dialogue on an unsynchronized magnetic tape recorder and

Jean Rouch, in *Chronicle of a Summer* (1961) was the first to use the Nagra 3. Rouch, a filmmaker–ethnologist, was always on the lookout for cutting-edge, ultra-lightweight technology. Reducing his crew to a minimum was vital to his work, and this opened the documentary to fictional methods. With his characteristic responsiveness, Godard at once grasped the possibilities of this new tool: the result was *My Life to Live* (1962), in which the fixity of view, which ranged from the coolness of journalistic inquiry to the dryness of police statistics, forces the viewer to listen carefully to the young and attractive Nana,

Filming *Le Signe du Lion*

Jess Hahn in *Le Signe du Lion* (Éric Rohmer, 1959–1962)

inserting it during editing.
The creative use of editing in *Breathless* was dictated in part by the limitations of sound recording when the film was shot. To some extent these limitations were responsible for the sense of innovation that contributed to the film's success.

The Nagra 3 was introduced in 1958. In 1959 the Italian radio station, Rai, signed a contract for a hundred recorders, which it paid for in cash, to cover the Olympic Games held in Rome during the summer of 1960. The machine was an immediate success. In fact, it was so successful that one year later the factory had to expand to increase production to 800 units per year. At first the Nagra 3 was of greatest interest to radio stations and television newsrooms. It was only after 1962 that lightweight cameras and recorders began to make their way into the film market.

In this case a sporting event of global importance engendered the technological revolution the New Wave directors had hoped for but didn't have access to for their first films. It confirmed the need to break with the heavy technical requirements of documentary (especially narration) and replaced them with the immediacy of reporting. The tape recorder finally acquired its independence. Now on an equal footing with the camera, it possessed flexibility. It satisfied the aesthetic need to get as close as possible to the fullness of life's movement and the multiplicity of its varied expression, enabling filmmakers to penetrate the sonorous texture of a lived reality.

exploited, prostituted, and tragically consensual. From this point on sound in Godard was as important, if not more important, than the image.

"Ever since we've been able to work without being tied down with heavy equipment for live recording, people have started talking, they've come alive on screen as never before. Our freedom is also their freedom, and by improving our ability to listen, we sharpen our ability to look." This quote from Nestor Almendros, chief camera operator for Rohmer and Truffaut, perfectly

223

Jean Le Poulain and Jess Hahn, *Le Signe du Lion*

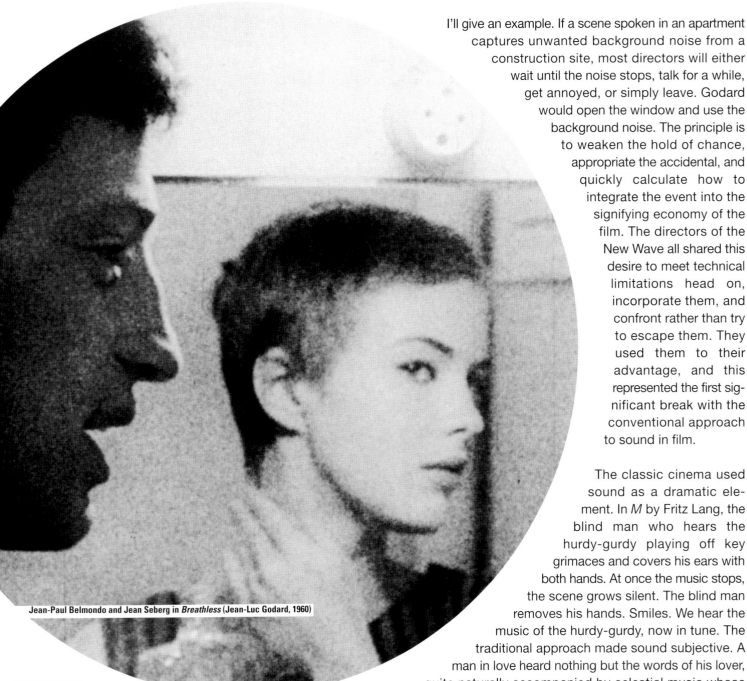

Jean-Paul Belmondo and Jean Seberg in *Breathless* (Jean-Luc Godard, 1960)

I'll give an example. If a scene spoken in an apartment captures unwanted background noise from a construction site, most directors will either wait until the noise stops, talk for a while, get annoyed, or simply leave. Godard would open the window and use the background noise. The principle is to weaken the hold of chance, appropriate the accidental, and quickly calculate how to integrate the event into the signifying economy of the film. The directors of the New Wave all shared this desire to meet technical limitations head on, incorporate them, and confront rather than try to escape them. They used them to their advantage, and this represented the first significant break with the conventional approach to sound in film.

The classic cinema used sound as a dramatic element. In *M* by Fritz Lang, the blind man who hears the hurdy-gurdy playing off key grimaces and covers his ears with both hands. At once the music stops, the scene grows silent. The blind man removes his hands. Smiles. We hear the music of the hurdy-gurdy, now in tune. The traditional approach made sound subjective. A man in love heard nothing but the words of his lover, quite naturally accompanied by celestial music whose purpose was to transport him to another world and obliterate earthly sounds. For the New Wave background noise had as much importance as conversation, and it was heard with the same intensity, the same presence as in reality. Sound was no longer subjective and dramatic. It was the sound of life.

expresses
the revolution
ushered in by the arrival of
the Nagra 3. It enabled filmmakers to capture all the sounds of the city, to establish a kind of equality among them. The murmur of Paris now became as important as the film's music, and it blended with the dialogues. Godard pushed this idea to the extreme by masking—as if to better visualize sound—what the characters were saying: concrete, real, exterior sounds obscure their speech and prevent a clear understanding the words being spoken. For Godard the microphone's range is much greater than the frame; it is not limited by and to the image. Sound has a radius of action so large that it necessarily and simultaneously covers what is both in and out of the frame. The directors of the New Wave played with this idea of off-screen sound and tamed it. They were determined to explore and control what was referred to as "sound pollution."

This approach led the New Wave to combine and compose sound tracks from natural elements, the concrete and trivial components of everyday sound. As I indicated above, this began long before the appearance of the Nagra 3. Even though they were unable to shoot their first films with live sound in the modern sense of the term, that is sync-

Breathless

sound, they managed to overcome the handicap by using lightweight portable tape recorders, which accurately reproduced the beauty of the sounds of Paris. This was unimaginable only a few years before. The documentaries about Paris made during the fifties, unable to use the heavy equipment of the period (sound trucks and bulky batteries), substituted off-screen narration for the absent sounds of the city. In fact, in terms of sound, the filmmakers at *Cahiers du cinéma* remembered the lesson they had learned (again) from Renoir. At the beginning of the talking period, Renoir had the audacity to record in the street and unwrap his mikes. The result? Can anyone forget the river of raw sound flowing into *La Chienne* and *Boudu Saved from Drowning*? Today, these films remain a valuable record of the unique physicality of the sounds of Paris in 1931–1932.

Le Petit Soldat (Jean-Luc Godard, 1960–1963)

Unlike Godard, who had no qualms about "fooling reality," Rohmer, in the tradition established by Renoir, was rigorous in his use of live sound: the sound that wound up in the film should be the same sound recorded during the take. Even if it had to be added later on. If a bird was singing in a tree at five in the morning during shooting, Rohmer would later return alone to record the song of that same bird, under the same tree, at the same time. This notion of presence, of *thereness*, explains and justifies a primordial aspect of the sound revolution initiated by the New Wave. They never manufactured a sound track from tired and dusty clichés (the sound of gulls that was added if the scene took place by the sea or the well-known motorcycle in the night). They rejected traditional ambient sounds, and never considered using a sound library, much less a sound effects technician. They were careful to use real sounds, to scrutinize the grain of sound that characterized the moment, its

Anna Karina, *Le Petit Soldat*

continuity. Today it is easy to combine a sound track using digital audio. But the essential element will always be missing: the fleshiness, the roughness, the materiality of sound. A beach in *Conte d'été* has nothing in common with an artificial beach.

Sound is used to establish the climate of a film and in Rohmer this climate is a separate character. The beauty of the sound in his films has its origin in this authenticity: a sound is beautiful only if it is accurate. In the tradition of Renoir, the filmmakers of the New Wave played with sound ambiance. Unlike the "atmosphere-atmosphere" typical of filmmakers of the French quality tradition, now sound discreetly introduced reality into a situation.

Anna Karina and Peter Kassowitz in *My Life to Live* (Jean-Luc Godard, 1962)

Anna Karina, *My Life to Live*

From a theoretical point of view, little work has been done on the New Wave's interest in sound and its formal revolution. By abandoning traditional ambient sound (where the viewer was bombarded by sounds he was cinematically familiar with) and using an unexpected sound associated with a real environment, the New Wave filmmakers created a sound track that was always unique and caused both the image and the viewer to react; it sparked their attention and visual focus. Confronted with sounds he does not recognize, the viewer's auditory attention was heightened and directed. This was the opposite of what was generally done in film—and which is so often, and badly, done

As a result, when scouting for locations Rohmer first took into account the sound elements even before the visual elements of a scene. Chabrol and Truffaut approached sound from a more traditional point of view, but Rivette remained faithful to these principles and the sound of brush on canvas in *La Belle Noiseuse* (1991) is one of the most beautiful sounds of material ever recorded; handled rhythmically and melodiously, it becomes a musical accompaniment. The same is true of those directors who refused to abandon this approach to sound. Jean Eustache put tremendous effort into finding a rough sound full of imperfections for his films (the café scenes or the record player in the interior scenes in *The Mother and the Whore*). The same is true of Philippe Garrel. The limit was reached by Jean-Marie Straub and Danièle Huillet, who used nothing but the sound made during the actual take, without any alterations. They completely rejected the use of independent or ambient sound.

Anna Karina, *My Life to Live*

228

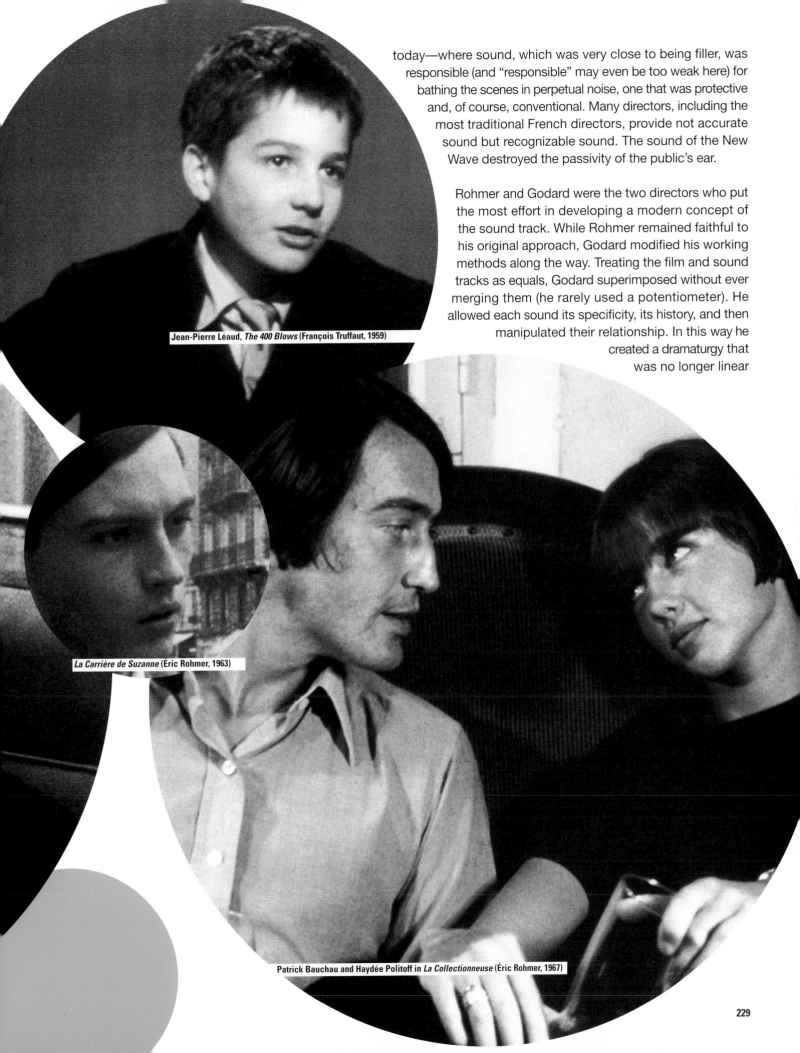

today—where sound, which was very close to being filler, was responsible (and "responsible" may even be too weak here) for bathing the scenes in perpetual noise, one that was protective and, of course, conventional. Many directors, including the most traditional French directors, provide not accurate sound but recognizable sound. The sound of the New Wave destroyed the passivity of the public's ear.

Rohmer and Godard were the two directors who put the most effort in developing a modern concept of the sound track. While Rohmer remained faithful to his original approach, Godard modified his working methods along the way. Treating the film and sound tracks as equals, Godard superimposed without ever merging them (he rarely used a potentiometer). He allowed each sound its specificity, its history, and then manipulated their relationship. In this way he created a dramaturgy that was no longer linear

Jean-Pierre Léaud, *The 400 Blows* (François Truffaut, 1959)

La Carrière de Suzanne (Éric Rohmer, 1963)

Patrick Bauchau and Haydée Politoff in *La Collectionneuse* (Éric Rohmer, 1967)

but multiple, plural. The incessant transition from one track to another created a network of counterpoints and voice-overs between words, noises, sounds, and music, which gave rise to emotional response. In Godard the sound track is always fundamental, sometimes the primary element in the film (recall that he named his own production company Sonimage); it gives birth to the image or alters its nature. Godard skewed the visual image with sound, for he knew different sounds used with the same image changed its meaning and tone.

La Collectionneuse

La Collectionneuse

The filmmakers of the New Wave all shared the characteristic of being good listeners and knowing if a take was good or not by listening to it. They worked like Guitry, Renoir, and Pagnol, who rather than remain on the set, stayed in the sound truck to get a better idea of the scene, convinced that if the rhythm sounded right it would look right, and that the acting and blocking would consequently also be good. They listened to the actors' rhythms, the timbre and song of their speech, the musicality of their words (one of the reasons for their frequent use of voice-overs). They loved accents and especially, like their three old masters, the authentic and inimitable charm of a foreign accent. Subsequently, the casting in their films was often dictated by the beauty of the actor's voice. Jean Moreau, Marie-France Pisier, Jean Seberg, Jess Hahn, Anna Karina, and others had melodious voices or quirky accents, which these directors knew placed as much importance on

Jean-Paul Belmondo and Anna Karina in *Pierrot le fou* (Jean-Luc Godard, 1965)

Brigitte Bardot in *Contempt* (Jean-Luc Godard, 1963)

the way words were said as their meaning. From an aesthetic and financial point of view, the way in which New Wave filmmakers used sound had a lasting effect on French film. Their methods on location, which were very economical (they eliminated post-sync work and studio rentals), were in nearly all respects the same as those in use today. Shortly after the flowering of the New Wave, a number of French sound engineers and live sound specialists developed a following and went abroad to work (in Italy films were still being dubbed, as they were in Spain, where dialogue was censured by the Franco government).

In 1962 the former staff of *Cahiers du cinéma*, those who had now become directors, and the current editorial team prepared a special issue on the New Wave (issue 138). This special issue was extemely successful, completely surprising the magazine's writers, who simply wanted to make a point. Among the various articles, interviews, and roundtables listed in the magazine's table of contents, there appeared a dictionary comprising the names of 62 young directors who had completed their first or second film within the past three years. Each of them was given a thoughtful article, many of which remain surprisingly relevant forty years after their publication. The entries concerning former *Cahiers* staff, however—Kast, Doniol, Truffaut, Chabrol, Rohmer, etc.—while based on material excerpted from their own articles, had been turned over to the two worst critics of the time (Georges Charensol and Louis Chauvet, both of whom were aesthetically, and politically, reactionary).

For example, the article on Godard begins as follows: "From nonchalance to insignificance is but a short step. Jean-Luc Godard has just crossed that threshold. It looks like our new directors will soon be 'breathless.' After *Shoot the Piano Player*, *A Woman is a Woman* burst the bubble of New Wave euphoria. The leaders of the movement are looking more and more like plagiarists who haven't even bothered to dissimulate their sources" (Charensol, *Les Nouvelles littéraires*, Sept. 14, 1961). In his article on Truffaut, Charensol writes, "I've come across quite a bit of fat but very little tasty broth in Truffaut's soup. He obviously doesn't believe that the shortest jokes are the best and seems to take pleasure in pointing out all the absurdities in his scripts" (Charensol, "*Shoot the Piano Player*," *Les Nouvelles littéraires*, Nov. 1960). The articles on Chabrol, Rohmer, Rivette, and the others are similar. Aside from the juvenile pleasure of skewering the mistakes of the directors, this private

PHICAL
ARY OF
WAVE

joke had the advantage of highlighting the anger—which has not entirely dissipated even today—of the New Wave's adversaries, such as Charensol and Chauvet, who spearheaded the anti-New Wave movement.

This makes the inclusion of a biographical dictionary of the New Wave all the more important. To be effective such a dictionary should be complete, objective, alphabetically arranged—in short, easy to use. Unfortunately, like all human activity, the following effort is personally motivated and thus incomplete. I have settled for a simple companion to film. Any omissions, intentional or otherwise, judgments, and comments thus assume relative importance, and a somewhat detached quality guided only by memory.

This biographical dictionary is divided into two sections. The first contains a list of directors, classified as follows: pre-New Wave, New Wave, and contemporary directors more or less related formally and intellectually to the New Wave. The second part covers the various individuals, from screenwriters to producers, who helped make the New Wave successful.

DIRECTORS

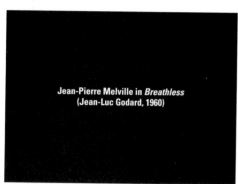

the New Wave, he did almost all his work in the studio (a small one, but his own), and used Delon as his leading man. Unclassifiable, a faux classicist, intentionally different, Melville is mythomaniacally American and terribly French, but a great director.

JEAN-PIERRE MELVILLE. Melville burst upon the dreary world of French film in 1948. In his adaptations of literature he rejected "visual equivalence" in favor of a closer approximation of the writer's text. Through the use of voice-overs, he was able to give *Le Silence de la mer* a sense of presence. His directorial methods made him the mentor of the New Wave. *Bob le flambeur*, which appeared in 1956, inspired the day's critics with its freedom, its washed-out scenes of the Parisian dawn, its romantic stylization based on hackneyed photographs of the place Clichy and its gangsters. It is this same stylization, pushed to its limits, that distanced Melville from the New Wave that claimed to be his heir in *Breathless*. Melville himself, gradually distanced himself from the movement. And, unlike

JEAN ROUCH. "The great originality of his approach . . . is his reflexiveness. It offers us not only an informed cinema, but a critical cinema, and an awareness of this knowledge. . . . It is through this dialectic of questioning and authentification that Rouch's work is for us so important." These words, which appeared in *Cahiers du cinéma*, reveal the importance of Rouch's method (after 1950) of giving the present—along with the past and the habits and traditions that constitute it—a presence. Initially, this involved the privileged spectator, the subject-viewer of the anthropologist's film. He observed himself as if in a mirror and it was this act of self-examination that became

the ethnologist's subject. Rouch's procedure, which was intentionally subjective, contrasted sharply with the claimed objectivity of other ethnologists. But Rouch also insisted on the use of the techniques (camera, film, sound, sequence of shots, etc.) of cinéma-vérité in his work. He is thus both pre- and post-New Wave. Rouch

embodied a form of journalism in its purest and most original state, and there is a direct line connecting him with Lumière, Griffith, Flaherty, Rossellini, and Renoir.

ALEXANDRE ASTRUC. Initiator and victim of the New Wave, Astruc was younger (1923) than Doniol-Valcroze, Kast, Rohmer, Marker, and Resnais, and yet he achieved recognition before them. Extremely brilliant, he was considered a prodigy ever since the publication of his article on the "camera-as-pen" in 1948. He was awarded the Delluc prize in 1953 for *Le Rideau cramoisi* and made his first feature, *Les Mauvaises Rencontres*, long before the others. Because of this, the second generation of directors (Truffaut, Godard, etc.) turned to Astruc for guidance, without admitting that his plots perpetuated the literary discourse of the thirties. His lyrical and romantic tragedies of adolescents in search of absolutes but forced to make compromises by an adult world was no longer topical. Astruc's extreme classicism (his camera movements resemble Preminger's), the sharp dialogues, and tendency to abstraction, gave his style a forced quality that ultimately led nowhere. He intellectually and practically excluded himself from the contemporary world that the New Wave was intent on discovering. After making several films, including two superb shorts (*Évariste Galois* and *Le Puits et le Pendule*),

Jeanne Moreau,
Ascenseur pour l'échafaud (Louis Malle, 1958)

Astruc stopped directing in 1968 and devoted his life to television, journalism, and writing. His withdrawal from the cinema can only be viewed with deep regret.

LOUIS MALLE. Born in 1932, favored by a not inconsiderable personal fortune, he codirected *Le Monde du silence* with Jacques Cousteau in 1955 and made his first film, *Ascenseur pour l'échafaud* in 1957. Malle employed a number of technical innovations in his work (high-speed film, portable cameras), which established him as one of the precursors of the New Wave. Still, the *Cahiers du cinéma* said of Malle in issue 138 that "He's still in search of a 'subject.' Disturbing, honest, hard working, he's looking for 'his' vision of the world, but it seems that so far it's managed to evade him." This may have been the reason for his feverish search for a style. His careful framing, for example, is physically faultless but not very inspired. Seen from today's vantage, his work includes a few

successful films that are primarily the result, as in *Lacombe Lucien*, of good scripts and an interesting story.

ROGER VADIM. "He is aware that eroticism contains an explosive charge that can annihilate the old, worn bastions of convention, prejudice, and morality" (*Cahiers du cinéma*, no. 138). This brief summary reveals the undeniable and very New Wave aspect of *And God Created Woman* (1956), particularly its treatment of morality. But Vadim's fame as a director is due more to his character than his films, which are now seen as sophisticated, frivolous, dull, and hopelessly out of fashion.

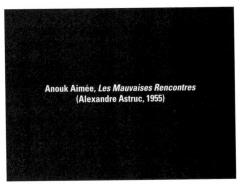

Anouk Aimée, *Les Mauvaises Rencontres*
(Alexandre Astruc, 1955)

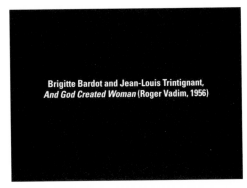

Brigitte Bardot and Jean-Louis Trintignant,
And God Created Woman (Roger Vadim, 1956)

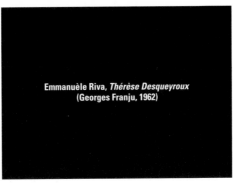

Emmanuèle Riva, *Thérèse Desqueyroux*
(Georges Franju, 1962)

GEORGES FRANJU. Having made his first feature in 1958, it's only by accident that Franju is classified as part of the New Wave. A nonconformist and anarchist, Franju is difficult to label at all. He had an unquestionable passion for cinema, however, as witnessed by the fact that he cofounded the Cercle du cinéma in 1935 with Henri Langlois and the Cinémathèque française in 1936, at the age of 24 (his models were Louis Feuillade and Fritz Lang, masters of the serial). He firmly believed that cinema was an art form whose works had to be conserved, and became executive secretary of the Fédération International des Archives du Film (FIAF). Between 1945 and 1953 he was secretary to Jean Painlevé (a friend of Antonin Artaud and the surrealists). A master of scientific cinematography and intent on revealing the "fantastic" aspect of all reality, Painlevé had a profound influence on Franju, whose own documentaries (*Le Sang des bêtes*, 1949, *Hôtel des Invalides*, 1952) and features (*La Tête contre les murs*, 1959, *Eyes Without a Face*, 1960) were all based on a form of "magical realism." Yet his style remained classical. His often literary subjects were primarily concerned with the past. There was nothing very New Wave about such aspects of his work. It was rather his unique personality and his heightened sensibility that was carried into the current of the movement. In the end, whether Franju was technically part of the New Wave or not has little importance. He remained faithful to his vision.

JACQUES DONIOL-VALCROZE. Although no director was more typically "New Wave" than Doniol-Valcroze, he's been largely forgotten by posterity. He was a contributor to *La Revue du cinéma*, and along with J. G. Auriol, cofounder of the Objectif 49 film club and the Festival du Film Maudit at Biarritz. As a cofounder, shareholder, editor in chief and writer for *Cahiers du cinéma*, and a critic for *L'Observateur* he militated for a renewal of French cinema. A highly cultured man of impeccable manners, he was a victim of self-doubt and that led him to adopt an attitude of remoteness. This attitude, although not without an element of humor, infused his work, which was eclipsed by the second generation of New Wave directors. His first feature film, *L'Eau à la bouche* (1960) appeared too late in his career. Not strong enough to surprise audiences, the film received a "sympathetic" response from the critics. His subsequent career, however, was marked by a period of critical neglect and distance.

PIERRE KAST. Kast began his career as a critic, participated in Objectif 49 and the Festival of Biarritz, wrote for *Cahiers du cinéma*, worked as an assistant to Grémillon (whom he considered his mentor), Preston Sturges, and Renoir, and after 1953 made several highly regarded short films. More than any other director of his era, Pierre Kast embodied the intelligence, culture, and literary imagination favored by the first generation of New Wave directors. For this generation the camera served as the instrument of the modern writer. His films, beginning with *Le Bel Âge* (1960), were perceived as brilliant cinematic essays. His sensuality drew its

In the center, Pierre Kast, seated

inspiration from the best sources: the eighteenth century, Sade, Stendhal (whom he worshipped), Queneau, Boris Vian, Vailland, etc. But he was unable to provide a physical embodiment for the amorous gameplay in his films, which remained more aural than visual. His dialogues are excellent but highly intellectual and disembodied.

Corinne Marchand, *Cléo from 5 to 7*
(Agnès Varda, 1962)

AGNÈS VARDA. She initially worked as the official photographer for Jean Vilar's productions at the Théâtre National Populaire. She then turned to the cinema and directed *La Pointe courte* (1954). Blithely unaware of contemporary developments and impatient to make her first film, Varda was an innovator and created a New Wave of her own. She started a cooperative, filmed without the CNC's authorization, and worked on a minimal budget (120,000 francs). Because she was unable to distribute her work commercially and couldn't compete for award money, she was forced to make shorts so she could apply for the government subsidies that were essential to cover her film expenses. What is striking about Varda's work is her astonishing stylistic freedom and the manifestation of authorial will. This helps explain Varda's preeminent position within the New Wave. This was true of both the documentary filmmakers of the time, such as Marker and Resnais (who was the editor on *La Pointe courte*) as well as the *Cahiers* group, which was glad to lend their support to her subversive activities. In this light her marriage to Demy appears logical, given his interest in both

documentary and narrative filmmaking. Varda's own work uses two modes of language or two kinds of speech. She attempts to emphasize "the confusion of the world of objects" caught between the "material" world (which always has the upper hand) and culture. An attitude that helps explain the preciousness that resulted from and characterized Varda's femininity.

ALAIN RESNAIS. *Hiroshima, mon amour* (1959) remains one of the three landmark films of the New Wave. But

unlike his younger colleagues, Resnais achieved celebrity with his shorts, including *Night and Fog* (1955), *Toute la mémoire du monde* (1956), and *Le Chant du Styrène* (1958). Like Varda, Resnais's intention was to "overlay a (love) story on a context that takes into account the misfortune of others" and expose "the perpetual seesawing of the individual happiness one tries to

preserve in the face of collective suffering." From this Resnais worked out a principle of "fearful tenderness," that consisted of using tenderness as a way to frame the most terrifying aspects of our era. Deeply concerned with photography, Resnais established a dialectic between the still photograph and the moving image that remained at the core of his work. His filmic style did not drive the action of the film forward or promote an illusion of reality. On the contrary, it stripped away any sense of movement and drained vitality from moments of stillness, from all forms of fixity: memories, the mechanism of remembering, and the incessant repetition of affective models, such as in the Pavlovian mental programming of the songs in *On connaît la chanson* (1997). He achieved a kind of calm artificiality, especially in his last films. In Resnais's work, life, as in Dr. Morel's invention, is inexorably attached to the cinematic machine and its illusory succession of images at 24 frames per second: *Smoking/No Smoking*. Because of the independent character of the individual image, in Resnais montage and its infinite possibilities remain the focus of his aesthetic concerns.

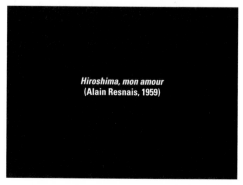

Hiroshima, mon amour
(Alain Resnais, 1959)

CHRIS MARKER. Marker belonged to the small band that consisted of Resnais, Varda, and himself. Distant, secret, austere, his love of paradox made preciosity—a chiseled preciosity that sometimes came close to Gongorism—his favorite weapon. His texts, incisive and alive, harbor a strong sense of irony and self-awareness, but they are not devoid of poetry. Bazin noted that,

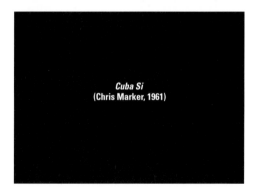
Cuba Si
(Chris Marker, 1961)

ÉRIC ROHMER. He is the link between the first generation of the New Wave, to which he belonged chronologically, and the succeeding generation, which he resembled in spirit. This second generation (with the exception of Chabrol) admired and respected Rohmer, and saw him as a kind of older brother. His "Cinema, the Art of Space" appeared in number 14 of *La Revue du cinéma* (June 1948) and remains, along with Astruc's "The Camera as Pen," one of the fundamental texts of New Wave thought. Under his real name, Maurice Schérer, Rohmer wrote, between the ages of 18 and 25, the majority of the subjects he later filmed. He observed a strict sense of fidelity to his theoretical opinions, which he also developed very early in life and never abandoned, and he applied them when constructing a story, writing a dialogue, and establishing the mise-en-scène for a film. He always relied strictly on an existing reality. While there is no obvious sign of progress or development in his work, it is nevertheless of paramount importance. The enjoyment of his last films has little to do with plot, but with the science and perfection of his style. As a New Wave director, Rohmer has made aesthetics the driving force of his creativity.

unlike the engagé documentary filmmakers, who thought the image was film's raw material, Marker believed that "its raw material is intelligence, its immediate expression is speech, and the image serves only as a reference to this verbal intelligence. . . . Moreover, the primary element is the beauty of sound and it is through sound that intelligence must leap into the image. Montage takes place from the ear to the eye." A friend of Resnais for nearly fifty years, together they codirected several shorts, including the well-known *Les statues meurent aussi* (1950–1953), a documentary about African art. Creating a comfortable distance for the viewer through a simple commentary, the film gradually changes into a strong anti-colonialist polemic. The film was banned, but Marker would later

transform many of his censors' prejudices. Using still and moving images, he created *La Jetée*, a masterpiece of science-fiction, constructed on the principle of the photo-novel. Here too, the commentary drives the movement of the film and the text leads us into the poetic realm of the bizarre. Marker is unlike anyone else. Unclassifiable, he is, like Varda in *La Pointe courte*, a New Wave all to himself.

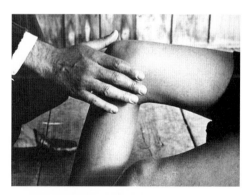

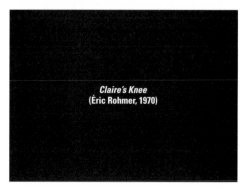
Claire's Knee
(Éric Rohmer, 1970)

JACQUES RIVETTE. He was the power behind *Cahiers du cinéma* and the man who shaped its aesthetics. Rivette initiated the battles fought by the New Wave, although he left the job of fighting them to Truffaut. A native of Rouen, he was the first to lead the assault against the old guard of professionals. In *Le Coup du berger* (1956) he demonstrated that it was possible to make a film without

the scene remains open, free to live its own life. Rivette is not only an experimental filmmaker but a modern one.

Jacques Rivette on the set of *Pont du Nord*, 1982

FRANÇOIS TRUFFAUT. Truffaut was the New Wave's most illustrious representative. A fearful polemicist and ferocious critic who had an ability to single out the defects in a film and the sworn enemy of academic French cinema, it was assumed that his first film would be met with fists, guns, tanks, and canons. Instead it was

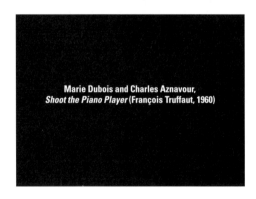

Marie Dubois and Charles Aznavour, *Shoot the Piano Player* (François Truffaut, 1960)

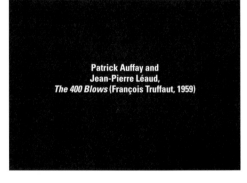

Patrick Auffay and Jean-Pierre Léaud, *The 400 Blows* (François Truffaut, 1959)

worrying about censorship. His short film marks the beginning of the New Wave. A sense of conspiracy saturates his films. He experiments with time, restricts and compresses it, reduces it until it is no more than a utilitarian vector of the action. Tone serves as an empty vessel, one devoid of decorative artifice, from which Rivette creates a scenic space (he showed a marked preference for the theatrical stage) that must be kept bare (*Paris nous appartient*, *L'Amour fou*). For cinematic time, the *dead time* of film, can't be furnished, it must be occupied. In Rivette's films life erupts through a complex interplay between staging and improvisation. Duration becomes Rivette's raw material and play his primary instrument. The beginning of a scene in Rivette thus never intimates its ending;

greeted with flowers and an ovation. At the Cannes Festival in 1959, *The 400 Blows* was triumphant. In one evening the film profession became "young" again and the radical cinephiles won public acceptance. The name, New Wave, could be heard around the world. After this initial explosion, Truffaut's work followed several different paths (autobiographical, sentimental, literary,

etc.). Truffaut's oeuvre contains a number of beautiful, yet unclassifiable objects, such as *The Wild Child* (1970) and *La Chambre verte* (1978). He was the best known and best loved director of the French New Wave. One of the reasons for this is that his work spanned two different arenas: commercial success and auteurist film. As a lover of literature, he always considered the screenplay to be an essential stage in the production of a film. This helps explain his admiration for Lubitsch and Hitchcock, whom he considered masters of the screenplay. Yet the screenplay for Truffaut was only a succession of words whose only purpose was their ultimate realization in the image. He felt *To Be or Not to Be* was the greatest screenplay in the history of film, simply because it couldn't be understood in words or writing but was immediately understandable on screen. He felt the same way about the dialogues of Renoir and Guitry. Without Truffaut the New Wave as we know it wouldn't have existed.

CLAUDE CHABROL. He began working with *Cahiers du cinéma* in 1953 and had a fondness for detective and suspense films. For Chabrol, no film within the genre, from B series films to the masterpieces by Lang and Hitchcock, was without interest. With Rohmer he wrote an insightful book on Hitchcock; Chabrol covered the first part of Hitchcock's career, from his silent films

for destruction, his sudden need to reject social existence to prove, in and through sensation, the very existence of his being. With a mixture of amusement and terror, Chabrol observes his ordinary characters evolve, quietly, innocently, into monsters and plunges them into an abyss from which they can never return. There is a heightened sense of dramatic and tragic morality

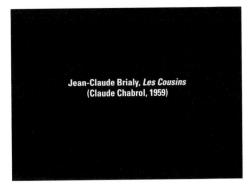

Jean-Claude Brialy, *Les Cousins*
(Claude Chabrol, 1959)

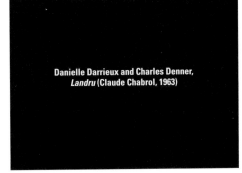

Danielle Darrieux and Charles Denner,
Landru (Claude Chabrol, 1963)

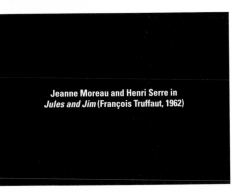

Jeanne Moreau and Henri Serre in
Jules and Jim (François Truffaut, 1962)

through *Under Capricorn* (Rohmer covered the second part) and was primarily interested in the way Hitchcock managed his career in England as a steppingstone to Hollywood, where he was an immense success. Judging by the way Chabrol skillfully managed a career that enabled him to maintain his independence, it's obvious that he took the lesson to heart. Yet he distinguished himself from his master in both the scope and the structure of his films. It isn't crime so much as the ineluctable series of events that lead up to a crime that interests Chabrol. In his work crime creates, attracts, and feeds off the guilty individual, rather than the reverse. He is its prey and victim. In Chabrol's *comédie humaine* we observe with fascination the human being's attraction

associated with the pleasure that arises from true Epicureanism. His flowing style sustains and propels a slow, furtive moral drift, as if the earth had somehow shifted beneath one's feet, at least on the surface of his films. In reality the construction proceeds through a series of sudden shocks, like the movement of tectonic plates in the darkness beneath the surface of the earth. Chabrol's films have gotten better as he has matured, as demonstrated by the superb *Rien ne va plus* (1997), the director's fiftieth film.

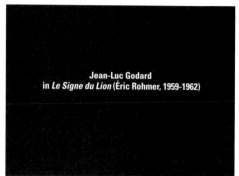

Jean-Luc Godard
in *Le Signe du Lion* (Éric Rohmer, 1959-1962)

JEAN-LUC GODARD. The quintessential New Wave director, a filmmaker who has made reference (or quotation) one of the pillars of his cinematic style, Godard shows that we live within the disintegration of a civilization forced to navigate among fragments of culture that float around us as the ultimate signs of a world that is disappearing before our eyes. We exist in a mirror

Peter Kassowitz and Anna Karina
in *My Life to Live* (Jean-Luc Godard, 1962)

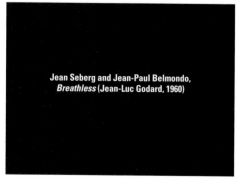

8
LES APRÈS-MIDI - L'ARGENT - LES
LAVABOS - LE PLAISIR - LES HÔTELS

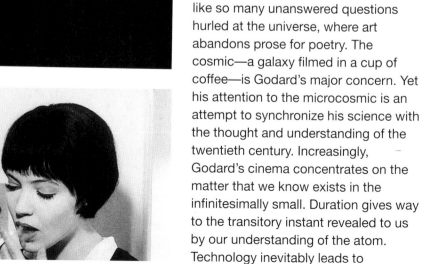

Jean Seberg and Jean-Paul Belmondo,
Breathless (Jean-Luc Godard, 1960)

world, crisscrossed by laser beams that attempt, discontinuously and without any apparent consequences, to establish a line of communication between what we have become and what we once were. A world of echoes, like so many unanswered questions hurled at the universe, where art abandons prose for poetry. The cosmic—a galaxy filmed in a cup of coffee—is Godard's major concern. Yet his attention to the microcosmic is an attempt to synchronize his science with the thought and understanding of the twentieth century. Increasingly, Godard's cinema concentrates on the matter that we know exists in the infinitesimally small. Duration gives way to the transitory instant revealed to us by our understanding of the atom. Technology inevitably leads to incessant ruptures and forces us to experience and live in a world now subject to modern science. Godard's cinema is the cinema of a researcher. All its components (story, dialogue, mise-en-scène, locations, graphics, camera movements, framing, lighting, sound, editing, mixing, etc.) are ground down, broken apart. These serve, not to extract the answer to Bazin's well-

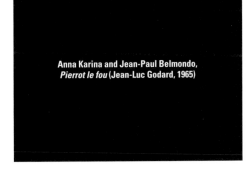

Anna Karina and Jean-Paul Belmondo,
Pierrot le fou (Jean-Luc Godard, 1965)

Anna Karina and Jean-Paul Belmondo,
A Woman is a Woman (Jean-Luc Godard, 1961)

Brigitte Bardot and Fritz Lang,
Contempt (Jean-Luc Godard, 1963)

known question "What is cinema?" but to push our investigation to the extreme, to prove its existence. The great musician seeks only music, the poet poetry, the painter painting—Godard seeks only cinema.

JACQUES ROZIER. He was the only New Wave director to have completed, though perhaps in somewhat random fashion, the IDHEC program. He worked as an assistant director for French television during its formative years, a period in his life he would later cover in *Adieu Philippine*. There is no inherent reason why he should be included in this section. It's important to

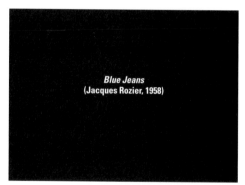

Blue Jeans
(Jacques Rozier, 1958)

remember, however, that he was also an assistant-intern on Renoir's *French Cancan*. But it's his first short films, *La Rentrée des classes* (1955) and especially *Blue Jeans* (1958) that, in their informality and freedom and in the accuracy of their portrayal of a new generation of young people, unite Rozier in spirit and sensibility to the New Wave. He became an integral member of the group, and Godard, with the assistance of his producer, helped put together the financing for *Adieu Philippine* (1960–1963), the most new wave of New Wave films. It is a film in which "the virtues of the young cinema shine through in all their purity and the plausibility of its methods are most convincingly demonstrated, whether this involves shooting on a shoestring budget, the use of unknown actors,

borrowing from TV, or the freewheeling nature of the story, the theme of youth itself" (*Cahiers du cinéma,* no. 138). It is also one of the rare French films of the period to have addressed the shameful silence surrounding the war in Algeria. Since then, Rozier has made short films and a few, all too infrequent, features, including *Du côté d'Orouet* (1970) and the marvelous *Maine Océan* (1986). In the tradition of Renoir, Rozier has perpetuated a style obsessed with naturalness to the point of artifice, which intelligently blends improvisation and control, the spontaneity of his characters, and careful directing.

JEAN-MARIE STRAUB and **DANIÈLE HUILLET**, his companion and codirector. Director of the Metz film club, Straub became friends with Truffaut, Rivette, and Godard toward the end of the fifties. He began making films with Danièle Huillet in Germany and Italy after going AWOL during the Algerian war. Straub and Huillet radicalized certain New Wave principles. They practiced a cinema of poverty, a fundamentally Marxist economic stance that responded to their ethical, political, and aesthetic beliefs. Intransigent and radical, their films have the brilliance and hardness of diamond.

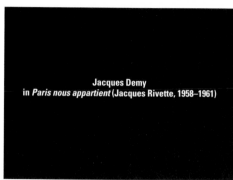

Jacques Demy
in *Paris nous appartient* (Jacques Rivette, 1958–1961)

JACQUES DEMY. Demy was the first to combine the two New Wave currents, that of the documentary (Resnais, Marker, Varda) and that of the *Cahiers du cinéma*. His sense of determination—as a child he designed and built complex stage sets—led him to follow a path that he never swerved from throughout his life: he would do film and nothing but film. His formal training included studies at the École des beaux-arts in Nantes and the École Louis Lumière on rue Vaugirard in Paris, where film (Demy was in the cinematography section) and sound technicians were trained. This was followed by several months working for Paul Grimault, the leading French animator of the time. He then worked as an assistant for Georges Rouquier, who was considered the leading French documentary filmmaker when he made *Farrebique* (1946). Rouquier produced his "student's" first film, *Le Sabotier du Val de Loire*, in 1956. Demy quickly became friends with the group at *Cahiers du cinéma* and followed the rise of the New Wave that led to *Lola*, his first feature, made in 1961. In 1957 he made a screen adaptation of a one-act play by Cocteau, *Le Bel Indifférent*. The film, which was in color and shot in a studio using sequence-length shots, marked a turning point in the development of his style. Sets assumed a major importance in his work and Demy designed them so they would mesmerize viewers. His magic captivated and charmed audiences, but it was his sharp, often strident colors, that revealed his true power to fascinate. Demy's approach was based on a desire—one that was contradictory, ambiguous, and convoluted—to ravish the viewer through enchantment. His films incorporate sweeping camera movements, often using a boom, which follow the incessant back-and-forth of the complex emotional (and physical) aspirations of his characters. Yet every film Demy has made breaks this spell and leads the viewer, inexorably, toward their own disenchantment. His films constantly sound a note of melancholy. With the passage of time, the greatness of Demy's work increases.

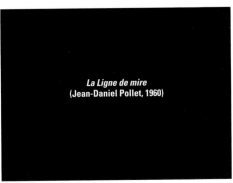

La Ligne de mire
(Jean-Daniel Pollet, 1960)

JEAN-DANIEL POLLET. Pollet stands apart. Using family money, he financed his first short film, *Pourvu qu'on ait l'ivresse* (1958). He followed this with a feature, *La Ligne de mire* (1959–1960), in which he broke every rule in the book. His attitude brought down the wrath of the CNC, and since the film wasn't a success, the "profession" used it as an example when it launched its counterattack on the New Wave. In issue 138 of *Cahiers du cinéma*, the author of Pollet's entry wrote, "the only thing left to this ultra-New Wavist is to learn how to tell a story or, what amounts to the same thing, how to do without one." He continued, "He possesses that gift, which the greatest directors have, of being able to transform everything he looks at. . . . Of all the directors listed in this dictionary, Pollet is the one whose future direction seems the least obvious." This last comment turned out to be the case. Pollet's career went from short to feature-length films but followed two separate paths: one was to make tragicomedy starring his favorite actor, the Keatonesque Claude Melki; the other, more abstract and poetic, was to make a cinema of pure contemplation based on texts by Philippe Sollers and the music of Antoine Duhamel.

LUC MOULLET. He was the youngest writer at the *Cahiers du cinéma* prior to 1960. His attitude toward the world was unique and Moullet cultivated an offbeat and unsettling sense of humor, not unlike that of Alfred Jarry. The subjects of his films, as reflected in their titles (*Un Steack trop cuit*, *Genèse d'un repas*), are highly unusual but remain interesting in spite of the fact that they have been marginalized. Through its economy of means—minimalist and often embracing an aesthetic of poverty—and its attitude, his work falls well within the tradition of the New Wave.

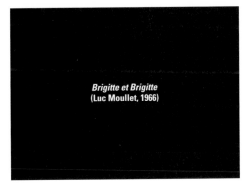

Brigitte et Brigitte
(Luc Moullet, 1966)

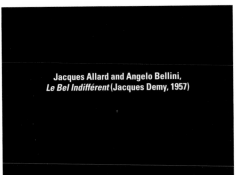

Jacques Allard and Angelo Bellini,
Le Bel Indifférent (Jacques Demy, 1957)

Jean-Pierre Léaud, Bernadette Lafont, and Françoise Lebrun
in *The Mother and the Whore* (Jean Eustache, 1973)

JEAN EUSTACHE. Eustache did not belong to the group of writers who contributed to the *Cahiers du cinéma* before 1960, but subsequently saw them on a regular basis, admired, and soon developed friendships with them. He absorbed the principles of the New Wave but reworked its approach. Fiercely independent, his career included shorts, feature films, documentaries, and journalism. But his unwillingness to follow production and distribution standards jeopardized his work. Beginning with his first two short films (*Du côté de Robinson*, 1963, and *Le Père Noël a les yeux bleus*, 1966), later shown together as *Les Mauvaises Fréquentations*, Eustache displayed a strong personality, a directorial temperament, and a marked sensitivity toward poverty and the working-class world of his childhood, later depicted in *Mes petites amoureuses* (1974). In this sense he distanced himself from the middle-class context of the New Wave. In *The Mother and the Whore* (1973), Eustache addressed post-1968 France and its new approach to emotional crisis; it was the most important film in French cinema of the seventies and has become a cult film since. Although a very personal film, it carries a clear imprint of the New Wave.

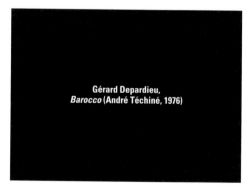

Gérard Depardieu,
Barocco (André Téchiné, 1976)

ANDRÉ TÉCHINÉ, PHILIPPE GARREL, BARBET SCHROEDER. All three are inheritors of the New Wave. André Téchiné (born in 1943) wrote criticism for *Cahiers du cinéma* during and after the sixties, and made his first film, *Paulina s'en va*, in 1969. Since then he has become one of the most important directors in French cinema. Philippe Garrel (born 1948) filmed *Les Enfants* *désaccordés* when he was sixteen and made *Anémone* in 1967, both of which are directly influenced by Godard. Because of his ideal of an absolute cinema, Garrel refused to compromise with commercial art. His work introduces the themes of origin, childhood, and family ties. More than any other filmmaker, he radicalized the New Wave's fundamental principles in terms of both attitude and technique. Barbet Schroeder (born 1941) began frequenting the *Cahiers'* offices in 1959, and became a friend of Rohmer and, later, his producer. He produced *Paris vu par ... ,* which claimed to follow all the criteria of a New Wave film and thus became the movement's manifesto. Schroeder moved on to directing with *More* (1969), one of the first films about drug use during the sixties. Throughout his films he never lost sight of the concreteness provided by journalism, a genre he employed in *Idi Amin Dada* (1974) and *Koko the Gorilla* (1977). This Rohmerian attention to the truth of the smallest detail served as a touchstone in the films he made in Hollywood after 1987.

André-S. Labarthe

ANDRÉ S. LABARTHE. One of the most influential critics at *Cahiers du cinéma*, which he joined in 1956. Beginning in 1962, he launched, together with Jeanine Bazin (André Bazin's widow), the now famous and historically important series known as *Cinéastes de notre temps*. The series was intended to continue, on the small screen, the celebrated interviews—serious, intelligent, and well- documented that had contributed to the international fame of *Cahiers du cinéma*. Labarthe, who was equally interested in literature, philosophy, painting, and eroticism, became a specialist of the cinematic essay. His work is characterized by careful analysis, an oblique and searching attitude toward his subject, and a refined style.

JEAN-LOUIS COMMOLI began working with *Cahiers du cinéma* in 1962 and later became its editor in chief. Because of his political concerns, in 1968 he made *Deux Marseillaises* with Labarthe, one of which referred to the film by Renoir, the other to the events that took place in May of that year. He began making narrative films, but they were generally considered too political and received little attention, and he later turned to documentary, a field in which he has garnered considerable acclaim.

JEAN-CLAUDE BIETTE, CLAUDE GUIGUET, PAUL VECCHIALI. Jean-Claude Biette joined *Cahiers du cinéma* in 1964, before going to work with Pasolini. After making a few shorts in Italy and France, he made his first feature in 1977, *Le Théâtre des matières.* Biette quite intentionally developed a low-budget approach to cinema. Because of his antipathy for figuration and aestheticism, he reduced his films to the barest essentials of dramaturgy and separated the plot from any overt motivation. With theatrical flourish, he presents his film to the viewer and invites him to watch it throb with pleasure. Jean-Claude Guiguet also began as a critic, but outside the circle of the *Cahiers du cinéma*. He made his first feature film, *Les Belles Manières*, in 1978. His reserved and sensitive films contrast the sentimentality and rules of melodrama (Grémillon in France, Sirk in the United States) so often associated with the upper class, to the day-to-day realities of French life. His work is a bit like the Visconti of *Death in Venice* ("beauty is dying, youth is waning") except for his predilection for the emotional upheaval, strength, and wisdom of the middle-age woman faced with the disappearance of her sexuality. Guiguet filmed emotion, and recorded not only the motivation of melodrama but also its effects on his characters. Paul Vecchiali, the producer of Biette and Guiguet's films, studied at the École polytechnique, was a combative cinephile, and only incidentally became a critic (*Cahiers du cinéma*, *La Revue du cinéma*). Like his idol, Jean Grémillon, whom he considered the master of French cinema, Vecchiali wanted to unite violently contradictory elements in his first films (*Les Petits Drames* (1961) and *Les Ruses du diable* (1965)). His films display a sense of melodrama, directness, suspense, false realism, forced stylization, American-style action, and emotional analysis *à la française*. Like his master, Grémillon, his films were not immediately understandable, and he suffered at the hands of the public and the critics for the pronounced sense of uncertainty that characterized his work. Fortunately, films like *L'Étrangleur* (1970), *Femmes femmes* (1974), and *La Machine* (1977), were well, and often enthusiastically, received by amateurs.

CONTEMPORARIES OF THE NEW WAVE

MAURICE PIALAT. It would be difficult to ignore one of France's most important contemporary filmmakers. Yet, it's hard to consider Maurice Pialat as belonging to the New Wave when he himself has so strongly distanced himself from the movement. And in one sense, his rejection is justifiable. His career followed a very different course than

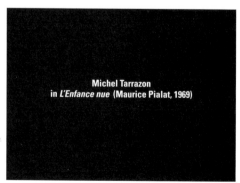

Michel Tarrazon
in *L'Enfance nue* (Maurice Pialat, 1969)

that of his predecessors; a painter, Pialat studied at the École des Arts Décoratifs and the Beaux-Arts, then, around 1955, became interested in theater before becoming an assistant director in film and television. In 1960 Pialat made his first short film, *L'Amour existe*, which received an award at the Venice film festival, and began his first feature, *L'Enfance nue*, in 1969. He

incorporated certain fundamental New Wave principles in his work, however, beginning with his penchant for realism. All his films are documentary in spirit, and there is a sense of "live" action about them. Yet there is little that distinguishes Pialat's naturalistic approach from Renoir's naturalism or his master's, Erich von Stroheim. His work is violent, disturbing, asocial, with sparks of brilliance here and there. He produced three masterpieces, *L'Enfance nue*, *La Maison des bois* (a series made for television), and *Van Gogh* (1991), along with other excellent films.

ALAIN CAVALIER. Cavalier could be considered a New Wave director but his career was so unique, so singular, that it's more accurate to include him among its contemporaries. He studied at IDHEC, was an assistant to Malle and Molinaro, and made his first film, *Le Combat dans l'île*, in 1962, followed by *L'Insoumis* in 1964. He was a complex director from his earliest films, both in terms of his characters and his style, which was highly interiorized. After making several films that were more accessible to the public, but all of which were failures, he took refuge in a cinema that was radically different. *Thérèse* (1986) is an austere, though highly aesthetic, film that makes few concessions to its audience. It was well received—more or less. The director's extreme, almost maniacal, sense of accuracy, plunges the viewer into a state of fantasy that is undeniably unique. The most common detail of everyday life is transcended by Cavalier's cinematic vision.

JEAN-PIERRE MOCKY. There is nothing in Mocky's background that would have predisposed him to the New Wave. After a career as an actor in theater and film (he appeared in the French segment of Antonioni's *I Vinti*), he decided to become a director. In 1958 he adapted Hervé Bazin's *La Tête contre les murs* for the screen, but the producers balked at his lack of experience and turned the direction over to Franju. As compensation, they gave him the principal role. The New Wave phenomenon that was sweeping through the profession gave him an opportunity to direct his first film, *Les Dragueurs*, the following year. Because of its subject, the film is characteristic both of Mocky's attitude and, at the same time and seemingly without his awareness, of the New Wave itself. After *Les Dragueurs* he continued to make films almost without interruption. His work is based on a sense of caricature that is, in spirit, very close to

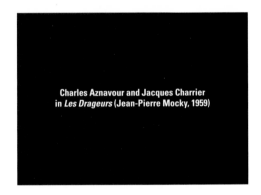

Charles Aznavour and Jacques Charrier
in *Les Drageurs* (Jean-Pierre Mocky, 1959)

CLAUDE LELOUCH. I feel a certain reticence in including Claude Lelouch here. Yet, his inclusion can be justified. His first (*Le Propre de l'homme*, made in 1960) and subsequent films, all the way through *Un homme et une femme* (1966), were all conceived within the New Wave spirit. The spirit is plain to see: the handheld camera (journalistic style), the lyrical camera movements (Russian cinema of the sixties), the washed out black and white (Melville, Godard), the frenetic editing (a lot like Scopitone, the video of its day, in which Lelouch specialized). To this he added sentimentality, character simplification, and action sequences that had no basis in concrete reality. There is a lot of movement in Lelouch's films. Many ideas are thrown out to the viewer. But there is a lack of thought in his films, beginning with a missing and vital conception of cinema—rather than a dream, desire, or passion. Although there is no question that Lelouch adored cinema, it can't be said that cinema appreciated the gesture.

Unwürdige Greisin, which met with considerable success. Strongly influenced by Brecht, he explored the notion of realism in his work, and initially he tied his narrative, or the moral of his stories, to reality. Later in his career he attempted to extract reality's fictional element, as in his most impressive film, *Moi, Pierre Rivière, ayant égorgé ma mère, ma soeur, et mon frère* (1976). In this film the action becomes increasingly politicized but in distinct ways: Allio tries to resurrect the popular account of a true story, which indeed remains the truth of the story. He subsequently rejected the professional and ideological centrality of Paris's film industry. For *Retour à Marseille* (1980) Allio built a regional production facility that exemplified his ideas about film and focused on life in Provence. Forty years later he resumed work on the project begun by Marcel Pagnol. Needless to say, his approach was radically different.

La Vieille Dame indigne
(René Allio, 1965)

Dubout. In Mocky two irreconcilable worlds collide with one another. One or more characters from the first world are in conflict with the inhabitants of the second and their conventions. There is a constant parade of supporting characters, whose own stories interfere with that of the hero. The entire film is built up, scene by scene, from an accumulation of details that provided the actors (who adored Mocky) with tremendous freedom of expression. This was accompanied by a an element of improvisation both on screen and in his screenplays.

RENÉ ALLIO. René Allio was a painter, art director for theater, and set designer who created an animated film that was used in a production of Gogol's *Dead Souls* in 1959. After making a short in 1963, he began working actively in film in 1965. His first feature was an adaptation of a Brecht short story, *Die*

There were a number of directors who got their start during the sixties, including **JACQUES BARATIER,** an ambitious, private, and often perplexing director. He liked working with poets (Schéhadé or Audiberti). *La Poupée* (1962) received a certain amount of critical acclaim and *Dragées au poivre* (1963) came close to meeting with popular success. **HENRI COLPI,** a fine editor (Colpi worked on some of Resnais's shorts), began making his own films in 1960. His first was *Une aussi longue absence*, based on a novel by Marguerite Duras. This was followed by *Codine* in 1962. He developed a slow, careful, unidimensional style based on the notions of memory and forgetfulness common to Resnais and Duras. **ALAIN ROBBE-GRILLET,** one of the best known practitioners of the nouveau roman, was the first writer, after Cocteau, to attempt to use cinematic means to write with film (Pagnol and Guitry were interested in theater, and Malraux was only involved in one film, *L'Espoir*, 1939, based on his novel, and was to promote the book's politics). Robbe-Grillet made *L'Immortelle* in 1962, then in a succession of films, yielded to an increasingly simplistic representation of his obsessions and fantasies. Unwittingly, Robbe-Grillet demonstrated that literary and cinematic style are unrelated. **JEAN PÉLÉGRI,** an excellent writer, codirected with **JAMES BLUE,** an American director, one of the best films of this period, Les *Oliviers de la justice* (1962). The film addressed one of the most crucial issues of its day: the injustices committed during the French occupation of Algeria. **MARGUERITE DURAS** worked with both Resnais (1958) and Colpi (1959) on screenplays for their films and began directing a few years later. Working with very little money, Duras created a written body of work intended for the screen. Her films are "modern" and ultimately very New Wave. A cousin of Jean-Pierre Melville, **MICHEL DRACH** directed *On n'enterre pas le dimanche* (1959), an introverted and tortured work; both he and **MARCEL HANOUN** (*Une simple histoire*, 1958, and *Le Huitième Jour*, 1960) had difficult careers. Hanoun's work constantly flirts with the experimental, which has alienated it from the public and some critics. **LÉONARD KEIGEL** intentionally distanced himself from the New Wave, although he was the son of **LÉONIDE KEIGEL,** the founder of Objectif 49 and managing director of *Cahiers du cinéma*. Keigel saw himself as an atypical director, and this is evident in his adaptations of Julian Green's *Leviathan* (1961) and Pushkin's *Queen of Spades* (1965).

Marcel Hanoun.

Abdoulaye Faye, *Un coeur gros comme ça*
(François Reichenbach, 1962)

of stock photos skirted with sensationalism. A television producer, **FRÉDÉRIC ROSSIF** later specialized in commercially lucrative nature films. "Without Truffaut and Chabrol, those of us who came up through ordinary channels would have remained cinematic bureaucrats." The "us" in this sentence refers to the first group of assistant directors who benefited from the New Wave and became directors in their own right, ten years earlier than would have been expected. This includes **ÉDOUARD MOLINARO,** who made the above comment, a director of several fine films; it also includes **PHILIPPE DE BROCA,** an assistant to Henri Decoin, Georges Lacombe, Truffaut, and Chabrol, who produced De Broca's *Les Jeux de l'amour* in 1960. In his work De Broca wavered between delicate comedies and robust adventure films. **MICHEL DEVILLE** began his career in 1961 with a comedy, *Ce soir ou jamais*. The genre became a specialty of his, along with detective films. **CLAUDE SAUTET** made *Classe tous risques* in 1960 and is considered a poet of everyday life—his films are often about love affairs—which he examines more from the point of view of morality than sociology. **JACQUES DERAY** began

making films in 1961, specializing in detective films. One of his best in this genre is *La Piscine* (1969), starring Alain Delon and Maurice Ronet. **GEORGES LAUTNER** continued the longstanding French tradition of the "dialogue" film, using screenplays by his friend Michel Audiard. In *Môme aux boutons* (1959) and *Marche ou crève* (1960), he successfully bypassed most of the New Wave. **ROBERT ENRICO** made a number of short prizewinning films, and began directing features in 1963. His skill as a technician served him as a means of advancing in the industry. His most successful film was *Vieux Fusil*, made in 1975. To some extent all these directors continued the pre-New Wave tradition of the French quality film and have thus kept the small shopkeepers of French cinema in business.

Documentary filmmaker **FRANÇOIS REICHENBACH,** the cousin of producer Pierre Braunberger, created an original body of work in film. "Born with a camera in his hand," a connoisseur of painting, and a self-taught filmmaker, his work is filled with images of bewildering variety; they define the "Reichenbach style." From *L'Amérique insolite* (1958–1960) and *Un coeur gros comme ça* (1961) to *F for Fake* (1975) (in which he appears as Orson Welles's accomplice), this sensitive yet pliable filmmaker provides a worldly portrait of cultural celebrities, American prisons, and marine training camps. **FRÉDÉRIC ROSSIF** specialized in politically oriented montage films. *Le Temps du ghetto* (1961) and *Mourir à Madrid* (1963) both received a certain amount of recognition although the director's use

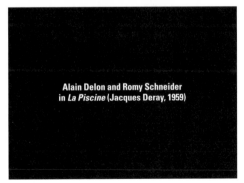

Alain Delon and Romy Schneider
in *La Piscine* (Jacques Deray, 1959)

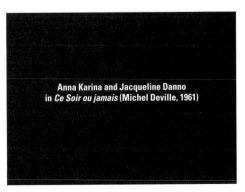

Anna Karina and Jacqueline Danno
in *Ce Soir ou jamais* (Michel Deville, 1961)

SCREEN-WRITERS, CINEMATO-GRAPHERS, AND SOUND TECHNICIANS

the majority of his writing for lesser-known directors such as de Broca, Rappeneau, Malle, and so forth. **JEAN GRUAULT,** also a screenwriter, worked with some of the best directors of the time. He got his start in the theater and later became a friend of the group at *Cahiers du cinéma*. He wrote screenplays for Rossellini (*Vanina Vanini* and *The Rise of Louis XIV*), Rivette (two films), Truffaut (four films), and Resnais (three films), and worked as an actor in films by Godard, Truffaut, and others. Although **GÉRARD BRACH** was also a close associate of the *Cahiers* staff at the end of the fifties, he didn't work with any New Wave directors. His scripts were used in films by Berri, Annaud, Ferreri, Antonioni, Risi, Kontchalovski, Rossellini, and Polanski. As screenwriters **ALAIN ROBBE-GRILLET** and Marguerite Duras worked with Alain Resnais on his first two feature films; **JEAN CAYROL,** wrote splendid texts for *Night and Fog* and *Muriel*, also by Resnais.

SCREENWRITERS

PAUL GEGAUFF played an important role in the intellectual and cultural adventure known as the New Wave. In one sense his nonconformist attitude led to its development. A novelist by trade, he wrote scripts for Rohmer and Barbet Schroeder, but devoted most of his time to working with Claude Chabrol, and wrote the scripts for twelve of his films. Gegauff's scripts provided the director with an opportunity to develop a more personal approach to his films. His writing is devastatingly cynical and marked by an attraction for scathing dialogue that reveals an individual's true self. He had a fascination for any form of stupidity, which was admirably displayed in *Les Bonnes Femmes*, his best script. **DANIEL BOULANGER,** a novelist and currently a member of the Académie Goncourt, is perhaps better known as an actor than a screenwriter. He appeared in *Breathless* and *Shoot the Piano Player*, and in both he was excellent. He had a talent for narration and sharp, penetrating dialogue but did

CINEMATOGRAPHERS

HENRI DECAI worked on Jean-Pierre Melville's first three films. In the superb *Bob le flambeur*, shot in black and white, he employed most of the techniques that would later be used by the New Wave. After working with Melville, Louis Malle suggested he do the lighting for *Ascenseur pour l'échafaud* and *Les Amants*. Decai also did the lighting on Chabrol's first four films and shot *The 400 Blows* for Truffaut. It was **RAOUL COUTARD,** however, who had the greatest effect on the new cinematography. A photographer and reporter in Southeast Asia for *Life* and *Paris-Match*, he became a cinematographer in 1957. At the time current lighting conventions failed to correspond to Coutard's own rough and tumble approach to cinematography. Since he didn't have a reputation to defend, he was able to be more experimental, more daring in his work. Pushed by an iconoclastic and provocative Godard, his filming in *Breathless* was so new that it radically—and permanently—altered the cinematic image; earlier lighting methods suddenly appeared old fashioned. Coutard worked with Godard on nearly a dozen films, and was also the cinematographer for Truffaut (four films), Demy, Kast, Rouch, Garrel, and others. **NICHOLAS HAYER,** who began his career in journalism, was a great classically trained cinematographer who managed to adapt to new demands in film and

Raoul Coutard

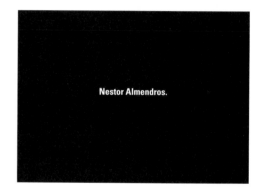

Nestor Almendros.

and sex) while the war in Algeria was raging off screen. Two years later he filmed the flat and unremarkable scenes in *Muriel* to better represent a life that the forced repression of conflict had rendered tedious and painful. Vierny also worked with Kast, Buñuel (*Belle du jour*), Duras, and Ruiz. **NESTOR ALMENDROS** was a relative latecomer to the New Wave. He began his career in 1964 with *Paris vu par . . .* and worked primarily with Rohmer, Truffaut, and Barbet Schroeder. At the same time, Almendros began working in Hollywood, and he eventually won an Oscar for Terence Malick's *Days of Heaven*. Almendros continuously improved the New Wave's approach to cinematography. This involved the use of natural lighting, the incessant modification of reflectors to alter composition, the use of fill lights, the search for colors that were accurate, and so on. It would be unfair not to include **PIERRE LHOMME** here. Lhomme was Hayer's assistant on *Le Signe du lion* and became chief cameraman in 1960. He worked on films by Cavalier, Marker, Bresson, Eustache, and Jacquot.

later worked with Rohmer. In *Le Signe du lion* he accurately captured the particular quality of light in Paris during an August heat wave. **GHISLAIN CLOQUET** worked closely with a number of directors of the period, including Pierre Kast, Jacques Becker in his masterpiece *Le Trou*, Malle, Demy (two films), Bresson (three films), Doniol-Valcroze, Duras, and Polanski (*Tess*).

Two other cinematographers played an important role within the New Wave. **SACHA VIERNY** was a longtime collaborator on many of Alain Resnais's films. He photographed the superb, high contrast, black-and-white images for *Last Year at Marienbad*. Vierny's images implicitly critiqued the beautiful academic images of a vain and sterile bourgeois cinema, entirely focused on its own problems (mostly sentimentality

SOUND TECHNICIANS

The New Wave thought it should be direct, that it should be recorded live with lightweight, portable instruments. For technological reasons, the need for live sound was somewhat delayed (1963–1964), but the New Wave was resourceful in overcoming its absence, and anticipated its arrival. The appearance of the Nagra on the film set was inevitable to the New Wave's use of sound. Young technicians eager for technical novelty in a field that was constantly changing had been preparing for the revolution in sound since 1959. Their goals matched those of the young directors of the time. Jean-Pierre Ruh, one of the finest sound engineers in France, worked with Resnais, and with Rohmer on *My Night at Maud's* (1969) and *Perceval le Gallois* (1978). Following Ruh, GEORGES PRAT worked with Rohmer for several years. JEAN-PAUL MARCHETTI provided sound for Truffaut's *The 400 Blows* and worked with Chabrol from 1958 (*Beau Serge*) to 1965 (*Tigre se parfume à la dynamite*). He was followed by GUY CHICHIGNOUD, who worked with Chabrol between 1966 and 1975, one of the director's most fertile periods. One of the best known and most respected sound engineers of the period was ANTOINE BONFANTI, who worked with Resnais. Two other well-known sound engineers were WILLIAM SIVEL and BERNARD ORTHION.

EDITORS

The upheaval introduced into the plot structure by the New Wave inevitably resulted in changes to directorial style. But the changes in editing technique were even more dramatic. Continuity had been the credo of the period prior to the New Wave. The sense of fluidity, the continuity of movement and space, the use of dissolves, the highly attenuated, muffled sound and balanced mixing—all worked in concert so that nothing disturbed the magical sensation of being carried away by the story. But it wasn't the story inscribed in the script that interested the New Wave; the script was merely the medium or conduit to the confrontation between the singular story and the truth of life. This struggle between fiction and journalism gave rise to the real story that the film related.

Skillful editing was used to promote the unforeseen, the accidental. There was no longer any point in stringing together a sequence of predetermined scenes. Directors were interested in the visual and aural breaks, pauses, and ruptures caused by events that burst—or sometimes stole—into the camera's field of view. Discontinuity became king; the viewer's discomfort signalled its reign. Alain Resnais and Jean-Luc Godard were the first to experiment with such techniques. This is only logical since both directors had worked with film directly, cutting, splicing, experimenting. Resnais edited several of his own short films and ever since *Histoire d'eau* in 1958, Godard has attempted to exhaust the infinite expressive, stylistic, and poetic possibilities of editing. Similarly, Marker, Rohmer, Demy, Straub, Rozier, Rivette, Eustache, and many others preferred to personally edit their own films.

This didn't always prevent them from using outside editors. Once the young technicians were made familiar with the goals of the directors, they too broke with the rules and conventions of the editing profession. One such editor was CÉCILE DECUGIS. She got her start working with Godard in 1957 with *Tous les garçons s'appellent Patrick* and continued working with him until 1960, when *Breathless* came out. Decugis edited *Shoot the Piano Player* (1961) for Truffaut before succeeding JACKIE RAYNAL as Rohmer's editor. She worked with Rohmer between 1969 (*My Night at Maud's*) and 1984 (*Les Nuits de la pleine lune*). AGNÈS GUILLEMOT worked with Godard almost continuously between 1960 (*Petit Soldat*) and 1967 (*Weekend*), then was Truffaut's editor between 1968 and 1970. Similarly, Chabrol worked with editor JACQUES GAILLARD for fifteen years; Truffaut worked with CLAUDINE BOUCHÉ between 1962–1967, and Demy worked with ANNE-MARIE COTRET between 1961 (*Lola*) and 1980 (*Naissance du jour*). Resnais, however, since he always considered himself an editor, had difficulty working with anyone over an extended period of time. He asked his great friend HENRI COLPI to do the editing on his first two features, but it wasn't until 1968 that he met ALBERT JURGENSON, who functioned as Resnais's alter-ego and worked with him for the next twenty years.

255

COMPOSERS

Until the sixties relatively little genuine creative collaboration existed between directors and composers. Prokofiev and Eisenstein or Hermann and Hitchcock are exceptions. In general the musician didn't see the film until the final stage of editing and then provided either a pleasant, decorative, accompaniment or the musical support for the narrative; sometimes the musician worked with the director, sometimes he worked only under the direct supervision of the producer. There was a period of time during the fifties, however, when composers insisted on highlighting the least dramatic effect in a story. They were careful to occupy the entire duration of the film (increasing their royalties) with a psychologically suffocating continuum of sound. Since the prime victims of this system were the cinephiles and critics of the fifties and sixties, it's hardly surprising that the New Wave considered the relationship between music and film to be important and paid careful attention to it.

Directors of the New Wave and composers worked together (in doing so they followed in the footsteps of Rossellini and his brother Renzo, and Bresson and Jean-Jacques Grünewald). They discussed the musical implications of individual scenes and the optimal duration for any specific musical accompaniment, which could range from nothing to an entire passage. Some directors, like Rohmer and Straub, decided not to use any music at all in their films unless it came from a source within the film that was visible on screen. In those rare instances where Rohmer did use

contemporary music for a film, as he did with Sauger for *Le Signe du lion* (which hardly contributed to the film's commercial success at the time), or when Straub worked with Bach or Schönberg, the music was conceived as a documentary element of the film, a block of aural matter. The musician thus became an independent contributor in the process of making a New Wave film.

A number of New Wave composers had been working in film for years. One of them was **PAUL MISRAKI,** a pop musician and author of several popular songs, including *À la mi-août* and the huge post-War hit, *Tout va très bien madame la Marquise*. Beginning in 1932 he began writing music for a number of what might today be called Saturday matinee films. Misraki had more talent than these films would indicate and true melodic sensibility, which could be heard in films by Henri Decoin starring Danielle Darrieux. After the Liberation he worked with Jacques Becker on *Ali Baba* and *Montparnasse 19*, with Welles on *Mister Arkadin* and Buñuel on *Death in the Garden* and *Republic of Sin*. He also began to take an interest in the New Wave. Misraki composed music for Vadim's *And God Created Woman*, Godard's *Alphaville*, and Chabrol's *Les Cousins*, *À double tour*, and *Les Bonnes Femmes*.

A number of young, talented composers arrived on the New Wave scene. **MAURICE JARRE** wrote scores for Resnais, Demy, and Mocky. But he did most of his work with Franju, for whose films he was able to provide an atmosphere of unsettling strangeness. The music he wrote later in his career, which garnered him success in Hollywood and an Oscar, was never as effective as his scores for Franju's *Eyes Without A Face* and *Judex*. Jarre's musical idiosyncrasies, which make his music immediately recognizable, were here dissolved into the atmosphere of gentle and sophisticated cruelty created by the director. In the tradition of the great Maurice Jaubert (who worked with Jean Vigo), the talented **GEORGES**

DELERUE had the ability to create and continuously build upon a melodic line. An extremely prolific composer, he wrote scores for Kast, Resnais, Truffaut, Varda, Melville, Cavalier, Malle, de Broca, and especially Godard, with whom he worked on *Contempt*. His unforgettable score in Godard's film has the seeming ability to cling to flesh and blood and follow the rhythm of our breathing. The music doesn't underline the dramatic action but becomes part of the drama, the way a Greek chorus accompanies a tragedy. Later in his career, Delerue was immensely successful in Hollywood. **ANTOINE DUHAMEL** was approximately the same age as Delerue and Jarre. He was a student at the Conservatoire, where he studied with Olivier Messiaen and participated in Pierre Schaëffer's experiments in musique concrète. Duhamel is a genuinely modern composer, willing to write accessible music for certain directors. He worked with Astruc, Resnais, Truffaut (*Stolen Kisses* in 1968, *The Wild Child* in 1970), Tavernier, and others. He wrote the superb score for Jean-Luc Godard's *Pierrot le Fou* (1965) and *Weekend* (1967). But Duhamel did most of his work for Jean-Daniel Pollet, composing the music for nearly all of the director's films. Similarly, **PIERRE JANSEN** worked extensively with Claude Chabrol, writing music for the director from 1960 (*Les Bonnes Femmes*) to 1980 (*Cheval d'orgueil*).

It was inevitable that jazz, which had won over Paris's young artists and intellectuals in the nightclubs of Saint-Germain-des-Prés after the Liberation, would provide the accompaniment for the New Wave. It was *the* sound of their generation, even if the petty-bourgeois staff of *Cahiers du cinéma* stayed away from the nightclub scene. Astruc, one of the high priests of the period, a habitué of Tabou, and great friend of Boris Vian, never used jazz in his own films because he felt it wasn't serious enough. Louis Malle, however, in spite of his upper middle-class background, not only liked jazz but had **Miles Davis** compose the score for his first film *Ascenseur pour l'échafaud*. Vadim, who frequented Paris's jazz clubs at the time, hired **John Lewis** and the Modern Jazz Quartet to write the music for his second film, *Sait-on jamais?* (1957). It was quite natural, therefore, and in keeping with the tastes of his generation, for Godard to use **Martial Solal,** at the time considered the best jazz musician in France, to write the score for *Breathless*.

Then there was **Michel Legrand**. Son of the composer Raymond Legrand (who had studied in the United States with jazz musician Paul Whiteman), Legrand had developed all the attributes of an accomplished musician early in his career. He was a "precocious virtuoso pianist, a much sought-after accompanist, star orchestra leader, and a highly regarded jazz musician," wrote Dominique Rabourdin. He worked with François Reichenbach before his decisive meeting with Jacques Demy. Between 1961 (*Lola*) and 1988 (*Trois places pour le 26*), Legrand wrote nearly all Demy's film scores. His scores for *The Umbrellas of Cherbourg* and *Demoiselles de Rochefort* are still internationally popular. Legrand also worked with Godard (*A Woman is a Woman*, *My Life to Live*, *Band of outlaws*) and Varda (*Cleo from 5 to 7*). He worked with a number of American directors as well, including Norman Jewison, for whom he wrote the score to *The Thomas Crown Affair* (1968). Two other well known musicians of the period are **Maurice Le Roux** who worked with (Godard and Truffaut) and **Philippe Arthuys** who composed for Rossellini, Godard, and Resnais.

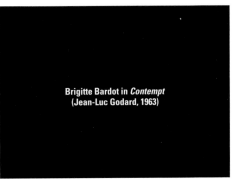

Brigitte Bardot in *Contempt*
(Jean-Luc Godard, 1963)

ACTORS

It would be impossible to list all the actors who appeared on screen at the time the New Wave made its debut. I've only included those who are, in one sense or another, the embodiment of the New Wave phenomenon. Perhaps the most obvious is **Brigitte Bardot.** The prototype of the new woman, Bardot rose with the New Wave, gave it a physical presence. (A fuller description of Bardot is given in the chapter entitled "The Body.") **Jean-Paul Belmondo** is her male counterpart, except that he didn't help launch the New Wave. The New Wave launched Belmondo. He owes his fame to Godard's *Breathless*. With this film he became the symbol of masculinity, the tough, seductive, liberated, and romantic male of the sixties generation. He transformed

Jean-Paul Belmondo and Jean Seberg
in *Breathless* (Jean-Luc Godard, 1960)

Godard's *Pierrot le fou* into a representation of the mythic figure of the modern hero, who is drunk with freedom, love, and self-awareness but tragically at odds with the criminal materiality of money. As long as Belmondo worked with Godard, Chabrol, Truffaut, Melville, Resnais, even Malle and Lelouch, or de Broca and Sautet, he was able to maintain the liberating spontaneity and natural insolence that were his trademarks. Unfortunately, these traits became affectations later in his career. With success—and wealth—he began to stereotype his own character, to formalize it. He became a poseur, the caricature of the great actor he once was, providing a prosaic and sadly bourgeois ending to a Pierrot no longer fou.

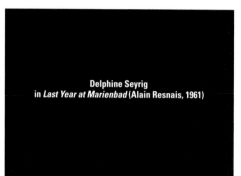

Delphine Seyrig
in *Last Year at Marienbad* (Alain Resnais, 1961)

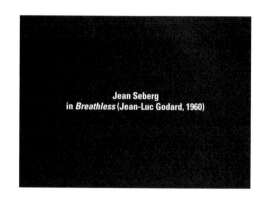

Jean Seberg
in *Breathless* (Jean-Luc Godard, 1960)

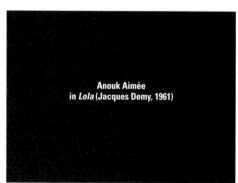

Anouk Aimée
in *Lola* (Jacques Demy, 1961)

Although **ANOUK AIMÉE** is very much a part of the New Wave, her inclusion has little to do with the parts she played for Astruc, Becker, Franju, Mocky, Demy, Bellocchio, Fellini, Cukor, and others. Like Garbo, it was her aura of mystery and absence that made her fascinating, her ability to pass through a film and remain impassive and distant, but in reality hypersensitive, vulnerable,

wounded, fragile, and highly desirable. The screen persona of **DELPHINE SEYRIG,** unlike that of Aimée, although equally skewed, is that of the ethereal diva, precious and mannered, superbly artificial, and true to her femininity. The musicality of her voice—its strange and unexpected inflections—introduced the possibility of subtle variation within the tradition of the apparently inaccessible woman, a tradition which she used and not without humor, for Resnais, Truffaut, Demy, Duras, Buñuel, Losey, Akerman, and Soutter.

The choice of **JEAN SEBERG**—made a young Hollywood star by Otto Preminger—for a film by Godard, introduced the irresistible charm of a foreign accent into French cinema. Viewers let out an audible gasp at the end of *Breathless*, when Seberg asks "What did he say? He said, It's despicable. What's despicable?" She remained in France, however, and her career went nowhere. A brief return to Hollywood for Robert Rossen's *Lilith* (1964) reminded audiences of her greatness and sensitivity as an actress. Another foreign actress, a heroine and character in her own right, without whom the New Wave would never have been what it was, is the Danish actress

ANNA KARINA. She appeared in seven films for Godard and illuminated one of the most inspired periods in his career. Like Bardot, she had a dancer's body, her movements are aristocratic and graceful. Yet, Karina also possesses an interior beauty that can illuminate or darken, like a passing cloud, the fascinating landscape of her enigmatic face. She also worked with Rivette (*La*

the course of four films, Antoine Doinel—Léaud interprets the life of Antoine Doinel—Truffaut. As the latter, Léaud was the hero in *Two English Girls* (1971) and the lead in *Day for Night* (1973). Léaud starred in four films by Godard, including *Masculin féminin* (1966). He later appeared in films by Rivette, Skolimowski, Bertolucci, Benoît Jacquot, Varda, Kaurismaki, and Assayas.

Religieuse, 1964), Delvaux, Deville (*Ce soir ou jamais*, 1961), Visconti, Fassbinder, and Ruiz.

If there is one actor who could be classified as most typically New Wave, it's **JEAN-PIERRE LÉAUD.** Discovered by Truffaut for *The 400 Blows*, he became the director's double in later films. In this fictional biography, which developed from adolescence to adulthood over

Jean-Pierre Léaud
in *The 400 Blows* (François Truffaut, 1959)
and *Le Père Noël a les yeux bleus* (Jean Eustache, 1967)

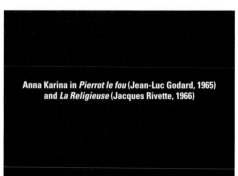

Anna Karina in *Pierrot le fou* (Jean-Luc Godard, 1965)
and *La Religieuse* (Jacques Rivette, 1966)

But it is doubtful he will ever be as great or as unforgettable as he was in Jean Eustache's *The Mother and the Whore* (1973). Léaud is a unique actor, explosive, unpredictable, abrupt, and almost clinical in his roles, to which he brings a schizoid alienation.

STEPHANE AUDRAN was discovered by Chabrol and later became his wife, starring in more than ten of his films. Her cold beauty, the inflection of her voice (which oscillated between accuracy and imprecision and reflected the unconventionality of her theatrical diction), the way she held herself, watched, and behaved (even when playing a criminal), make Audran a unique and highly unusual actress. She also appeared in films by Rohmer, Buñuel, Fuller, Kast, Sautet, and Tavernier.

A group of young actors appeared in Chabrol's *Le Beau Serge* (1959) who were to become inextricably associated with the New Wave: **JEAN-CLAUDE BRIALY, BERNADETTE LAFONT,** and **GÉRARD BLAIN. BRIALY** worked with Chabrol, Astruc, Godard, Rivette, and Rohmer when they were just getting started in film. His character was relaxed, seductive, elegant, and often cynical. His style as an actor, direct and confrontational, resembles that of Jules Berry and enabled him to affect a certain distance between himself and the characters he played, to constantly form judgments about others as well as himself. He embodied the kind of dandyism affected by Paul Gegauff,

Gérard Blain and Jean-Claude Brialy in *Les Cousins* (Claude Chabrol, 1959)

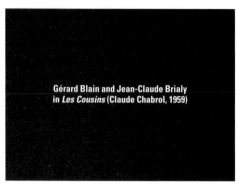

Bernadette Lafont in *Une belle fille comme moi* (François Truffaut, 1972).

which fascinated inexperienced directors. In later life he placed fewer demands on himself as an actor and also began directing. **BERNADETTE LAFONT** made her debut (with her future husband Gérard Blain) in Truffaut's *Les Mistons* (1957) and later worked with him in *Une belle fille comme moi* (1972), one of her finest roles. Within a period of three years (1958 to 1960) and four

films (*Le Beau Serge*, *À double tour*, *Les Bonnes Femmes*, and *Les Godelureaux*), Chabrol provided Lafont with an opportunity to develop into a free, sensual, nonconformist, coquettish, mocking, and spontaneously intelligent character. She appeared in films by Rivette, Garrel, Eustache (she was outstanding in *The Mother and the Whore*), Nelly Kaplan, Juliet Berto, Jean-Henri Roger, Laszlo Szabo, and others. Although later a director, **GÉRARD BLAIN** began his career as an actor for Jean-Pierre Mocky. His earliest screen appearance was in 1954. He appeared in films by Cayatte and Duvivier, and later Truffaut and Chabrol. Hawks gave him a supporting role in *Hatari!* (1962). But beginning in 1971 with *Les Amis*, he abandoned acting for directing (there were exceptions, however: for example, Blain appeared in *The American Friend* by Wim Wenders in 1977). His own directing career continued the tradition of the New Wave. In Blain's case he wrote his own scripts, shot on relatively low budgets, was influenced by Bresson's style, and used relatively unknown actors, with the exception of Robert Stack in *Un second souffle* (1978). His pared down style resulted in an original, secretive, and

Jeanne Moreau in *La Baie des Anges* (Jacques Demy, 1963) and *Jules and Jim* (François Truffaut, 1962)

tenacious body of work that included *Le Pelican* (1974), *Le Rebelle* (1980), and *Pierre et Djemilla* (1987).

JEANNE MOREAU had a somewhat unusual career in film. Classically trained (Conservatoire, Comédie française), she began in film in 1950 in a series of second-rate films, the one exception being her supporting role in *Touchez pas au grisbi* (1954) by Jacques Becker. In 1958 the New Wave served as her vehicle to stardom when she appeared in Louis Malle's *Ascenseur pour l'échafaud* and *Les Amants*. In his *Dictionnaire du cinéma*, Christian Viviani writes, "She introduced an authentic sensuality in place of a fabricated eroticism. Although close to being stilted, her acting introduced a subtle sense of displacement into her roles, which she compensated for by her astonishing intuitiveness. This gave her characters an authenticity that had previously been unknown in France." Since then she has appeared in commercial and auteurist films, as well as works by younger directors. Moreau has appeared in films by Welles, Renoir, Losey, Buñuel, Antonioni, Kazan, Truffaut, Chabrol, Demy, Duras, Téchiné, Mocky, Varda, and Fassbinder.

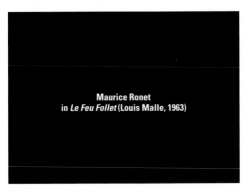

Maurice Ronet
in *Le Feu Follet* (Louis Malle, 1963)

MAURICE RONET was also a graduate of the Conservatoire. His first serious role was in Jacques Becker's *Rendez-vous de juillet* (1949), but his career didn't take off until he starred opposite Jean Moreau in *Ascenseur pour l'échafaud*. After this, Malle offered him the principal role in *Le Feu follet* (1963), a role perfectly in keeping with Ronet's own character: that of an elegant dandy who feigns detachment and conceals an ironic sense of pessimism. It was Ronet's finest performance and one of Malle's two or three best films. Unfortunately, Ronet's distant and amused attitude alienated a number of directors, and only Astruc and Chabrol were able to take advantage of his qualities as an actor. His performance in Michel Deville's *Raphaël ou le Débauché* captured

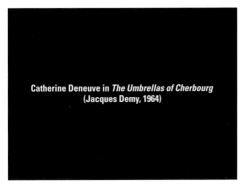

Catherine Deneuve in *The Umbrellas of Cherbourg*
(Jacques Demy, 1964)

some of these qualities. His roles in René Clément's *Plein Soleil* and Jacques Deray's *La Piscine* demonstrate that, in terms of physical attraction, seductiveness, presence, and capability as an actor, he was more than a match for Alain Delon. Ronet was a subtle actor whose sense of the contingency of things prevented him from becoming the star he could have been.

No discussion of the period would be complete without mentioning the sisters **FRANÇOISE DORLÉAC** and **CATHERINE DENEUVE.** Dorléac made her debut in 1960 at the age of eighteen but her career was tragically cut short when she died in an automobile accident at the age of twenty five. Her finest roles are associated with the New Wave. She appeared in Michel Deville's *Ce soir ou jamais* (1962), de Broca's *L'Homme de Rio* (1963), and Norbert Carbonnaux's *Gamberge* (1962) (Carbonnaux was a marginal filmmaker, fond of burlesque and goofball comedy, and popular with the writers at *Cahiers du cinéma*). Truffaut provided her with dramatic roles in his films. She generally played a modern young woman, the victim of conventions and prejudices from which her fashionable but genetically middle-

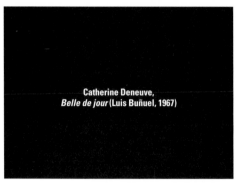

Catherine Deneuve,
Belle de jour (Luis Buñuel, 1967)

class lover (and writer) is unable to free her (*La Peau Douce*, 1964). Roman Polanski, during his English period, having given the lead to her sister in *Repulsion* (1965), offered Dorléac the starring role in *Cul-de-sac* (1966). They shared star billing in the celebrated *Demoiselles de Rochefort*, in which Dorléac, one year older than Deneuve in real life, plays the role of her impulsive and free-spirited twin sister. It was Dorléac's last film. She was a great actress, capable of representing the young, modern women of her generation. **CATHERINE DENEUVE** went on to become one of the biggest stars of French film. She made her debut in film in 1957, at the age of 13, a year before her older sister. She played in a number of second-rate films until 1963, when she appeared in Pierre Kast's *Vacances portugaises*. She then had an unremarkable role in the pseudo-Sadean *Le Vice et la Vertu* by Roger Vadim, to whom she was once married. But it was Demy who made her internationally famous with *The Umbrellas of Cherbourg*, in 1964. Since then Deneuve has appeared in a

number of excellent films. She has had a remarkable career, characterized by both the quality and variety of her roles. She could have been the ideal Hitchcock heroine, had the master of suspense ever cast her in one of his films (*Marnie*, 1963, was the last time Hitchcock used this type of female character in a film). Both Truffaut and Buñuel were able to make use of her personality as a cold, remote, untouchable beauty, simultaneously hysterically virginal and neurotically fierce. Directors like Polanski (*Repulsion*) pushed this aspect of her screen persona to the point of psychosis. She is the ever-present and transparent actress, eminently pliant, subject to the fantasies imposed on her by her directors, viewers, and even her characters. She has become an essential element in the landscape of French film and has been directed—or used—by nearly every French director (with the exception of Godard, Rohmer, Rivette, and Pialat).

Once we understand how a sense of stylistic displacement, of distance between actor and character, and personal reserve characterize the New

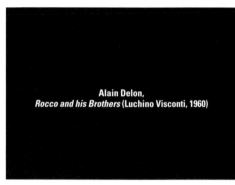

Alain Delon,
Rocco and his Brothers (Luchino Visconti, 1960)

Wave actor, it is clear why an actor like **ALAIN DELON** was of little of interest to the New Wave. An exception was Godard, who cast him in a double role as himself in the 1990 *Nouvelle Vague*. An excellent actor and superb leading man, who was used to good effect by Visconti, Antonioni, Zurlini, and Losey, Delon was incapable of dealing directly with inflated egos. So it was perhaps inevitable that he would work with the most megalomaniacal director of the pre-New Wave, Jean-Pierre Melville. Their collaboration led to a series of magnificent films. **JEAN-LOUIS TRINTIGNANT'S** appearance in *And God Created Woman* inspired a number of young directors of the sixties. These included Franju, Lelouch, Astruc, Rohmer (*My Night at Maud's*, 1969),

There were a number of other remarkable actors, such as **MICHAEL LONSDALE,** an intelligent and independent actor on both stage and screen, whose roles ran the gamut from James Bond (he played the villain in *Moonraker*) to films by Peter Handke and Marguerite Duras. He also appeared in films by Welles, Buñuel, Losey, Molinaro, Carné, Costa-Gavras, and Annaud. Debonair and phlegmatic in appearance, he preferred to work with New Wave directors, including Truffaut, Resnais, Rivette, Eustache, Hanoun, and Ruiz. **CLAUDE MELKI,** a kind of suburban Keaton, was "discovered" by Jean-Daniel Pollet. **LASZLO SZABO** fled Budapest in 1956 and became friends with some of the best known New Wave directors—Godard, Rohmer, Rivette, Chabrol—with whom he had exciting and unusual supporting roles. He made several films of his own, which were strange and endearing, a lot like his own character on screen.

Chabrol, Truffaut, Demy, Téchiné, Kast, Doniol-Valcroze, Robbe-Grillet, Bertolucci, Soutter, and Tanner. From film to film, Trintignant displayed an impressive and enigmatic nonchalance devoid of affectation. **LAURENT TERZIEFF'S** career, however, is more difficult to place. A film and stage actor, he refused to exploit the cinematic fame that followed his appearance in Marcel Carné's *Les Tricheurs*. On stage he was a sensitive yet reserved actor, with a somewhat Dostoyevskian aspect to his character. Yet he worked only with auteurist directors, such as Rossellini, Buñuel, Zurlini, and Pasolini, or traditionalists such as Clouzot, Bolognini, and Autant-Lara. This explains his rare appearances in New Wave films: Kast's *Le Grain de sable*, 1964, Garrel's *Les Hautes Solitudes*, 1974 and *Voyage au jardin des morts*, 1977, and Godard's *Détective*, 1985.

Laurent Terzieff and Jean-Louis Trintignant in *Les Sept Péchés capitaux* (sketch by Jacques Demy, entitled "La Luxure," 1961)

PRODUCERS

RAUL LÉVY. A bold, sometimes scandalous, producer, he shook up the staid environment of French quality cinema. When he produced *And God Created Woman*, he had the audacity to request that Vadim, Bardot, Marquand, and Trintignant be sold as a package, although they were all more or less unknown. His insistence on pushing the "youth" angle helped launch the future New Wave. Once it was underway, however, Lévy returned to more traditional projects. He cast Bardot, his "discovery," in roles with his favorite director, Autant-Lara (*En cas de malheur*), along with Christian-Jaque (*Babette s'en va-t-en guerre*), and Clouzot (*La Vérité*), and failed to realize that a director like Godard or Malle could have put her talents to better use. Having missed the New Wave, he initiated a series of large-scale projects. One of his last films, *Marco Polo*, led to his ruin and ultimate death. Lévy committed suicide in 1966.

PIERRE BRAUNBERGER. Failure never deterred Braunberger, who weathered a number of flops during his career. The old man of the cinema, Braunberger entered the business during the period of the silent film and produced films by Renoir (*Nana*, 1925, *Tire-au-flanc*, 1928, *La Chienne*, 1931, *Partie de campagne*, 1936–1946), Man Ray, Fejos, Florey, and so forth. He also worked with Buñuel on *Un Chien andalou* (1928) and *L'Age d'or* (1930). The war interrupted his activities until 1946. Specializing in short films, he launched a number of young directors, both in and out of the New Wave. These include Resnais, Rouch, Doniol-Valcroze, Godard, Truffaut, Rohmer, Rivette, Pialat, Reichenbach, Lelouch, Guy Gilles, René Gilson, and many others. His ability to discover new talent extended to foreign directors as well, and his extensive distribution network allowed him to get their work into theaters. Although he was a tough, some would say unscrupulous, businessman, everyone that worked with him admired his

intellect, artistic ability, and humanity, and he was well liked by those who knew him.

ANATOLE DAUMAN. Dauman can be considered as more of a gifted and cultured amateur than a professional producer, and he followed a consistent production policy throughout his career. Through his company, Argos Films, he sought out personal films by auteurist directors and made quality, intellectual ambition, and the film's politics paramount. Although a challenging goal, it was one he managed to live up to, beginning with the production of Alexandre Astruc's *Le Rideau cramoisi* in 1953. He was Resnais's producer and, following *Night and Fog*, worked with the director on his next four features. He also produced films by Roger Leenhardt, Robert Bresson (*Au hasard Balthazar*, 1966, and *Mouchette*, 1967), Godard, Pollet, Rouch (who worked with the sociologist Edgar Morin), Chris Marker (*Lettre de Sibérie*, *La Jetée*, *Sans Soleil*), Oshima (*Empire of the Senses*, 1976, and *Empire of Passion*, 1978), as well as Volker Schlöndorff (three films), Robbe-Grillet, Wim Wenders (three films), and Andreï Tarkovsky.

GEORGES DE BEAUREGARD is the producer most often associated with the New Wave. After producing two films in Spain (Bardem's *Death of a Cyclist*, 1955, and *Main Street*, 1956), he returned to France and was near bankruptcy at the time of the 1959 Cannes festival. Spurred on by Truffaut's success, Godard had raced to Cannes. Truffaut introduced Godard to Beauregard and gave them the screenplay for *Breathless*. Beauregard, unsure of Godard, who was then unknown, insisted that Truffaut and Chabrol's names appear on the credits. At the time, Godard's method of shooting the film could hardly be said to be conventional and gave rise to reasonable doubts about his abilities. But the film's critical and popular

success saved de Beauregard's production company from failure, and de Beauregard subsequently had a free hand to produce what he liked. Since the two men had become close friends, this also meant what Godard liked. The director made six more films for de Beauregard (*Le Petit Soldat*, *A Woman is a Woman*, *Contempt*, *Les Carabiniers*, *Pierrot le Fou*, *Made in USA*, *Numéro deux*), and recommended films by several new directors, including Demy's *Lola* (1961), Rozier's *Adieu Philippine* and Varda's first feature, *Cleo from 5 to 7* (made in 1962). That same year, de Beauregard produced *Léon Morin prêtre* by Melville, starring Jean-Paul Belmondo, and paired actor and director again the following year for *Le Doulos*. He produced two films by Chabrol and Rivette's *La Religieuse*, which caused a scandal in France, was banned, and resulted in Godard's sending a scathing letter to André Malraux, then minister of culture. Later de Beauregard helped Rohmer and the fledgling Les Films du Losange complete *La Collectionneuse* in 1967.

MAG BODARD. Another influential producer of the sixties was Mag

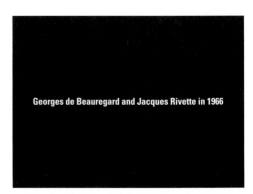

Georges de Beauregard and Jacques Rivette in 1966

Bodard. She produced Demy's *Umbrellas of Cherbourg*, *Les Demoiselles de Rochefort*, and *Peau d'âne*, four of Deville's films, including *Benjamin* (1968), two for Bresson (as coproducer with Dauman), two for Varda (including *Le Bonheur*, 1965), two for Godard in 1967 (*Two or Three Things I Know about Her* and *La Chinoise*), *Je t'aime, je t'aime* by Resnais in 1968, and launched Pialat's career with the sensational *L'Enfance nue* (1969). Like de Beauregard and Dauman after him, she too fell victim to commercial pressure and abandoned film production for television. She worked with another producer, **PHILIPPE DUSSART**, who was her production manager for several years. He helped shepherd the New Wave into existence and continues to have an influence on independent French film.

A number of young directors formed production companies of their own after giving considerable thought to ways of maintaining their artistic independence through the strict control of film budgets. **CLAUDE CHABROL** was the first to implement the idea when he founded Ajym Films. In addition to producing his own films, he helped Rivette complete *Paris nous appartient*, which had been shelved for lack of funding. He financed Rohmer's *Le Signe du lion* and helped Philippe de Broca, his first assistant, with *Les Jeux de l'amour*. But, as mentioned in a previous chapter ("History of the New Wave"), an unscrupulous accountant ran off with the company's funds and bankrupted Ajym Films. **FRANCOIS TRUFFAUT,** like Chabrol, set up his own production company, Les Films du Carrosse. But Truffaut was somewhat more cautious than Chabrol, and after a few abortive attempts at producing his friends' films, he devoted his efforts to exclusively producing and distributing his own work. Similarly, in 1963, Barbet Schroeder founded Les Films du Losange. The company, which is still in business, has maintained a production

Claude Berri on the set of *Le Vieil Homme et l'Enfant* (1967)

policy very much in keeping with the ethos of the New Wave. Les Films du Losange has produced nearly all of Rohmer's films, for example.

CLAUDE BERRI could have been listed here as an actor (Chabrol's *Les Bonnes Femmes*) or director (*Le Vieil Homme et l'Enfant*, 1967, *Le Cinéma de papa*, 1970). Yet his greatest success was as a producer. At the beginning of his career, Berri was very much a part of the New Wave. He directed several short films and sketches for de Beauregard and was a friend of Truffaut, who influenced Berri's first features as well as his efforts as a producer. As the years passed, however, Berri's attitude came to be increasingly at odds with that of the New Wave. He combined skill, intelligence, and business savvy in producing increasingly big budget films (his own and films by Polanski, Patrice Chéreau, and others). His brother-in-law, **JEAN-PIERRE RASSAM** didn't enter the business until the end of the sixties. Although he also promoted big-budget films, he remained faithful to the spirit of the New Wave. Rassam was a brilliant and extremely active man, who brought to French film the intensity of the

tycoons that dominated Hollywood's golden age.

Like them he had a style and an aesthetic agenda. Hervé Le Roux, writing in *Cahiers du cinéma* (issue 139), provided an accurate portrait of Rassam: "Hotheaded, brash, hypercreative, not always easy to get along with, but at bottom quite charming. At the time (1972 to 1975) New Wave film came to resemble him in its provocativeness and innovation. He produced Marco Ferreri (*La Grande Bouffe*, 1973, and *Touche pas à la femme blanche*, 1974), Jean Yanne, Schroeder (*Idi Amin Dada*, 1974, and *Maîtresse*, 1976), and Eustache (*The Mother and the Whore*), Bresson's *Lancelot du Lac*, and Jean-Luc Godard's videos and *Numéro Deux* (1976). French cinema at the beginning of the seventies was as much a product of Rassam's efforts as it was the directors he produced. He was a demanding producer whose name is synonymous with the vitality of cinematic art." Such intransigence, coupled with his complete disdain for any form of mediocrity and his all-embracing love of life, could only lead Rassam to ruin. He committed suicide in 1985 at the age of 43.

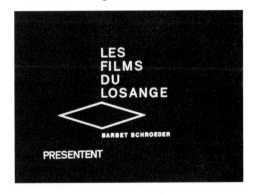

LES FILMS DU LOSANGE

BARBET SCHROEDER

PRESENTENT

Opening credits for *La Boulangère de Monceau*

1963

LE DOULOS

LA BAIE DES ANGES

LE PETIT SOLDAT

LES CARABINIERS

LE FEU FOLLET

CONTEMPT

CUBA SI

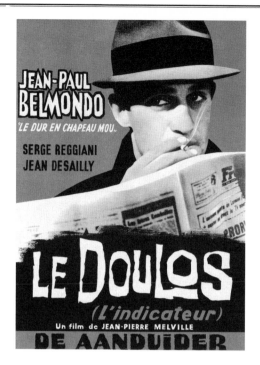

LE DOULOS

Jean-Pierre Melville

RAZOR-SHARP ACCURACY

We're a long way from Montmartre and the novel—a pretty good detective thriller by the way. Melville maintains his distance from the written word (recall the zoom shot from the Sacré-Coeur at dusk) and has no interest in picturesqueness or anecdote. It's man, aging but with his nobility intact, that concerns him. Lying is something too serious to discuss by allowing a voice to fade into the background. The only appropriate setting is the bareness, the violent contrasts of mournful light in which Nicolas Hayer excelled, or the surprisingly exotic set in the film's final sequence. Melville's sets bear no resemblance to Bresson or Fritz Lang (*Le Doulos* is a bit like an anti-Lang, just as *Léon Morin* is something of an anti-Bresson) but are closer to those used by Howard Hawks in *Scarface* or *The Big Sleep*. Harsh light lashes, as it might during an interrogation, the faces of the liars that form one of the most astonishing rogues gallery film has given us in a long time: failed liars (Faugel), successful liars (Silien), massive liars (Kern), pathetic liars, like the drunken doctors we so often find in westerns (Christian Lude),

sardonic (Clain), drugged (La Criminelle's masculine hands, so similar to those of Nuttheccio). All of this is presented without fanfare and with razor-sharp accuracy. Melville renders his world and his characters by refusing to get sidetracked from the main story, rejects the slightest expansiveness. His film has a kind of frigid humanism. ■
Claude Beylie, *Cahiers du cinéma*, March 1963

FRENCH CINEMA AMERICAN-STYLE

Melville has gone back to the source. His admiration for American cinema is well known, as is his knowledge of the field (he lists some 64 American directors among the pre-War directors he admires). *Le Doulos* is an homage to those directors. It would be tempting to take him at his word when he says, "But the times I feel I'm not an amateur, I consider myself the most technical of all French directors. I'd gladly agree to take a test with my colleagues to find out who is the best technician. I'm probably the only one who knows how to use a camera, except for those chief cameramen who have become directors themselves, like Agostini. Outside of them I don't know anyone who can use a camera or who even knows what a photograph is."

However, in writing this article I had several doubts. Once the enjoyment of watching *Le Doulos* is over, what remains? As time passes Melville's film begins to grow smaller and smaller in memory. Yes, it's good cinema, French cinema shot like an American film. No doubt film aficionados will be delighted. Who else? ■
Bernard Dort, *France-Observateur*, February 7, 1963

LA BAIE DES ANGES

Jacques Demy

I LIKE THE FILM FOR THAT "MAYBE"

He's a good kid, honest, a hard worker. He lets himself get talked into gambling, first

by his so-called friend, then by a disturbing woman in white. Together, they win, lose, win, lose. . . . Meanwhile they fall in love. A little? A lot? Not at all? They escape together, running from the fatal casino. For how long? We don't know. And none of us has any illusions about what will happen next. Not Demy, not you, and not me. There's a good chance they'll soon find themselves at the roulette table. All we know is that the lady in white's best girlfriend one day decided to stop gambling. All by herself. So maybe, the two of them. . . . I like this film for that "maybe" that Demy includes. Because, all things considered, there aren't that many different ways to end a film. And Demy has chosen the right one, which is to say the most difficult one, the open door that leads to freedom, and the freedom to destroy oneself.

The screenplay may have no value in itself. The film is good for the way it's directed. But it so happens that Demy also wrote the screenplay, and I see no reason to separate Demy the screenwriter from Demy the director. The story is rather simplistic and it soon becomes obvious that gambling is not its true subject. *La Baie des Anges* is no more a film about gambling than *Lola* is a film about cabaret. In case anyone has any doubts, I'll compare

the two films: The first scene in *Lola* reveals a luxurious American car and a mysterious profile, Michel's white shadow. Who is this character who haunts the entire film but only appears at the very end? He's the obstacle between Roland and Lola. Michel's white shadow could be reflected and multiplied until it came to resemble Frankie and the Americans. It's what makes love impossible. At the same time, it's what makes us want to love this thorn in Lola's heart that Roland can't prevent himself from touching. He frees Lola but wounds himself. We're back in the world of Visconti's *Le Nuits blanches*.

Michel is nowhere to be seen in *La Baie des Anges*. But gambling is to Jackie what Michel was to Lola: the shadow that fascinates Jean. "Why do you gamble?" he asks her as they dance. It's his way of saying, "I love you." He loves Jackie for this passion, the passion that will drive them apart and reunite them with the same force. From this perspective the end of *Lola* casts a pall over the "happy ending" of *La Baie des Anges*: gambling, like Michel, will soon reclaim its white heroine. ■

Jean Collet, *Cahiers du cinéma*, April 1963

GAMBLING, NOT LOVE

While the smoker, as everyone knows, consumes the object of his passion, the gambler is consumed by it. Demy shows us a woman, Jackie (played by Jeanne Moreau), who is consumed, who ruins herself without hope. The film is ostensibly about gambling, and although this isn't the film's only theme, it's one of the most significant elements in it. Gambling wastes, erodes, and destroys, and Demy pitilessly frames the thinness, the ugliness of his heroine, and later renews Jeanne Moreau's character by showing how she's changed physically. In Malle, Truffaut, Vadim, and Losey (and in a somewhat more complex way in Antonioni), Moreau has always been the sensual woman, whose wrinkles, circles, and bags were the physical manifestation of a particularly active sex life. Bardot is an invitation to sex. Moreau reveals its most prosaic effects. In Demy's film it's gambling and not love that possesses her. In making this transfer,

Demy has managed to reveal something that's rarely shown on screen: the destruction of a human being by gambling. There's nothing surprising, therefore, when the love scenes between Jean and Jackie are systematically ignored, since love doesn't exist for Jackie and she's the film's central character. Demy's use of close-ups is justified in this context. They enable him to isolate the two protagonists, leaving Jackie to her gambling and Jean to his fascination for her. ■

Michel Ciment, *Positif*, July-August 1963

LE PETIT SOLDAT

Jean-Luc Godard

SINISTER, SHAPELESS, RIDICULOUS. . .

On the basis of recent censorship you would have thought that Godard had made a fascist film. All he did was dump one garbage pail into another. *Breathless*, aside from the talent of its actors, is by comparison heavily "constructed." Bluff for bluff, Godard recites—even tells us he's reciting—a page from Cocteau, but simply "borrows" a passage from Nietzsche, whose meaning he distorts by projecting it on a building where torture is supposed to take place. It's true that Nietzsche is no longer

around to cry genius before this gelatin-crazed hack, who lacks both intelligence and generosity, violence and candor. I can only hope that Godard manages to make himself repulsive to Brigitte Bardot, since she had the bad judgment to appear in a Moravia story under his "direction." Sinister, shapeless, ridiculous not merely for its dialogue and "photography," *Le Petit soldat*, is no longer *contempt*, but *boredom*: death without further comment. ■

Gérard Legrand, *Positif*, June 1963

LES CARABINIERS

Jean-Luc Godard

A MORALITY OF INDULGENCE

In *Les Carabiniers*, as in all great works of inspiration, cinema becomes atonal. It no longer indicates events but actions, no longer sentiments but motives. We shouldn't try to discover who loves whom, or who misses what, but watch the characters live, let ourselves be swept away by their charm, and sample the world's richness from a suitcase. The essential stages of the plot are found in the ellipses.

The things this film conceals, more or less indirectly—that stupidity, envy, rapacity, and pride are sentiments created or unleashed by war—are not its most important aspects. Nor is the absurdity of political parties, or the fact that Communism and Christianity are outdated, anachronistic, or even the fact that the artist alone has the right to our respect. The importance of this film can be found in its immense love of life, once again demonstrated through the absurd. What is important is the film's preoccupation with ideals, its tranquil appetite for beauty, which reveals monstrosities to be less monstrous, errors to be less serious, criminals to be less responsible, victims less innocent. The importance of this film is its ability to make us acknowledge a higher, more lucid morality, that of total goodness: a morality of indulgence. ■

Paul Vecchiali, *Cahiers du cinéma*, July 1963

A SCHOOLPLAY

The protagonists do what they like, how they like, any way they like. Jean-Luc Godard, a dedicated expert of *farniente*, gives the impression of not knowing the exact outcome or content whenever a scene is being shot. He gives in to casual improvisation that works against him and looks contrived on screen.

More pitiful than furious, the viewer has to listen to a succession of childish paradoxes on war, better suited to an annual school play at the local grammar school. The carabiniers, bums, and their "ladies," speak like second-rate Brecht, but in snippets, as if even pastiche would have been too difficult for them to bring off. The film is bathed in an atmosphere of cerebral nothingness, based on interminable silences that interrupt the few falsely ironic remarks mumbled by amateur actors, or the sudden appearance of a verbal cataract. The director doesn't skimp on padding the dialogues. Take, for example, that incredible description of post cards. The film's heroes bring back a suitcase full of them as bounty from their odyssey. The description lasts ten minutes but feels like a hundred.

Outrageously disconnected, the film has all the earmarks of a slow, lazy mind, someone confused, fuzzy; it's the work of an "auteur" who lacks even the desire to create: the horrors of war as seen by an apathetic and untalented bumbler, always ready to lapse into bad taste. From time to time, he inserts a small Ubuesque joke, a bit of burlesque worthy of the silent film, an intellectual sarcasm. All of it trickles away in the sand. ■

Louis Chauvet, *Le Figaro*, June 5, 1963

THE HORRORS OF WAR

In the screenplay, which he wrote with Roberto Rossellini (based on an Italian play I'm unfamiliar with), Godard has multiplied the allusions to the Second World War. The soldiers-carabiniers carry a two-armed white cross (equivalent to the swastika in Chaplin's *The Dictator*). The king is obviously Hitler. The battles take place near Rostov, according to the subtitles, for the film is subtitled as if it were silent.

Yet the conflict takes place not at the beginning of the forties but the sixties. The automobiles and fashions are those of today. The female Resistance member whom the two carabiniers capture and execute is dressed as if she were spending the winter in Megève.

This image of contemporary war is much more striking than a reconstruction of the years 1940–1945 would have been, with its old front-wheel drives and orthopedic shoes. The horrors of war and its monstrous stupidity are even more shocking because the fusillades, rapes, massacres, Resistance fighters, and fires, belong to our time and not some epoch in a distant and historic past. The story is told in a deadpan manner with that black humor so characteristic of Godard.

He casts a cold sardonic eye at the savagery and irrationality of militarism, war, and fascism. Even though they are closer to *commedia dell'arte* than a carefully developed story, the scenes in the film have a poignancy all their own: the shooting of the hostages or the arrival of the soldiers at the house of a poor family, where they lift the girl's skirt with the barrels of their machine guns. ■

Georges Sadoul, *Les Lettres Françaises*, June 6, 1963

UNBEARABLE

I don't want to trash *Les Carabiniers* under the pretext that the film is, in so many words, badly done, badly written, badly acted, badly edited, badly lit, just bad. It's all of that, of course. But it's worse: it's a disaster and to screen it in a normal movie theater with a box office and seats is a bad move, which will have a negative effect on good films, whether by Godard or someone else. In fact, Godard should have shown *Les Carabiniers* outside, in a vacant lot, on an old sheet tacked to a wall, letting his friends sit on empty milk cans. When you start out as badly as this, you don't end up in velvet seats in the orchestra.

Godard's film is neither seductive nor moving. It's totally exasperating, sickening. The viewer can't wait until it ends, until the war ends. Could such cynicism in presenting a situation be possible without an equal degree of cynicism in the way it was filmed? Alas, I don't think so. The qualities missing in Godard's film are those which would have sunk his project. The least concession would have risked looking good on screen.

Les Carabiniers is the representation of ignominy. The film is unbearable because it is so badly tied together and because it explodes the misunderstandings and ambiguities that make war films bearable. Stupid because of its intelligence, revolting because of its honesty, disjointed because of its intellectual rigor—in the end *Les Carabiniers* proves that a successful war film is morally impossible. In truth Jean-Luc Godard has sacrificed himself: he's the first director of a war film who dared make himself unbearable. ∎
Michel Cournot, *L'Express*, June 13, 1963

LE FEU FOLLET

Louis Malle

"YOU ARE YOUR OWN WORST ENEMY"

I no longer recall who wrote the following (Godard?), "Tragedy is a lot like the close-up." I don't know if Louis Malle has read it. But I know that, thanks to his use of close-ups, he's succeeded in giving *Le Feu Follet* a tragic intensity. The film opens (without credits) with a series of close-ups: the face of a man, and the face of a woman, talking after making love. There are circles under their eyes, their mouths look defeated, and already there is a great distance between this man and this woman, the distance associated with ordinary politeness. The film ends with a close-up: a close-up of a revolver going off, followed by this disenchanted, almost indifferent face, fixed in the gelatin of the image. Between the opening close-ups—the solitude of love—and the final close-up—death as the final form of solitude—Alain's destiny is played out. There are close-ups of people, faces, to whom he offers his own face. Close-ups of objects toward which he extends his hand—in vain. Occasionally there is a long shot: a street, a dinner, other people, life, noises, automobiles, gestures, words, the

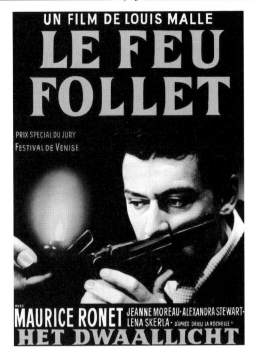

world outside. But it's impossible to breathe. Once again we are confronted with a close-up of the hero obsessed with himself, prisoner of himself: his head, heart, and ears occupied by his own voice to the point of nausea. "You are your own worst enemy." Rarely have the formal properties of a film (especially the use of voice-overs, here readings from Drieu la Rochelle) appeared as essential as they do here. *Le Feu Follet* never gives the impression of virtuosity. You only notice it afterwards, the sign of true elegance. ∎
Jean-Louis Bory, *Arts*, October 23, 1963

ANGUISH, DESPAIR, AND A REFUSAL TO GO ON

It's not easy to forget the voice of Maurice Ronet playing Alain, "I'm clumsy, I'm heavy. I've worked hard to make it easy. There was sensitivity in my heart, but not in my hands." Later on he says, "I wanted to be loved so badly that it seems like I love myself."

Drieu la Rochelle has often been accused of writing an apology for suicide. Maybe Louis Malle will have succeeded in making his film clearer than the book ever was, since it is continuously interpreted on the basis of Drieu la Rochelle's life and politics. In *Le Feu Follet*, anguish, despair, the refusal to live, belong neither to the right nor the left. They express only the

questioning of an extremely sensitive individual in the face of existence. ∎
Henri Chapier, *Combat*, September 3, 1963

CONTEMPT

Jean-Luc Godard

THE SHIPWRECKED OF THE WESTERN WORLD

Moravia's novel is a vulgar but amusing popular novel, filled with conventional but old-fashioned sentiments, in spite of the modernity of the situation. But from such novels beautiful films are often made.

I kept the basics and simply transformed some of the details, starting from the principle that anything that's filmed is automatically different than what is written, and thus original. There's no need to try to make them different, adapt them for the screen. You simply need to film it as it is. Just film what's written, more or less, for if cinema wasn't primarily about film, it wouldn't exist. Méliès is the greatest director, but without Lumière, he would have been completely unknown.

The subject of *Contempt* revolves around people who observe and judge themselves, and who are in turn examined and judged by cinema, here represented by Fritz Lang playing himself. He's the film's conscience, its honesty. (I shot the scenes for *The Odyssey*, which Lang shoots in *Contempt*, but since I play the role of his assistant, Lang would say that those scenes were shot by his second unit.)

Aside from the psychological story about a woman who feels contempt for her husband, *Contempt* is like the story of the outcasts of the western world, the survivors of the shipwreck of modernity, who, like the heroes of Verne and Stevenson, suddenly discover a deserted and mysterious island, whose mystery is inevitably the absence of mystery, or truth. The odyssey of Ulysses was a physical phenomenon; I filmed a moral odyssey. The way the camera examines the characters looking for Homer replaces the way the gods looked down on Ulysses and his companions.

It's a simple film, without mystery, an Aristotelian film, stripped of appearances. *Contempt* proves, in 149 shots, that in cinema, as in life, there are no secrets, nothing to discover, just life—and film. ∎

Jean-Luc Godard, *Cahiers du cinéma*, August 1963

YOU SHOULDN'T MEDDLE WITH SIMPLE EMOTIONS

J.-L. G. You know that, roughly speaking, *Contempt* is the story of a woman who stops loving her husband because she discovers that the man is weak. To make money, he agrees to rewrite the screenplay of *The Odyssey*, which Fritz Lang is supposed to shoot. Lang is arguing with his American producer, Jeremie Prokosch, played by Jack Palance. The screenwriter, who really shares Lang's opinion of *The Odyssey*, sides with the producer, to show off and to neutralize his wife's anger.

The couple's disagreement is represented as an intellectual conflict that appears distinct from the argument. But Piccoli, the screenwriter, makes the mistake of looking for interference between fiction and life. This conjunction exists, since it's the motive for the film, but he's wrong to consciously mix two worlds as different as this. His efforts lead to all sorts of catastrophe.

This "duel of opinions" about *The Odyssey* contains something extremely important. To get at this I modified Moravia's novel by giving the producer ideas that the novelist attributes to the director. I wanted Fritz Lang to represent classicism. Thus, in the film, the producer has his own theory about *The Odyssey*. He thinks that Ulysses waited so long to get back to Ithaca because he didn't get along with his wife. Fritz Lang disagrees with this Freudian interpretation. He feels that Homer and his heroes were simple people, without any "modern" complications, and that it's important to keep *The Odyssey's* purity, preserve the incomparable harmony of the ancient world.

The producer is crazy, like all producers. Paul, the scriptwriter, only agrees with him because he's opportunistic and because he's looking for a fictional image of the difference that separates him from his wife. **M. M.** Prokosch may be crazy but he's not completely wrong, since life has confirmed

BRIGITTE BARDOT
JACK PALANCE
MICHEL PICCOLI

IL DISPREZZO

UN FILM DI
JEAN LUC GODARD

the accuracy of his concept of the screenplay. There's definitely a break between Paul and Camille, the screenwriter and his wife.
J.-L.G. Naturally, the producer is comfortable within his system, and he's always right since he never steps outside it. The drama involving the others arises because they try to belong to two worlds. They make the mistake of meddling with simple emotions, which can't be transplanted. Culture and intelligence change nothing. The contemporary world has lost the secret of the ancients. Recall the well-known serenity of antique statuary. Our smile is forced. We look for complications.
M. M. Your vision is a contemporary vision of this ancient world, after 25 centuries have elapsed.
J.-L. G. The problems may have been the same. There were punks in Athens. But our outlook isn't the same. *Contempt* is conceived on that other point of view. It's based on a few essential things: the sea, the earth, the sky. My characters are no longer in harmony with nature as the ancients were. Yet I treated this landscape as a character, giving it as much presence as the actors.

My primary goal was this return to classicism and serenity. *Contempt* was

filmed using very long takes (there are barely 150 shots), and the long shots, where the actors are "lost" in the background, were very important during the editing.

My concern for color was similar. I used only primary colors: red, blue, white, green. And always very pure, unadulterated tones. You can't imitate a painting by playing with color, it's pointless. You have to film things with simplicity. ∎

Interview with Jean-Luc Godard conducted by **Michel Mardore**, *Les Lettres Françaises*, December 25, 1963

EMPTY, STUPIDLY PRETENTIOUS, AND INTELLECTUALLY VAPID

Upon leaving the Vendôme, where *Contempt* is playing, I hurried to a late-night bookstore to buy a copy of Moravia's novel. It seemed inconceivable that the book would be as empty, as stupidly pretentious, as intellectually vapid as what I had just seen. Upon reading it, I found that it involved the story of a psychological analysis (a genre for which Godard has about as much talent as his left foot) and that the "additional" dialogue, as it's referred to, in the film, amounted to such immortal phrases as, "Get in your Alfa, Romeo." Without being a partisan of fidelity (which would be something new), I'm amazed that Godard's *Contempt* would, by some strange mechanism, involve Moravia.

What he's produced is easy to understand. For the first time in his career, the director of *Le Petit soldat* was faced with a *story* and characters with realistic motivations. All he could do with this was superimpose his own bluestocking taste for citations (Brecht, Hölderlin, Louis Lumière, and André Bazin), his adolescent facetiousness, his fuzzy and complacent direction. In *Contempt* excerpts from a number of books are read aloud, Hindu fables are related, Bardot is given a string of profanity to repeat, Michel Piccoli and his hat are filmed in a bathtub, but not for a single moment does anyone behave as if they were in a film. Jack Palance, who plays the part of a producer and speaks English, is left to his own devices and is as fatuous and as obnoxious as he is in real life. Fritz Lang, who is supposed to play himself, passes through the film like the survivor of a one-act play, left with nothing but the dignity of his monocle.

It required (long live America!) repeated requests on the part of the producer, Joseph E. Levine, before the director consented to film Bardot in the long introductory nude scene, the best in the film and the only one to provide a brief glimmer of hope. Bardot unclothed is an ever-renewing, always inspiring spectacle, that changes color like the sea and transforms the grumpy viewer into a grateful pup. I'm afraid that Bardot's presence, as sublime as it is, won't save *Contempt*. The nude scenes come at too high a price, resulting in a vague uneasiness resembling the discomforts of insomnia. ■

Robert Benayoun, *France-Observateur*, December 24, 1963

INTENTIONAL OBSCURITY

An average writer named Alberto Moravia once wrote a story (in first person) about a poor intellectual, consumed by doubt, stuck in the labyrinth of an Italian film production, who is despised by his wife, an intrepid but rather conventional and "uneducated" (if not brainless) woman. Jean-Luc Godard felt there was enough here to make a film.

But a film by Godard is generally nothing more than the argument of an intrepid autodidact, unable to make up his mind about cinema, the world (ancient or modern), or any of his concerns no matter how varied: from looking for an apartment to the anguish of "artistic creativity." In this sense *Contempt* is no more successful than his other films. It is even less excusable since Godard had several major advantages at his disposal, none of which he managed to put to good use. He's probably a very unhappy man, but unhappiness is no excuse for this.

Contempt begins with a long shot in which Godard himself is filming the studios from a crane while a sepulchral voice reads the credits (the name of Joseph E. Levine, the man who took all the risks, fails to appear). This is followed by the following sentence from André Bazin, whose only mistake is his optimism, "In place of our gaze, cinema substitutes a world that conforms to our desires." An even more sepulchral voice follows this careless remark, "This film is the story of that world." The camera's lens then turns on the viewer.

Ninety minutes later the same viewer sees a flat and overexposed expanse of sea, which through violent efforts, eventually turns blue. During this scene, whose limpidity is taken straight from Bresson, the same voice concludes with this enigma, "Yes, this is the last scene in the film. Ulysses has returned to his homeland." There's no sign of Ithaca on the horizon.

What happened in between? Yielding to a perverse mania that certainly won't make him the French Samuel Fuller, Godard has "switched" the roles drawn by Moravia, and in the process made the story unintelligible to the viewer as soon as he tries to interpret the characters' true destinies. The screenwriter no longer struggles to impose his conception of *The Odyssey*. In the book it was Rheingold, the director, who wanted to "psychoanalyze" Homer. Here, it's the screenwriter who confronts his own emotional problems at every turn. Their violent opposition, however, is replaced by a courteous colloquy.

The "overall intention" of this film terminates in nothing more than an avalanche of contradictory quotes that introduces a number of incomprehensible elements into the film and slows down Godard's direction. Even Vadim's *Repos du guerrier* looks good in comparison. The most astonishing lapses don't bother me overmuch and I'm not very good at logic, but I'm still trying to figure out why Michel Piccoli is supposed to write the script for a film whose rushes Lang has already screened. At the start of the film, when Palance (the producer) asks him to write the script, Piccoli questions him about whether Lang will go along with it. It's the missing *how* that bothers me not the *why*.

Behind the name of Hans Lucas, Godard once wrote scholarly elegies, obscure but peremptory, on "classic directing." No matter what he claims, however, the uncertain pleasure of complicating matters purely for the sake of complication, reveals him to be a man increasingly dependent on the mannerisms of an armchair director. ■

Gérard Legrand, *Positif*, May 1964

CUBA SI

Chris Marker

THE METAPHORIC EXISTENCE OF CROCODILES

Cuba Si has been waiting two years for its censorship license. It was rejected in 1961 by Mr. Terrenoire, a long forgotten Minister of Information. Like Joseph Prudhomme and his reference to the sword used to defend and, if need be, "combat" the government, Mr. Terrenoire wanted to be remembered by posterity for declaring that any film containing "ideological propaganda" could not be shown on screen. Although he never censured the filmed speeches of His General, Terrenoire made it understood that *Cuba Si* would be authorized only on condition that its narration contain no "ideological content."

Chris Marker had been out of Cuba for several months when the anti-Castro forces landed in the Bay of Pigs and were turned back. Such an event had to appear in *Cuba Si*. Another documentary filmmaker would to edit a sequence using the abundant current news footage of the event. Chris Marker selected from his negatives a sequence about the life and habits of crocodiles in Cuba's swamps, and used these images to evoke the Bay of Pigs and the defeat of the anti-Castro forces.

The words of his narration give a new (metaphoric) meaning to those crocodiles. Tomorrow, we may discover the failure of a new anti-Castro attack, and those who have seen *Cuba Si* will mentally view the assailants not as parachutists or legionnaires, but as caymans in the swamps. What would *Cuba Si* have been with a *Terrenoirian* commentary? "Many crocodiles can still be found in this tropical island. Their skin is greatly valued by the leather goods industry, which produces handbags and shoes that are coveted by tourists, etc." ■

Georges Sadoul, *Les Lettres Françaises*, September 26, 1963

THE NEW WAVE AROUND THE WORLD

Any attempt to present the French New Wave as the beginning and end of all modern cinema would not only be incorrect but ridiculous. Roughly similar causes, in different contexts, would have produced similar effects in the end. If the New Wave hadn't originated in France, it would have appeared somewhere else at about the same time. Of course its impact would have been different; rather than being global, it would have remained local. It is thus difficult to judge the New Wave's direct influence on cinema. It would be more accurate to say that all the new waves—along with their idiosyncrasies—that sprung up around the world during the sixties, came into being because they were necessary to the evolution of their country and its cinema. But that the French New Wave contributed to their growth is both certain, relative, and ultimately questionable.

The above remarks certainly apply to John Cassavetes, whose work appeared at the same time as the New Wave but was never influenced by it. A promising young actor with a future in Hollywood, Cassavetes refused to conform to its demands. After his first film, he broke with the taboos of traditional American film. Financed by a subscription campaign announced on the radio, acted by students in his drama course, and filmed in 16 mm on the streets of New York, *Shadows* (1959) was innovative in every respect. To the routine of the Hollywood bureaucrat, Cassavetes responded with creative freedom and the search for a new form to express new ideas. *Shadows* was the story of a young black woman who passes herself off as white and loses her white boyfriend when he meets her brother, whose own skin color leaves little room for racial doubt. Cassavetes's audacity in portraying such a subject in 1959, at the height of the Civil Rights movement, immediately labeled the young filmmaker as an innovator. For the first time, New York's youth, its minorities, and its problems—the entire film is constructed around a succession of problems (racial, financial, emotional)—are candidly portrayed. Cassavetes sacrificed conventions and technical concerns on the altar of realism. In *Shadows* the emphasis is not on the story but the characters and their movements, which determine the film's own incessant movement. The film is not psychological; the characters' actions are never judged. Their behavior, the subtleties and details of their life, are observed from the outside.

After a brief detour with the major production companies, which obviously didn't agree with Cassavetes (*Too Late Blues*, 1962, *A Child is Waiting*, 1963), he returned to working as an independent in 16 mm, and created a cruel, uncompromising portrait of the American middle class. *Faces* (1968) pushed the system examined in *Shadows* even further, radicalized it. What is left is a clinical study that reveals a society's innermost, neurotic truth. The film shows what happens to people living in the midst of a powerful ideological system, and how its myths are falsified, how the illusions are broken. It is an uncompromising film that, in the end, shows the American dream to be nothing more than a painful hangover in the face of a pale dawn. Cassavetes shows America's tragedy to be that its people live without authentic, necessary goals; life is nothing but a block of time to be filled up or squandered with jokes, drunkenness, wild laughter, or hysterical tears. The cult of success intended to spur the country's triumphant march forward produced a society that moves in "fast-forward." America is pure facade, a mask. The forced smile cracks to reveal a sense of desolation, whose sudden bursts of infinite despair are tracked by the camera.

Emphasizing reality never implied that events have priority over style. Art occurs when reality is on a par with its expression. It is as much for his aesthetics and his probing camera that Cassavetes is a revolutionary. No one was better able to capture in real time the fluidity of behavior. The length of his takes has nothing to do with naturalism but is essential to his quest for self-revelation and the spectacle of man's ruined existence. The filmmaker rejects the condensation of life inherent in classical dramaturgy. This in turn determines the mobility of his camera, required for the revelation of intimacy. In Cassavetes the hand-held camera is no longer liberating and exhilarating, but stifling and alienating. It tracks his characters at any cost, encircles and encloses them. They are incapable of escaping its eye. The concentration of energy that "signifies" American cinema is turned upside down in Cassavetes, revealing itself as a form of irremediable waste and loss. A giant of the independent film scene in New York, Cassavetes continued his work on the alienation of American life by not accepting outside financing or studio interference. Like Welles, he preferred to appear as an actor in television and minor films to finance his projects.

Brought to public attention with *The Connection* at the start of the sixties, Shirley Clarke is one of the major talents of the New York School. The film is about a group of drug addicts waiting for their fix. What sets Clark apart is her ability to establish a relationship of force between her subject and her audience. Clark isn't satisfied with simply providing an image for those without one—junkies in *The Connection*, black delinquents in *The Cool World*, prostitutes in *Portrait of Jason*—

Gena Rowlands in *Faces* (John Cassavetes, 1968)
John Cassavetes (second from right) with his crew during the shooting of *Shadows* (1959)

Guns of the Trees (Jonas Mekas, 1961)

but directly implicates the viewer in their situation. In *The Connection*, a film within a film, the director addresses the viewer directly, has the actors look into the camera, gives on-screen advice to the characters about how to act, and so forth. Using a reality that is foreign to the audience, she draws attention to our presence as voyeurs.

This flowering of young independent filmmakers concerned with realism was beneficial for theoretical questions about reality and its film image. How could the director show what had never existed? How far could he go? These are the kinds of questions that haunted the first films by the critic Jonas Mekas (*Guns of the Trees*, *The Brig*), who was head of the New American Cinema Group (founded in September 1960), and who demanded that films be "tough, maybe even badly done, but alive."

Then there was Drew Associates, founded by Robert Drew in 1958. Unlike Clarke and Mekas, Drew wasn't interested in a specific synthesis of documentary realism and formalism, but the total obliteration of the filmmaker in favor of the event represented. Richard Leacock, Don Alan (D. A.) Pennebaker, and Albert Maysles produced a number of "live" film portraits and invented a new form of journalism (approximately thirty films were made until the breakup of Drew Associates in 1963) of citizens, politicians (a campaigning John F. Kennedy in *Primary*), and film and music stars.

The interest in what is referred to as "direct cinema" became the credo of the new Canadian filmmakers who appeared at this time. They were Francophone Canadians, for the English-language cinema in Canada lacked individuality and seemed to be nothing more than a pale imitation of American film. The desire to draw attention to Québécois identity generated a sense of cultural euphoria, stimulated a need, a demand for political existence. Québécois cinema, in its search for representative characters and the unique character of "la belle province," had to explore the new Canadian reality. A return to their roots became the focus of young filmmakers, many of whom had worked in television (Radio Canada). Four names dominated this new cinema: Pierre Perrault, Michel Brault, Jean-Pierre Lefebvre, and Gilles Groulx. Claude Jutra and Fernand Dansereau were also part of this movement but produced work of inconsistent quality. In spite of their diversity, the films produced all had something in common: fiction was revealed through the technique of direct cinema, and it was invented as it was being made. Freed of the heavy and sententious documentary bias that characterized the style of the National Film Office, the reality described in the first films of the young Canadian New Wave metamorphosed before the viewer's eyes into a story. The technique was employed in the series of televised news spots on Isle-aux-Coudres by Pierre Perrault and in the short film, *Les Raguetteurs*, made by Michel Brault and Gilles Groulx in 1958.

The ambition of Québécois filmmakers was to grab hold of an identity and a way of life that was changing. After having lived for two years among the inhabitants of Isle-aux-Coudres, Perrault began his trilogy (*Pour la suite du monde*, 1963; *Le Règne du jour*, 1966; *Les Voitures d'eau*, 1969). The characters speak in their own dialect, connect with the roots of their identity, and thus provide Québec with a distant memory that suddenly becomes immediate. Lefebvre and Groulx are painters of Canadian youth with their moral and political uncertainty. *Le Chat dans le sac* (1964), which was well received in Cannes, uses a cinéma-vérité style to sketch the portrait of two adolescents and their discontent. *Révolutionnaire*, made in 1965, is nonchalant and easygoing, but the film's ideological satire caused a scandal when it came out. Cinema, Godard said, provided an ID card to the country that was looking for one. His remark certainly applies to Québec at this time.

The new Brazilian cinema, which appeared during the early sixties, followed a similar course. After the important critical movement and growing interest in film of the preceding decades (which resulted, as it had in France, in the creation of film clubs and cinémathèques), a generation influenced almost exclusively by film began to question a Brazilian reality in crisis. Underdeveloped and excluded from the modern world, Brazil was in a perilous situation. Rebellion was brewing. The military units associated with ultra-conservative elements were on alert. But the handful of filmmakers present preferred to close their eyes and continued to pursue a lifeless craft devoid of artistic ambition or naturalism. The Cinema Novo group made a violent break with Brazilian film tradition. In parallel with the nationalist claims made at the end of the fifties, Nelson Pereira dos Santos, Alex Viany, and Roberto Santos were the first to point their cameras at the realities of the country. Independent, sometimes produced cooperatively, their films wavered between a transposed neorealism and a socialist realism. They were followed by the first films of Gustavo Dahl, Leon Hirszman, Carlos Diegues, Paulo César Saraceni, Ruy Guerra, and especially Glauber Rocha.

For these filmmakers it was no longer sufficient to be a realist, one had to assume a critical stance in light of the national situation. Cinema was not just an

Le Dieu noir et le Diable blond (Glauber Rocha, 1963)

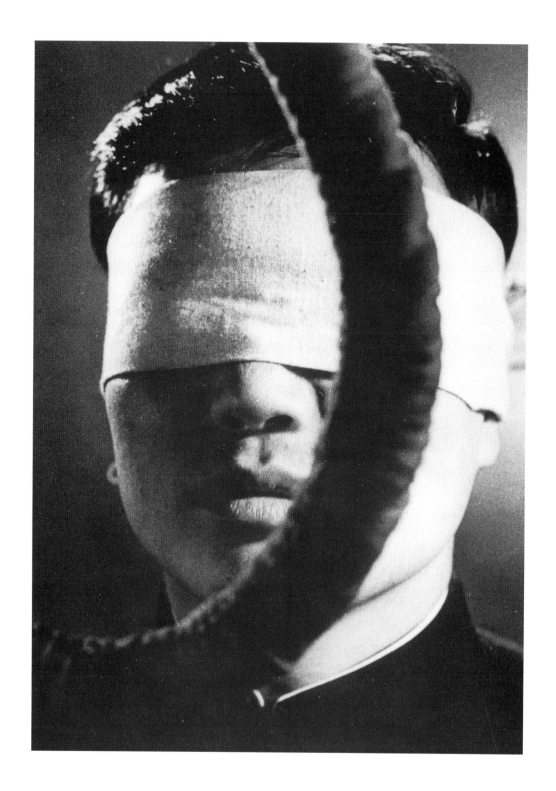

Death by Hanging (Nagisa Oshima, 1968)

instrument of knowledge but an active tool of political agitation, an art that was less didactic than polemic. Unlike the Québécois filmmakers, those of the Cinema Novo were not searching for the meaning of their country, but reaffirming a national identity with remote origins. In contrast to other new wave movements, which were only interested in the present, young Brazilian filmmakers investigated Brazil's past (*Os Fuzis* by Guerra, *Ganga Zumba* by Diegues). They revealed the foundations of a national culture that the present had forgotten and which it was essential to reintroduce. Glauber Rocha, a spokesman for the movement, didn't locate the action of his films in the past but practiced a kind of syncretism, blending the religions, cultures, rituals, and popular representations that had *made* Brazil, to describe a contemporary situation considered intolerable and desperate. In Rocha's case there was no sense of political reductionism. Hysterical and violent, his liberating films (free from the influence of traditional American cinema, which had colonized the Brazilian screen) are devoid of academicism and blend, in baroque fashion, a variety of chaotic and spontaneous styles that do less to destroy an earlier cinema than they do to construct a new one.

The situation in Japan was very similar to the emergence of the French New wave. Japanese filmmakers were interested in shaking up the great classical tradition, which they found stifling and overly dominating (a cinema of revered, formidable "masters," represented by the work of Kenji Mizoguchi, Yasujiro Ozu, Mikio Naruse, and Akira Kurosawa). The desire to separate themselves from the classical way of working was made stronger by the fact that the majority of them had been assistant directors and were forced to undergo the oppressive dictatorship of the studio system. The young directors—Yoshishige Yoshida, Masahiro Shinoda, Shohei Imamura, Kiriro Urayama, and Nagisa Oshima—wanted to get out, get a breath of fresh air, and confront an external reality. Freed of the Japanese tradition, Oshima's *Cruel Story of Youth* evokes the dynamism of American film and the adolescent emotional faults found in the work of Nicholas Ray. Oshima's film reveals the reactions of a younger generation that is already violent and no longer willing to tolerate the lies in which Japanese society cloaked itself. This ideologue of the Japanese New Wave rejected comparisons of the movement with its French homologues, whose films Oshima reproached for lacking political conscience. And yet, it was after seeing *Night and Fog* by Resnais that Oshima determined the direction his country's cinema would now follow. The Japanese intelligentsia of the time (Mishima and others) was driven by a general sense of revolt that had become increasingly ideological. With his next film, *Night and Fog in Japan*, Oshima gave his work a more overtly political flavor (the film is about the consequences of renewing the Japanese-American treaty) that grew stronger with time.

After the sixties the Japanese financial sector switched its investment allocation. It abandoned film and invested heavily in television, which was considered a more strategic media. The new directors who came on the scene at this time had great difficulty in trying to produce their own films. Their revolt in the face of this injustice politicized them even further and led them to espouse the revolutionary dogma that animated anti-authoritarian movements around the world. The spirit of '68 hung over the raw films of Yoshida and Imamura. Oshima was influenced by this as well, and questioned Japanese society directly and politically (*Death by Hanging, Boy, Ceremony*). After 1975 and the decline of anti-authoritarianism, Oshima, like Kurosawa, had to obtain financing in the West to pursue an increasingly politicized body of work (although without any particular ideology), which attacked society and its sexual taboos.

England

The energy and sense of liberation of the New Wave affected other areas of Europe. At the end of the fifties, the large British studios and majors (such as Korda or Rank) went bankrupt and liquidated their assets. The rise of high-quality television, eager for documentary material, quickly adopted a hands-off policy with respect to the conditions and means of production. This permitted the Free Cinema rebels (Lindsay Anderson, Tony Richardson, Karel Reisz) to film their first news pieces and fictional films on location in 16 mm. Many of these rebels had been writers for the magazine *Sequence* (which folded in 1952) and then *Sight and Sound* (the more pragmatic and sociological London counterpart to the Parisian *Cahiers du cinéma*). With the exception of *Saturday Night and Sunday Morning* (Karel Reisz), *The Knack and How to Get It* (Richard Lester), *If* (Lindsay Anderson), and *The Loneliness of the Long Distance Runner* (Tony Richardson), the production of the English New Wave was disappointing. Once again, British cinema reflected the lack of affection the country felt for it as an art form, in spite of Chaplin, Hitchcock, and Stephen Frears.

Sweden

In Sweden it was again a former critic who created a sensation. After rebelling against the stifling psychoanalytic introspection of Ingmar Bergman, Bo Widerberg went on to direct *Barnvagnen* (1962). Like his compatriots Mai Zetterling and Jan Troell, the only aspect of the French New Wave Widerberg seemed to retain was its technical features (stripped down production techniques, location shooting, and improvisation) rather than any genuine aesthetic.

Russia

Even Soviet cinema was no longer impervious to change. During the Krutschev era, production increased and enabled new filmmakers (Grigori Tchoukhraï, Sergei Bondartchouk, Lev Koulidjanov) to make their first features. A new realism made its appearance, freed of the ideological weight and pomposity of socialist realism; it was more lyrical and closer to the Soviet people, and described their everyday life, their problems. And it took an interest in the individual rather than the collective. At the beginning of the sixties, far removed from the naturalist obsessions of socialism, two great filmmakers arrived on the scene. They created an uproar in the Soviet cinema: Andrei Tarkovsky and Sergei Paradjanov. For both filmmakers, the visible revolution was more aesthetic than political. They were followed by Andrei Kontchalovski, who had written screenplays for his school friend Tarkovsky, and the Georgian Otar Iosseliani, who began making his first short films.

Poland

In Poland, after the first wave during the fifties (Wajda, Kawalerowicz, Has, Munk), two young directors responded to the changes in France and began making films about their country's youth: Roman Polanski and Jerzy Skolimowski. Although more faithful to illusionist cinema than to cinéma vérité, in his first film, Polanski combined an isolated setting (a boat) with representatives of the two social groups that formed the new Polish society (a very recently arrived bourgeoisie, the product of the nomenklatura, and a rebellious youth movement). All of Polanski's interests can be found in *Knife in the Water*: the claustrophobic setting, the intruder who upsets a world we know little about, the playing with perception (the problem of point of view is conveyed through the optical phenomenon of accommodation), and the elements of the thriller inserted into the most banal everyday setting. Skolimowski, who wrote the dialogues for Polanski's film, was deeply influenced by the French New Wave when working on his first films (*Rysopis* in 1964, *Walkover* in 1965). He added a sense of irony all his own, however. Although his films are based on the everyday and its familiar banality, Skolimowski

Following pages: *Knife in the Water* (Roman Polanski, 1962)
Pier Paolo Pasolini in 1968 on the set of *"Che Cosa sono le Nuvole"* (sketch from *Capriccio all'Italiana*)

is not content to describe the situation he presents but emphasizes its pathetic side, its emptiness and broken dreams. Exiled in the West, Polanski and Skolimowski naturally used New Wave actors. Polanski shot a film with Catherine Deneuve and another with Françoise Dorléac; Skolimowski used Jean-Pierre Léaud for *Le Départ*.

Italy

By the end of the fifties, Italian neorealism and its post-war Christian Democrat inspiration were dead and buried. Rossellini entered his period of historical films before he began making didactic films in 1965. Visconti abandoned the neorealist populace of *Rocco and His Brothers* (1960) and turned to a decadent and refined baroque aristocracy in *The Leopard* (1963). De Sica turned his back on his realist beginnings and began working on a series of mediocre comedies. The years 1959–1960 marked a radical turning point in the work of Fellini, beginning with *La Dolce Vita* and especially *8 1/2*, which was characterized by a dreamlike realism. Similarly, Antonioni made a violent break with his past in *L'Avventura*, a film that quickly became a symbol of cinema's modernism.

At this time, when the major figures of the first era of neorealism were distancing themselves from their origins, a new wave of young filmmakers came on the scene. They were united by a common desire: to revive the still warm corpse of neorealism by combining it with a materialist, Marxist approach to society. They included the Taviani brothers, Francesco Rosi, Vittorio de Sica, and, of course, Pier Paolo Pasolini. Pasolini acknowledged the influence that Godard's *Breathless* had upon him; its freedom of tone and style, its poetic treatment of narration, encouraged Pasolini to make films. Godard proved that cinema also belonged to poets. Bernardo Bertolucci, the son of a poet, met Pasolini and became his assistant. Bertolucci boasted of this affiliation with Pasolini when he was filming *La commare secca* (1962) and later aligned himself with the tradition of young French filmmakers when he made *Before the Revolution* (1964). Although these first films indicate no more than an ability to follow fashions and trends, there are signs of definite talent. Another young filmmaker, Mario Bellocchio, filmed *Fists in the Pocket* (1966). This angry film created quite a sensation, marking its author as part of the New Wave tradition.

The Third World

While the arrival of Egyptian filmmaker Youssef Chahine in 1958 could be considered part of the general phenomenon of the New Wave, the same wasn't true of third-world cinema as a whole, especially African cinema. After their independence many of these young nations, contemporaries of the New Wave, were directly or indirectly influenced by it through the work of directors who had studied in Europe. But their subject matter did not reflect the economic boom that preceded its development in Western Europe. The very existence of a national cinema and the problems of survival were far more urgent matters for these young directors than knowing whether or not they should imitate an aesthetic model that, ultimately, was foreign to them. A similar process took place in North Africa and the African republics, as well as Iran and Turkey.

For political or cultural reasons, many western cinemas were unable to take part in the early New Wave and were forced to wait several years to make their appearance. Their arrival depended on a sense of freedom that didn't manifest itself until 1965–1966. This was the case in countries still under the thumb of Stalinist dictatorship, such as Hungary and Czechoslovakia. The former Federal Republic of Germany was dominated by a crippling sense of shame and guilt. The New Wave's influence on cinema in the United States was likewise delayed.

Czechoslovakia and Hungary

As intellectuals began to openly criticize state dogmatism (the 1977 charter) and as social, political, and artistic demands became increasingly urgent, destabilizing the apparatchiks, the young Czech cinema started buzzing with activity, eager to participate in the debate. Stimulated by the French New Wave and the excitement of Italian neorealism, a handful of new directors made films that were "cheap and shot on location." In escaping the artificial comfort of the powerful Barrandov studios, they also escaped the control of the censors. Jan Nemec (*Diamonds of the Night*), Vera Chytilova *(The Ceiling, A Bagful of Fleas, Something Different,* and especially the wonderful, stylized *Daisies*), Stefan Uher (*Sinko v Sieti*), Pavel Juracek (*Josef Killian*), Vojtech Jasny (*When the Cat Comes*), and Ivan Passer (*A Boring Afternoon, Intimate Lighting*), were part of a group of directors intent on breaking with earlier cinema and eager to represent Czech society, especially its youth, whose reality was an everyday life that was dull and drab but where people clung to whatever hope was left to them.

This was the world in which Milos Forman, a young Czech assistant director,

Following page: *Loves of a Blonde* (Milos Forman, 1965)

grew up. He saved enough to buy a camera and directed his first film, *Konkurs* in 1962. This film was a slightly dramatized documentary about an audition for aspiring young singers held in a nightclub and a local concert that two young men escape to watch a motorcycle race. The following year Forman made his first feature, *Black Petr*, which won the grand prize at the Locarno Festival, over Godard and Antonioni. But it wasn't until *Loves of a Blonde* (1964) that Forman developed an international reputation as a director. The film was enormously successful at home and an immense critical success elsewhere. The (forced) liberalization of the government between 1965 and 1968 stimulated the growth of new Czech cinema, and Forman directed his most biting and prophetic work, *Fireman's Ball* (1967).

Konkurs, *Black Petr*, and *Loves of a Blonde* form a kind of trilogy on Czech youth of the time. Like the New Wave elsewhere, Forman's style was journalistic. Through a grisaille of black and white, his indiscreet camera candidly records the misadventures of several young girls at an audition, a trainee-guard at a supermarket, and a naive young lover; their adventures are tinged with the gravity and melancholic awareness of failure. Yet Forman is careful not to overdramatize or *melodramatize* any of these situations. He allows us to watch, to observe. He follows the itineraries of his characters as if the film were a gossip column and tracks what is most trivial in the daily lives of these young people, who so desperately want to be hip and cool. The films are saturated with a tender humor. Forman's realism is based on this sense of naturalism and amusement. His fluid camera captures the spirit of the moment and the adventures of Czech youth, and with gentle irony establishes the fact that the clock is ticking for the young people on screen. In his films innocence, idealism, and the naiveté of late adolescence are threatened by adulthood and a responsibility that is still difficult to accept (the same theme appeared twenty years later in the character of Cécile, the pure young girl in *Valmont*).

Banality, daily life, and the observation of routine gestures are the natural subjects of Forman's early films. In *Black Petr*, the structure of the story is characterized by the way the director "adds" moments together, the bits and pieces of life. There are no straight lines, no neat, clearly marked paths, only short melancholic moments without any action to speak of. Just the flow of everyday life devoid of a sense of underlying drama. The story behind Forman's first feature is broken up into a series of anecdotes, digressions without any apparent purpose. The same is true of *Loves of a Blonde*, in which each sequence appears as a small, uneventful block of time, each without any real effect on the overall action. This purposeless temporality

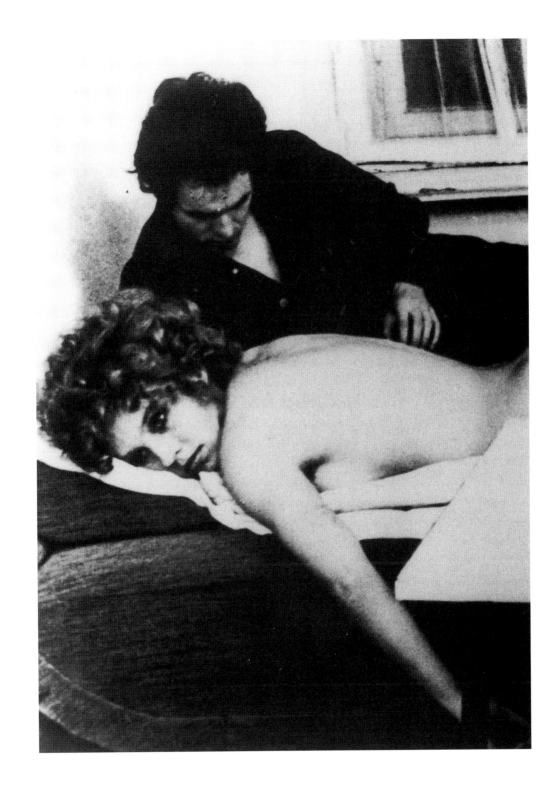

Love is Colder than Death (Rainer-Werner Fassbinder, 1969)

culminates during the discussion in bed between the young girl and Milda, the pianist, where what is said serves no *dramatic* purpose as in Godard.

Later in his career, *Ragtime* (1981) enabled Forman to follow several known and unknown characters on screen and make them the temporary *vehicles* of the story. The importance given to minor characters, frequently more typecast than the principals, enables Forman to focus the narrative. Thus Petr, the buffoon who gives his name to the title of the film, forfeits the narrative to Cenda, the drunk young mason, during the long party scene. *The Fireman's Ball* is constructed around the addition and multiplication of burlesque situations (for instance, the theft of the raffle prizes during the beauty contest) in such a way that no single character carries the full weight of the story. A metaphor of communist society, the film provided an elegant mechanism for showing that this society was based on stripping responsibility from the individual, and therefore from society as a whole.

Like the New Wave, Forman refused to provide neat endings for his films: the sudden freeze frame in *Black Petr*, the looping narrative (the return to the starting point) in *Loves of a Blonde*, the lack of denouement in *Taking Off* and its open ended finale, as if the narration had "senselessly" followed its characters the way Petr pointlessly tracks the shoplifter in the supermarket. Foreman is perhaps the foreign director most influenced by the New Wave, which, in turn, admired him and his work. It is interesting to note that when Russian tanks invaded Prague in 1968, Forman was in Paris and couldn't get out. The producers and brothers-in-law Claude Berri and Jean-Pierre Rassam, borrowed Truffaut's car, snuck into Prague and brought back the director's wife and children. In 1968 Forman began a brilliant career in America. Other Czech filmmakers also went into exile, as Czech and Slovak cinema began to fade with the arrival of the Prague Spring.

The flowering of the Hungarian New Wave closely followed the rebirth of Czech cinema. The historical events of 1956 and the subsequent anguish undermined the bleak, heavy films produced by the national cinema industry at the end of the fifties. With the liberalization of power in the sixties, new filmmakers with new subjects arrived on the scene: Istvan Szabo (*Age of Illusions*, *Father*), Ferenc Kosa (*Ten Thousand Days*), Andras Kovacs (*Cold Days, Walls*), and especially Mikloš Jancšo, the most important Hungarian director of the period. His epic trilogy (*The Hopeless Ones, The Red and the White, Silence and Cry*) destroyed the sentimental romanticism of earlier cinema and questioned Stalinist power. In Jancso's films there is a raw sense of action, which is shown without psychologizing or explanations. It is action as ritual.

Federal Republic of Germany

An insurrection took place in the German film industry in 1962, during the short-film festival in Oberhausen. Access to the powerful individuals who ran the festival was impossible, and young filmmakers were surviving only on the small grants handed out by the government. During the festival, 26 new directors and scriptwriters published an angry manifesto that marked the birth of a new German cinema. They demanded freedom from current commercial interests and government oversight. "The old cinema is dead. We believe in the cinema of tomorrow" they claimed. But it wasn't until 1965 that their hopes became reality, and the "Committee for Young German Cinema" was created along with a Film Promotion Office. It was within this context that Volker Schlöndorff (*Young Torless*), Werner Herzog (*Signs of Life*), Jean-Marie Straub (*Machorka-Muff*, *Not Reconciled*), and Alexander Kluge (*Anita G.*) got their start. After an important period working in the theater (The Antitheater), Rainer Werner Fassbinder made his first film in 1969 (*Love Is Colder Than Death*). He became the most important German filmmaker of the second half of the century.

What sets his work apart is its overt refusal of the techniques of cinéma-vérité and any attempt to blindly reproduce reality, which was so important to young directors of the period. Fassbinder rejected *presentation* for *representation*. For him, it was the heart of reality and life. His characters are victims of the social need to "play" a role they don't believe in, one that is foreign to them. They are willing to go along with the "spectacle" imposed by society but are unable to find either their place in it or their identity; they play a role from which their "self" is missing. This is the reason for the constant, obsessional, neurotic use of mirrors in Fassbinder's films. They serve to feverishly verify whether or not the image they reflect matches the one the world expects.

Fassbinder marked the end of the New Wave. His work began with the culmination of a course that, over a ten year period (1958 to 1968), made the transition from an intoxicating sensation of liberty to a critical and rebellious analysis of an artificial freedom suffused with anguish. Fassbinder's films are an illustration of the society of the spectacle that Guy Debord wrote about. They incorporate the events and ideology of 1968. Their mise-en-scène was based on the truth of German expressionism and denounced a society that continued to embody signs of nazism and forced individuals to assume an attitude of hypocrisy and deformation of the self.

Following page: Rainer-Werner Fassbinder in *Fox and his Friends*, 1974

The flexible and self-contained movements of his camera reveal the networks, the invisible codes that turn representation—the instrument of domination—into a spider web in which his characters are caught and ultimately destroyed. The lateral and circular dolly shots that capture these beings cease to function whenever representation itself suddenly breaks apart; close-ups and direct, head-on framing, are thus used to reveal his characters in their true light.

Like Fassbinder, Daniel Schmid (*Tut alles im Finstern, eurem Herrn das Licht zu ersparen*, 1970, *Heute nacht oder nie*, 1972), and especially the baroque and fascinating Werner Schroeter (*Eika Katappa*, 1969, *The Death of Maria Malibran*, 1971), though formally opposed to the New Wave, nevertheless resemble it in attitude. Schmid and Schroeter eventually developed a friendly and professional relationship with Rohmer and Schroeder's Films du Losange. The former critic, Wim Wenders, extended the New Wave approach but put his own stamp on it. He shot his first film in 1970 (*Summer in the City*) and was already dreaming about America.

Switzerland

Unable to accept the naive vision of a country without problems, the French-speaking Swiss developed a contentious cinema that created a scandal in the country. Alain Tanner, inducted as head of the movement, made two films, *Charles Dead or Alive* in 1969 and *La Salamandre* (starring the marvelous Bulle Ogier) in 1971. *La Salamandre* in particular was to become a symbol of May '68. It is difficult to determine the influence of the British Free Cinema group that Tanner (and Goretta) associated with in London before his return to Geneva in 1968 or the influence of the French New Wave, which his films of the period resemble in several respects.

Two other young directors deserve mention alongside Tanner. Claude Goretta, who codirected a short with Tanner entitled *Nice Time* (1957), got his start on Swiss television before he made his first feature, *Le Fou* in 1970. His best known film is *The Lacemaker* with Isabelle Huppert, shot in 1977. Goretta has always been interested in the common man, in those who, in his words, "have missed their rendez-vous with history." Michel Soutter, although younger than his two compatriots, got his start with them. He made his first feature film, *La Lune avec les dents*, in 1966. It was shot in 16 mm, as were his next few films. The success of Tanner and Goretta, however, enabled Soutter to abandon low-budget methods and direct films using professional equipment. His films, secretive and reserved, had only limited success. All three directors were declining in popularity when Godard moved back to Lake Leman, the region of his childhood, to set up a production studio. Once he had taken up residence in the country, Godard seemed to embody all of Swiss film.

Belgium

It would be a serious oversight to omit the Belgian director André Delvaux. Delvaux attempted to merge the influence of Rouch and the New Wave with Fellini's oneiric vision. His cinema insinuates itself in the strange and phantasmagoric imagination of Flanders. It supplies a fictional counterweight to the long proletarian tradition of engagé Belgian documentary. These two veins helped renew Belgian cinema. Twenty years later Chantale Ackerman and the Dardaene brothers would become its most illustrious representatives.

France

A passionate cinephile and friend of *Cahiers du cinéma*, although he never wrote for the magazine, Benoit Jacquot was interested in the psychoanalytic theories of Jacques Lacan and admired Robert Bresson. He was also an assistant to Marguerite Duras. Jacquot constructed and refined a body of work that was both sensitive and severe. Sexuality become the object of his study, and he treated it as simultaneously fascinating and mysterious. His style is restrained, abstract, and informed; yet it strives for the simplicity and obviousness of the written word. Jacques Doillon directed a utopian film, *L'an 01* (1973) in which Resnais and Rouch each appear. Since then his films have been divided between stories about children and adolescents, and emotional crises between adults. They are part of the "realist" trend characterized by Eustache and Pialat, without the energy of the first or the violence of the second.

Pierre Zucca's films are both more emotional and more personal. His work, which is unusual for its quantity and quality and rarely shown, is admired by many directors, including Rohmer. What Rohmer finds interesting in Zucca's work is its esoteric undercurrent, which is both modern and very close to the rigor of classic cinema. This is true of Zucca's *Roberte* (1978), written by Pierre Klossovsky, whose wife plays the title role. For Rohmer, the influence of Gegauff on *Alouette je te plumerais* is obvious (strengthened by the fact that Chabrol acts in the film), just as he sees the influence of Stevenson on *Rouge-gorge* (1985). Zucca, who also directed *Vincent mit l'âne dans le pré* (1975), possesses a genius for subtle humor and intimation that fascinates, enchants, and offers a unique vision of the world. Jean-François Stevenin held many jobs in film and was assistant director to François Truffaut. Yet he is most frequently credited with being an actor (one of the few in France built like an American). He directed only two original and quite remarkable films: *Passe-montagne* in 1978 and *Double Messieurs* in 1986.

A definite, yet remote New Wave influence can be found among directors who were shaped by the spirit of '68. These include Romain Goupil, Jean-Pierre Gorin, Marin Karmitz, René Gilson, and Philippe Condroyer. Its influence, however, was greatest on Juliet Berto and Jean-Henri Roger, who collaborated with Godard on the militant films he made between 1968 and 1972. As an actress, Berto stood out in Godard's *Two or Three Things I Know About Her* (1967), *La Chinoise* (1958), and *Weekend* (1967). She also appeared in films by Rivette, Tanner, Glauber Rocha, and others. As a director she produced a vibrant, tense, rebellious, and passionate body of work that also managed to be joyful and humorous. She died in 1990 at the age of 43.

Once the *Cahiers* had passed its Maoist stage, which led it not only into a political dead-end but financial ruin, the magazine regained its bearings. It appealed to a generation of young, passionate critics, animated by a desire to become directors, like their well-known predecessors. With the rebirth of the *Cahiers* a number of new directors appeared on the scene: H. le Roux, J. P. Limosin, P. Kané, Danièle Dubroux, Serge le Péron, A. Bergala. All of them retained the mark of a political conscience that made its way into their films.

At the same time an anti-New Wave current appeared. This had begun rather modestly when Bertrand Tavernier began directing in 1974. As a form of protest, as well as a provocation, he returned to using the scriptwriters of the French quality tradition that Truffaut had damned twenty years earlier. He gave precedence to the formal attitudes of documentary film, which enabled him to maintain his distance from the film (not to be identified with Brechtian alienation) to the detriment of journalism's sense of immediacy and urgency. Nevertheless, his style more than his subject matter retains certain elements of the New Wave. His best work occurs when he is filming as a journalist. Bertrand Blier is the son of the excellent actor Bernard Blier, the great friend of Michel Audiard. Audiard was the talented specialist of ultra-French dialogue and had a considerable influence on the young Bertrand Blier, who continues to use his sing-song dialogue in his films. But beginning in 1980 a new generation of young directors made their appearance in France, many of them

(Besson, Beinex, etc.) virulently anti-New Wave. Their approach to cinema, however, is less concerned with art than with production. It is their false naiveté that has so far served as their salvation ... and their excuse. In general they have been unable to justify a profession, which on the whole remains hostile to the New Wave and has aligned itself with commercial success as a way to help it navigate in what can now only be described as troubled waters.

The American cinema at the beginning of the sixties fell into a kind of vacuum. Disoriented by the decline of Hollywood, it needed time to reflect on itself. Out of convenience Los Angeles became its capital. But it also became the center of a Californian cinema that exploited a debased and demeaning version of Hollywood and attempted to "Disneyfy" the world. During the years 1960–1970, there were three important filmmakers who not only maintained the earlier traditions but helped ensure the transition to a new cinema: John Cassavetes, Jerry Lewis, and Sam Peckinpah. But the older directors, who were once the remarkable "young" directors of the fifties, were having greater and greater difficulty working within the system (Nicholas Ray, Anthony Mann, Joseph Mankiewicz, etc.). The directors of an earlier generation (Fritz Lang) either left, emigrated (Chaplin, Welles), declined (Hitchcock after *Marnie*), or disappeared after one or two last masterpieces (Hawks, Walsh, Ford and his sublime *Seven Women*). After 1965 the landscape changed: Hollywood died and Los Angeles took its place. The attitudes and stakes changed radically, as did the management and conception of film, now considered nothing more than a simple audiovisual object. The dream factory was busy with marketing.

Traditionally, a new generation would take advantage of this profound upheaval and jump into the void that had been created. This typically New Wave phenomenon also took place in California. What makes it unique, however, is the approach taken by these directors. The right foot advanced proudly along the institutional path. Young directors studied film in college (UCLA), absorbed different techniques, analyzed and dissected the great classics, and generally took advantage of school in a way that the French New Wave had adamantly and categorically refused to do (IDHEC). At the same time, the left foot tentatively explored the Z-series circuit, which was fundamentally marginal in terms of the profession but highly commercial. Here they had a first-hand opportunity to learn the tricks of the trade and the craft of cinema. Their professor was an astonishing

Following pages: *Goodfellas* (Martin Scorsese, 1990)
The Godfather, Part III (Francis Ford Coppola, 1990)

character, an intrepid producer and magnificent director of small, genre films, hastily shot on a shoestring, that were ten times better than many of the bloated productions cranked out by the majors. The man was Roger Corman. He was the real teacher of the rising generation and the first to give an opportunity to the young Francis Ford Coppola with *Dementia 13* (1963).

Impregnated with a love of film as strong as that of the *Cahiers du cinéma*, deeply influenced by the French New Wave, linked to the changing attitudes that led to the hippie, beat, and rock movements, affected by the revolutionary spirit that in 1968 inspired youth movements around the world, these new directors rocked Los Angeles and the majors. Within five years they rose to the top of the film industry, where they remain to this day.

Although initially united, this group soon split into two separate movements and followed two different paths. Led by Steven Spielberg and George Lucas, one path embraced capitalist ideology, promoted a Californian cinema whose intelligence was on a par with that of the surfers who populated its beaches, made products that were superbly constructed but without substance, that were pumped up with special effects hormones, and created a form of cinema that headed straight for the wall of the virtual image.

The other path held directors who reflected on the nature of the image and continued to view cinema not only as their subject, but a reality inseparable from fin-de-siècle America. The basic idea behind the work of Francis Ford Coppola, Brian De Palma, and Martin Scorsese is that cinema is no longer a new art form. Consequently, the filmmaker's eye is contaminated, is no longer pure; they focus on reworking the theme of a lost paradise, so essential to the Anglo-Saxon imagination. Their films incorporate an entire system of references to cinema's founding fathers (Ford, Hitchcock, Welles, Nicholas Ray), which not only underscored the way their films were directed but also the behavior of their characters. They prove that although Hollywood may be dead, its spirit lives on in the minds, lifestyles, and imaginations (dreams) of Americans. Cinema is the heart of the American imagination and has become one of the parameters of American reality. Coppola's *Apocalypse Now*, the *Godfather* trilogy, *One from the Heart*, and *Rusty James*, Scorsese's *Mean Streets, Who's That Knockin', Taxi Driver*, and *Goodfellas*, and De Palma's *Dressed to Kill, Body Double*, and *Scarface*, reveal only that the characters who "constitute their cinema" are unreal, exist only as Hollywood heroes, and enclose themselves in an outdated mythic universe whose victims and prisoners they have become. More perverse than Coppola and Scorsese, De Palma has pushed this destabilization of the character onto the viewer, plays with his knowledge of cinema (Hitchcock especially), and the loss of cinematic innocence. This is what separates Spielberg (who pretends to believe in innocence, glorifies it, wraps it in sentimentalism, and further alienates the viewer) from Coppola, who reveals the origin of evil, the old Hollywood and its modern bastardization, California cinema. Coppola's work defends another American cinema, which traditionally examined and criticized the means and effects of its style and technology to better reflect the world, to believe in the world.

These new American filmmakers have been able to analyze the American dream that was conveyed, fashioned, and projected by Hollywood, and what remains of it. Hollywood created myths that have become outdated and useless, which once made sense but have now caused us to lose our sense of reality. Coppola, De Palma, Scorsese, Michael Cimino, and others belong to the generation that experienced the shock of the Kennedy and King assassinations, witnessed the Vietnam War, and lived through a moral crisis exacerbated by economic recession: events that undermined their confidence in America and its system. Their cinema is critical of the American dream and questions the very foundations of the nation. This critical dimension is missing in the films of Spielberg and Lucas, and even more so in their followers. It is a form of pernicious senility on the part of those who claim they have preserved their "childlike soul."

1964

THE UMBRELLAS OF CHERBOURG

LA PUNITION

DES PISSENLITS PAR LA RACINE

THE NUTTY PROFESSOR

BAND OF OUTSIDERS

for
all
the young
lovers
of the
world

THE LANDAU COMPANY PRESENTS

The Umbrellas of Cherbourg
IN SONG AND COLOR

THE UMBRELLAS OF CHERBOURG / Written and Directed by JACQUES DEMY / Set to music by MICHEL LEGRAND / Starring CATHERINE DENEUVE · NINO CASTELNUOVO · ANNE VERNON · MARC MICHEL / A MAG BODARD PRODUCTION FOR PARC FILMS-MADELEINE FILMS / Distributed by AMERICAN INTERNATIONAL

THE UMBRELLAS OF CHERBOURG

Jacques Demy

SMILES AND TEARS

If *The Umbrellas of Cherbourg* needs to be defended, it is its proponents rather than its detractors (there are few of them and their arguments are limited) that we should be concerned about. Unlike Renoir, Rouch, and perhaps Jacques Rozier, but like Godard and Bresson, Demy communicates directly with his audience for no more than a few brief, but astonishing, moments. Everything else is hidden beneath irony and mannerism, or refinement, as Godard's work is behind provocation and quotation. Often we must overlook the film's beauty to discover its virtues. Ophuls's memory is there to remind us of this. "All beauty has its source in suffering" (Jean Genet).

One sign of the film's success is the way it conveys emotion. Not since *An Affair to Remember* has there been such balance between smiles and tears. But unlike what transpires in McCarey's film, Demy doesn't try to hide the film's structure. His protagonists aren't puppets improved upon by the direction; they are men and women of flesh and blood, who feel the same contradictions and feelings we do, live the same life as we, one in which tears do not imply improvement, but defeat or disappointment.

There's also a sense of harmony in this film: it exists within the individual frame. And it's this harmony at the elementary level that makes me believe that the integration of beauty is more than accidental. I still laugh when I hear film being *dissected* as something linear (this color, that music). Cinema is not a language, or several languages together, but an art that begins with everything at once, starting with the individual shot. ■
Paul Vecchiali, *Cahiers du cinéma*, May 1964

A WORLD OF SOFT COLORS

It would be a mistake to compare this film with Gene Kelly or Stanley Donen simply because people cry or sing in the rain. Musical comedy reorganizes space, but not in Demy's film (the exceptions are the credits and the overhead shot and the *directed* movement of the umbrellas). Musical comedy reorganizes space, modifies it, remodels the perspectives for dance, and more generally, for the fantasy that allows the impossible (dreams, happiness, flight, laughter) to become possible; it makes visible the unreal. Musical comedy requires at least one imaginary dimension, even if it's only the elimination of gravity. Nothing of the sort happens in *The Umbrellas of Cherbourg*, which is profoundly anchored in a day-to-day banality—natural sets, streets, the houses of Cherbourg, the systematic platitude of the dialogue, the adventures that aren't. It's an everyday story.

The second unique aspect of the film is that this *Geneviève* isn't called *Geneviève* but *The Umbrellas of Cherbourg*. This changes, if not everything, then just about everything. We would expect a lighthearted film, agreeably amusing, but modern. The switch displaces our attention from the story (which resembles Charpentier's *Louise*) to the sets, while asking that we see this set as more than a set. The umbrellas thus become the symbol of the grace that bathes Demy's Cherbourg in both happy and melancholy charm. The umbrellas are so many fairy's wands. As soon as they touch a service station, a café, a mechanic in his overalls, prostitutes, an old woman dying in her bed, everything begins to sing, starting with the colors. In the third act of Giraudoux's *Ondine*, the scullery maid, through supernatural action, begins to speak in verse. This is exactly what has happened in Cherbourg. Because of a magic charm, everything in the ordinary world is hitched up a notch above its everyday level. The most boring prose becomes song and song becomes breath. The young people are, naturally, beautiful, the girls are beautiful, the mother, the old dying stepmother are beautiful. The dresses are beautiful, and we find it quite normal that the woman with money problems wears exquisite clothes. Even the wallpaper in the bedrooms is breathtaking, and the harmony between the dresses and the sets is enchanting. It snows at Christmas, already an unusual event in Cherbourg, and the snow is like a mountain of sugar. It's impossible to imagine this snow turning into slush. This Cherbourg is to the real city of Cherbourg what Geneviève's umbrellas are to the streetcorner variety: a miraculous universe, poetic, *musical* in the most profound sense of the term. It's easy to understand why the music is inseparable from the overall sense of well-being. It's the very expression of that well-being. The film's music bathes the actors' words the same way its colors bathe the city's walls. ■

Jean-Louis Bory, *Arts*, February 26, 1964

LA PUNITION

Jean Rouch

STILL THE SAME INSIPID GIRL

It's been clear for some time that Jean Rouch has had nothing to say and his latest film confirms this. To those who may have been lulled into complacency by *Chronique d'un été*, we recommend they see *La Punition*. I'm sure there are some critics who will maintain that Rouch has achieved a kind of truth. I'd like to know who they are, since it would give me a better idea of the intellectual level of French film.

Nadine, who still plays the same insipid young girl as in Rouch's earlier films, is sent home from school one day, which provides

an opportunity for her to meet three boys. Rouch appears to be parodying himself here, with his characters again playing the same old story. They seem to be playing Rouch in life as in fiction, the way others play Godard. As for the dialogue, obviously Rouch was unable to decide between directing and complete improvisation. ■

Robert Grelier, *Positif*, January 1964

YOU COULD SEE LA PUNITION THREE OR FOUR TIMES

From French television viewers to specialists in cinéma vérité, nearly everyone has condemned *La Punition* as a kind of *cinema lie*. Their attitude is unjustified because it confuses three very different elements: film, truth, and cinéma vérité. For example, we have no right to say that *La Punition* is bad *because* it's untrue (Rossif's documentaries are true, but look at the result), or because it's not real cinéma vérité (neither is *The Rules of the Game*), or because its director or, more precisely, its producer (and who should we believe if they disagree?) might incorrectly claim it is. In such a case it would have been enough if they had said nothing, or were from a place (Afghanistan) or time (1909–1914) forgotten by interviewers, for the film to be considered good.

The truth of *La Punition* isn't apparent without the active participation of the television viewer, who in talking or doing the dishes while trying to watch the film, fails to comply, fails to participate. This is not the kind of passivity that a nerve-wracking dramatic intrigue forces you into. The audience has to actively interpret the film to understand at which level of truth the film situates itself. If we relax our attention, we lose the sense of the film. It's possible to watch *La Punition* three or four times without it ever being the same film. Even if it were eight hours long, it would be equally compelling. In this light, it seems rather unnecessary to cut six or eight minutes out of *La Punition*, simply to broadcast the full version of *Cuba Si* afterwards.

Here we have an exciting film devoid of exoticism and accessible to everyone, which would shatter box office records if the French didn't prefer, in place of simple, direct cinema (*La Punition, Adieu Philippine, Procès de Jeanne*), the preciosity of indirect cinema (*Mélodie en sous-sol, La Grande Évasion, La Guerre des boutons*),

whose useless digressions, dullness, and repetitiveness in the end reflect purely commercial values. Such values enable viewers to turn their attention from films in which a handful of powerful scenes leave lasting impressions on minds no longer required to confront the disturbing reality of unadorned facts. ■

Luc Moullet, *Cahiers du cinéma*, May 1964

DES PISSENLITS PAR LA RACINE

Georges Lautner

A CORPSE IN THE DOUBLE-BASS

In a strange way, *Des Pissenlits par la racine* marks the triumph of intellectualism over commercial cinema. Lautner's film, which appears to be very much an industrial "product," manages to get caught up in its own game and finds itself nose to nose—which is both good and bad for the film—with its true theme.

Georges Lautner appears to have constructed his film around an incessant stream of wordplay and verbal puns, a rich combination of slang and everyday speech, although there's something gratuitous about it. But aside from the "useless" verbal fireworks, the film intentionally obscures an "essential" detail: the body disappears without leaving any trace. The solution to the mystery is only indicated, never explained. The same fuzziness can be found in Queneau's short stories, where the details work to hide the essential point that would justify their presence. This is done less to make that point disappear than to surprise, to communicate the sentiment of a void whose only reality exists in those sparse details.

Reversing the structure of commercial cinema, Lautner has turned this film into an empty shell in which fools and maniacs, madness and lucidity destroy one another (a madwoman declares, "There's a corpse in the double bass"). In doing so he couldn't help but project his own situation (the formal qualities of his cinema prove it as much as this film, which describes the underside of reality), that of an intellectual who plays the game of being a "professional" (Serrault, the musician, a one-dimensional figure, gets into a fight out of love) and who nevertheless manages to beat them at their own game. It's the kind of skill that enables him to bet the derby (or commercial cinema) and switch the tickets in the envelopes at the appropriate moment. The operation here takes place in secret; it's not filmed. In spite of all the calculation and planning, Lautner shows nothing is determined until the envelope is opened. At worst, while playing commercial cinema's game, Lautner has swung in the direction of true filmmaking, closer to *Les Bonnes Femmes*, only to encounter the same incomprehension at that end of the race. ■

Jean-Claude Biette, *Cahiers du cinéma*, June 1964

ALL IN GOOD FUN

Des Pissenlits par la racine provides plenty of amusement for comedy fans. The film is a kind of thriller that verges on the burlesque. You don't have to handle it with kid gloves. The actors take center stage here. Their expressions are straight out of cabaret, the parody is obvious, the deceit clever. Michel Serrault, Mireille Darc, and Francis Blanche are especially good. They follow their own intuition, not exactly a harsh mistress.

I won't go so far as to say this is a brilliant film. But it's all in good fun. And it cleverly lampoons the conventions of commercial cinema. Regardless of the screenplay, Lautner always manages to deal himself a winning hand. He's marked the deck. ■
Arts, May 13, 1964

TWO OR THREE FITS
OF HYSTERICAL LAUGHTER

The title is silly, the story ridiculous. The director doesn't succeed in making us die laughing and the actors' jokes are pretty stale by now. But anyone who can watch *Des Pissenlits par la racine* without at least two or three fits of hysterical laughter should probably give up on film altogether. ■
Henri Gault, *Paris-Presse*, May 15, 1964

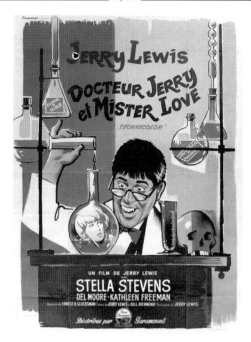

THE NUTTY PROFESSOR

Jerry Lewis

THE BEST COMIC DIRECTOR

The Nutty Professor is, along with *Ladies' Man*, Jerry Lewis's best film. The many gags are top notch and well acted. They begin at the start of the film when, after an explosion in the lab, Jerry leaves the wreckage as a kind of Dracula. They continue when a barbell he can barely get off the ground, much less lift, stretches his arms. There is another scene in a bowling alley when he "knocks down" a group of bowlers, and another hysterical scene, where he tries to direct the president of the university as Hamlet. But there are too many gags to mention here. One thing is certain though, this movie is funnier than just about any film recently made.

Lewis has tremendous creative talent, a touch of sentimentality, an interest in self-analysis, and a sense of conscience (perhaps because he's Jewish). He's one of the best comic directors of our time—author, actor, director—and embodies many of the complexities, including some of his own, now facing modern America. Today's answer to today's enigma is Jerry Lewis. ■
Paul-Louis Thirard, *Positif*, February 1964

OUTRAGEOUSLY FUNNY

This week's contenders in Paris are, on our right, *Cleopatra*, a three-hour extravaganza by Joseph Mankiewicz, a supershow with three big-name stars, whose cost you're familiar with, and, on our left, *The Nutty Professor*, by Jerry Lewis, starring Jerry Lewis (who is twinned in the film), and which cost just under a hundred times less. It's an unfair fight. On one side we have deathly boredom, pretension, heavy-handed editing, and a mess of overwrought production that's tough to swallow. On the other we have an imaginative film, outrageously funny, which arrives with no preconceptions, and whose content, though it hardly competes with Plutarch or Seutonius, is complex enough to poke fun at sociology.

The comparison is unfair to Mankiewicz, who had to struggle with time, illness, the paralyzing opulence of his budget, Mr. Darryl Zanuck, Lloyd's of London, and Elizabeth Taylor. Yet I do want to compare an outdated concept of entertainment that has sunk a large part of the film industry to a personal and relatively intimate method of creation, which, although typically Hollywood, is not insignificant. All of Jerry Lewis's films, without exception, have had outstanding commercial success. The actor, who has become his own producer and director and works with his own studio, with the same group of actors and technicians, appears, from our point of view, to be one of Hollywood's independents, an industry within an industry, and a source of joy. ■
Robert Benayoun, *France-Observateur*, October 31, 1964

BAND OF OUTSIDERS

Jean-Luc Godard

CINEMA IS A GAMBLE

J. C. Your film *Band of Outsiders*, is based on a detective thriller, *Pigeon vole*, by D. and B. Hitchens. I haven't read the book. Why did you use it as the basis of the film?

J.-L. G. What I liked about the book, was the tone of the story, the dialogues, which I tried to retain in the film. This tone may have been the result of the translation, which was bad. But the translation at least gave the book a certain style that interested me. I kept it in the narration that accompanies certain scenes in the film. It resembled a novel I've always wanted to film, *Banlieue Sud-Est* by René Fallet. It's a similar story: two guys, one girl, a bicycle race. You find the same thing in the majority of pre-War novels. In the trailer for the film, I say, "A French film with a pre-War flavor."

J. C. Like *Quai des brumes*?

J.-L. G. More like those pre-War novels that weren't filmed but were already films. Some of Simenon's novels, Queneau. *Loin de Rueil*, for example. I was trying to render this populist and poetic pre-War climate. Not in any pejorative sense, by the way.

J. C. In watching the film, which is, after all, a B-series film, it seemed to me that you were more comfortable in hiding any references or quotes. You've often been criticized for quoting so much. I don't even think there are any in this film.

J.-L. G. Yes, I wanted to make a simple, perfectly comprehensible film. For example, when the distributors see *Muriel* or *Contempt*, they can't figure them out. For them, the films are unreadable. But *Band of Outsiders* is perfectly clear. This didn't prevent me from putting in what I liked. I took advantage of every situation, every moment of the film. For example, if there's a scene in a car, the two characters discuss the cars they like best. In selecting the names in certain dialogues, in certain parts of the narration, I added the things that are important to me.

J. C. You took a risk in shooting this film in 25 days, a record. Why so fast?

J.-L. G. I always like to harmonize the shooting and financing of the film, the budget and the subject, or what I think is the subject. When you go to a party, you get dressed one way and not another. Even if it has nothing to do with what you're going to see, hear, or do. You prepare yourself. For example, you pay for a taxi because you're going to a "chic" party, whereas ordinarily you'd take the subway. That's why I made the film in 25 days. I always try to put constraints on the way I work. To the extent that I'm free, I need to create my own data for myself, impose my own rules. I never agree with the data that

the producer wants me to use because they're not the right data for the subject. So I have to find and use the right data myself. For example, I've always been told that I've "ruined" my films. People are very happy if I shoot the film in four weeks rather than six. But if I shoot in three weeks, they're upset. They say, "Hey, there's no need to ruin it." But that has nothing to do with it. It's a gamble and I try to win.

J. C. You also don't write the dialogues. Why?

J.-L. G. I write them at the last moment. I do this so the actor doesn't have time to think about the dialogues, to prepare. This means he has to give more of himself. He is both more awkward and more whole. I give the actors a great deal of freedom. ■

Interview conducted by **Jean Collet**, *Télérama*, August 16, 1964

THE NEW CONFORMITY

Just because Jean-Luc Godard always makes more or less the same film doesn't mean I always have to write the same article. On the contrary, I try to vary the overall effect. I get no particular pleasure in doing the same routine three times a year (Godard never seems to be out of work).

I'm aware, therefore, of the possible staginess of the whole thing. A good Godard? There's nothing unusual about this. It's normal for a young director who shoots constantly to make progress. And since I detest habit, I get no satisfaction in being constantly negative, a vicious naysayer. All my good resolutions need is a film to test them on. And if there's only one left....

"This is where my story begins," intones Godard's rather ordinary voice on the sound track. However, the film (*Band of Outsiders*) has already been going on for a few minutes. The director is late and we're already in the middle of that familiar drone that should delight film buffs. Nothing resembles a Godard more than another Godard. We can count on a ritual that is as indifferently structured as Audiard-Verneuil's films. We've found a new conformity that we can accept with complete equanimity, a reassuring conformity that enables the viewer, any viewer, to suddenly feel terribly intelligent, clever and cultivated (by contrast, of course). The ingredients never change.

There are bad puns . . . There are private jokes (the camera insistently lingers in front

of the window of a store called "New Wave"). There are scenes where nothing happens, that are used merely as filler. The characters read the newspaper, observe a minute of silence, execute dance steps before the camera until they're bored. The actors read from books. A scene from Romeo and Juliet is read aloud, a complete passage from "Nadja," Poe's "Purloined Letter," etc. There's the obligatory vulgarity. "Look, she's still moving." Anna Karina is beaten, a woman is gagged by shoving a rag down her throat with the barrel of a revolver. ("Look, she stopped moving.") Any of these scenes could have appeared in *Les Carabiniers*, *Le Petit Soldat*, or *My Life to Live* . . . There's something euphoric about this complete lack of surprise.

In discussing Godard, there's always someone who'll say, "In any case, whether you like it or not, it exists." Unquestionably. Like De Gaulle, Godard is there. He makes films, speaks, and repeats himself, but don't take it personally. Between himself and his public he introduces a kind of mocking, though slightly idiotic, presence. "His films exist because he exists," wrote Jean Collet, whose moribund words have been briefly rejuvenated by the use of italic type. They are, we are told, based on the "obvious.". . . It's an attitude that results in a stupefying catatonia: what you see is unquestionably there, you perceive it, and you should accept it, if possible, with a little gratitude. *A Woman is a Woman*. "Life is life," intones Godard. "A film is a film," Collet happily responds. Godard, this vegetative creature *sans pareil*, digests his prey in public like the boa in the city zoo. ■

Robert Benayoun, *France-Observateur*, August 13, 1964

NOTHING HAPPENS

What is it about? As far as I can tell, it's a film about banality, boredom, melancholy, and emotional uncertainty. Two young men complain; a young woman is inexplicably sad. The film takes place in an ugly suburb. This apathetic trio kill time by talking. The minutes pass, interminably. Nothing happens, other than a few morose dance steps. The camera casts a tired eye on faces worn by weariness, landscapes drowned in gray. God, how boring the picture of boredom can be. ■

Michel Aubriant, *Paris-Presse*, August 12, 1964

INFLUENCE
AND
DECLINE

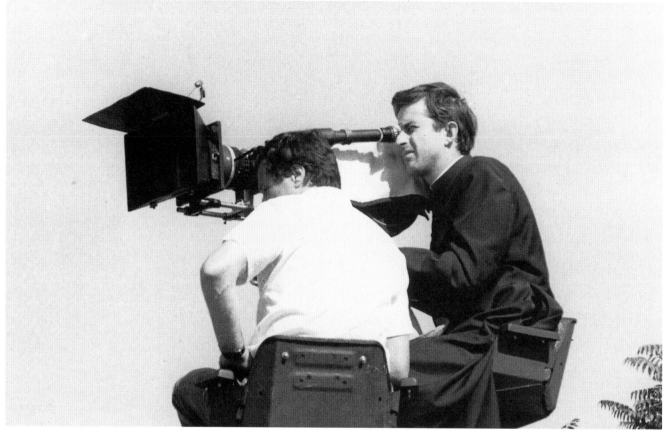

Nanni Moretti on the set of *La messe est finie* (1985)

A hundred years after its birth the cinema appears more strongly divided than ever between the two choices present since its inception: Méliès or Lumière. From a commercial and financial point of view, spectacles, special effects, and diversions have won the day. The cinema of fact, of observation, is in the minority and resists these influences as best it can. Although the consequences of the New Wave's contribution to cinema's development are obvious, they have not always found their way into the mainstream.

The New Wave has always attempted to undermine both these approaches to film: the former is mannerist, the latter naturalist. In mannerist films, an unrestricted formalism presides in which a knowledge of cinema is systematically interspersed with and blended with the act of representation, obscuring the film's true legibility. In such films, the use of references is no longer liberating but stifling, no longer creative but alienating. Appreciation and imitation remain the only education necessary to understand them. Reworking older forms should serve, however, to filter the world and the reality of an epoch, not obscure it. Unusual angles, an affected style, incidental formal inventions—they may be interesting but are useless when they become only self-referential: too much cinema destroys cinema. In opposition to this interest in form for form's sake, a mindless naturalism developed, which is content to merely copy reality. But imitation alone is not art. Without a style of its own, cinema can never soar. It remains satisfied with a "human" presence that it can drag across the screen and wallows in the tired clichés of a cinéma vérité that the New Wave rejected long ago. Both approaches are alive and well and threaten the future of cinema. They have not gone unchallenged though. The true descendants of the sixties continue to restore to fiction its

And Life Goes On (Abbas Kiarostami, 1996)

power to represent and question the real. They create a mechanism that doesn't copy life but questions certain aspects of living. The New Wave continues to roll.

Abbas Kiarostami is an Iranian director. All of his films without exception are involved with the elaboration, the construction of a means for accessing reality. The heart of his cinema is based on a concern with tracking reality. His characters are only instruments, enigmatic figures of whom we know little. Their existence is less important than the quest they have been charged with, and their personal history leaves room for their movement across time and space in voyages of initiation. The car that carries them is the site where this activity takes place. A cinematic metaphor, the window frame provides access to a succession of images in perpetual movement, like a series of passing photographs.

Kiarostomi's characters are able to understand the real by means of a device that is unique to cinema (the succession of images displayed by the projector). Among the ruins of the earthquake that devastated northern Iran in 1990, the heroes of *And Life Goes On* leave in search of the two child actors of *Where is my Friend's House?* They do not find them during the course of the film, but along the way they come face to face with a reality that assumes greater and greater significance in their mind. Kiarostami's belief in cinema as an instrument of knowledge, his method of working, of giving priority to its means (whose presence the filmmaker systematically reveals), make him one of the most subtle descendants of the theories developed by the New Wave.

Although Kiarostami claims to be unfamiliar with the new cinema of the sixties, **Nanni Moretti** has acknowledged its influence and describes himself as one of its descendants.

La Messe est finie (Nanni Moretti, 1986)

Moretti formed his own film company (Sacher Films), which guarantees him independence and loyalty to the economic and aesthetic principles of the New Wave. As a result Moretti has been able to combine the subject of his films with the means at his disposal (Super 8, 16 mm, video, 35 mm). He doesn't hesitate to use his friends or family as his principal actors, and based in Italy, has refused to dub his films to maintain the authenticity of his documentary style. His entire body of work rejects and resists the bland standardization of contemporary Italian cinema, just as the water-polo player in *Palombella Rossa* rejects the journalistic language of his time. The singularity and solitude this implies are his subjects. His characters are not marginal individuals but people who have been displaced within the new world taking shape around them (the curé in his cassock, the math professor, the amnesiac communist party boss). This failure to comply with standards destroys their attempts to approach others and isolates them. It provokes only aggressiveness and a desire to reinstitute a world they are subjected to. Only the main character in *Dear Diary* is able to accept that he is different from those he encounters and listens to them. The open-ended and digressive story line, freer than ever before in Moretti's work, the chance encounters that occur within it, the narration, which is structured around the geography of the places the characters pass through (Rome, the Lipari islands, etc.), the purely autobiographical and documentary elements—all recall the sense of dramatic revolution and release ushered in by the New Wave. Moretti appears to have found a balance between Italian comedy, without the element of farce, and the political cinema whose nagging didacticism he has rejected in favor of a description of his country's identity crisis and its people's doubts.

Goodbye South, Goodbye (Hou Hsiao-Hsien, 1997)

The New Wave's influence on the Taiwanese director **Hou Hsiao-Hsien** would be less obvious if his work hadn't recently taken a new and radical turn. Temporarily abandoning the contemporary history of Taiwan, *Goodbye South, Goodbye* plunges its petty criminals into today's melancholy insularity. Like listless younger brothers of Michel Poiccard in *Breathless*, Hou's young hoodlums dream only of getting off the island, but their efforts lead nowhere. Hsiao-Hsien's representation of youth leaves no room for self-aggrandizement or strong emotions, only a sense of purposeless movement, a weariness of place, and futile attempts to locate money. This lost time is not just the subject of the film but its heartbeat. Everything that happens on screen is part of everyday life and never serves a dramatic purpose (endless conversations on a portable phone, riding on motorcycles, waiting, eating, drinking). The anecdotes follow one another with the same indifference to the minimal requirements of narration. A worthy descendant of Naruse, Hsiao-Hsien turns daily life and its infinite repetition into the confined space in which his characters evolve without ever managing to get out. Like Godard, Hsiao-Hsien is a filmmaker of the moment. He doesn't force cinematic duration to conform to the requirements of the story, but turns it into a measurable quantity. Plot hasn't been eliminated entirely from *Goodbye South, Goodbye*, a film he prepared while teaching, but it is only one of the elements of the melancholy and lyrical story that his characters experience. This is the reason for Hsiao-Hsien's long takes. They are essential for this gradual transition toward the sense of affective duration, which was already present in *The Puppetmaster* and the nightclub scenes in *Good Men, Good Women.* His indifference to

A Brighter Summer Day (Edward Yang, 1991)

continuity shots, the way he turns each scene into a self-contained whole that ignores everything that follows, and his need to adapt his style to the rhythm of the modern world, make Hou Hsiao-Hsien the best representative of the New Wave ethos within a traditionally anti-New Wave environment.

There are other great Taiwanese directors: **Edward Yang** (*A Brighter Summer Day*), who portrays newcomers growing up in China, **Tsai Ming-Liang** (*Vive l'amour*, *The River*), and the ultraformalist **Wong Kar-Wai**. Of course, no survey of Asian cinema would be complete without mentioning **John Woo**. A cinephile as well as director, Woo grew up on the work of the French New Wave and the American New Wave of the seventies. Today, the director of *A Better Tomorrow* remains the leading proponent of the current Hong Kong school of mannerism.

In Woo's world cinema is everywhere. Like earlier French (Michel Poiccard, Nana in *My Life to Live*) and American film characters (the young heroes in Scorsese and Coppola), the characters in his films barter their personality against a substitute identity based on the cinema. Thus Jeff in *The Killer* sees himself as a local Alain Delon. Woo owes as much to the Chinese as he does the Western action film, to the western as much as to melodrama, to comedy as much as to suspense. A brilliant mimic, Woo borrows freely from the work of his favorite directors: choreography from Demy, breakdown of movement from Godard, an American edginess, Cimino's sense of epic, etc. The only problem with Woo's work is that since his characters are so deeply embedded in cinematic history, they have trouble existing as real characters during scenes of emotional intimacy (*Face/Off*). The skill and boldness Woo demonstrates during

A Brighter Summer Day (Edward Yang, 1991)

the action scenes is not always obvious once the on-screen situation has calmed down.

This post-New Wave mannerism found in Asian cinema is not quite as rich in its American homologues. As well-crafted as they are, **Quentin Tarantino's** (*Reservoir Dogs*, *Pulp Fiction*) and **Roger Avery's** films (*Killing Zoe*) represent contemporary cinema's tendency to be self-referential. Cinema bites its tail. Although the construction of a film like *Pulp Fiction* is dazzling and draws on the entire range of cinematic resources, his characters' archetypal load—no matter how faithful to the genre—and their way of systematically "doing cinema" eventually become grating. In the end the film amounts to nothing more than a form of clever yet sterile craftsmanship. Of Tarantino's contemporaries, **Hal Hartley** is too imitative, **Jim Jarmusch**, too mannered. But **Abel Ferrara** has proved to be an extraordinary successor to the French and European New Waves. An independent filmmaker in every sense of the word, Ferrara has managed to buck the system, produces films at a frenetic pace, and transforms works-for-hire into political manifestos (*Body Snatchers*). Far from the sentimentalism and evasion of Hollywood, his work reflects a radical crisis and weakening of American society, a civilization in decline. Every genre Ferrara has explored (thriller, science fiction, vampires, the Mafia) is treated as if it were exhausted, used up. The hero is no longer a part of myth and has given up trying to conquer the world. Like the tortured beings in Nicholas Ray, Ferrara's heroes see themselves in a negative light and can only judge their actions through the responses of those around them. The brothers in *The Funeral* and Frank White in *King of New York* or *Bad Lieutenant* are all trying to save their self-image. Looking at those around them, they see only a corrupted version of

Abel Ferrara on the set of *Bad Lieutenant* (1992)

themselves. Surreptitiously present in every scene, death is the inevitable outcome of this moral rift.

Wim Wenders is the oldest of the European descendants of the New Wave. He borrowed from it the idea of displacement, which has become an end in itself in his work. Although a sense of movement lies at the heart of his films, it leads nowhere. The liberating road movie, the voyage as coming-of-age novel is over. We set out to understand the world and return dumbstruck (*The Wrong Move*). All we are left with is the contemplation of the landscapes we have crossed, a contemplation that is closer to the fixity of still photography than the triviality of cinema. Because of this obsession with photographic and plastic composition (Edward Hopper's hyperrealism) Wenders's films often result in a sophisticated but lifeless impasse. The increasingly systematic reflection on the image and its power has unfortunately failed to infuse new life into his work and seems, on the contrary, to have led him into a deepening confusion from which he has been unable to extricate himself.

The sophistication of **Pedro Almodovar's** cinema stems from a curious mixture of Hollywood and the brutality of Latin-American melodrama. It is through Fassbinder that Almodovar is a descendant of the New Wave. Almodovar borrowed Fassbinder's use of melodrama as a means to study society and its system of representation, and he borrowed the Hollywood "genre" to portray minorities rather than high society. His use of loud color, which Fassbinder himself had stolen from Douglas Sirk, is idiosyncratic and disturbing. Such a desire to create an Iberian Hollywood is far from the preoccupations of the young Portuguese director **Pedro Costa**. Rigorous and sober, Costa's *Ossos* makes

Bones (Pedro Costa, 1997)

use of a sound track that is taken chapter and verse from the New Wave: the mikes are kept open, the sound is never limited to the frame, but makes a break with the insipid ambient sound characteristic of conventional productions. It is a sound that captures and restores the perpetual murmur, the color, taste, and odor of the neighborhood in which his films are shot (for Costa, the creole neighborhoods of Lisbon).

Television was largely responsible for the "rebirth of British cinema" during the early eighties. Three directors were successful in using the methods employed to produce theatrical dramas for their own ends: **Mike Leigh**, **Ken Loach**, and **Stephen Frears**. Like their predecessors in the Free Cinema group (Frears was Lindsay Anderson's assistant and Karel Reisz helped with the editing of his first films) they would walk joyously down the street, aiming their cameras at the "proles" of the conservative movement that followed the sexual revolution of the sixties. Their willingness to reveal the disastrous effects of Thatcher's politics, and their hatred of the woman herself, repoliticized their films at a time when English cinema was represented primarily by David Puttnam and his mind-numbing productions (spouting nostalgia for a United Kingdom that no longer existed, portraits of the upper classes, etc.). Making films about modern England led to the arrival of a new "romantic naturalism," in which any hope of cinematic style is sacrificed to the search for truth in human relations. The working class is presented as a prisoner, mired in a stifling social situation from which even the idea of escape seems remote. Frears alone was able to jettison this sociological naturalism and make films of substance. Whether his subjects are unemployment, immigration, or the life of gay Pakistanis, the work place is idealized and organized as a territory that

Fatherland (Ken Loach, 1986)

needs to be defended against outside aggression. Frears doesn't idealize the resigned and tragic melancholy of the working class; he captures its vitality and the energy of its characters, who openly and sometimes aggressively display both sexuality and vulgarity. His work is organized around two types of character: those whom society forces to hide their true nature (*My Beautiful Laundrette, Mary Riley*) and those who, reacting against society, flaunt it openly (*Prick Up Your Ears, Sammy and Rosie Get Laid, The Snapper, The Van*). This enables Frears to draw on the political aspect of the cinema's tradition of "angry young men" without falling into the sentimental trap of working-class idealization or the opposite (and typically French) one of smug contempt.

We can also add two true directors. First, **Jean-Claude Brisseau**. While he was working as a teacher, he managed to produce two full-length films on an amateur basis. Eric Rohmer championed his work and subsequently helped him to produce *Un jeu brutale* (1982), a film whose promise is confirmed by *De bruit et de fureur* (1987), *Noce blanche* (1989), and *Celine* (1992). And second, **Catherine Breillat**, a writer and comedienne who has produced four films over the course of twenty years: *Tapage nocturne* (1979), *36 fillette* (1987), *Sale comme un ange* (1991), and *Parfait Amour* (1997). Her work is provocative and speaks bluntly of female desire and the fear men have of it. But it does so with a mastery that is at once tender and curiously modest, and it is this that positions her as one of the only authentic women directors in French cinema.

In France, **Leos Carax** was the first director to be "haunted" by the memory of the New Wave (especially Godard). Although his means are heavy-handed, every aspect

Paris s'eveille (Oliver Assayas, 1992)

of his work is an attempt to incorporate a sensation of lightness and a vanished celestial grace. Carax's films revolve around the idea of making poetry, of being airborne, by using sophisticated and complex methods. It's an admirable goal but one that embodies a fundamental contradiction (the rift between ends and means is too great) that is a far cry from the New Wave's attempt to combine aesthetics and economy, the subject and the means of expression.

The most interesting filmmakers of the succeeding generation were not those who replaced the poetic stylization of the eighties with a sudden return to social realism, but those who attempted to restore to French cinema a romantic density based on a tragic reality—**Xavier Beauvois**, for example. Everything in his work that is not real is a distraction. His characters have to feel that reality has left them without a future; it is the only way they will want to live a life that is different and intense. Sometimes they escape (*N'oublie pas que tu vas mourir*), and sometimes they don't (*Nord*). Their goal is to confront the world and take control of their own life once more. Condemned to die, the young Benoît turns the rest of his life into an elliptical existence in which all the possible sensations of a full life follow one another in breathtaking succession—risk and pleasure, drugs and art, war and love, nature and dependence. His hero enables Beauvois to identify the clichés of a period (Yugoslavia, AIDS, heroin) and give them a new reality by filming them with unflinching directness. The uniqueness of his films is based on the application of this kind of raw observation (a characteristic found in Pialat, Cassavetes, and Godard after 1975) of people who live as if their existence were romantic or heroic.

Nord (Xavier Beauvois, 1991)

Arnaud Desplechin is another French director who has made confrontation the focus of his work. Overgrown adolescents, his characters are subject to and invaded by reality. They are forced to undergo a succession of humiliating trials to prove their existence and gain access to an adult perception of their environment. Overcome by doubt and uncertainty, they lose themselves in this sudden plunge into the heart of reality before discovering who they are. Desplechin's films, like *La Sentinelle* or *Comment je me suis disputé*, expand beyond the narrow and sophomoric universe that characterizes the work of many young directors in France. Desplechin's way of juxtaposing the imaginary with the reality of the world, of tracking a character's inner thoughts by filming from within, is similar to the work of Alain Resnais. His rejection of naturalism, the way he uses the intimacy so typical of French film as a genre (with as many codes, required transitions, and fundamental principles as an American thriller), his use of narrative possibilities and voice-over, make Desplechin's cinema one of the most experimental successors of the New Wave seen to date.

The generation of young directors that exploded onto the French screen after 1990 has been called a new New Wave. Their subject matter, their form, their approach to reality and their willingness to shoot on shoestring budgets have a lot in common with their illustrious predecessors. There are a number of such directors and many of them are genuinely talented. Unfortunately, it would be impossible to list them all here. This summary, however, would be incomplete without some mention of **Nicolas Philibert**, who helped renew the French documentary school made famous by **Raymond Depardon**, or **Olivier Assayas**. Ex-critic of *Cahiers du*

cinéma and author of *Une nouvelle vie*, Assayas succeeds in combining the notion of movement and chance encounter so typical of the French New Wave, with the predisposition to experimentation characteristic of American independent filmmakers of the late sixties. Then there is Jean-Pierre Léaud. Léaud remains the ghostly representative of a bygone cinema and Asseyas has cast him as such in his films. In conclusion, it is probably safe to say that a number of young filmmakers still feel the presence and weight of the New Wave. Some of them identify with it, others try to distance themselves from it, and still others attack it openly. Yet, whatever the attitude toward it, the New Wave remains a force to be dealt with by anyone making films today.

Jean-Pierre Léaud and Maggie Cheung, *Irma Vep* (Oliver Assayas, 1996)

CHRONOLOGY OF THE NEW WAVE IN FRANCE

1946

February 15. Banned when it first appeared in 1933, Jean Vigo's *Zero for Conduct* receives its export license from the Film Board. "I had the good fortune to discover Jean Vigo's films during a Saturday afternoon performance in 1946 at the Sèvres-Pathé, thanks to the Chambre Noire film club run by André Bazin and others from *La Revue du Cinéma*. When I entered the theater, I didn't even know Jean Vigo's name, but I soon became a great admirer of his work, which all told doesn't amount to more than two hundred minutes of screen time." François Truffaut.[1]

May 28. The Byrnes-Blum agreement is signed in Washington, providing France with a loan in return for less restrictive import measures. For the industry this meant that American films would now be shown in French movie theaters (388 were shown during the first half of 1947).

1948

March 24. Release of the first feature-length film by critic Roger Leenhardt, *Les Dernières Vacances*.

March 30. Alexandre Astruc publishes his manifesto, "Birth of a New Avant-Garde: The Camera-as-Pen," in *L'Écran française*, number 144.

October 26. The first film museum is opened in Paris on avenue de Messine. The museum is the work of Henri Langlois, cofounder and director of the Cinémathèque française.

December. First screening by the Objectif 49 film club at the Studio des Champs-Élysées. The film, *Parents terribles*, was introduced by Jean Cocteau and André Bazin.

1949

April 22. Release in theaters of the first feature film by Jean-Pierre Melville, *Le Silence de la mer*. Made outside the traditional production system (Melville never worked as an assistant director and didn't have his work card), the film is an adaptation of a novel made without the author's approval. There are no stars; the film is shot on location, and the budget is small.

July 29–August 5. First Festival du Film Maudit at Biarritz, organized by Objectif 49 and devoted to "outlaw" and independent filmmakers. It's an anti-Cannes event. Those present include Astruc, Bazin, Grémillon, Doniol-Valcroze, Cocteau, and Kast. A second festival was held in 1950.

December 6. Release of Jacques Becker's *Rendez-vous de juillet*, a film about the crossed destinies of young men and women in Paris.

1950

May–November. Appearance of *La Gazette du cinéma*, which published five issues with articles by several then-unknown directors: Maurice Schérer (Éric Rohmer), Hans Lucas (Jean-Luc Godard), and Jacques Rivette.

1951

February 7. Release of *Journal d'un curé de campagne* by Robert Bresson. The film is both a model of its kind and a new type of literary adaptation. Three years later Truffaut recalls Bresson's film in his attack on some of French cinema's most prominent screenwriters. ·

March 6. Release of *The Flowers of St. Francis* by Roberto Rossellini.

April. *Cahiers du cinéma* no. 1. The issue is dedicated to Jean George Auriol, who died the previous year and was cofounder of *La Revue du Cinéma* before and after the war.

1952

January. Special issue of *Cahiers du cinéma* devoted to Jean Renoir (*Le Fleuve*, shot in India, was released the previous month and appeared on the cover). The first article by Jean-Luc Godard (under the pseudonym Hans Lucas) appears in the same issue.

May. *Positif* no. 1. Founded in Lyon (the publication moves to Paris in 1954). Soon, the magazine would take issue with *Cahiers du cinéma* and its "auteur policy" and describe the New Wave as politically reactionary.

December 21. Roger Vadim marries Brigitte Bardot, who is 18. She was introduced to him three years earlier by the producer Pierre Braunberger.

1953

February. Release of *La Vie d'un honnête homme* (Guitry), *Monkey Business* (Hawks), *The Golden Coach* (Renoir), and *Les Vacances de Mr. Hulot* (Tati). First article by Jacques Rivette appears in *Cahiers du cinéma*.

March. First article by François Truffaut appears in *Cahiers du cinéma*. Truffaut takes aim at the French film industry and extols "minor" American films ("a cinema that proves each week it is the greatest in the world").

April 6. French law institutes the Fonds de Développement de l'Industrie Cinématographique and establishes an "award for quality" for short films.

May. An article by Jacques Rivette, boldly entitled, "The Genius of Howard Hawks" appears in *Cahiers du cinéma*. The concept of the auteur is underway.

November. First article by Claude Chabrol in *Cahiers du cinéma*.

1954

January. *Cahiers du cinéma* no. 31 publishes "A Certain Tendency of the French Cinema" by François Truffaut. The article is a polemic against the methods of the most prominent directors and screenwriters in France. During this month, *Le Blé en herbe* by Claude Autant-Lara, based on a story by Colette (Aurenche and Bost write the screen adaptation and dialogues), is released. In the same issue of *Cahiers du cinéma*, Jacques Rivette writes a glowing article about the rise of CinemaScope. The article concludes with these words: "For forty years the masters have shown us the way. It is our job not to ignore their example but follow it to its completion. Yes, our generation will be the generation of CinemaScope, *metteurs en scène* finally worthy of the name—the creatures of our imagination moving across the unlimited stage of the universe."

May 14. Release of *Monika*, starring Harriet Andersson. Five years later, the young Doinel will steal the stills of Bergman's film from the lobby of a movie theater (*The 400 Blows*).

July. Truffaut begins writing for *Arts* (and continues to do so until the end of 1958). He uses the publication to consistently take issue with the French film establishment. Due to his efforts, others soon begin to write articles for the weekly magazine, including Rivette, Rohmer, Godard, Bitsch, de Givray, and Douchet. *Arts* will remain strongly pro-New Wave until August 1961, when it makes an abrupt about face.

July–August. Shooting of Agnès Varda's *La Pointe courte* begins in a fishing village near Sète, starring two actors from Jean Vilar's Théâtre Nationale Populaire. In Varda's film actors and crew work cooperatively, an approach that didn't meet the professional standards of the Centre National de la Cinématographie. Editing is by Alain Resnais.

October. Special issue of *Cahiers du cinéma* devoted to Hitchcock. The magazine's credo: the master of suspense is an idealist.

1955

February. In *Cahiers du cinéma* no. 44, André Bazin asks, "What Does it Mean to be a Hitchcocko-Hawksien?" In the same issue Truffaut responds with "Ali Baba and the Concept of the Auteur," a critique of Jacques Becker's latest film.

April. Release of *Viaggio in Italia* by Roberto Rossellini. In opposition to current attitudes, Rivette publishes his "Letter on Rossellini" in *Cahiers du cinéma* no. 46. The article is brilliant.

April 20. The offices of the Cinémathèque française on avenue de Messine in Paris, are closed. The Cinémathèque moves to the rue d'Ulm (where it will remain for twenty years).

October 21. Release of Alexandre Astruc's *Les Mauvaises Rencontres* on the same day as Jean Delannoy's *Chiens perdus sans collier*.

December 23. Release of *Lola Montès* by Max Ophuls. Hated or admired, the film serves as a rallying cry for the young critics of the day.

1956

July 1. When the results of the competition at the Conservatoire are announced, Jean-Paul Belmondo, who had until then received only honorable mention, is carried out in triumph. He gives the finger to the jury on his way out.

Summer. Jacques Rivette films a 35-millimeter short, *Le Coup du berger*, in Claude Chabrol's apartment (Chabrol is coproducer and helps write the screenplay). The actors include Jacques Doniol-Valcroze and Jean-Claude Brialy. Pierre Braunberger remarks, "*Le Coup de Berger* is the first truly New Wave film."

November. Second Festival du Court Métrage in Tours. The grand prize is awarded to Chris Marker for *Dimanche à Pékin*. Other films shown at the festival include *Le Sabotier du Val de Loire* (Demy), *Toute la mémoire du monde* (Resnais), *Impressions de New York* (Reichenbach), and *Le Coup du berger* (Rivette).

November 26. *And God Created Woman* by Roger Vadim is released in Paris. The film is in color and CinemaScope, and stars the twenty-two year old Brigitte Bardot.

1957

Spring. François Truffaut founds the production company Les Films du Carrosse to produce *Les Mistons*, *The 400 Blows*, and films by his friends.

May. Special issue of *Cahiers du cinéma* on "The Situation of the French Cinema." The young generation of critics continues to attack the bastion of "French quality," which they deem beyond repair.

October 3. The weekly *L'Express* publishes an inquiry on French youth entitled "The New Wave Arrives!"

1958

January 30. The cover of *L'Express* displays a photograph of Maurice Ronet in *Ascenseur pour l'échafaud*, which has just been released. The picture is accompanied by a caption written by Louis Delluc, "Good boys aren't the only ones playing with pictures."

May. Release of *Mon Oncle*. *Cahiers du cinéma* includes interviews by Truffaut and Bazin with Jacques Tati.

July 8. Like Rossellini when he filmed *Open City*, Jacques Rivette begins shooting *Paris nous appartient* with borrowed money and equipment, an unpaid crew, and credit from the film lab. Shooting stops when money runs out, then resumes, and the film

finally releases in December 1961. The producers are Ajym Films (Chabrol) and Les Films du Carrosse (Truffaut). In *Arts* Truffaut writes a long article entitled "The Agony of the New Wave." The film is a commercial failure.

October 10. Release in Paris of the new film by Marcel Carné, *Les Tricheurs*. The film is the biggest success of the 1958–1959 season.

October. Release of Chris Marker's *Lettre de Sibérie*.

November 11. Death of André Bazin the day after shooting begins for *The 400 Blows*. *Les Mistons* is released at the same time.

November. Festival du Court Métrage in Tours. The films in competition include *Blue Jeans* (Rozier), *Le Chant du styrène* (Resnais), *Du côté de la côte* (Varda), and *Le Bel Indifférent* (Demy).

December. Special issue of *Cahiers du cinéma* entitled "French Cinema's Younger Generation." In 1958 this generation included Malle, Marker, Rouch, Chabrol, Rivette, Norbert Carbonnaux, Truffaut, and Resnais.

1959

February 11. Release of *Beau Serge*, the first feature film produced and directed by Claude Chabrol. The film stars Bernadette Lafont, Jean-Claude Brialy, and Gérard Blain. The low-budget film is a popular success and receives the Prix Jean Vigo.

March 11. Release of Chabrol's second film, *Les Cousins*. Stéphane Audran stars in the film; Paul Gegauff writes the script. The film wins a Golden Bear award at the Festival of Berlin. Also released in March are Jean Rouch's *Moi, un Noir* and the first feature film by Georges Franju, *La Tête contre les murs* (with Jean-Pierre Mocky).

April 29. Release of first film by Jean-Pierre Mocky, *Les Dragueurs* (with Charles Aznavour).

May 4. *The 400 Blows* is shown during a preview at the Festival of Cannes (and also out of competition, along with Rossellini's *India* and Resnais's *Hiroshima, mon amour*). Truffaut and Léaud are triumphant, with Truffaut winning for best direction. Georges de Beauregard meets Godard in Cannes. During the Festival, Unifrance Film[2] promotes a colloquium on new French cinema in La Napoule. André Malraux, recently made Minister of Cultural Affairs, sends a representative. There are presentations by Truffaut, Godard, Chabrol, Pollet, Malle, Vadim, Hossein, and Molinaro. The proceedings are immediately published in *Arts* magazine.

May. Henri Jeanson, the leading screenwriter for "quality" French cinema writes a virulent article in *Arts* attacking the newcomers, whom he refers to as "fakers." However, in the March 14, 1960, issue of *Paris-Presse*, Jeanson will write, "I like *Breathless* and I'm jealous of the film. It's the first film of revolt in French cinema or of cinema in general."

June. *The 400 Blows* appears on the cover of *Cahiers du cinéma*. The film is released on June 3 and seen by 450,000 people in France.

June. *Présence du cinéma* no. 1 appears. This new review, which later became the fiefdom of "Macmahonism,"[3] aligns itself with the New Wave and devotes its first issue to "new French cinema." The magazine publishes a number of writers from the *Cahiers du cinéma* (Kast, Moullet, Doniol-Valcroze) and interviews Mocky and Franju.

June. André Malraux institutes a program of advances on ticket sales. Initially reserved for completed films, beginning in 1962 it is extended to cover screenplays, and in 1963 it is offered to promising directors.

June 24. At 82, rue de Courcelles, in Paris, André Malraux and Henri Langlois inaugurate the new offices of the Cinémathèque française.

August 11–14. *Le Monde* asks "Is There Really a New Wave?"

August 17–September 12. Filming of *Breathless* by Jean-Luc Godard, based on an original story by François Truffaut. The cinematographer is Raoul Coutard. The film stars Jean Seberg and Jean-Paul Belmondo. The film is released on March 16, 1960. During its exclusive Paris screening, 259,000 tickets are sold. The film wins the Prix Jean Vigo.

October. Release of *Déjeuner sur l'herbe* (Renoir) and *General Della Rovere* (Rossellini). Issue 100 of *Cahiers du cinéma* appears with a cover by Jean Cocteau.

1960

January–May. Release of *L'Eau à la bouche* (Doniol-Valcroze), *Le Bel Âge* (Kast), *The Testament of Orpheus* (Cocteau), *Eyes Without a Face* (Franju), *Breathless* (Godard), *Les Bonnes Femmes* (Chabrol), *Les Jeux de l'amour* (de Broca).

June. The magazine *Esprit* publishes a special issue devoted to French cinema.

September 2. Release of *Vieux de la vielle* by Gilles Grangier. The film accurately reflects its title[4] and stars Jean Gabin, Noël-Noël, and Pierre Fresnay.

November. Release of *Shoot the Piano Player* (Truffaut) and *Un couple* (Mocky), second films by both directors.

1961

March 3. Release of *Lola*, first feature by Jacques Demy, dedicated to Max Ophuls. The cinematographer is Raoul Coutard, the chief cameraman for *Breathless*. Only 35,000 tickets are sold.

March 3. Director Jean-Luc Godard and Danish model Anna Karina are married in Béguins, near Lausanne. They met during the filming of *Le Petit Soldat* in 1960, a film that is still on the French censor's list at this time.

August. Jean-Michel Frodon notes that at this time "Thirty six recent films by young directors have been waiting for at least three months, sometimes more than a year, for distribution in theaters. True control over film financing and distribution is held by the distributors" (*L'Age moderne du cinéma français*, Paris: Flammarion, 1995).

September. Release of *Last Year in Marienbad* (Resnais, with Delphine Seyrig), *A Woman is a Woman* (Godard, with Anna Karina), *Léon Morin prêtre* (Melville, with Emmanuelle Riva and Jean-Paul Belmondo).

October. Interview in *Cahiers du cinéma* with Jean-Pierre Melville, "creator of the New Wave."

November 17. Paris release of the *Testament du docteur Cordelier* by Jean Renoir. The film was shot with several cameras (from four to eight) on sets at the Buttes-Chaumont film studio. The evening before its release, the film is shown on French television, which coproduced the film.

1962

January 24. Release of *Jules and Jim* (Truffaut) starring Jeanne Moreau.

April–May. Release of *Cleo from 5 to 7* (Varda) and *Le Signe du lion* (Rohmer).

May. Raymond Borde, Freddy Buache, and Jean Curtelin publish a small pamphlet entitled *Nouvelle Vague*, which attempts to reduce the phenomenon to a successful media campaign. In the preface Bernard Chardère, founder of *Positif* and editor of the publication, denounces "the sycophants, epigones, eclecticists, and others who claim that Godard is a leftist and that the New Wave exists. It is very vague and hardly new."

June. In *Positif* no. 46, Robert Benayoun denounces the "cinematic imposture" of the New Wave as a "muddleheaded cinema ... [a] mystique of blind approximation that pays homage to the sketch and glorifies the incomplete," a cinema that "finds refuge in formalism" and is suspect for its suspicious apolitical stance. Benayoun's article is entitled "The Emperor Has no Clothes" and the entire issue "Spotlight on French Cinema."

July 11. Release of *My Life to Live* by Jean-Luc Godard.

September. Interview in *Cahiers du cinéma* (Rohmer) with Henri Langlois.

December. *Cahiers du cinéma* publishes a special issue on the "New Wave," which includes a (slightly inflated) list of 162 new French directors. It also includes interviews with Chabrol, Godard, and Truffaut.

1963

January 25. After three years on the censor's list, Godard's *Le Petit Soldat*, about the war in Algeria, is finally released. The film stars Anna Karina.

February. Release of *La Baie des anges* (Demy), *Le Cri de la chair* (Bénazéraf), and *Le Doulos* (Melville).

May 31. Release of Jean-Luc Godard's fifth feature film, *Les Carabiniers*. It's the New Wave's biggest flop (less than 3,000 tickets sold), and critics tear the film apart. Godard answered them point by point in issue 146 of *Cahiers du cinéma* ("Fire on les carabiniers").

June 5. The Cinémathèque française moves to the Palais de Chaillot and presents a tribute to Charlie Chaplin.

September 27. Release of *Adieu Philippine* by Jacques Rozier. Shooting began in 1960.

October 1. Barbet Schroeder, a twenty-year old cinephile, founds Les Films du Losange with Pierre Cottrell, future producer of Jean Eustache. The first films produced by the new company are by Éric Rohmer.

December 20. Release of *Contempt* by Jean-Luc Godard. The film is in CinemaScope and stars Brigitte Bardot, Michel Piccoli, Jack Palance, and Fritz Lang.

1964

February 19. Paris release of Demy's *Umbrellas of Cherbourg*, a color film in which all the dialogues are sung. The film wins the Prix Louis Delluc for 1963 and the Grand Prize in Cannes in 1964.

October. The journal of the New Wave changes color. Number 159 of *Cahiers du cinéma* is the last issue to appear with yellow covers.

December. Release of *A Married Woman* by Jean-Luc Godard. In August of the same year Godard released *Band of Outsiders*. In May of the following year, he releases *Alphaville*.

1965

October 13. Release of *Paris vu par ...* , a series of sketches by Pollet, Rouch, Douchet, Rohmer, Godard, and Chabrol, filmed with live sound and in 16 millimeter. The production company is Les Films du Losange.

November 3. Paris release of *Pierrot le fou* by Jean-Luc Godard.

November. *Cahiers du cinéma's* noticeably changes its attitude to the concept of the auteur and American cinema.

1966

April 1. *La Religieuse* by Jacques Rivette, based on the novel by Diderot, is banned under pressure from the Catholic church. An editorial in *Cahiers du cinéma* sounds the call to arms, "War has begun."

May 11. Release of *La guerre est fini* by Alain Resnais.

1967

March 2. Release of Éric Rohmer's *La Collectionneuse*, the fourth of his six moral tales. The first two tales were *La Boulangère de Monceau*, (1962), and *La Carrière de Suzanne*, (1963).

1968

February. Henri Langlois is fired as director of the Cinémathèque française by the Gaullist government. *Cahiers du cinéma* enters the fray. Filmmakers, including Truffaut, Godard, and Chabrol join forces. By April 1968 Langlois is back.

Chronology prepared by Bernard Bénoliel.

---

1 The quote was written in 1970 and appeared in Truffaut's Les Films de ma vie, Paris: Flammarion, 1975.

2 Unifrance was a part of the Centre National de la Cinématographie that was responsible for promoting French cinema abroad.

3 A cinematic tendency based on an exclusive interest in certain directors (Losey, Lang, Preminger, Walsh) and the rejection of "intellectual directors" (Welles, Antonioni, Bergman), and later, the New Wave.

4 The expression refers to someone who is a veteran, or who has extensive professional experience.

INDEX

YVES ALLÉGRET
THE CHEAT, 1950

P. 141

RENÉ ALLIO
LA VIEILLE DAME INDIGNE, 1965

P. 249

OLIVIER ASSAYAS
IRMA VEP, 1956

P. 325

ALEXANDRE ASTRUC
LES MAUVAISES RENCONTRES, 1955

P. 125

P. 125

P. 125

P. 125

P. 200

P. 236

ALEXANDRE ASTRUC
END OF DESIRE, 1958

P. 48

P. 48

P. 48

ALEXANDRE ASTRUC
LA PROIE POUR L'OMBRE, 1961

P. 48

ALEXANDRE ASTRUC
LE PUITS ET LE PENDULE, 1963

P. 48

BORIS BARNET
THE GIRL WITH THE HATBOX, **1927**

P. 62

XAVIER BEAUVOIS
NORD, **1991**

P. 324

JACQUES BECKER
PARIS FRILLS, **1945**

P. 137

JACQUES BECKER
CASQUE D'OR, **1951**

P. 69

INGMAR BERGMAN
SUMMER WITH MONIKA, **1953**

P. 66

ROBERT BRESSON
ANGELS OF THE STREETS, **1943**

P. 68

ROBERT BRESSON
LE DIEU NOIR ET LE DIABLE BLOND, **1944**

P. 281

ROBERT BRESSON
LADIES OF THE PARK, **1944**

P. 31

LUIS BUÑUEL
L'ÂGE D'OR, **1930**

P. 65

LUIS BUÑUEL
EL, **1952**

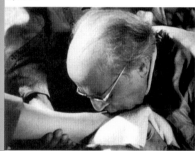

P. 65

LUIS BUÑUEL
BELLE DE JOUR, **1966**

P. 262

MARCEL CARNÉ
GATES OF THE NIGHT, **1946**

P. 119

332

JOHN CASSAVETES
FACES, **1968**

P. 275

CLAUDE CHABROL
LE BEAU SERGE, **1959**

P. 198

CLAUDE CHABROL
THE COUSINS, **1959**

P. 118

P. 118

P. 167

P. 167

P. 198

P. 241

P. 260

CLAUDE CHABROL
BLUEBEARD, **1962**

P. 241

CHRISTIAN-JAQUE
LA SONNETTE D'ALARME, **1935**

P. 116-117

HENRI-GEORGES CLOUZOT
THE RAVEN, **1943**

P. 23

HENRI-GEORGES CLOUZOT
THE MYSTERY OF PICASSO, **1956**

P. 141

FRANCIS FORD COPPOLA
THE GODFATHER PART III, **1990**

P. 304-305

333

PEDRO COSTA
BONES, 1997

P. 319

JACQUES DEMY
LE BEL INDIFFÉRENT, **1957**

P. 245

JACQUES DEMY
LOLA, **1960**

P. 171

P. 171

P. 171

P. 258

P. 258

JACQUES DEMY
LA LUXURE, (LES SEPT PÉCHÉS CAPITAUX), **1961**

P. 263

JACQUES DEMY
LA BAIE DES ANGES, **1963**

P. 199

P. 260

P. 260

JACQUES DEMY
LES PARAPLUIES DE CHERBOURG, **1963**

P. 141

P. 214

P. 214

P. 215

P. 261

P. 261

P. 261

P. 261

JACQUES DERAY
LA PISCINE, **1969**

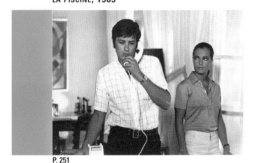

P. 251

MICHEL DEVILLE
CE SOIR OU JAMAIS, **1960**

P. 251

JEAN DOUCHET
SAINT-GERMAIN-DES-PRÉS (PARIS VU PAR...), **1964**

P. 96

CARL THEODOR DREYER
LA PASSION DE JEANNE D'ARC, **1928**

La mort !

P. 62

JULIEN DUVIVIER
CHAIR DE POULE, **1963**

P. 136

S. M. EISENSTEIN
THE BATTLESHIP POTEMKIN, **1925**

P. 62

JEAN EUSTACHE
ROBINSON'S PLACE, **1963**

P. 127

P. 165

JEAN EUSTACHE
SANTA CLAUS HAS BLUE EYES, **1966**

P. 15

P. 165

P. 259

JEAN EUSTACHE
THE MOTHER AND THE WHORE, **1973**

P. 126

P. 126

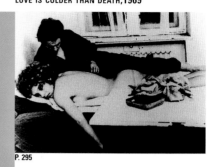

RAINER-WERNER FASSBINDER
LOVE IS COLDER THAN DEATH, 1969

P. 295

P. 126

P. 126

RAINER-WERNER FASSBINDER
FOX AND HIS FRIENDS, 1975

P. 298-299

P. 126

P. 155

P. 126

P. 246

JOHN FORD
SHE WORE A YELLOW RIBBON, 1946

P. 126

P. 64

JEAN EUSTACHE
MES PETITES AMOUREUSES, 1974

P. 200

MILOS FORMAN
LOVES OF A BLOND 1964

P. 126

P. 292-293

GEORGES FRANJU
BLOOD OF THE BEASTS, 1949

P. 76

GEORGES FRANJU
HÔTEL DES INVALIDES, 1952

P. 76

GEORGES FRANJU
THÉRESE DESQUEYROUX, 1962

P. 237

PHILIPPE GARREL
ANÉMONE, 1967

P. 187

JEAN-LUC GODARD
ALL THE BOYS ARE CALLED PATRICK, 1957

P. 81

JEAN-LUC GODARD
BREATHLESS, 1960

P. 120

P. 120

P. 120

P. 120

P. 120

P. 120

P. 120

P. 120

P. 154

P. 169

P. 169

P. 184

P. 184

P. 184

P. 184

P. 185

P. 185

P. 185

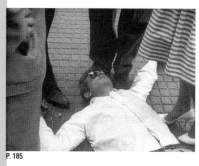

P. 185

P. 197

P. 213

P. 225

P. 225

P. 235

P. 242

P. 257

P. 257

P. 258

P. 258

JEAN-LUC GODARD
A WOMAN IS A WOMAN, 1961

P. 182

P. 243

P. 243

P. 243

JEAN-LUC GODARD
LES CARABINIERS, 1962

P. 208

P. 208

P. 209

JEAN-LUC GODARD
MY LIFE TO LIVE, 1962

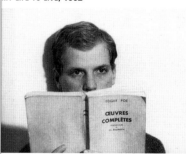

P. 20

P. 119

P. 123

P. 123

P. 151

P. 164

P. 227

P. 228

P. 228

P. 242

P. 242

P. 242

8
LES APRÈS-MIDI - L'ARGENT - LES
LAVABOS - LE PLAISIR - LES HÔTELS

P. 242

P. 242

P. 242

P. 242

JEAN-LUC GODARD
CONTEMPT, 1963

P. 105

P. 118

P. 143

P. 143

P. 146

P. 146

P. 147

P. 152-153

P. 152-153

P. 204

P. 231

P. 243

P. 243

P. 243

P. 243

P. 257

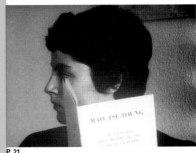

P. 21

P. 96

P. 96

P. 97

P. 97

P. 226

P. 226

JEAN-LUC GODARD
BAND OF OUTSIDERS, 1964

P. 151

JEAN-LUC GODARD
ALPHAVILLE, 1965

P. 187

JEAN-LUC GODARD
MONTPARNASSE-LEVALLOIS (PARIS VU PAR...), 1965

P. 122

P. 122

P. 122

P. 122

P. 122

P. 122

P. 122

P. 122

JEAN-LUC GODARD
PIERROT LE FOU, 1965

P. 17

P. 20

P. 21

P. 67

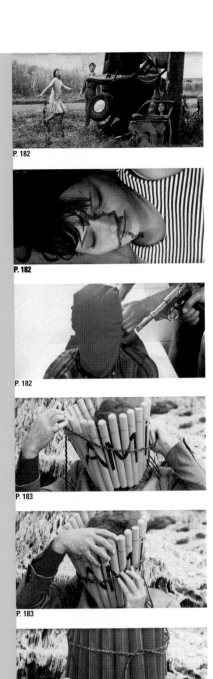

P. 182

P. 182

P. 182

P. 183

P. 183

P. 183

P. 183

P. 202

P. 203

P. 205

P. 206

P. 207

P. 231

P. 243

P. 243

P. 243

P. 258

P. 259

JEAN GRÉMILLON
GUEULE D'AMOUR, 1937

P. 65

D. W. GRIFFITH
INTOLERANCE 1916

P. 58

P. 114

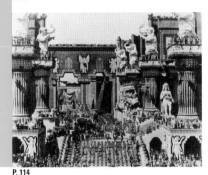

P. 114

SACHA GUITRY
QUADRILLE, 1937

P. 63

HOU HSIAO-HSIEN
GOODBYE SOUTH, GOODBYE, 1996

P. 314

BUSTER KEATON
THE NAVIGATOR, 1924

P. 59

ABBAS KIAROSTAMI
AND LIFE GOES ON, 1992

P. 317

FRITZ LANG
BEYOND A REASONABLE DOUBT, 1956

P. 61

ROGER LEENHARDT
NAISSANCE DU CINÉMA, 1946

P. 39

RENÉ LEPRINCE, FERDINAND ZECCA
LA LUTTE POUR LA VIE, 1914

P. 112

KEN LOACH
FATHERLAND, 1986

P. 322

ERNST LUBITSCH
TO BE OR NOT TO BE, 1942

P. 61

LUMIÈRE
LA SORTIE DES USINES LUMIÈRES, 1895

P. 57

LUMIÈRE
ENFANTS PÊCHANT DES CREVETTES, 1896

P. 58

LUMIÈRE
LONDRES, ENTRÉE DU CINÉMATOGRAPHE, 1896

P. 57

LOUIS MALLE
ELEVATOR TO THE GALLOWS, 1957

P. 236

LOUIS MALLE
LE FEU FOLLET, 1963

P. 17

P. 261

P. 261

P. 261

JOSEPH L. MANKIEWICZ
THE BAREFOOT CONTESSA, 1954

P. 67

CHRIS MARKER
SUNDAY IN PEKING, 1956

conseil sinologique: AGNES VARDA

P. 79

P. 79

P. 79

P. 79

CHRIS MARKER
CUBA SI, 1961

P. 239

INMINENTE
INVASION YANQUI
ROA A LA ONU PARA DENUNCIAR EL ATAQUE

REVOLUCION

P. 239

P. 239

P. 239

P. 34

P. 195

CHRIS MARKER
LA JETÉE, **1962**

P. 180

JEAN-PIERRE MOCKY
LES DRAGUEURS, **1959**

P. 195

NANNI MORETTI
LA MESSE EST FINIE, **1986**

P. 316

P. 180

P. 248

LUC MOULLET
BRIGITTE ET BRIGITTE, **1966**

P. 154

CHRIS MARKER
LE JOLI MAI **1962**

P. 166

P. 249

P. 188

JONAS MEKAS
GUNS OF THE TREES, **1961**

P. 278

P. 249

P. 245

346

F. W. MURNAU
SUNRISE, 1927

P. 59

MAX OPHULS
LE PLAISIR, 1951

P. 68

MAX OPHULS
THE EARRINGS OF MADAME DE..., 1953

P. 138

MAX OPHULS
LOLA MONTÈS, 1955

P. 140

P. 140

NAGISA OSHIMA
DEATH BY HANGING, 1968

P. 282

MAURICE PIALAT
L'ENFANCE NUE, 1969

P. 248

ROMAN POLANSKI
KNIFE IN THE WATER, 1962

P. 286-287

JEAN-DANIEL POLLET
LIGNE DE MIRE, 1960

P. 245

JEAN-DANIEL POLLET
RUE SAINT-DENIS (PARIS VU PAR...), 1965

P. 173

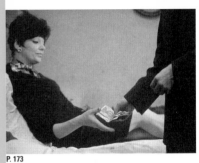

P. 173

P. 173

NICHOLAS RAY
JOHNNY GUITAR, 1954

P. 67

JEAN RENOIR
A DAY IN THE COUNTRY, 1936-1946

P. 63

JEAN RENOIR
FRENCH CANCAN, **1954**

P. 139

P. 139

ALAIN RESNAIS
NIGHT AND FOG, **1955**

P. 77

P. 77

P. 77

P. 77

P. 77

ALAIN RESNAIS
TOUTE LA MÉMOIRE DU MONDE, **1956**

P. 166

P. 166

ALAIN RESNAIS
LE MYSTÈRE DE L'ATELIER **15**, **1957**

P. 81

P. 81

P. 81

P. 81

P. 81

ALAIN RESNAIS
LE CHANT DU STYRÈNE, **1958**

P. 78

P. 78

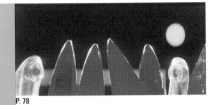

P. 78

P. 78

P. 78

P. 78

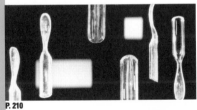

P. 78

P. 210

P. 210

ALAIN RESNAIS
HIROSHIMA, MON AMOUR, 1959

P. 191

P. 191

P. 194

P. 194

P. 238

P. 238

P. 238

ALAIN RESNAIS
LAST YEAR AT MARIENBAD, 1960

P. 181

P. 192

P. 258

P. 181

P. 192

P. 124

FRANÇOIS RICHENBACH
ON CŒUR GROS COMME ÇA, 1961

P. 124

P. 181

P. 251

P. 124

P. 181

P. 124

P. 197

JACQUES RIVETTE
PARIS BELONGS TO US, 1958-1961

P. 124

P. 124

P. 244

P. 124

P. 124

JACQUES RIVETTE
LA RELIGIEUSE, **1964**

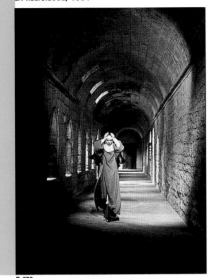

P. 259

P. 126

P. 172

P. 121

P. 121

ÉRIC ROHMER
THE BAKER OF MONCEAU, **1962**

P. 18

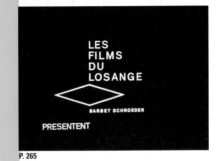

LES
FILMS
DU
LOSANGE

BARBET SCHROEDER

PRESENTENT

P. 265

P. 121

P. 126

ÉRIC ROHMER
LE SIGNE DU LION, **1962**

P. 121

P. 121

P. 121

P. 121

P. 126

P. 121

P. 121

P. 121

P. 121

P. 169

P. 223

P. 224

P. 242

ÉRIC ROHMER
SUZANNE'S CAREER, 1963

P. 172

P. 172

P. 229

ÉRIC ROHMER
LA COLLECTIONNEUSE, 1966

P. 229

P. 230

P. 230

ÉRIC ROHMER
MY NIGHT AT MAUD'S, 1969

P. 148

P. 149

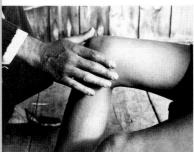

P. 149

ÉRIC ROHMER
LE GENOU DE CLAIRE, 1970

P. 239

ROBERTO ROSSELLINI
PAISAN, **1946**

P. 186

La nostra America non era ancora stata scoperta...

P. 186

JEAN ROUCH
MOI, UN NOIR, **1958**

P. 235

JEAN ROUCH
SIX IN PARIS, **1964**

P. 125

JACQUES ROZIER
BLUE JEANS, **1958**

P. 150

P. 244

JACQUES ROZIER
ÀDIEU PHILIPPINE, **1960-1963**

P. 122

P. 170

MARTIN SCORSESE
GOODFELLAS, **1990**

P. 304-305

VICTOR SJÖSTRÖM
THE OUTLAW AND HIS WIFE, **1917**

P. 58

JEAN-MARIE STRAUB
MAGDALENA BACH, **1967**

P. 187

JACQUES TATI
MY UNCLE, **1957**

P. 69

P. 138

ANDRÉ TÉCHINÉ
BAROCCO, 1976

P. 246

FRANÇOIS TRUFFAUT
THE MISCHIEF MAKERS, 1957

P. 79

P. 79

P. 79

P. 79

FRANÇOIS TRUFFAUT
THE 400 BLOWS, 1959

P. 12

P. 47

P. 47

P. 47

P. 127

P. 229

P. 127

P. 127

P. 168

P. 168

P.

P. 240

P. 240

P. 240

P. 259

P. 259

P. 259

FRANÇOIS TRUFFAUT
SHOOT THE PIANO PLAYER, 1960

P. 170

P. 170

P. 240

FRANÇOIS TRUFFAUT
JULES AND JIM, 1962

P. 150

P. 170

P. 170

P. 241

P. 241

P. 260

P. 260

FRANÇOIS TRUFFAUT
UNE BELLE FILLE COMME MOI, 1972

P. 260

ROGER VADIM
AND GOD CREATED WOMAN, 1956

P. 236

AGNÈS VARDA
LA POINTE COURTE, 1954

P. 80

P. 80

P. 80

P. 80

DZIGA VERTOV
THE MAN WITH A MOVIE CAMERA, **1929**

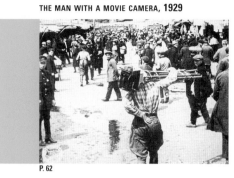

P. 62

ORSON WELLES
CITIZEN KANE, **1941**

P. 180

AGNÈS VARDA
DU CÔTÉ DE LA CÔTE, **1958**

P. 166

LUCHINO VISCONTI
ROCCO AND HIS BROTHERS, **1960**

P. 262

ORSON WELLES
DON QUIXOTE, **1955-1972**

P. 68

AGNÈS VARDA
CLEO FROM 5 TO 7, **1961**

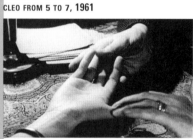

P. 188

P. 199

P. 238

JOSEF VON STERNBERG
MOROCCO, **1930**

P. 64

ERICH VON STROHEIM
QUEEN KELLY, **1928**

P. 60

EDWARD YANG
A BRIGHTER SUMMER DAY, **1991**

P. 318

P. 316

PHOTOGRAPHIC CREDITS

The reproductions in this book are taken from films produced or distributed in France by the following:

Acacias (*Monika*), AFMD (*Faces, Jules and Jim, Les Mistons, Paris nous appartient, The 400 Blows, Shoot the Piano Player*), Archeo Pictures (*Citizen Kane*), Argos (*Dimanche à Pékin, Hiroshima, mon amour, La Jetée, Night and Fog, La Pendaison*), Arkeion (*Battleship Potemkin, Man with a Movie Camera, The Girl with the Hatbox*), Artedis (*Barocco*), Association Lumière (*La Sortie des usines Lumière, Londres*), Atlantic Films (*Hôtel des Invalides*), Bernard Verley Films (*Nord*), Canal Plus Image Audiovisuel (*Breathless, Alphaville, Belle de jour, Casque d'or, Ce soir ou jamais, Last Year at Marienbad, Chair de poule, The Navigator, Sonnette d'alarme, Le Corbeau, Contempt, Le Petit Soldat, Les Carabiniers, Pierrot le fou, Un drôle de paroissien, A Woman is a Woman*), Ciné Classic (*La Religieuse, Landru, Morocco*), Cinéma Public Film (*Adieu Philippine*), Cinémaris (*Baie des anges, Cleo from 5 to 7, Du Côté de la côte, La Pointe courte, The Umbrellas of Cherbourg, Lola*), Columbia (*Une belle fille comme moi*), Connaissance du Cinéma (*Love is Colder than Death, Fox and his Friends, Queen Kelly*), Filmel (*Thérèse Desqueyroux*), Films Ariane/TF1 (*And God Created Woman, Les Dames du bois de Boulogne, La Proie pour l'ombre*), Films Roger Leenhardt (*Naissance du cinéma*), Les Films de l'Atalante (*Loves of a Blonde, Le Sang des bêtes*), Les Films du Jeudi (*Le Chant du styrène, Don Quichotte, Lola Montès, Moi, un Noir, La Partie de campagne, Tous les garçons s'appellent Patrick, Toute la mémoire du monde, My Life to Live*), Les Films du Losange (*Gare du Nord, La Boulangère de Monceau, La Carrière de Suzanne, La Collectionneuse, Claire's Knee, Le Signe du Lion, My Night at Maud's, Paris vu par…*), MK2 (*A Brighter Summer Day, El, Fatherland, Goodbye South, Goodbye, La Messe est finie, Le Mystère Picasso, Mon oncle*), Films Sans Frontières (*Amore, Le Dieu noir et le Diable blond, Paisan*), Francécrans (*Johnny Guitar, L'Enfance nue, Rocco and his Brothers*), Gallimard (*Les Anges du péché*), Gaumont (*Band of Outsiders, La Passion de Jeanne d'Arc*), Gemini (*Ossos*), Les Grands Films Classiques (*And Life Goes On, L'Âge d'or*), Haut et Court (*Irma Vep*), Hollywood Classics (*She Wore a Yellow Ribbon*), Jacques le Glou Audiovisuel (*The Mother and the Whore, Mes petites amoureuses*), Kotor Financial Corporation (*La Vieille Dame indigne*), Jean-Pierre Mocky (*Les Dragueurs*), Luc Moullet (*Brigitte et Brigitte*), Pandora (*La Piscine*), Pathé (*La Lutte pour la vie, Le Bel Indifférent, Les Portes de la nuit*), Pyramide (*Ascenseur pour l'échafaud, Feu follet*), Robur (*Manèges*), Sofracima (*Le Joli Mai*), Teledis (*French Cancan, Les Cousins, Madame de …, Le Beau Serge, Le Plaisir, Le Silence de la mer, Quadrille*), Action Gitanes (*Chronique d'Anna Magdalena Bach, Beyond a Reasonable Doubt, The Barefoot Contessa, Knife in the Water, To Be or Not to Be*), UGC (*Falbalas*), UIP (*The Godfather III*), Warner (*Goodfellas*).

All reference documents were supplied by the Cinémathèque française except for the following:

BERNARD MARTINAND
24, 25, 26, 27, 28, 29, 70, 75, 82 (bottom), 83, 84, 86, 109, 110, 128, 129, 130, 131, 132, 135, 156 (bottom), 157, 158, 159, 160 (bottom), 162, 177, 216, 217, 266, 268, 269, 270, 312.

BIFI
23, 25, 32, 33, 40, 41, 55 (top), 59, 62 (bottom center), 71, 72, 74, 82 (top), 85, 107, 109, 119, 156, 160 (top), 161, 174, 175, 178, 179, 218, 221, 267, 310.

PRODUCTIONS GEORGES DE BEAUREGARD
169.

CAHIERS DU CINÉMA
36, 37, 42 (R. Joachim), 43 (P. Zucca), 51 (J. Belin), 52, 62 (bottom right), 65 (right), 67, 81, 92, 93, 141, 173, 211, 212, 240, 244, 245, 246, 247 (J.-P. Biesse), 248, 249, 250, 251, 254, 262, 264, 275, 276, 277, 278, 288, 289, 293, 295, 304, 305, 315, 320, 321, 323 (I. Weingarten), 324, 325.

MK2
314, 316, 317, 318, 319, 322.

RAYMOND DEPARDON/MAGNUM
55.

ORIGINALLY PUBLISHED AS *NOUVELLE VAGUE* BY ÉDITIONS HAZAN/CINÉMATHÈQUE FRANÇAISE.

FIRST ENGLISH LANGUAGE EDITION PUBLISHED BY D.A.P./DISTRIBUTED ART PUBLISHERS, INC. IN ASSOCIATION WITH ÉDITIONS HAZAN/CINÉMATHÈQUE FRANÇAISE, 1999.

COPYRIGHT ©1998 BY ÉDITIONS HAZAN/CINÉMATHÈQUE FRANÇAISE.
TRANSLATION COPYRIGHT ©1998 BY ROBERT BONONNO.

PRINTED IN ITALY

ISBN 1-56466-057-5

TRANSLATOR: ROBERT BONONNO
EDITOR: JULIETTE HAZAN
BOOK DESIGN: ATALANTE/ PARIS
COMPOSITION AND EDITORIAL, USA: POLLEN DESIGN/NEW YORK
COPY EDITOR: BERNARD BÈNOLIEL
COPY EDITOR, USA: MARK BOREN
PROOFREADER: JEAN-YVES REUZEAU
PROOFREADER, USA: MARY CAROL DEZUTTER
PICTURE RESEARCH: BERNARD BÈNOLIEL AND JULIETTE HAZAN
PRODUCTION: FÈDÈRIQUE CADORET
PRODUCTION, USA: ELISA FRÖHLICH, BETH KESSLER, JACK DONNER
COLOR SEPARATION: PRODIMA, BILBAO
PRINTER: MILANOSTAMPA, FARIGLIANO

Douchet, Jean.
   [Nouvelle vague. English.]
   French new wave / by Jean Douchet. —1st ed.

p.   cm.
   Includes bibliographical references.
   ISBN 1-56466-057-5
   1. New wave films—France—History.   I. Title.
   PN1993.5.F7D6813 1998
   791.43i0944—dc21
                                      98-26522
                                      CIP